Education and Social Transition in the Third World

Education and Social Transition in the Third World

Martin Carnoy and Joel Samoff

with
Mary Ann Burris
Anton Johnston
Carlos Alberto Torres

PRINCETON UNIVERSITY PRESS
PRINCETON, NEW JERSEY

Library of Congress Cataloging-in-Publication Data

Carnoy, Martin.
Education and social transition in the Third World / Martin Carnoy
and Joel Samoff; with Mary Ann Burris, Anton Johnston, Carlos
Alberto Torres.
p. cm.
Includes bibliographical references.
1. Social change—Developing countries—Case stu. 2. Education
and state—Developing countries—Cross-cultural studies.
3. Socialism and education—Developing countries—Cross-cultural
studies. 4. Social change—Cross-cultural studies. 5. Developing
countries—Economic conditions—Cross-cultural studies.
6. Education and state—China. 7. Education and state—Cuba.
8. Education and state—Tanzania. 9. Education and state—
Mozambique. 10. Education and state—Nicaragua. I. Samoff, Joel.
II. Title.
LC98.C37   1990   370.19-dc20   89-39164

ISBN 0-691-07822-X—ISBN 0-691-02311-5 (pbk.)

This book has been composed in Linotron Caledonia

Princeton University Press books are printed on acid-free paper,
and meet the guidelines for permanence and durability of the
Committee on Production Guidelines for Book Longevity of the
Council on Library Resources

Printed in the United States of America by Princeton Academic Press

10 9 8 7 6 5 4 3 2

For Alan Carnoy, whose elegance and sense of justice touched all who knew him, and Bernard Samoff, who did not accept a disjunction between the intellectual and the practical and for whom everyone was an equal.

Contents

Tables

Acknowledgments

THIS BOOK originated when a group of us at Stanford—students and professors—began meeting to discuss educational change in Third World transition societies. We were stimulated both by our own curiosity and by the only partly rhetorical queries we had heard from colleagues in transition societies: "Now that we have assumed power, what must we do to achieve what we have set out to accomplish? What specific programs are essential? Which tasks should have the highest priority? How do we get the old schools to nurture the new people?"

Carnoy had already written about Cuba, and Samoff about Tanzania. Mary Ann Burris had taught in China, Carlos Alberto Torres had done research on adult education in Nicaragua and Mexico, and Jeff Unsicker was writing his dissertation about Tanzania. The time seemed opportune to compare notes and, if possible, develop a more general understanding of the contents and processes of social transformation in these societies that distinguished them from others in the Third World.

At about the same time, the Institute of International Education (IIE) at the University of Stockholm and the International Development Education Program at Stanford, under the sponsorship of the United States Information Service (USIS), agreed to a three-year faculty exchange and a program of collaborative research. Swedish expertise in countries such as Ethiopia, Mozambique, Zimbabwe, and Vietnam provided added dimensions to our original project. Anton Johnston, who had spent many years in Mozambique and was writing his dissertation on educational change there, became our Stockholm collaborator.

Special thanks is due to all the faculty and students at the IIE. They extended our knowledge and commented on various aspects of the research. The USIS made possible the interchange between our faculties. This had many benefits, among them the presentation of our research to one anothers' university communities. Of course, the USIS bears no responsibility for what we have said in the book. Jeff Unsicker, who was deeply engaged in his Tanzanian study, nevertheless took time to comment on what we were writing, and was a major contributor to formulating the structure of the study. All of us consider him one of the authors even though his name does not appear on any of the chapters. Although we have identified authors with principal responsibility for particular chapters, all of us are present throughout the work.

We are grateful to several organizations that provided support for both field research and periods of reflection and writing. The Latin American Studies Center at Stanford University supported travel to Nicaragua for Carnoy and Torres. Samoff's work in Tanzania over several years was supported by the Rockefeller Foundation and the Fulbright-Hays Program, and the African Studies Center at Stanford University and the Spencer Foundation supported supplementary research and writing. The Fulbright-Hays Program and the Social Science Research Council enabled Unsicker to conduct his field reserch in Tanzania. Fellowships and grants from the Committee for Scholarly Cooperation with the People's Republic of China and the Spencer Foundation supported Burris's research in China. The Swedish International Development Authority and the Swedish Agency for Research Cooperation with Developing Countries supported Johnston's work in Mozambique and Sweden.

We appreciate the thoughtful readings that Manuel Castells, Sherry Keith, and Jonathan Barker gave these many pages. We are grateful as well to our colleagues in the countries we have studied, who made room for us—indeed, often energetically assisted us—amidst what has been for many of them a time of social reconstruction under siege. And many thanks to Sandy Thatcher, our editor at Princeton, who was able to see good qualities in the thicket of detail we felt essential to our work.

Martin Carnoy
Joel Samoff
Palo Alto, January 1989

PART I

Education and Transition: Theory and Method

CHAPTER 1

The Search for Method

THIS IS A STUDY of education in five developing countries undergoing profound social, political, and economic change. Four have had revolutions. All have rejected capitalism as the basis of production relations in their economies, and all are attempting to construct the foundations of a new social system on a national scale.

Much has already been written about the social transformation process occurring in many Third World states, but that process is still not widely understood. Where understandings have emerged, they are usually clouded by ideological controversy. The more important goal of coming to terms with the nature of the transformation and what it helps us understand about change itself remains elusive.

We want to reexamine such transformations from both a theoretical perspective and in practice. We support the aspirations of these societies. Their leaders have committed themselves to broad-based social and economic development anchored in significant social structural change—a change that even many critics of these societies agree is desirable. And the development that has taken place, for all its problems, offers important insights into economic and social alternatives to capitalist development—alternatives that may be especially relevant in a Third World context.

Analyzing education, we believe, is an important way to understand larger economic and political change, or the lack of it. But our aim is also to compare educational change itself across societies, and to analyze whether and why education develops differently in societies that seek to make a transition from capitalism to socialism than in their Third World capitalist counterparts. The existence of significant differences in educational policy will tell us something about how political and economic policies differ in countries with different social organizations. The comparison will also help us understand the barriers to reforming education in capitalist societies. Is it possible, for example, to duplicate the main lines of educational change across societies without developing similar social and economic reforms? Conversely, is there something about each of the societies we study here that makes the way their educational systems developed unique to particular sociohistorical conditions?

We develop an analysis of change—including educational change—that focuses on the state and politics. It is the state, much more than the production system, we argue, that is the source of the dynamic of revolutionary societies, and politics, much more than relations in production, that drives their social development. The importance of the state and politics is not limited to the analysis of societies undergoing social transformation. We also make a case for increasing focus on the state and its relation to the economy in understanding how social structures in Third World capitalist societies remain relatively unchanged. But it is in the "transition" to new structures that the state and politics become dominant in understanding the nature of change.

DEFINITIONS

The five states in our study are often referred to as marxist, socialist, communist, or "in the transition to socialism." But the definition of such terms has always been difficult and controversial: There exists no real world example of the kind of society to which they are in transition; their own divergent programs and histories obscure any single, clear picture of a "socialist" society; and defining idealistically in advance what the end product or the process of the transition ought to be is inconsistent with a dialectical or materialist approach.[1]

We therefore do not refer to these societies as "socialist" or "transitional-to-socialist," and thus avoid assuming all the theoretical baggage inherent in those terms. Where the states we study do not refer explicitly to themselves as "constructing socialism" (which some do not), we use the terms "social transformation" and "transition" to describe the process of transforming one social structure into another.

We do consider, however, that the dialectical approach to studying this process case by case is also a contribution to research on "socialism"— carried out by examining the practice of those who say they are constructing socialism. With such an approach, we can (1) identify what is common and what varies among the cases; and (2) use these similarities and differences as the essential elements for the development of the theory of the transition and the role of education within it.

In these states' political programs and practices we are able to distinguish various common features a priori. Some indicate what the states are against, and others identify elements of goals to which they are in transition.

A common initial distinguishing feature is that the states in our study have not come about from the set of circumstances predicted by Marx. (This is yet another reason to worry about the premature use of the term

---

[1] Even in terms of a theoretical goal, "socialism" is portrayed by Marx and Lenin as being one stage in a continuum of development, characterized by the establishment of global socialist hegemony, which will lead into a transition to communism.

"socialism.") All these states have appeared historically in predominantly agricultural, industrially underdeveloped countries with a large peasantry, a weak national bourgeoisie, and a very small proletariat. We argue that it is in part the peripheral position of these countries in the world economic system that prevented the capitalist state from finding the political and economic resources necessary to maintain its hegemony. This helped create the conditions for the accession to state power of popular-based movements.

A second common feature of the new state's program is its noncapitalist or anticapitalist orientation. The new state stems from social movements organized to oppose the more extreme manifestations of peripheral capitalism—land expropriation, forced labor, tyrannical dictatorships, colonialism, and neocolonialism. Its problem is to replace the social system underlying these manifestations with one that guarantees that previous social relations and the institutions associated with them do not return. The new state therefore aligns itself against exploitation for individual gain and against those most intimately connected with economic and political power in the previous social structure. In doing so, it automatically comes into conflict with the interests of those industrialized countries that supported the previous regime. The result is that the new state often faces sanctions and even military confrontation as part of establishing and defining itself. Implementing a non- or anticapitalist program also means that the state has to rely for support on peasants and workers, and, initially, it directs much of its effort to the mobilization of mass participation in social change.

A third common feature is that these states seek to collectivize production through public rather than private ownership. The state seeks in collectivization the route to a nonexploitative, highly productive, and eventually classless society. The state's policies are not only collective, but also oriented toward a much more equal distribution of goods and services. This combination underlies the attempt to replace individual gain by equitable collective consumption—notably through social services, of which education is one of the most important. Building an equitable society also involves efforts to guarantee the right to work, a narrowing of wage differentials, and equal status in law and in employment for women and men. The expansion of public ownership binds the state ever tighter to direct dependence on economic success for its legitimacy. This relationship raises tensions, which come to play a central role in determining the future direction of development.

The coincidence of the hostility of powerful industrial economies toward the new state, the state's hostility to capitalism and dependence, and the program of collectivization and public ownership in the economy bring about another common series of features in the countries under study. The state tries to redefine its whole system of relations with the outside world, especially its relations with external military and economic systems. It seeks new trading partners and allies with similar collectivist goals, reducing previous dependencies (at the risk of further antagonizing capitalist powers and of incurring new forms of dependence). Particularly for the smaller economies (all but China in our study), an international approach to changing domestic social relations becomes a material necessity.

A fourth common feature of these states is the dominant role of the state in all spheres of social transformation and development—and with that role, a fundamental tension between the respective domains of central authority and local democracy. On one hand, the new state's legitimacy and its development program depend on its ability to mobilize and incorporate the citizenry. On the other hand, the new state—often permeated by the old state's bureaucrats, structures, methods, and philosophies—not only has a direct economic interest in steering the country's social transformation from the center but is impelled by outside aggression and internal resistance to intensify centralization and authoritarian practice. The result is that these states have always made significant large-scale efforts to develop new organs of popular democracy at various levels of the society, but have simultaneously developed a bureaucratic and authoritarian structure, which manages to undermine and circumvent people's power. The tension between these two forces simultaneously impedes and dynamizes the process of social transformation.

The events of the Beijing summer of 1989—dramatic student-led protests and hunger strikes with mass popular mobilization and support, followed by heavy-handed political repression—highlight a fifth common characteristic of these states: a sense of hope. Like the student demonstrators and their working-class allies in Western Europe and the United States in the spring of 1968, Chinese protesters in 1989 shared an optimism about the possibility of change and about their potential role in the change process. They believed that citizen initiatives and mass mobilization could not only confront the awesome power of their authoritarian state but, indeed, transform it. Perhaps even more striking, they believed that China's army was a people's army, drawn from the citizenry and unwilling to raise arms against it. Contrast this sense of the possibility of change and the viability of citizen action with the widespread cynicism and depoliticization in the United States and Western Europe. Where in the North Atlantic do student protestors consider the citizenry their protectors, the workers their allies, and the army their ideological and perhaps even experiential comrades?

For an extraordinary moment, when unarmed citizens defied the state and turned away the tanks, the Chinese demonstrators' optimism seemed founded. In the short term, however, state coercion overwhelmed their hopes, their organizations, and their bodies. At this writing it is impossible to assess fully either the impact of the protests or their longer-term durability. It would be politically naive and analytically superficial to romanticize what was necessarily a shaky coalition of diverse interests. As Mary Ann Burris stresses in her study of Chinese education, widespread economic reforms in China have thus far not been accompanied by similarly broad-gauged political reforms. At the same time, it is striking that while the popular mood in the liberal capitalist democracies is one of political cynicism and self-centered individualism, in the transitional states we study here, and indeed in the perestroika and glasnost of socialist Europe, we find high expectations about how the society ought to be organized, democratic political engagement, and optimism about change.

WHY EDUCATION?

In studying such societies, why should we focus on education and not some other institution, such as factories, farms, or the health care system? The most important reason is that the leaders of these states themselves attribute great importance to education as part of the means of achieving social transformation. The same kind of optimism exists about the role of education in development that characterized international agencies in the early 1960s. However, the education in question is not just the same old education as before. Education itself is seen as having to be changed and renewed. The leadership in these societies does not just mouth rhetoric about changing and developing education. They expand it more rapidly and reach out to more people of all ages than in any previous efforts in history. They mobilize entire populations to achieve universal literacy over a short period and invent new ways to expand and deliver all levels of schooling to their citizenry.

Education is seen in such societies as a route to all things. It is expected to be the primary vehicle for developing and training skills to ensure that the next generation in the society is adequately prepared for the specific tasks that the society expects of it. It is expected to be the place where appropriate ideas, values, and worldviews will be developed so that from the process of schooling there emerges a new person—not simply someone with skills, but also someone with an understanding of his or her own role in the world and of what is important for that society. The schools are also expected to assume much of the responsibility for recruiting personnel for future leadership positions in these new societies. Religion, race, wealth, and gender are no longer to be the criteria for choosing the leadership. Rather, proven skills, social consciousness, and achievement are to be the mechanisms for determining who assumes power and holds positions of responsibility. How are those merits to be created and assessed? In and by the educational system. The redefinition of knowledge and schooling makes the school not only the place where cognition is developed but also the site of the pupil's first chance for organized participation in party activities, community work, and student government. The leadership believes that all these goals can be molded into the schools, and that the school can, and will, undertake the task of achieving them.

The schools are expected to have the same kind of responsibilities and perhaps even more than in societies where profound social transformation is not on the agenda. Moreover, in the countries we study here, the leadership counts on schools to achieve these transformations of social structure and consciousness in the immediate postrevolutionary (or, in the case of Tanzania, less a postrevolutionary than a postcolonial[2]) transition period.

The analysis of education is therefore a logical point of entry into the analysis of the overall process of change in such societies. But where to start? There have been a number of studies of education in Third World revolutionary societies (for example, Löfstedt 1980; Carnoy and Werthein 1980; Arnove 1986). Yet none of these studies develops a coherent framework for comparing the role of education in peripheral capitalist societies to education in the transition.

Here, we develop the theoretical basis for such an analysis by turning to theories of the state and directly to the experiences of the five Third World countries we studied. Our search for method, then, is rooted in previous theoretical approaches and the practice we observed in the case studies.

THE STATE AND EDUCATION

Notions of correspondence, cultural reproduction, and contradiction are important in developing an analysis of education's role in social transformation (see Bowles and Gintis 1976; Carnoy 1974; Apple 1982c; Giroux 1981). Yet even this insightful analysis of change in capitalist societies fails to develop a coherent theory of the relations among economy, ideology, and political system (the state) and, in turn, a theory of the relationship between the state and the educational system. We shall argue

[2] Tanganyika became independent in late 1961 without significant conflict after nearly a half-century of British rule. Less than three years later, there was a minirevolution in Zanzibar (the African majority overthrew an Arab minority government), and in 1964 Tanganyika joined with the revolutionary government in Zanzibar to form the United Republic of Tanzania.

that a theory of the state is even more crucial in understanding present-day transition societies in the process of social transformation, for in them politics is the primary arena in which that transformation is played out.

Carnoy and Levin (1985) provide such a theory, at least for an advanced capitalist society. They begin by arguing that critical analysis must explain not only education's role in maintaining relatively unchanging social structures in capitalist societies but also its role in those social changes that do occur. The democratic capitalist state, they contend, is an institution that necessarily allows for change by allowing for political democracy but simultaneously is inherently obliged to reproduce capitalist social relations by being a capitalist state. The educational system is part of that state and also plays both roles: It must produce political democrats and economic capitalists. The tension between the dynamics of social democratization and those of social reproduction—both inherent and conflicting parts of the democratic capitalist state and its educational system—explains why the state and education in some historical periods act to promote social mobility and greater social equality and in other periods act to reduce social mobility and contribute to increased inequality. Education's conflicting roles create a contradiction in capitalist development by exacerbating the conflict between democratic demands—which include demands for social mobility and greater economic equality—and the demands of the hierarchical, highly unequal economic system.

Even with greater attention to the state in this critical theory, however, its usefulness for our purposes is limited by two factors. The analyses of education using various versions of state theory have concentrated on capitalist economies, and primarily on industrialized, politically democratic capitalist economies.[3] Third World countries in the process of social transformation have generally overthrown capitalist states through revolution, but the states they have overthrown were substantially different from advanced capitalist states. Furthermore, the economies inherited by these revolutionary regimes are hardly industrialized, and their prevalent social structure and social relations are also very different from those in the North Atlantic. Our task, therefore, has been to apply relevant elements of the critical theory outlined above to a very different setting: a process of change from a peripheral capitalist political economy, which differs significantly from advanced capitalism, to a political economy which is no longer capitalist.

To carry out this task, we needed to build on existing theories of the capitalist state in the periphery and to develop a theory of the transition

---

[3] Among the many excellent recent analyses of education in peripheral capitalist societies are Cunha 1975; Saviani 1983; Torres 1983; Rama 1984; Gadotti 1987.

state for an earlier view of these problems, (see Fagen, et al. 1986). We also have to come to understand the similarities with capitalist development and differences in the role that education plays in such a transition. There is the danger that a critical analysis of education in capitalist societies (where the goals of the private capitalist sector are often in conflict with those of the democratic public sector) is not applicable to transition societies, where, allegedly, there is no conflict between the goals of civil society and the state. Developing an analysis of education in transition societies requires a systematic and detailed examination of the actual experiences of these five countries and extensive discussion of their implications for a theory of education in the transition.

THE CASE STUDIES

The case studies are the particulars from which we develop the general. In these studies, we were guided by a set of common concerns. The first of these concerns is the pretransition inheritance. The countries we study were, at the time of their revolution (or independence, in the case of Tanzania), in the periphery of the world capitalist system, that is, they were part of that system but had little control over their economic and social development process. We define this pretransition situation as "conditioned" capitalism.[4] The legacy of this era preceding both the revolution and the transition is not only important but much more important than we had anticipated. History does not begin anew with the revolution or with independence. Revolutionary movements have to pay attention to the legacy of the past. That attention has to be systematic and

---

[4] In our view, the term "conditioned" rather the widely used term "dependent" should be used to describe periphery-center relations for two reasons: (1) "Dependency" somewhat misdefines these relations. As we show in succeeding chapters, "dependency" implies a degree of correspondence between economic and social change in the center and the periphery that fails to account for many social structures and social changes in periphery countries, changes that are also shaped by a local dynamic. Cardoso and Faletto (1979) have argued that political formations and economic development in the periphery depend not only on the dominant world economic structure but on local resources, the development of a local class structure, and the development of local social movements. The term "conditioned" better captures this more complex relationship between center and periphery. (2) The semantic substitution of "conditioned" for "dependent" also serves to distinguish between the more stereotyped "structural" version of dependency theory as found in the works of Frank (1967) and Amin (1970) and the more dialectical conception of dependency in Cardoso and Faletto's work (see Chapter 2 of this volume). We wish to focus on this second version. And although it can be argued that all social relations are conditioned, Cardoso and Faletto highlight important differences among periphery countries regarding the *degree* of conditioning and the political and economic forms that emerge from various degrees of conditioning. The importance of such differences becomes even clearer in studying transition societies.

coherent and has to have a sense of what is to be done in terms of what is inherited. In turn, existing structures and consciousness shape the political and social transformations that take place. We pay considerable attention, then, to the economic and political conditions in each country before the revolution.

The second concern is with the relevant political history of the change from a capitalist to a transition society. In each country, we trace the emergence, character, and trajectory of the revolutionary or independence movement that is now shaping that society's social transformation, with particular focus on the role that education plays in the movement's definition of social transformation. Each of the movements studied, we find, had a partially different understanding of what the transition—the process of social transformation—should be, how it should be achieved, what its essential ingredients and characteristics were, and what was important but less central. The process by which the current government came to power in Cuba and shaped the transition there is different from the process that occurred in Tanzania, and both are different from the process whereby power and social transformation were achieved in China. In three of the countries—Cuba, Mozambique, and Nicaragua—foreign-financed, armed counterrevolutionary interventions were a prominent feature of the transition. The understanding of the transition therefore differs across the five countries. We had to bring these differences into an overall, wider analysis of education in that transition.

A third concern in the case studies is to develop a periodic history in which the particular options chosen can be situated in terms of whatever else is happening in that society. For example, what are the social and political origins of a country's focus on basic education or, alternatively, on higher level skills? How does the emergence of those priorities fit with other events that were occurring in the society, for example, with changing needs for new skills and with the development of new consciousness? or with the traumatic consequences of armed intervention against the revolutionary state? How do the priorities that are assigned to different educational orientations emerge, and why do they emerge at that particular time? Who in the society are the carriers of particular policies? What are the tensions and conflicts in the choices made, and how do these shape the nature of education? How, in turn, do educational choices shape subsequent political and economic conditions?

Our fourth concern is with the outcomes of these choices. Even though the time period we are studying in some of these countries is very short, we ask what have been the principal outcomes for education, for the political, social, and economic structures, and for the link between education and these other structures. To what extent are the particular outcomes we observe—for example, increases in the level of literacy among adults or increases in primary school enrollment—associated with changes in political and economic participation, with higher levels of productivity, with changes in people's concept of their role in society? We also discuss in each study the outcome of the tension between emphasis on skill development and commitment to equality, the tension between formal and informal schooling, and the tension between the expansion of education and direct investment in production or defense. In each case, our concern is not only with outcomes but with how these outcomes shaped the transition itself.

TOWARD A THEORY OF EDUCATION IN THE TRANSITION

Our study of theory and practice leads to some important methodological conclusions. The analysis of transition societies, to an even greater extent than that of capitalist societies, must focus on the political process and the state and place less emphasis on economic relations. In the revolutionary and postrevolutionary transition, we argue, economic conditions and changes influence political change, as they do in capitalist societies. But in the transition, the state, not economic institutions, is the principal shaper of social structures. We recognize that transition states exist in a world economic system together with conditioned and advanced capitalist societies at various levels of economic development. In this sense, economic conditions out of the control of individual transition states influence their local politics and the form of their states. However, in contrast to the scenario in conditioned capitalist societies, shifts in international economics are not played out in the transition society through their impact on dominant economic groups. Rather, the shifts reflect directly on the legitimacy of the transition state and its personnel as they respond to the changes in local economic conditions that result. Social movements with deep roots in civil society do play an important role in this legitimacy. But again, even more than in capitalist societies, the focus of the social movements in the transition is the state and the state's relation to economic restructuring. Thus, in transition societies, peasants occupying land are aiming their movement solely at the state personnel, not at the landowner. Unions in conflict over the organization of production are in conflict with the state, not with a private factory owner. The struggles in these societies have shifted sharply from a conflict over private rights in conditioned capitalism to a conflict over public rights in the transition.

Education in such a change process, we find, must also occupy a somewhat different role than in capitalist societies. The conflicts over the direction education is to take are much more political and are embedded in the conflicts within the state (or revolutionary party) over national development strategies. In turn, educational strategy is much more central to political alternatives in the transition state than in capitalist societies. All transition strategies involve, in some sense, mass mobilization—and a crucial element in mobilizing masses is education.

Our focus on the political process and the state is a necessary foundation for comprehending educational changes in the countries under study. Although the countries' political structures and economies differ considerably, important threads are sufficiently common to discuss more generally.

Chapter 2 focuses on the theory of the state in periphery capitalism and in the transition. In that chapter we attempt to build a theory of the transition state. In Chapter 3 we attempt the beginnings of a theory of educational change in that context. We consider such a theory a crucial element in our understanding of why and how education developed under new conditions and the role of education in a new kind of educational and political development.

Part II of this volume presents the case studies of Cuba, China, Tanzania, Mozambique, and Nicaragua. Although we have not followed an identical outline in each study, each does address the common concerns discussed above. But each also develops different dimensions that are important to the particular transition of the individual countries.

The concluding chapter draws together the lessons from the case studies for understanding education in the transition. We show that as a group these transition societies provide valuable insights into the rewards and difficulties of expanding schooling in an economic/political system where the state and education focus on labor rather than capital and education has an explicit role in defining the nature of the state itself.

CHAPTER 2

The State and Social Transformation

Martin Carnoy

THE STATE is the principal arena where the transition from a capitalist to a postcapitalist society is shaped and implemented. It is the dominant institution where the currents of civil society are crystallized and transformed during this social transition. The transformation of a capitalist society is therefore largely a political process, carried out through a state which is itself in the process of transformation.

THE CENTRALITY OF POLITICS

A fundamental difference exists between the growth of capitalism and that of alternatives to capitalism—namely, that capitalist structures could mature within a precapitalist society but anticapitalist structures have not matured within a capitalist state. Banking and manufacturing came into being and matured in feudal society, as economic phenomena in civil society: "For centuries bourgeois man lived alongside feudal man, sometimes in uneasy accommodation, sometimes in mortal combat, but always advancing and reaching out for more power, eventually conquering and even assimilating his ancient rival. When the time finally came for bourgeois man to step forward as the master of his universe, his nature was fully formed and faithfully reflected the newly emergent ensemble of social relations" (Sweezy and Bettelheim 1971, 109). But alternatives to capitalism in civil society (in production itself)—such as militant worker organizations demanding greater control of production or worker-owned and -managed enterprises—appear (particularly to capital) as explicitly anticapitalist and hence are resisted by the bourgeoisie. Such alternatives do not flourish and mature within capitalist society.

Several arguments could be made here. First, capitalism may be still too young and energetic for alternative economic organizations to appear spontaneously. It took the Oriental trade, the discovery of the New World, and rampant corruption in the Church for feudalism to collapse and for the nascent merchant class to develop capitalist production and overthrow the absolutist state.

Second, it could be argued that economic alternatives to capitalist production are, in fact, appearing spontaneously in mature capitalist societies. One alternative is the cooperative, or worker-controlled, enterprise. These have developed in most capitalist societies and have sometimes been successful (Carnoy and Shearer 1980; Simmons and Mares 1983; Thomas and Logan 1982; Jackal and Levin 1984). Another is the "soft" management alternative within capitalist firms, which gives employees greater control over work time and the process of production and includes stock ownership plans ("Beyond Unions," 1985). A third is the labor union, not only as a bargaining unit in capitalist production but as the holder of vast amounts of capital in union pension funds. Although most unions do not (and cannot) use their funds to develop alternative production organizations, the potential for such an alternative is there.

Third, it could be argued that the principal alternatives to capitalism already coexist with it but in political rather than economic forms. The development of socialist and social-democratic parties that gain state power (in Austria, Spain, Sweden, and France, for example) could be thought of as the beginning of a new dominant form of social organization. This raises the important issue of whether the growth of such political forms are extensions of capitalism or an incipient postcapitalism. It also raises the issue of whether the existence of capitalist markets alone means that a society is capitalist or, rather, whether it is their relationship to the state that gives capitalist society its underlying character (just as it could be argued that it was not religious institutions alone but their dominance of economic and political institutions that gave feudal society its particular character).

There is no inherent reason to assume that alternatives to capitalism should arise in the form of economic institutions, even if such alternatives have their "origins" (Althusser's "last instance") in the relations of capitalist production. As Althusser (1971) has argued, the principal moment, or dynamic, of feudalism was ideological, and the institution fundamental to its cohesion was the Church. The state, to the degree that it existed under feudalism, was invested with legitimacy by the Church. Capitalism did not first surface in its ideological form but as a new economic dynamic, and its power still lies in its superior ability to accumulate capital. Merchants could flourish in feudal society because their activity did not initially conflict with its ideological base. Socialist ideology stresses its superiority as an economic system, particularly from the point of view of the working class, but it is as a sociopolitical dynamic that it emerges to make good on economic demands.

Marx insisted that capitalism could develop only by increasingly exploiting labor; hence socialism could make workers much better off than they were under capitalism. Socialism emerged as a response to unfavorable economic conditions for a new social class—wage labor. Both the existence of that class and the unfavorable—and worsening—material conditions facing it were, according to orthodox Marxism, necessary for capitalist development.

Marx and Engels's answer to this situation for the working class was not, however, the formation of alternative, worker-run production units. Instead, they called for direct political action, primarily against the capitalist state, but also against individual enterprises. Lenin did the same, and succeeded in organizing a political movement that overthrew the Russian state—itself in transformation from absolutism to capitalism—by force. Gramsci, in light of a failed attempt at worker revolt in Italy immediately after World War I, developed the concept of counterhegemony—an ideological sociopolitical struggle against capitalist cultural dominance in industrial societies.

The call to political action by socialists was a recognition of the crucial role played by the state in capitalist development. The assumption was that labor's economic situation would not and could not improve under capitalism. Capitalists would have to rely on the state to repress political opposition while capitalism expanded. But such was not universally the case. In more industrialized capitalist societies, the very political struggle engendered by workers' movements changed the capitalist equation. One of the immediate effects, even in Marx's lifetime, was that the working class won suffrage and expanded political democracy. Labor unions gained increasing bargaining rights. Finally, the state itself—through the parliamentary system that Marx and Engels (and Lenin) considered a "bourgeois facade"—altered the legal claims that labor had on national resources. In the industrialized countries, the crisis of the 1930s prompted the capitalist state to incorporate organized labor as an element in the policymaking structure of the capitalist state. This changed the very nature of the capitalist state (Buci-Glucksmann and Therborn 1981). The result was that in the post-World War II expansion, Keynesian stabilization policies tended to maintain the labor share in output or even increase it (Przeworski and Wallerstein 1982; Bowles and Gintis 1982).

Not all societies in the transition to capitalism have been able to adjust to working class political demands. Revolutions in Russia and China succeeded in overthrowing states in transition to capitalism that were incapable of either repressing armed uprisings or, alternatively, compromising sufficiently with workers and peasants to maintain capitalism as an economic-political system. But the success of these revolutions (although economic exploitation was a critical root cause of dissatisfaction and unrest) was also directly the result of the inability of the state to respond to political crises (Skocpol 1979). In Russia, the final crisis was generated by the Tsar's and then the Duma's continued participation in an unpopular war. In China, it was the Kuomintang's disorganized response to Japanese invasion.[1]

---

[1] Antonio Gramsci's concept of hegemonic crisis (Gramsci 1971; Buci-Glucksmann 1980) analyzes such historical moments in terms of the inability of a dominant fraction of the

Later revolutions all occurred in the Third World, and all involved prolonged armed struggles against the military forces of corrupt dictatorships or colonial regimes—military forces that were ineffective in containing the struggle primarily because of their political illegitimacy. This suggests, first, that there is something about capitalism in periphery capitalist countries (including pre-World War I Russia) that makes it more difficult for capital to compromise with labor demands for greater economic participation in capitalist development and, second, that the state in those societies is much less capable, as a state, of responding to political action by workers and peasants demanding social and political change.

The fact that successful revolutions have been confined to the periphery has led some analysts (Baran 1957; Frank, 1967; Amin 1970, for example) to argue that revolution (armed overthrow of the capitalist state) is inherently a Third World phenomenon. The expansion of political democracy in the advanced industrial countries has enabled the working class to make material gains within capitalism. Such gains have precluded (at least until the present) the need to replace capitalism there with an alternative economic system that would raise wages and reduce worker alienation, but only at the cost of extracting more surplus from the Third World, hence making similar changes in the periphery impossible. Revolution is therefore a logical result of metropolitan economic and social development and the only possible solution to Third World underdevelopment.

Other analysts (Cardoso and Faletto 1979, for example)—and we agree with these—argue that economic and political conditions in the Third World are not strictly determined by conditions in the metropole but rather by a combination of metropole-periphery economic relations and sociopolitical conditions in each peripheral society. In that model, although the possibilities of compromise with the working class in the metropole do emanate in part from the capability of the metropole to extract surplus from the periphery, they also are the result of political conditions (the nature of the social struggle and the development of the state apparatuses) in the metropoles themselves. In these advanced industrial societies, the state has expanded greatly in the context of increased economic demands by the working class (Buci-Glucksmann and Therborn 1981) or by the "employee society," as it is called by some analysts (see *Business Week*, July 8, 1985). This type of politically democratic capitalist state is characterized by a significant degree of political participation or

---

bourgeoisie to organize state power to reproduce bourgeois hegemony. Skocpol (1979, 1985) views the state bureaucracy as having considerably more autonomous political power than in the Gramsci analysis. Hence, the crisis for Skocpol develops largely because the state leadership is unable to respond adequately to reproduce its power.

accountability (Schmitter 1983), and the institutions of the state are thus well organized to deal with political conflict.

In the periphery, the possibilities for such a compromise are much more limited, but cannot be completely excluded, especially in the larger economies. The armed overthrow of the capitalist state is viewed as one path to a postcapitalist society and the most logical path in those societies where political action by subordinate groups for increased political and economic power cannot be diffused by existing institutions.[2]

Whether social democracy is a viable political form in the periphery (or even in the metropole) and whether social democracy represents a stage of the transformation of capitalism is beyond the scope of our study, but our analysis suggests that the control of state apparatuses by regimes committed to the working class could represent the beginning of the transformation of capitalist society—a democratic political alternative to the capitalist state cohabiting with capitalist economic institutions.[3]

At present, we cannot observe a democratic transition to a postcapitalist society in the Third World (or, many would argue, anywhere else).[4] The transition societies we analyze in this study are existing forms of al-

[2] It may be difficult to imagine alternatives to capitalism developing in a society with a participative and/or accountable capitalist state. Even though contradictions arise in capitalist development, until now politically democratic capitalism has had the flexibility to transcend them. But, at the same time, these adjustments—such as social democracy (in Austria and Sweden, for example)—have altered capitalism significantly by transforming the capitalist state. If alternatives were to develop in such societies as a response to new contradictions, the juridical, economic, and political systems, whereas necessarily having to undergo change, would probably do so through the existing parliamentary democracy.

[3] This is the implication of the argument in, for example, Carnoy and Shearer 1980, or Bowles and Gintis 1986. Bowles and Gintis also claim that changing family (gender) relations could be a source of the transformation of capitalist society. It seems, however, that the major changes in family relations in capitalist societies (and, indeed, in "socialist" societies) occur through women's organized political action to change social legislation. The success of such action comes about more, it seems, because of "consciousness-raising" by women in the state (through politicians' necessary responsiveness to women's votes) than in the family (through interaction of individual women and men and children).

[4] A country such as the Philippines was initially viewed as possibly providing a good case study of a peripheral economy implementing significant social change as a social democracy (see "Aquino's Acceptable Left," *In These Times* 10 [September 10–16, 1986]: 8–9). But Aquino faces the same problem faced by most Third World conditioned democracies attempting to equalize the distribution of income and wealth. The military—as the repressive apparatus of the state—is not committed to the profound social change necessary to transform such societies. Its hierarchy is partly "revolutionary" but still largely tied to traditional socioeconomic elites. At the same time, the military remains much more politically powerful, as an institution, than in highly industrialized countries, primarily because of its social base in the traditional, landowning bourgeoisie, but also because of its symbolic power as a force for social order among the petite bourgeoisie and liberal professions. These latter groups are particularly important for the reproduction of state power in these Third World social democracies.

ternatives to capitalism, forms that have developed out of the particular historical conditions of these societies. Four of the five countries studied (all but Tanzania) underwent armed revolution. Evidently, in the peripheral capitalism that preceded the revolution, the state was unable to come to terms with the political and social conflict facing it.[5]

LIMITS ON THE CONDITIONED STATE AND THE
REVOLUTIONARY ALTERNATIVE

What is it about these states, in general, that limits their responsiveness to such conflict? We will argue that the state the revolution overthrows in such societies is highly restrictive in its participative base and its accountability to various groups. The institutions of the state are accessible to only a limited few. The prerevolutionary state apparatuses overthrown by revolutions in Russia and China, for example, can be best characterized as postfeudal states in transition to capitalism (see Skocpol 1979), even though the most dynamic sectors of their civil societies were dominated by capitalist relations of production. Although there is a great deal of controversy over the nature of the state in present-day Third World capitalist countries (see Carnoy 1984, ch. 7), it is considerably different from the state in industrialized capitalist societies. We can characterize that Third World state as a "conditioned" capitalist state. It is conditioned by the nature of the peripheral role that its economy plays in the world system and the corresponding enormous influence that the dynamic of metropolitan capitalism has on its development process. The Third World state is also conditioned by the significant noncapitalist (postfeudal) elements in its own political system.[6]

The nature of these states and their inability to respond to demands for greater popular political participation and increased accountability of state personnel are crucial factors in the birth and success of local revolutionary movements and shape their ideology. Such movements are not primarily anticapitalist. Rather, they are either anticolonialist, in those cases where a foreign power controls the state directly, or anti–local corruption and authoritarianism. The very "backwardness" of these states makes the revolutions that overthrow them often less socialist than nationalist, and—at least initially—often more committed to redefining the relationship of the state to civil society than to replacing capitalism.

[5] That such failure to deal with social conflict is often but not *necessarily* the case is borne out by the existence of Third World capitalist states that have confronted attempted revolutions and survived, and by the move toward political democratization in some authoritarian capitalist states.

[6] See our reasons given in note 4 to Chapter 1 for using the term "conditioned" rather than "dependent" to describe the Third World state.

Offe (1973) contends that the principal functions of the advanced capitalist state are to foster capital accumulation in private production units that are separate from the state (and over which the state has no direct control) and to resolve crises that occur in the capital accumulation process. Since the personnel of the state have no power base of their own, they need some mandate for action derived from an alternative source of power—this source of power is the legitimation afforded by the symbolism of mass participation in the selection of the state personnel (Offe 1973). It is precisely this mandate that allows the capitalist state to resolve crises in capital accumulation and to reproduce itself as a state.

However, the personnel of the conditioned Third World state bureaucracy, although allied with important sectors of industrial and financial capital (including transnational business), still operate largely as if they were independent of the long-term needs of those groups. The bureaucracy promotes capital accumulation but does so within the context of enriching state bureaucrats, and state funds are used primarily to enhance the political networks of those in power. These are also secondary characteristics of the advanced capitalist state, but in the conditioned state they are primary. This primitive capitalist state defends capitalist interests without itself being fully developed as a capitalist state. In Offe's terms, the state bureaucracy does not assume the function of promoting capital accumulation as such; rather, it primarily promotes accumulation that is directly useful to the power of state bureaucrats. Further, the state is primarily dedicated to reproducing a particular configuration of political networks, rather than a set of bureaucratic institutions related to the accumulation of capital.

Most important, the conditioned state—as opposed to the advanced capitalist state—does not have a mandate for action (legitimacy) derived from mass participation in the selection of the state personnel (or at least of those who pick the state personnel). It therefore never develops institutional legitimacy. Instead, it seeks its mandate through populist policies and charismatic leaders. The state bureaucracy derives its power from personalistic ties to various individuals and institutions in civil society. Those who are not in the state network are outside it. The state, in turn, in the absence of populist, charismatic leadership, has legitimacy for the small minority tied into it directly. Consequently, its capability for handling accumulation crises is limited.[7]

[7] Nicaragua and, more recently, Haiti are cases where economic difficulties became magnified when extremely particularistic regimes could not—in their limited network structure—maintain political legitimacy in the face of increasing economic difficulties. Relying on more intense police repression (a usually reliable alternative for particularistic states' populist leadership) only exacerbated counterviolence in these cases and further delegitimized the regimes.

This is not to say that all conditioned capitalist states are conditioned by the same degree of particularism. Because of the very size of their economies, some, such as India, Brazil, Argentina, and Mexico, have developed a dynamic in which internal factors are particularly important. The local state is somewhat autonomous vis-à-vis international capital.[8] The dynamic of these societies is heavily conditioned by the world economy, and their states operate more particularistically than those in advanced capitalist societies. However, their states are also marked by mass participation in choosing the leadership. The more flexible conditioned state apparatuses in the larger economies are also more capable of dealing internally with popular-based conflict.[9]

When revolutions have been successful, therefore, it has been against particularistic and authoritarian states. Such states' bureaucracies do not base their legitimacy on mass participation; hence, they are not able to incorporate dissident political elements. Difficulties in accumulating capital also make this incorporation difficult (as we discuss below). However, we argue that these factors are not sufficient to explain the state's incapacity for compromise.

LIMITS ON THE TRANSITION

Once the state is overthrown, the revolution has to face the difficulty of developing new state apparatuses in the context of a conditioned capital-

[8] Evans (1979), in his study of conditioned development in Brazil, discusses a triple alliance of international capital (embodied in transnational corporations), local capital, and the state. In this alliance, "the centrality of the state to accumulation on the periphery is incontrovertible" (p. 43). The role of the state is "to redirect the global rationality of the multinational when it conflicts with the necessities of local accumulation. The state must continually coerce or cajole the multinationals into undertaking roles they would otherwise abdicate" (p. 44). Not all states have the bargaining power to achieve this redirected rationality, but where the state controls valuable resources, it can coerce the multinationals. Therefore, in these larger, newly industrializing economies, conflict is not limited to the ruling triple alliance with the popular classes, but may also take place within the alliance, resulting in more autonomy for the peripheral state. There are also struggles within the state concerning the nature of the bargaining to take place and the toughness of the bargaining position.

[9] The state has also developed new forms as part of dealing with this conflict. Mexico, for example, which had a popular revolution and civil war of its own between 1911 and 1917, produced a single party, "corporatist" state form, which co-opted popular movements into the ruling Partido Revolucionario Institucional (PRI). The PRI itself was the condensation of worker and peasant movements that had made the revolution, and was organized on a corporatist basis, preserving individual members' class identification through class-based organizations tied to the PRI. The Mexican state bureaucracy, on the other hand, continued to be particularistic in the traditional pattern, although, ultimately, through the PRI leadership, the state moved to distribute land and nationalize certain industries. The state also developed a public investment strategy that, with earlier reforms, was able to produce long-term, sustained capitalist growth.

ist society with particularistic and authoritarian political apparatuses. The absence of well-developed capitalist state apparatuses makes it unlikely that the new state will reconstitute itself as a political democracy—even as a new version of political democracy (where, for example, democratically constituted mass organizations control state decisionmaking and local political and worker organizations control production)—in either participative or accountability terms (Schmitter 1983). The lack of political democracy, in turn, raises serious questions about (1) whether the political/economic system that emerges from the revolution is capable of a durable alternative and (2) what form that transition will take. The problem as Ingrao (1977) and Bobbio (1977) have argued in the context of industrial capitalist societies, is that such alternatives must include a deepened political democracy and its extension and broadening to production and social life. Can it be argued, conversely, that a "true" and durable alternative to capitalism is impossible to achieve without a democratic state?

The development of a democratic state from a conditioned capitalist one is not a simple task. For most countries in Europe, the process took at least several generations. It was also a violent process. In the European case, a bourgeoisie with rapidly expanding economic and political power allied itself with the leftovers of the aristocracy to deny political rights to the mass of peasants and workers and to women. Eventually, despite fears that the working class would vote capitalists and landowners out of power, political compromises were made that provided universal suffrage for males. The juridical and constitutional bases for the capitalist states of the twentieth century evolved sporadically and through a series of internal conflicts and invasions by neighboring states.

The takeover of the particularistic, conditioned capitalist state by revolutionary forces necessarily requires a different political transformation of the state than occurred in nineteenth-century Europe. In the latter case, a capitalist economy dominated civil society, and even the state of Louis Napoleon (1850–1871) or pre-World War I Prussia depended on an "autonomous" bourgeoisie for capital accumulation and resultant government revenue. These were, for all intents and purposes, bourgeois states. Eventually, in a fitful and violent process, the postfeudal European state developed institutions that could reconcile capitalist development with working class demands—institutions that gradually reduced Bonapartist or Hapsburg particularist and authoritarian influence. The new state in revolutionary societies must simultaneously constitute itself and transform a dependent latifundia-capitalist and traditional subsistence economy into one that accumulates capital for collective rather than individual needs. Political transformation takes place simultaneously with economic transformation, but the state, rather than civil society, is the dynamic sector. The state's ideological apparatuses in formation are, at one and the same time, attempting to constitute themselves and to develop their hegemony in a new civil society in formation. Politics, rather than economics, is the dominant institutional base for this hegemony—hence, the form that the state takes is crucial for social and economic relations.

As Paul Sweezy has argued, "[T]he proletariat must not only change the relations of society but in the process change itself. And unfortunately, more than a century of subsequent history proves all too conclusively that there is as yet no guarantee that this can be successfully accomplished" (Sweezy and Bettelheim 1971, 116).

In theory, politics (revolutionary practice) in the transition society should replace economics as the sustenance of day-to-day life; that is, the quality of life in transition society should be increasingly viewed by the masses in terms of their political participation and less in terms of material gains. For a number of reasons, including the generally low standard of living inherited from the conditioned capitalist economy and the need to mobilize for the defense of the revolution against outside intervention, the transition state in formation and the conditioned capitalist state it replaces tend to share the necessity for capital accumulation as a primary basis for reproduction. But the need to accumulate capital and the focus on raising the standard of living is not determinant in and of itself. More important, it is the *political* decision by the hierarchy of the new state to allow economics to be defined as a technical (resource allocation) rather than as a political problem that halts the development of political institutions in transition society and, ironically, may make economic development more difficult.

In capitalism, capital is accumulated in private hands (although in many capitalist Third World countries, the state itself also accumulates capital). The state obtains resources in return for promoting the private accumulation process, at least for those with direct ties to the state personnel, and because it has a monopoly over the repressive forces in society. In the advanced capitalist states, the state can also appropriate resources for itself through taxation because it has legitimacy derived from mass participation in the political process and from the state's willingness to use resources as if it were representing mass interests (for example, redistribution of income and providing labor with free education and training).

In the transition, the state has the power to appropriate and redistribute resources in part because it has the support of the masses against the resource holders: landowners, former colonialists, foreign bourgeoisie, local rentiers, and local bourgeoisie. The state also has power because it has gained a monopoly of the repressive apparatuses. The legitimacy of the transition state depends, as in advanced capitalist society, on the acceptance of the dominant ideology—in this case, a "collectivist," redistributive ideology. In turn, this depends on the ability of the transition state to establish its hegemony (the dominance of a belief in collectivism) and in establishing an objective reality—both political and material—of which the majority of the citizenry approve. We argue that the role of the social wage (education, health care, job security, and old age security) is crucial in establishing this objective reality and that education is also important in establishing hegemony. Although many of the critiques of revolutionary societies and of Marxism in general focus on the efficiency with which socialism can increase material wealth and simultaneously distribute it more equitably (see Adelman and Robinson 1978), Marx, Lenin, and Mao were all much more concerned with the process of economic growth (who got the fruits of the economy and how distribution took place) than with the rapidity of increase. However, since Stalin's economic policies in the late 1920s, many Marxist analysts have contended that material wealth would increase more rapidly *because* of more equitable distribution and the elimination of alienating capitalist relations of production. In the more recent dependency literature, "stagnation" theorists, such as Frank (1967) and Amin (1980), claim that economic growth in the capitalist Third World is unlikely and even structurally impossible because of the economic relations between metropole and periphery. Essentially, they argue, economic growth in the metropole requires economic stagnation in the periphery—and hence, only socialism can produce material development.

But there is at best only mixed evidence that material wealth does increase more rapidly in bureaucratic, state-planned economies. Whereas the distribution of access to resources is more equitable in such societies, the difficulty of increasing material wealth is as great as in dependent capitalism. Poor countries in the transition to postcapitalist alternatives face many of the same limits to development that they had as economies in the transition to capitalism. Further, because the transition state has historically been attacked militarily by powerful capitalist opponents, capital accumulation is made more difficult on two counts: Production is sabotaged by metropole-sponsored, counterrevolutionary guerrillas, and an inordinately high percentage of state revenues goes to military spending. But the legitimacy of the transition state still relies on raising the material consumption of the population. To the extent that this legitimacy erodes, the state turns increasingly to the repressive forces at its disposal.

The transition state simultaneously reorganizes capital accumulation on a collective basis and reconstitutes itself as political *and* civil society. Under capitalism, the state develops as the condensation of economic relations. In transition society, the economy and social life are a condensation of political relations. The constitution of the state in revolutionary, transition societies is an attempt by revolutionary forces to rebuild political, economic, and social relations on different grounds—grounds that only exist theoretically. To some extent, this was also the project of early capitalist philosophers such as Locke, Hobbes, Rousseau, and Adam Smith. The classless, rational society they envisaged was a theoretical construct. Hence, the state they envisaged—for example, the state of the "general will" in Rousseau's social contract—depended for its existence on a degree of equality in economic and social relations that was never realized in objective reality.

The ideologues of the revolutionary transition also attempt to constitute a state that is based on idealized relations in civil society—on a theoretical construct of economic and social relations that is even more outside the experience of their society than the constructs of the early liberal philosophers. At least Adam Smith was able to observe markets, capitalist-employee relations and the division of labor at work in his own society. He idealized those concepts, giving them moral and political attributes that were ideological representations of reality. The model therefore failed to conceptualize the capitalist state and social relations as they developed. But much of what he said about the economic aspects of markets themselves was correct. The transition ideologues tend to make the mistake of basing their political model on a vision of collective relations of production in civil society that they have never seen work. Instead, from our perspective, they should begin with a construction of revolutionary political relations and their development, taking existing economic and social relations as given and as the object of change. The relations in civil society will have to be altered as part of a general transformation, but politics and the state are and must be the starting point of this transition, not vice versa. In both an empirical and normative sense, therefore, politics and the state are the primary focus of analysis in the transition—the beginning point of understanding the nature of structural change in revolutionary societies. This is precisely what we propose to do.

We will argue that four principal factors condition the nature of the transition state:

1. the state bureaucracy;
2. the legacy of the predecessor conditioned capitalist state;
3. counterrevolutionary foreign military intervention; and
4. the capitalist world economy.

The state bureaucracy is the principal dynamic force in shaping transition society. Politics, not economics, dominate the development and structures of transition societies. Hence, the economy and society are a condensation of political forces. The transition state attempts to develop a capital accumulation process based on collective goals and simultaneously constitute a new set of state apparatuses.

The capitalist state, we claim, has been overthrown by violent revolution only in societies with states best characterized as conditioned-capitalist or colonial-capitalist (a subset of conditioned capitalism), typified by particularistic and/or authoritarian characteristics, and underdeveloped in their ability to incorporate dissension and conflict. This may not be the only form of the transition. We pointed out that what have been called new forms of the capitalist state, such as those in Sweden and Austria, may actually be the beginnings of alternatives to capitalism. But the revolutionary alternative is the most visible in today's predominantly capitalist world. The political institutions of conditioned capitalist societies have shaped political culture in those societies. This is the "raw material" for revolutionary politics and the transition state. Thus, the starting point of the transition is not an advanced, liberal democratic capitalist state, organized around mass participation, but a conditioned state, marked by particularistic, authoritarian relations, severely limited participation in the selection of state personnel, and close ties to a single, dominant foreign power and its capital investment.

The revolutionary transition takes place in a world society dominated by powerful capitalist states. Their hegemony requires—and enables—opposition to alternative political and social forms, particularly those that might have appeal in societies with relatively inflexible, conditioned states. In the present historical conjuncture then, the transition state, in the first instance, is usually forced to defend itself militarily against counterrevolutionary interventions by hostile capitalist states. The military intervention of capitalist states against revolutionary transitions has usually been characterized as an expression of capitalist interests. It may have such roots. But capitalists themselves have, to a large extent, accommodated to the existence of noncapitalist economies, and, as we argue below, vice versa. A more persuasive explanation of such intervention is that the capitalist state, representing the hegemony of certain groups of capitalists in alliance with fractions of other classes, as well as the state personnel's own interests, uses counterrevolutionary actions and the threat of revolution in the Third World as a means of legitimizing power in the capitalist state itself. The threat of revolutionary regimes, real as it may be to the hegemony of that fraction of the capitalist class, is much less of a threat to capitalism itself than the development of political alternatives within industrial capitalist societies. And even though the physical costs to the revolutionary state of foreign-sponsored military actions are extremely high, they do provide to revolutionary regimes—which are fundamentally nationalist and antiimperialist in origin—an important source of legitimacy for the new state and its attempts to redefine national identity in revolutionary terms.

The transition also takes place in a world economy dominated by capitalism, in which advanced technology is in the hands of capitalist firms, consumer styles are set by capitalist markets, and those markets are the important sources of capital accumulation for both conditioned capitalist and revolutionary transition peripheral societies. There are two important implications of this dominance of capitalism in the world economy. The first, and most direct, is that transition states have to interact with the world capitalist system to develop their forces of production. The "smaller" a country's economy, the more trade and capital inflow from the capitalist world will play a role in its economic development, although separation from traditional sources of supply is an important part of the nationalist element of revolutionary transformation. But even the larger economies must import at least some advanced technology (often in the form of joint ventures with capitalist firms) if they hope to develop certain kinds of advanced industrial production capability and research and development capacity. The second, and more indirect, implication is that the dominance of capitalist consumption styles means that the legitimacy of the transition state will depend significantly on its ability to raise the material conditions of the citizenry, particularly on its ability to make available Western-style consumption goods. In the short run, and even medium run, there may be a trade-off between raising material consumption and the development of alternative values based on collective political participation and new kinds of social interaction.

The task before us is to understand this transition state as it develops in theory and practice—that is, under the conditions outlined above—and the crucial role that public education plays in this development. The context of this theory and practice is the conditioned capitalist society (including the conditioned state) inherited by the revolution. We contend that the sociopolitical transformation of conditioned capitalist society is heavily influenced by the historical context of its capitalist development, on the widely held assumption that at the moment of the overthrow of the capitalist state by revolutionary forces, the appeal of revolutionary ideology is primarily negative (eliminate the oppressive existing state) rather than a developed counterideology upon which the new state can transform the society. The new state must therefore transform *existing* values as part of the postcapitalist transition.

THE FORMATION OF THE TRANSITION STATE

Underlying limitations inhibit the conditioned capitalist state in its attempts to reintegrate the individual into a "people-nation" that symbolizes equality, social mobility, economic security, and political responsibility. These limitations have important implications for a revolutionary movement that inherits the history of a dependent capitalist society, even as the revolution changes the structural context in which that history is made.

As such movements attempt to transform a society by political means—through political movements and a revolutionary state in the process of transformation—they must do precisely what the advanced capitalist state does reasonably well: develop mass support to reproduce themselves. But in this case, the reproduction is to take place on a collective rather than a private basis and with collective rather than individual goals. With its direct, explicit, and primary political-social role (rather than the indirect, implicit supporting role that politics plays in capitalism to the primary social institution of the private market), the revolutionary state should, in theory, develop this mass support through much closer political, economic and social ties between state and the citizenry than in capitalist societies—even advanced ones.

At the same time, the very nature of the revolution in such societies—the process of political and physical struggle, itself conditioned by the structural conditions that allow the revolution to succeed—produces the new state that shapes the new society. This struggle requires close and direct ties between constituency and movement leadership in order to succeed.[10] But the long history of particularistic, authoritarian, and colonial structures of the conditioned capitalist state, which the revolutionary movement seeks to overthrow, has resulted in a highly underdeveloped political culture and, historically, usually low levels of political participation. The citizenry may therefore support the ideals of the revolutionary movement, but the institutions do not exist through which that support can be translated into direct political action or influence.

Revolutionary groups opposed to the capitalist state envisage a society that reintegrates the separated wage worker into a collective mode of production and is "led" in this transformation by a revolutionary party and a revolutionary state. In practice, the revolutionary state must constitute itself as part of the transformation. Nicos Poulantzas (1980) analyzed the capitalist state as a series of ideological elements that characterize its relation to civil society. The individual, law, the nation, and knowledge can be viewed as the major elements in the constitution of any state—capitalist or transition. The successful political constitutional-

---

[10] It is commonly assumed in the United States, on the basis of what happened in Soviet-controlled Eastern Europe after World War II, that revolutionary movements succeed through political-military coups by a small group directed from outside the country. This model is totally inconsistent with the history of the movements in the five countries we analyze in this study.

ization of these elements, given the limited political infrastructure and conditioned economic conditions inherited by revolutionary movements and the military intervention by foreign states after the revolution, both defines the society and forms the basis of the citizenry's acceptance of the state's legitimacy. In this study, we are particularly interested in the role that education plays in this reconstitution and the creation of the new, collective individual. But before turning to a detailed analysis of education in this process, it is important to set the context of political and social change in such revolutionary societies. We therefore first analyze how the revolutionary state attempts to reconstitute the four elements for an alternative development and an alternative basis for legitimacy.

THE CONTEXT OF THE TRANSITION

The movements that take over the dependent capitalist state—whether by military means or by nonviolent resistance—and set out to transform society and construct a new state have, by their very nature, an idealistic purpose. They are revolutionary. They would like to, and believe they can, create a new, classless society in which people are equal, will work collectively to satisfy individual and collective material needs, will participate politically on a daily basis to develop revolutionary practice, and will reach their maximum human potential through self-education, improved health, and mutual support. Through such political and social transformation, these movements believe that the new people-nation (and therefore its members) can eliminate dependency in all its forms, especially the violence and exploitation experienced by the masses in conditioned capitalist society, their low level of learning and skills, and the subordination of the economy and society to the necessities of the metropole powers. The revolution promises, overall, to seize history from the metropoles and their local agents and to put it in the hands of the mass of citizens. This ideal underlies the political dynamic of social reconstitution that takes place after the overthrow of the conditioned state. But there is also another ideal that emerges from armed overthrow of the state: Revolutionary movements that develop in armed struggle are committed to struggle itself. Revolutionaries have spent years fighting for their cause. They have overcome adversity by believing fervently in themselves as agents of history and in their cause as historic. Their struggle has produced victory, so further struggle, if necessary, will do the same. Many revolutionaries believe that revolutionary practice and struggle are inseparable.

Furthermore, those who overthrow the state (in Cuba, Mozambique, and Nicaragua, for example) are often not members of a political party with years of practice organizing political action at the local and national level, but rather a political-military organization used to overcoming obstacles by military means. The leaders who first take power in such cases—even though widely popular and enjoying mass support—have to organize the new state against continued internal political opposition, economic disruption and backwardness, and, in many cases, armed interventions supported by external powers. Ultimately, it is a political party that takes over the making and implementation of political and economic decisions, and this shift from military to political structure is crucial to understanding the nature of political development in revolutionary societies. But given their commitment to struggle and their primarily military experience, the movement's leaders' response to political and economic difficulties in the revolution's early years often has overtones of military organization. The more that armed opposition plays a role in the postrevolutionary phase of political reconstitution, the longer the revolutionary military will be an integral political force in the new form of the state.

Even so, there is a complex relationship between military-type authoritarianism and the new form of the transition state. The need to mobilize the population to overcome counterrevolutionary guerrilla forces also creates new forms of mass participation at the local level. The best defense that the revolution has to offer is the commitment of the population to the revolution. In both Mozambique and Nicaragua, for example, despite the fact that the revolutions in those two countries were very different, they shared an important political reality that is totally contradictory to traditional (European-based) Marxist theory: The mass of small-landholding peasants was a crucial revolutionary constituency. The protracted war against foreign-supported guerrillas ultimately forced the government to recognize the political importance of the local peasantry and mobilize them in ways that they had not envisaged in their earlier political-economic strategies. Such mobilizations have created greater political and economic participation, not less.

In the later stages of the transition, once the war against counterrevolutionary forces is won, the fact that the struggle was necessary makes military strength important (to protect against future possible invasions), giving a greater military hue to revolutionary ideology and political structures than they would otherwise have. As in capitalist societies, the military itself often tends to emerge as a conservative and hierarchical force in political decisionmaking, mistrusting social movements and other mass organizations, and often resisting economic and political democratization.

The revolutionary movement also inherits a conditioned society, including a low level of development of material forces and human skills. In all the cases of this study, the economy at the moment of the revolution was primarily an agricultural economy, which was both traditional and, in its most advanced forms, export oriented. The economy was characterized by low levels of capital per worker and low levels of worker education. Sociopolitical structures in civil society were repressive and traditional. The skills that did exist in the export sector were often foreign and left the country, to one degree or another, soon after the revolution.[11] All these societies except China were and continue to be heavily primary-export dependent, which means that the flight of these skills creates enormous difficulties for capital accumulation in the transition economy.

The agricultural base and relatively underdeveloped industry of all countries that have undergone revolutionary takeovers of their conditioned capitalist states confronts the revolutionary movements with an economic and sociopolitical situation little related to nineteenth-century Marxism. The "peasant issue" was dealt with in an extremely heavy-handed way in both Russia and China as part of the collectivization of peasant agriculture, on the assumption by both Stalin and Mao that kulak or Chinese family agriculture was an otherwise insurmountable barrier to socialism. In retrospect, it is unclear that those policies were correct. More important, the problem of market-oriented versus nonmarket-oriented agriculture for revolutionary movements is conditioned on the size of the economy they inherit and their need to maintain exports to finance imports. In Mozambique and Nicaragua, traditional socialist theory dictated that the new dynamic of economic development should be carried out by nationalized farms producing export crops and cooperatives of small holders. Both nationalized farms and coops were worked by "proletarianized" and therefore "conscious" agriculture labor. Individual peasants were considered inherently unmobilizable. However, under the exigencies of protracted struggle against counterrevolutionaries and significant management errors in the collectivized and cooperative sectors, Frelimo and the Sandinistas both have had to turn to mobilizing the traditional peasantry, giving them increased economic and political power and bringing them into the revolution as full participants. In Nicaragua, this also meant an important land distribution in the second wave of land reform, from the state farms (previously seized from the Somoza family)

---

[11] This is not always the case—Angola, for example, has managed to keep foreign oil companies operating the wells at Cabinda. But it is much more likely that the transition state can retain high-level skills in the export sector if those who have those skills, while perhaps opposed to the revolutionary movement, identify themselves closely with the people-nation whose state was overthrown rather than being foreign companies or individuals. Thus, Zimbabwe has, with some success, attempted to retain white farmers (who were the core of the Rhodesian economy), and much of Nicaragua's coffee crop and meat exports are still controlled by the private sector (few of Nicaragua's exports were controlled by foreigners before the revolution).

to the small peasantry. At a much different stage of the transition, China has also given much greater economic independence to individual peasants, with the apparent result of large increases in agricultural production and of simple consumer goods that can be manufactured in peasants' homes.[12] It is too early to tell what the implications of such moves are for the course of revolutionary ideology and economic development in these countries, but they definitely point to a much greater pluralism of interests in the transition and perhaps a different concept of revolutionary change.

Large countries, such as China or Russia, face economic choices that are not available to "small" economies such as Nicaragua, Cuba, Tanzania, and Mozambique. The former can think in terms of a long-term, autarkic economic development, with relatively small export sectors and internal demand providing the base for material development. The latter must, even in the long term, view exports and imports as crucial elements in their economic growth. In today's world, this means dealing with capitalist metropoles and subjecting a significant portion of the economy and the labor force to international market forces, including international pricing. One of the crucial elements of conditioned capitalism is therefore retained in such small economies as a "constraint" imposed on the transition state.

The export-oriented infrastructure of the conditioned capitalist state is therefore a mixed blessing in building a transition society. On one hand, different regions of the country are better connected to the metropole than to one another. This makes the task of creating the people-nation (of unifying different groups into an identification with one another, rather than each group's seeking a separate identification with the metropole) in large part dependent on developing a new "internal" infrastructure. On the other hand, well-developed communications with the metropole allow for the maintenance and development of export markets. Problems arise, however, when communications are particularly well developed with a country that is intent on opposing the development of the transition state (and economy), as in the case of Mozambique with South Africa, or Cuba and Nicaragua with the United States. In those cases, new international infrastructures have to be developed.

Similarly, the revolution inherits an infrastructure of knowledge that is rooted in the metropole's development process and in the problems of better developing those aspects of local society that can be related to the metropole. This externally oriented expertise is generally irrelevant to

[12] Cuba allowed free markets for agricultural products and certain artisan services beginning in 1981, but Fidel Castro closed the markets abruptly in mid-1986 when he allegedly discovered large fortunes being made in agriculture (and elsewhere in the society) through market activity (see Chapter 6).

the practice of the mass of peasants and workers in the postcapitalist transformation. When applied, it tends to reproduce the hierarchies and relationships of the conditioned society. It separates the state from its political base—separates theory from practice. However, in small countries, the need to interact with the outside world economically and politically may require such expertise, both to produce the kinds of goods demanded in the metropole and to defend the revolution militarily and ideologically. The move to an external orientation even in China in the last few years has meant a resurrection of externally oriented knowledge, including sending Chinese students to the West in droves and the reestablishment of Western-style Chinese universities. Can such conditioned capitalist knowledge be made consistent with transition development? Can it be incorporated into a politically and economically participative, collective society? Is the nature of the technology necessary for an information-based industrialization, such as China is now attempting to develop, insertable into a transition society?

Inversely put, what is the effect of the need of such knowledge for material development on the sociopolitical process—on the constitution of the transition state? The Chinese are facing not only the problem of the relation between private markets and collective politics, which is the principal issue for the smaller transition economies, but the problem of the influence on the social relations of transition society of transferring technical knowledge developed in the capitalist context. The revolution inherits not only the economic structures and technology of the conditioned society but also its political institutions. The conditioned state is overthrown but not destroyed. Even when this state is colonial and the colonizers leave, many of the staff positions in the state bureaucracy continue to be occupied by people who were integrated into the conditioned capitalist (or colonial) bureaucracy and are not necessarily sympathetic to the goals of the transformation. They are also tied into the particularistic, limited-access politics of the conditioned state. But lack of qualified personnel to fill administrative posts usually requires keeping most of these bureaucrats on in the state (China and Vietnam, however, rapidly purged the inherited bureaucracy). Indeed, their particularistic connections to various groups (their "private" constituencies) at the regional and local level can be helpful if they do not use such connections to subvert the constitution of the new state.

The inherited political structure also contains powerful economic groups in the civil society who are inherently opposed to the formation of a new politics, even if individuals in these groups are allowed to accumulate capital privately, precisely because it destroys their political power.[13] It is their relative political—and, by implication, economic—

---

[13] In all of the transition societies we studied, access to material wealth is distributed

position that such groups seek to defend, and they do so intensely. They are frequently supported by external forces, often through armed struggle: "If there is a logic of the majority, there is also a political logic of the minority, and that logic is non-participatory, obstructionist, and potentially subversive. There is thus what may be called an objective and inevitable basis for conflict" (Fagen 1986, 258–59). Necessarily, therefore, as in four of the five cases we examine (only Tanzania did not have to confront some sort of armed threat), the politics of forming a transition state are intimately entwined with organizing its armed defense.

One of the opposition groups worthy of special mention—especially in the Nicaraguan case—is the religious hierarchy. The Catholic Church, closely tied to power sharing with the conditioned state, directly opposes the constitution of the transition state, even as elements of the hierarchy (the liberation theologists) participate in organizing social and political transformation. The Church's mass base and its international connections make it a formidable foe. There is nothing in Catholic theology per se that should make it opposed to transition economics or politics, as evidenced by the teachings of the liberationists. It is the conditioned capitalist form of the religious hierarchy and the Vatican's (and all organized religions') international opposition to "atheistic," anti-Church communism that inevitably make the Church hierarchy side with antirevolutionary groups. Yet this opposition—whatever its logic—is a reality for the transition state, and it conditions both ideological transformation and attempts to reconstitute law and nation.

For an armed revolution or independence movement to succeed, it must simultaneously delegitimize the conditioned capitalist state and develop legitimacy as part of its gaining of power. In turn, a revolution or overthrow of a colonial power itself produces a significant change of consciousness—the act of liberation is an act of self-re-creation, both as an individual participating in making history and as a people-nation redefining itself vis-à-vis the rest of the world. The legitimacy of the overthrow of the conditioned state and the changed consciousness accompanying the liberation struggle give the movement that organized it and took over the reins of the state a broadly based and enthusiastic grant of authority.

Nevertheless, for the mass of members of the "new" people-nation, the change in consciousness that accompanies the revolution—the individual self-re-creation and national redefinition that comes from overthrowing the oppressive state—does not include a clear concept either of class struggle or of transition social relations. Most look to the revolution to

---

more equally in the transition, reducing the income and wealth of the business and professional classes. The freedom to use wealth for further accumulation is also sharply restricted. Hence, there is a material basis for the opposition of previously privileged classes to the transition state.

improve their material existence, to bring harmony instead of violence to their lives, and to offer them self-fulfillment rather than economic and social oppression.

The revolutionary or independence movement therefore has the legitimacy and popular base to develop a transition state, and even the beginning of a change in consciousness (and certainly a willingness to go farther if it seems to work). But it must deliver tangible gains in either material or political-psychic terms (or both) in order to retain this legitimacy. And it must successfully diffuse or combat the committed opposition without losing legitimacy.

In this context, how do the movements that overthrew the colonial or postcolonial conditioned capitalist state constitute a new one, and what is its nature? As Richard Fagen points out, "In fact, appearances to the contrary, in the period immediately following the victory, there is no such thing as the 'transitional state.' There is only the old state apparatus, captured and partially restaffed by revolutionaries, plus a political-military organization (often extremely popular and sometimes well-organized) that exercises state power in the name of reconstituting the nation and directing development to benefit the less privileged (what has been called in Nicaragua 'the logic of the majority'). The 'transitional state,' in both its constitutional manifestations, is still to be created" (Fagen 1986, 252).

Both the form and practice of transition politics are crucial to the constitution of this state. To describe this transformation, it is not enough to say that the revolutionary movement or vanguard party must lead in changing the consciousness of the masses (Sweezy and Bettelheim 1971, citing Lenin) or that the market economy with its private accumulation of capital must be replaced by collective ownership, worker decisionmaking, and a distribution system based on need. We have emphasized that in the transition, politics is the dominant element in the social dynamic, crystallizing the form and content of economic structures, social relations, and the individual's rights and obligations to other individuals and the collective people-nation. The transition state is the expression of this political practice.

Constituting the Transition State

To study this expression of political practice—what Fagen calls "transitional politics"—we turn to the four sociopolitical elements that Poulantzas (1980) used to analyze the capitalist state: individualism, the law, the nation, and knowledge. These are the political elements that those who overthrow the dictator, the colonial power, or, in the case of Zimbabwe or South Africa, an "indigenous" white minority must transform in order to create a legitimate transition state and a transition society with its own, self-reproductive dynamic.

The Individual

The capitalist state reproduces the fractionalization-individualization inherent in the capitalist division of labor and social relations of production by reintegrating the isolated individual into the state, no longer as a member of a social class but as a citizen-individual, equal to all other citizen-individuals (capitalists, workers, farmers) before the law, and in terms of his/her consumption possibilities, individual expression, and political power (one person, one vote).

To reproduce itself, the transition state also has to reintegrate the individual. Reintegration is generally carried out through participation in political organizations that defend and build the revolution, that is, the change in consciousness from an individual-oriented to a collectively oriented society, and through incorporation into collective (state-owned and -managed) production and distribution organizations. Individuals' separation from the means of production is, at least in theory, eliminated by the transformation of capitalist into worker-state production and by their political participation in collective efforts by the revolutionary party or state to deliver services and achieve social transformation. The capitalist state allegedly represents the best interests of a majority of diverse individuals; the transition state represents—for the collectivity of individuals—the revolutionary transformation of capitalist into transition society. How it constitutes itself to do this legitimately is one of the principal objects of our inquiry.

Building a nonmarket economic system that separates effort from material reward (work from consumption) and value from market price has been considered an essential element in developing a collective consciousness and creating the postcapitalist individual (Sweezy and Bettelheim 1971). Sweezy, for example, argues that only through collective economic goals for production and distribution is it possible to eliminate the competitive individualism that forms the basis for social classes and exploitation. And in order to have such an economy, it is necessary for the revolutionary party to develop collective consciousness in the working class (the masses). In other words, while politics must necessarily be behind the development of the collective economy, the nature of economic institutions inherently determines individual consciousness. Thus, while the vanguard political party builds individual consciousness, the state must collectivize the means of production.

But this model has not succeeded even in countries that can consider undertaking autarkic development, such as the Soviet Union or China.

In collectivizing the means of production, the transition state develops a state bureaucracy, which can be as limiting to political participation and almost as unaccountable to the citizens of the people-nation as the conditioned state it overthrew (Sweezy and Bettelheim 1971). The individual is integrated into a collectivized economy but not one that is genuinely collective. In other words, the individual is guaranteed work, income, and health care (a social wage)—that is, security from the violence of poverty—but is given no responsibility for the economic, social, and political decisions made by the "collective" state. Collective consciousness thus cannot be expressed positively through direct collective action, but only negatively, through lack of dissent.

One of the most important problems in the development of collective consciousness, then, is how to specify the units of collective participation in which this consciousness is developed. Traditional Marxist theory focuses on production units and social classes in capitalist societies as the logical elements of such development. During the transition in the cases we are studying, however, the autonomy of collective production units such as communes, brigades, unions, and cooperatives, has been severely restricted. The participants in these units are assumed to develop consciousness there or to have it, but not to exercise political participation through them. Early Soviets functioned in production units during the early days of the Russian Revolution, but soon ceased to exercise political power. Social classes are also obvious units on which to base collective participation. But again, the leadership in all the states we studied has sought to restrict the role of classes in political participation, sometimes even asserting that after the revolution classes no longer exist.

What are the alternatives for collective participation? Ethnic/tribal, religious, regional, and racial units all pose problems, and so do organizations based on gender and age (although women's organizations are active in Cuba, Mozambique, and Nicaragua, often clashing with the revolutionary political party). In all the countries we studied except Nicaragua, there is only one political party, so plural parties are not likely to be the participation units. Smaller units, such as Cuba's Committees for the Defense of the Revolution, do not seem very effective as collective units of participation, although they function well as service, monitoring, and control units.

The most active forms of political collectivity in the countries we studied are the single mass (in Tanzania) or vanguard parties and the mass organizations. Some mass organizations are production or class based, such as teachers' unions, peasant leagues, and central workers' organizations; some are age based, such as the youth organizations, and some are gender based. Another set of collectivities are the local villages or towns, with their more traditional interests, but also with the possibility of a local democracy that is capable of carrying mass-base demands to a central hierarchy. But the mass and local organizations do not have the power of sanctions over the vanguard or mass party. Neither do they have much say in who shall represent the interests of the members of these organizations in the councils of state.

The lack of sanctions constrains the meaning of participation. It also poses a highly significant political problem that is far from being resolved. In practice, it is the degree of mass participation in the party that establishes the influence that the "public" has on political decisions. But, in general, the party is an organization limited to those with a political commitment far beyond the norm, and the party itself is not very democratic, even in terms of its own limited membership.

This also raises the fundamental issue of how to collectivize the economy without reinforcing the inherited, conditioned state bureaucracy and without converting the revolutionary movement into an extension of that bureaucracy.[14] Sweezy (Sweezy and Bettelheim 1971) argues for sustained revolution as the basis for building collective consciousness through politics and preventing development of hierarchies and therefore a "new class." The Chinese case is especially interesting because economic collectivization was followed by a period of intense political activity during the Cultural Revolution. But the violence of this "consciousness-raising" apparently made it unsustainable. Moreover, it did not destroy the centralized power of the leadership of the state bureaucracy or increase permanently the level and quality of collective political participation. Rather, the Cultural Revolution produced a mass political reaction that sought to reestablish harmony, an increase in the material conditions of life, and even individual economic and cultural expression. It can be argued that the leaders of the state bureaucracy chose, in the wake of the Cultural Revolution, to increase economic output on the "capitalist road" for reasons independent of popular demands. But most evidence suggests that, to the contrary, the changes made in the last few years have considerable mass support (see Chapter 5).

"Sustained revolution," therefore, is difficult to maintain as the political basis of the transition state. Revolution is, by its very nature, a disruptive, intense political activity that few can tolerate over the long term.

Nevertheless, for institutions to be participative, accountable, and based on the equality of those who participate in them is the sine qua non of the transition ideal. The individual in transition society is re-cre-

---

[14] When we use the term "bureaucracy," we refer to the set of institutions that carries out government policy. This set of institutions is imbued with certain characteristics—it is hierarchical, compartmentalized, authoritarian/nonparticipatory, and shielded from public pressure. We do not use the term as a synonym for government officials or government personnel, although writers such as Claus Offe do employ it in this fashion.

ated in terms of the collective participation in those institutions and the nature of the equality, social relations and political participation they engender. Unless the transition state is able to build both equality and participation into economic and political activity, the new individual will be separated both from the means of production (controlled by the state bureaucracy) and from the state, as depoliticized as in conditioned capitalism, and incorporated into the people-nation primarily through state guarantees of employment and the social wage (an "adequate" level of material consumption, health care, education for all citizens). The capacity of the state to provide that social wage becomes the single measure of the bureaucracy's accountability to the citizen-individual, and the individual defines himself/herself primarily in terms of his/her social wage (size of apartment, car/no car, level of education, access to foreign travel).

In four of the societies we examine in this volume, as well as in other transition societies, the vehicle of the political re-creation of the transition individual is the "revolutionary party"—in China, the Chinese Communist party; in Cuba, the 26th of July movement and then the new Cuban Communist party; in Mozambique, Frelimo; and in Nicaragua, the Sandinista movement and then the Sandinista party. The nature of this vanguard party—as both the creator of the new collective consciousness and the arena of political participation and accountability—is therefore crucial to understanding what that recreated, reincorporated individual will be. As early as 1905, Rosa Luxemburg, in her critique of Lenin (Luxemburg [1905] 1961), argued for a democratic mass party and freedom of the press as absolutely essential elements in building democratic socialism. Gramsci's revolutionary party as the bearer of counter-hegemony was also a mass, democratic vanguard, with every worker an organic intellectual. But in practice, revolutionary parties have opted for limited membership in an elite vanguard, and mass organizations have been "charged with implementing state policies rather than representing the interests of their constituents to the state" (Fagen 1986, 260).

In Tanzania, the Chama Cha Mapinduzi party (CCM), formerly the Tanganyika African National Union (TANU), is not a vanguard party but a mass party, even though it is the only legal Tanzanian party. To an extent, it is also democratic, in that individuals compete in elections to gain seats in the legislature. Tanzanian socialism is criticized as "half-hearted" precisely because it lacks a vanguard party composed of those politically committed to transform the society. Instead, it is argued, CCM is infiltrated by the petite bourgeoisie and "capitalist-roader" technocrats, who are opposed to developing a collective dynamic.

The arguments for a "directive" party-state led by the vanguard are based on the necessity for a long period of consciousness-raising before the masses can be given responsibility for reproducing transition society (just as it took many years before the bourgeoisie allowed workers to vote) and on the necessity to defend the revolution from constant subversion from outside. The arguments against are the arguments for democracy itself—the need for competition and criticism in order to control bureaucratic abuses and develop responsive, accountable leadership and the need for practiced political participation and criticism in order to develop participative, socially-conscious individuals.

But as Fagen points out, it is not clear what particular institutional forms democratic practice might take in the formation of the transition state: "Elements of representative democracy and multi-party contestation? Vigorous intra-party competition of the sort envisaged by Lenin and others at certain points in their writings—but never practiced in the Soviet Union (or elsewhere) except very briefly? Mass organizations wholly autonomous from the state?" (Fagen 1986, 261). Furthermore, he argues, the liberal definition of democracy as a political system in which the results of conflict are "to some extent indeterminate with regard to positions which the participants occupy in all social relations, including the relations of production . . . [a system in which] . . . the current position within the political system does not uniquely determine the chances of succeeding in the future" (Przeworski 1980, 12) may be incompatible with the concept of a vanguard party.

Put most bluntly, does a commitment to democracy in the transition imply that in time the revolutionary vanguard may simply be transformed into just one more contender for power? If not, what are the specifics and limitations of the vanguard's right to rule (or lead, or guide, or orient)? (Fagen 1986, 252–53).[15]

THE INDIVIDUAL AND THE TRANSITION ECONOMY

What about the role of the economy in defining the new individual? Collectivizing the economy has not, in and of itself, developed collective consciousness. Unless the state is able to recreate the collectivized worker as a "collective" individual political actor-participant, he or she retains his or her isolation (although in a different form) from the means

[15] In our case studies, we observe intraparty competition (Tanzania); local "advisory" elections (Cuba); and, in the most interesting experiment, a national legislative election in which parties opposed to the revolution were allowed to participate and won more than 30 percent of the vote (Nicaragua). One possibility is to democratize the vanguard party over a "reasonable" period of time (open the party to all) and hold within-party elections all the way up to the leadership level. Almost anybody can try to join Frelimo, for example. The criteria are quite strict (no immorality, no oppression, no colonial fascist links, no one who hires labor), but do not exclude the majority in Mozambique. Inside the party there are elections, and many new people have come in, right up to the central committee. The very top figures, however, remain the same. The problem is that party loyalty is very strong and to change the very top of the party would be a direct criticism of the party as a whole.

of production. In this case, the now collectivized worker is alienated by state management rather than by private capital. It is almost the worst of all possible worlds as far as production is concerned: By guaranteeing a social wage, the state gives up the power to extract effort from workers through capitalist discipline (workers' fear of losing their livelihood) but does not replace that discipline with a collective consciousness that produces a new quality of worker effort. For Third World revolutionary movements, the experience of "established" transition states, such as the USSR, China, Cuba, and Tanzania, therefore poses important problems. On one hand, all of these states have tried to raise worker productivity in agricultural and industrial production through various forms of collectivization and moral incentives with only moderate success. On the other hand, increased material consumption of basic necessities is an important expectation of the revolution on the part of the masses. Revolutionary movements have to be concerned by these expectations and have to fulfill them in order to remain legitimate and to exact more collective effort on behalf of the people-nation. One of the reasons, after all, for overthrowing the conditioned state was that it misutilized resources and kept the masses in poverty.

The transition state also re-creates the individual as a collective consumer, and the state must deal with the issue of producing enough goods to raise material consumption over time. It may be able to reduce such demands through raising political consciousness, but it cannot avoid the necessity of also validating its legitimacy through material gains.

For low-income, conditioned societies, such as Mozambique, Tanzania, Nicaragua, and even Cuba (which had relatively well-developed forces of production in 1959), accumulating capital and raising consumption levels through collectivization is particularly difficult for two fundamental reasons: (1) The conditioned economy inherited by the revolution has a low level of productive factors and is badly organized to produce surplus in all but the export-import sector; and (2) the export-import sector least lends itself to collectivization because it is tied into the international capitalist economy, requiring market sensitivity, market pricing, and market skills.

In "small" economies, we have argued, the limitations on autarky force at least the export-import part of the economy to be "open." Is it possible to have (partly) a market economy and develop collective consciousness? What impact do market elements in the economy have on the nature of the transition state? Bettelheim and Sweezy have argued that a market economy forms individual consciousness that is necessarily anticollective—it necessarily tends toward private capital accumulation. Hence, the market creates an individual who cannot be integrated into transition collective politics. But to produce the necessary surplus in the export sector for financing necessary imports in the short and medium run, countries such as Angola, Zimbabwe, and Nicaragua rely heavily on private capital and management.

This is a very different problem from that posed by kulak production in the Soviet Union or the family farm in China, both of which allegedly constituted a political obstacle to the revolution by elements of the masses. In the present-day case, private capital in export production as a link to international markets means maintaining islands of capitalist production in the transition economy while separating that capital from its previous level of political power. These islands do not represent mass-based centers of conditioned capitalist consciousness, although they may try to link themselves to such centers through counterrevolutionary activity—for example, to the religious hierarchy, as in Nicaragua, or to popular dissenting groups, as in Angola (Union for the Total Independence of Angola, or UNITA) and Zimbabwe—in order to recapture control of the state. The problem for the transition state is not so much the effect of markets on the political consciousness of individuals working in the export sector, who may be among those with relatively high consciousness. Rather, it is the ability of private capital to affect directly the formation and reproduction of the transition state. The state must be able to convince private farmers in mixed economies, such as Nicaragua or Zimbabwe, to continue to produce for export even while separating them from political power. The transition state reintegrates the private farmer or importer into the state not with collective consciousness but disconnected from his/her previous relation with political power. [16] Since private capital accumulation separated from state power has considerably less influence on relations of production, private capitalists tend to refuse to participate on the new political ground rules. They invest less than before, reducing the short- and medium-run capability of the transition economy to produce surplus.

The continued existence of markets, including market pricing or wages based on skill and effort, exists to one degree or other in all transition economies, and will undoubtedly continue to do so. The principal issue we raise is whether markets in and of themselves are as crucial to the development of social relations that are alternatives to capitalism as the form and nature of transition politics. With markets, the individual retains a certain degree of capitalist consciousness in terms of price/wage response, or, if previously at the margin of market production (subsistence agriculture, for example), may be integrated more fully into the

---

[16] The announcement in Zimbabwe in 1986 that the 20 percent of seats formerly reserved for whites in the Parliament (whites represent only 2–3 percent of the population) are to be open to all candidates is part of this disconnection process.

price/wage system by the revolution than before. Real wages (consumption), inflation, and employment, remain important issues for the individual in transition economies to the degree that those economies rely on prices and wages to allocate resources and distribute consumption. Indeed, for some in the transition society, the revolution increases their integration into the wage-price system.[17]

Peasants and some merchants may even be permitted to accumulate capital, and therefore can be considered petty capitalists. Since they are engaged in private capital accumulation, they certainly would have capitalist mentality. But their ability to translate that consciousness into developing capitalist relations of production is severely limited or even prohibited by a state over which they—as capitalists rather than members of the revolutionary society—have little control. This reflects the fundamental role of the revolutionary state in defining transition ideology, political practice, and social relations independent of the remnants of capitalist ideology and especially of the imperatives of individual capital accumulation in transition society. At the same time that market influences exist in the transition economy, the state is committed to guaranteed employment and the guarantee of basic necessities to everyone, which greatly reduces the effect of wages and prices on consumption. The state protects workers' rights against employers, at the sacrifice of profits. Fagen points out that in Cuba after the revolution there was, for more than a decade, no significant unemployment, even though there were economic costs to such a policy: "[T]he political and social costs of open unemployment were greater than the economic costs of full employment!" (Fagen 1984, 11). The transition state also emphasizes collective consumption in the form of education, improved working conditions, health care, housing, and recreational activities rather than individual consumption. Either money wages are restrained, or, more usually, the state controls the production and importation of consumption goods so that there is little to buy other than basic necessities even if households have money income to spend. Collective consumption is therefore kept at a high proportion of the total, even with the existence of market wages and prices.[18]

[17] In the next chapter, we suggest that this increased integration makes the educational system *more* important for these groups in transition society than in conditioned capitalism. In contrast, the distribution of material rewards is greatly equalized, reducing the material value of attending school.

[18] The high proportion of collective consumption discourages private peasant production for the market as there is little to buy with the income made from such production. Other distortions also occur because of attempts to fix prices and currency rates and to control exports and imports, namely, black marketeering and smuggling, all of which reduces the surplus appropriable by the state.

The role of the market is different in the transition, then, largely because the state is no longer a capitalist state. Politics is organized for the purpose of enhancing the capacity of labor to produce and reproduce itself, not for capital. The individual, even one who operates economically in the context of the market, cannot escape that underlying political reality, and its power to shape individual action and self-conceptions.

The revolutionary movement and its crystallization in the state also substitute collective political engagement for individual consumption. To the degree that it is possible, collective engagement is used to produce public goods; that is, literacy campaigns, postliteracy schooling, preventive health care, the construction of housing, and crime control.

The trade-off between private consumption and collective political engagement is crucial to the definition of the individual in transition society. While there is little doubt that the existence of a market appropriate for goods and labor make it more difficult for the state to separate the individual worker from capitalist consciousness (especially as an individual consumer), it can induce the state to increase voluntary, collective political participation to develop state legitimacy. This is especially true if economic constraints make it difficult for the state to substitute more tangible social goods, such as health care and formal schooling, for private consumption. Such an increase in political activity requires, by its very nature, public institutions with a greater degree of participation and more opportunities for engagement.

In theory, then, the transition state reintegrates the worker separated from the means of production in conditioned capitalism into collective production and a state that represents the worker's collective interests. Since the nature of this collective production is a function of the degree of political participation of workers in the state, in practice the bureaucratization of the transition state has produced a new separation between the state and collectivized workers in production and in the meaning of "collective interests" as represented by the state. Yet, in the countries that we will study here, there have been different forms of greater political participation in both state policies and production that may reflect a greater degree of re-creating the individual as a socially conscious collective political agent, even while some of these economies continue to permit markets to operate (or even allow increased market activities).

WOMEN IN THE TRANSITION

The re-creation of the individual *woman* in the transition directly confronts traditional family relations predating capitalism, in which men's and women's roles are defined by a male-dominated organization of reproduction. All the transition societies we study attempt to redefine these roles, but not necessarily successfully. In *The Holy Family*, Marx and Engels declared that the emancipation of women was the most natural indicator of general emancipation, but like many of the Marxist theoreticians who followed them, they assumed an equality among all workers as forming the basis of the worker state. They also assumed that this equality would transform gender relations—men and women would enjoy equality in all areas of public life, and marriage would cease functioning as an economic unit. The elimination of capitalist relations of production, Marx and Engels claimed, would change not only political relations but family relations as well. In this sense, they fundamentally misunderstood the particularity of different sites of power and how these become interrelated in new ways as the basic structure of social relations changes (for the beginnings of an analysis of this point, see Bowles and Gintis 1986).

In practice, women do increase their *economic* equality with men in transition societies and this constitutes an important change in women's lives there. In Maxine Molyneux's opinion, "Whatever the failures of socialist society, it is evident that in the Third World its record is nonetheless impressive when matched against capitalist societies of comparable levels of development and religio-cultural background" (Molyneux 1982, 63).

This greater equality is achieved in three ways—incorporation into the labor force, equalization of income, and access to education. First, women are much more fully incorporated into the wage labor force: "Whilst women's employment under socialism remains subject to gender typing, the most onerous forms of economic exploitation of women, through unpaid family labour in the fields and sweatshops, have been substantially reduced if not eradicated completely" (Molyneux 1982, 64). Along with incorporation of women into the labor force, transition states have directed some social wages to women in the form of day care centers that allow them to work full time, support structures for maternity care, free health care, and equal education for women. Hence, as Marx and Engels predicted, women's economic role changes in the transition (as it is changing in advanced and even some of the larger conditioned capitalist societies). Like male workers, women receive the benefits of working in a society that favors labor over capital. Gradually, they gain equality in work because the state defines all workers as equally eligible to gain skills and to be paid equally according to those skills. Ideologically, then, the state is committed to labor, needs to alter the conditions of the labor market to incorporate women, and then is more likely to treat women equally in the work force than in conditioned capitalist societies, where profit-making employers have an inordinate influence over the conditions of and remuneration for work.

Second, since income differences among all individuals are drastically reduced, differences in rewards for the types of work people do are also equalized. Men may hold different jobs from women (gender differentiation in jobs continues to exist), but the pay differences between these jobs is reduced or even eliminated. In Cuba, for example, wages are set by general categories (unskilled worker, skilled worker, manager, and so forth). All skilled workers (men and women) receive the same pay, and although there may be more male than female managers, wage differentials between managers and workers are significant but much lower than in capitalist societies.

Third, women are encouraged to attend school to the same degree and with the same possibilities of reaching higher levels as men. Gender differences continue in selecting fields of study—there are far fewer female engineers, for example—but, again, the wage differences between those who pursue different fields of study are much smaller.

Socially and politically, however, women have made relatively limited progress in the transition, not only in the societies we studied here, but also in Eastern Europe and the Soviet Union. The question of women's political representation can be divided into two issues: (1) the degree of women's representation in the party and the state, and (2) the existence and influence of women's political organization, as well as their focus on feminist concerns as distinct from generic political issues (Molyneux 1982, 90).

The leadership of state bureaucracies and the vanguard parties (also, the mass party in Tanzania—CCM/TANU) is dominated by men. The increases over time in the number of women in politically important positions, even in the older transition societies, such as the Soviet Union, China, Cuba, and Tanzania, have been small. According to Molyneux, "In 1976, the Eastern European bloc together with Albania and China had between them a total of 197 Politburo posts: of these only ten were filled by women. . . . For the same group of countries there were a total of 557 such [top government] posts: only twenty-seven of them were filled by women" (Molyneux 1982, 90).

As far as women's organizations are concerned, where they do exist in transition societies, they are like other mass organizations, distinct from the vanguard or mass party but closely affiliated with it and designed primarily for mobilizing particular constituencies for the fulfillment of state goals. In the USSR and in China during the Cultural Revolution, women's organizations were dissolved despite some resistance from the women members (Molyneux 1982, 93): "Without any explicitly feminist component, these organizations do not generally encourage radical thinking or action, and many of the more subtle discriminatory structures are not tackled unless they are considered to be survivals from the pre-revolutionary period and obstacles to development" (Molyneux 1982, 93).

The limited representation of women in political leadership and the relatively conservative role played by women's organizations where they exist is largely the result of the transition state's reluctance to change social relations in the family. This has left women much more "equal" in terms of their contribution to production but unequal and dominated in terms of their role in reproduction. The male-controlled vanguard parties have been notoriously unwilling to raise male consciousness regarding women's social equality.

Among the societies we studied here, women in Cuba have made the greatest strides in changing gender social relations, permitting the creation of a women's mass organization that has pushed for and achieved significant legislation regarding male roles in the home. However, Judith Stacey (1983) claims that the Chinese revolution was "restorationist" where women are concerned because it sought in many ways to restore the Confucian family structure in rural areas. Stacey argues further that the bureaucratically controlled economic organization characteristic of transition societies may be more amenable to perpetuating patriarchal family relations than capitalism. Mozambique's revolution originally raised women to a primary role in the vanguard, but then reversed itself by emphasizing their role as wives and mothers.

The incomplete re-creation of women individuals in the transition compounds the limits already placed on them by their separation as workers from the control of collective production. The growth of a new, "directive" class in the bureaucracy keeps women as well as men from developing into full political and social participants in the transition society. Women as women, however, are excluded to an even greater degree than are male workers and peasants from political participation because they have even less access to directive positions. In addition, their unequal political and economic role in the family reproductive unit in those transition societies where this has not changed also separates them from political control of that aspect (the family) of reproduction. In order to preserve their control of the state production system (and, as we shall discuss, the state reproduction system—the schools), the new bureaucratic class may tend to hold back on emancipating women in the home in order to avoid action by male workers and peasants against the state.[19] In some "Westernized" countries, such as Cuba, this has not been the case, but moves by the women's organizations for family reforms have met with opposition within the bureaucracy and among the mass of male

[19] Molyneux points out that there may be some reason for moving slowly on radical change of women's roles: "Where they [socialist states] have tried to force a too rapid transformation of women's position without providing adequate support structures to help women make this radical transition the results have been disastrous" (Molyneux 1982, 60–61).

workers (Nazzari 1983). In Nicaragua, several women are "comman-dantes," the highest position in the Sandinista party, but women's social liberation lags far behind other reforms (Molyneux 1986).

Women acting to expand their rights in transition society, therefore, are apparently almost precluded, in the context of transition political structures, from developing movements that incorporate feminist values. But it is probably precisely such values that will be needed to advance women's rights beyond the important economic and education gains that have already been won through overthrowing the conditioned state.

The Law

Just as in capitalist societies, the law as constituted in transition societies redefines the rights and responsibilities of the individual vis-à-vis other individuals and the collective of the state. Under capitalist law, individualization itself is consecrated by making everyone equal before the law but at the same time legitimizing differences among individuals, both by protecting their property rights and by transforming class differences into new, ostensibly meritocratic hierarchies sanctioned by state legislation.

Capitalist law, therefore, accepts the inequalities of property and creates new forms of legitimatized inequality through schooling and other institutions, but simultaneously displaces these legalized individual differences by laws that homogenize individuals politically—rights to free speech, to vote in elections, to dissent in other forms (through a free press, for example), to be judged before the law by a group of peers, to secure a basic education, and so forth. All these political rights are independent of property or position in the division of labor.

The failure of the conditioned capitalist state to displace inequalities (instead, it affirms them in new forms) is an important factor contributing to the overthrow of that state. Although the basic legal system of the conditioned capitalist state is usually not very different from that of the metropole (both created in the image of late eighteenth and early nineteenth century bourgeois law), the development of that system in the metropole, largely through working class demands on the state, was not duplicated in the periphery. The practice of bourgeois law in conditioned capitalist states now differs greatly from that in the metropole, particularly in the unrestricted use of direct violence and the absence of protection of individual freedoms—free press, the vote, free speech, and the right to a trial.

Nevertheless, despite evidence (see Skocpol 1979, 1985) that the ability of revolutionary movements to overthrow the conditioned state is based on a widespread antagonism to the state itself and its unwillingness or inability to reincorporate the individual as a legal equal to other individuals in a people-nation, the emphasis of such movements in reconstituting the legal system of the transition state has been on those aspects that define the individual economically rather than on political grounds. The worker-state derives its new character fundamentally from the worker's new legal relation to capital rather than to the state. The worker is legally rejoined to the means of production, not through participative private ownership in the form of worker-owned or cooperative production, but through worker claims on the worker-state—which now owns the means of production.

Transition law as we know it in the Soviet Union, Eastern Europe, China, or Cuba, is therefore the Marxist-Leninist vision of capitalist law turned on its head. In that vision, capitalist law is solely the instrument of property relations, where capitalist ownership of the means of production defines all legal rights in the society, including the enforcement of the law to protect capitalist property and its inherent social relations. The new transition law is also constituted on the basis of a single class—workers—and only that class has absolute political rights, again through its ownership of the means of production. The transfer of the means of production to the workers through nationalization is seen as automatically creating legal equality for workers, since the fundamental basis of inequality has been eliminated. Similarly, other forms of legislated economic equality, such as full employment, the equalization of salaries, and equal access to the social wage (education, housing, health care, retirement, etc.), form the legal basis for re-creating the postcapitalist individual in the worker state.

But what is somewhat vague in this new legal system is an adequate definition of specific individual obligations and rights (limitations that the individual can place on the state) vis-à-vis the state itself. Allegedly this is not necessary (or may even be dysfunctional) because the state is the carrier of a revolutionary consciousness. The only legal right and obligation of the individual is to defend the new constitution, which includes the right and obligation to work (produce for the worker-state), to serve in the military (defend the people-nation physically), and to build revolutionary consciousness (develop the revolution). The state, in turn, must provide economic security for the individual, defend the people-nation, and embody the revolution.

The absence of individual rights and obligations in the bourgeois sense is defended on a number of grounds. The most important of these is the relatively low level of development of individual consciousness in the periphery concerning the use of such rights, especially in a situation where a state is in the process of constituting itself. Since the conditioned capitalist state does not develop the responsible practice of political rights, how can an unformed state put its own constitution into such unpracticed hands? The new sense of individual rights and obligations therefore has to be formed in the context of ongoing revolutionary politics. The individual, acting through the revolutionary party or other parastatal organizations, can criticize and develop new revolutionary practices. At the same time the state is accountable to individuals through its economic responsibilities and its ability to defend the revolution.

The assumption that the workers and peasants in a worker/peasant-state are incapable of leading the revolution, however, allows the revolutionary party and the state bureaucracy to develop definitions of revolutionary practice and the constitution of the transition state that do not necessarily reflect individual workers' interpretation of political reality, either as workers or as citizens of the people-nation. From that political point of view, the transition state reproduces the law of the conditioned capitalist state and its failure to homogenize individuals into a political equality represented by institutions of the state itself. The revolutionary party and the state become exclusive political bureaucracies with a dynamic that reflects bureaucratic needs.

To the degree that the bureaucracy of the transition state is made up of former workers and peasants and that these remain "organic intellectuals" in Gramsci's (1971) terms, they carry into the constitution of the state their previous class perceptions and therefore can develop institutions that incorporate worker and peasant reality and needs. But even if this development does not occur or is truncated as worker and peasant leaders take on the material trappings and ideals of a new bureaucratic class, the assumption that the popular classes are not capable of leading the revolution and reconstituting the state is contested by the mass organizations, which have a much closer connection to workers and peasants. For peasants in Nicaragua, for example, mass organizations have fought for access to land to be owned and farmed as individuals and cooperatives. When mass organizations also become bureaucratized, they often are contested by allegedly unconscious workers and peasants, as in Hungary, Czechoslovakia, and Poland.

The role of the military in this system of transition law is also shaped by the absence of clearly defined individual rights and obligations vis-à-vis the state. This absence is, we contend, partly due to the nature of the inherited conditioned capitalist political culture and its structure of authoritarianism and particularistic rights and obligations. But it is also the result of the revolutionary period itself. The revolutionary movement is initially a political-military organization. In all but one of the cases we studied here, and in almost all other cases as well, the revolution has been contested by internal antirevolutionary groups (who may have been for the overthrow of the conditioned capitalist or colonial state but are against the movement toward a transition society) aided by external military support from countries whose interests are both ideological and geopolitical (South Africa in Mozambique; the United States in China, Cuba, and Nicaragua). The revolutionary military is the first line of defense against such counterrevolutionary forces, and, historically, the military defense of the new state takes many years. It is this aspect of the constitution of the transition state that dominates much of its formation. Revolutionary consciousness, the rights and obligations of citizens, and individuals' economic functions become enmeshed with the military effort to preserve the new state. Military definitions of rights and obligations tend to overwhelm all other definitions; critiques of the state bureaucracy or demands for a diversity of views are interpreted by the military as a threat to the state related to the armed force being used against the state. And as the newly formed state encounters economic problems associated in part with external and internal sabotage, the military and the police are used increasingly to enforce internal order by crushing dissent. The militarization of the law is complicated by the fact that the military and the revolutionary party are essentially inseparable during the period of defending against external threat. Thus, the ideological and legal reconstitution of the state is dominated by military conceptions of politics.[20]

Although this military re-creation of the individual in the transition is consistent with the revolutionary ideal of struggle, it also means that revolutionary consciousness (and the transition state) will probably be hierarchical and possibly violent, neither of which is likely to lead to high levels of political participation or make for close identification of the individual with the party or the state. Thus a crucial issue in the development of transition law is whether to separate the military from the revolutionary party and from the legal apparatuses of the state, even as that same military is engaged in defense of the revolution and is an important mechanism for the integration of the individual into new crystallization of the people-nation.

The decision on separation is not so much ideological as practical: The state must develop the most effective means to defend itself against counterrevolutionary forces. In Mozambique, for example, the military was to a large extent separated from the party into a standing army with conscription, ranks, and strict hierarchy. Some critics of that arrangement blamed the failure of the army to defend against the counterrevolutionary Mozambican National Resistance (MNR) (financed from South Africa) on

[20] The role of repressive and military forces is also contested within the transition state. In Mozambique, for example, Machel's "socialist legality" speech charged the military, police, and secret service with all kinds of arbitrary oppression and resulted in severe purges in these organizations.

the army's "depopularization," and separation from the revolutionary party.

That criticism may be correct in the Mozambican context but not in others. In Nicaragua, the popular militia (an armed citizenry closely connected with the people and the revolutionary party) had difficulty coping with the "Contra" threat, and it was not until the Sandinistas built up and equipped a powerful, highly structured regular army, based on conscription, that the Contras began to be defeated. That army is also an ideological continuation of the Sandinista force that overthrew the conditioned Somosa state and is closely tied to the Sandinista party. Conscripts are given a heavy dose of political education throughout their two-year tour of duty, but it is difficult to assess whether more structure or revolutionary fervor is responsible for increased effectiveness.

Although defense is the overriding factor in organizing an effective military, the less hierarchical and more democratic the fighting forces, the more likely that the transition will be democratic, since the influence of the military is bound to be great in societies in armed struggle against external threat. The more the revolutionary party continues to be linked to the military, the more likely that violence will be incorporated into the transition's legal system (although the Sandinista regime has been marked by surprisingly little internal violence).[21]

The Nation

The conditioned capitalist state, we contend, fails to create an authentic people-nation and hence fails to attain legitimacy as the political representation of the nation-state. Revolutionary movements have seized on this failure, contesting the conditioned state's "illegitimate" nationalism with their own. Revolutions against the conditioned capitalist state have invariably called for dismantling the relationship of the state with dominant foreign powers and for the "nationalization" of the local economy and culture.

Revolutionary movements are therefore committed to creating an authentic people-nation based on a more autarkic economy, the dismantling of economic dependence on industrialized capitalist metropoles, and the development of a national, revolutionary culture, which includes an independent role in world politics. The transition state therefore aims to

[21] The first of the original conscripts into the Sandinista army were demobilized in the summer of 1986. As veterans, they will play important organizational and ideological roles in the mass organizations ("Conscripts Come Home, Well-Drilled Sandinistas," *New York Times*, September 12, 1986, 8). Time will tell how party policies will be affected by these thousands of new activists whose political ideas were developed as part of a military experience.

accomplish what the conditioned capitalist state could not: to re-create the individual as a member of the nation-state. The capitalist state achieves this through increased individual private consumption, individual voting, increased social consumption, and conflicts against external enemies (a mixture of individualized and collective acts). But the transition state relies on re-creating the individual as a member of the people-nation through collective acts: collective revolutionary practice, conflicts against external and internal enemies, and increased social consumption.

Nationalism is a key issue in the revolution, and a principal basis for the legitimacy of the transition state. The revolutionary movement develops a version of national history that is defined in terms of the revolutionary struggle itself. Once in power, the state builds national pride in terms of independence from colonial powers and the uniqueness of the nation's struggle for self-identity and control over its own destiny. Invasion by foreign forces or foreign-sponsored mercenaries contributes to the legitimacy of revolutionary history by extending the national struggle for self-definition and self-defense.

The territory of the transition people-nation is the revolutionary territory, and the incorporation of individuals into this territory takes place by extending and deepening the revolution. Literacy campaigns in Cuba, Mozambique, and Nicaragua, for example, were largely efforts to incorporate individuals at the margin of the revolution into the new people-nation (see Fagen 1969; Torres 1985). At the same time, the internal enemies of the revolution are often defined by the state as outside the people-nation and hence without political rights.

It is on this point that the legitimacy of the postcapitalist state is most contested: Who is a member of the people-nation and who is not? Put another way, how is the people-nation defined and who has the right to define it? Is the revolutionary party the embodiment of the people-nation, or is there a historical-territorial definition that precedes the revolution? If the latter is the case, all those who are incorporated in that historical-territorial definition (a history that in some nations is synonymous with the colonial or conditioned capitalist state) should have equal political and economic rights in the state, including equal treatment before the postcapitalist law, no matter what their level of consciousness or political views.

The issue is further complicated by the existence, in the territory defined physically by the conditioned or colonial state, of regional language groups who were not successfully incorporated into the people-nation governing that territory. Although the overthrow of the colonial state may unite the various groups temporarily in their common desire for a new order, group identifications again dominate once the definition of the new state begins. In some cases, like Tanzania, there are so many small language groups that no single one dominates and fractionalization is less. But in others, such as Zimbabwe, postrevolutionary struggles between such groups—each linked differentially to the colonial bureaucracy—threaten the formation of the new state.

The threat to the Soviet state posed by the German invasion in 1941–1942 and the state's response clearly illustrate all of these issues. During the first months of the invasion, some large minority groups, such as the Ukrainians, White Russians, and Cossacks, sided openly with the Germans, hoping to use the invasion as a way to gain independence from Russia. Their separate national identification preceded the revolution by hundreds of years. Furthermore, exhortations by the Soviet state to defend the revolution and to fight for the Communist party (the embodiment of revolutionary territory) were not particularly successful (Werth 1964). It was rather the threat that German invasion and occupation posed to Russians (including non-Great Russian Slavs, such as the Ukrainians and White Russians) in the prerevolutionary historical/cultural/territorial sense that mobilized the mass of the population to defend the motherland against a historical enemy. At the same time, the ability of the Soviet state to defend Russian soil against the invaders and defeat them created a new national identity of the mass of Soviet citizens with the Soviet state.

The current struggles in Angola, Mozambique, and Nicaragua are not primarily conflicts over the historical definition of national territory—even though this historical definition in all three cases is a colonial one—but conflicts over its revolutionary definition. And in each case, the revolutionary claim to define the people-nation is based on the defense of the historical territory against foreign invasion (even if, unlike the German invaders of the Soviet Union, the invaders are nationals of the contested territory). The relation of antigovernment guerrillas in Mozambique and Savimbi in Angola with the South African government and that of the Contras in Nicaragua with the "Yankee imperialists" is crucial to the revolutionary definition of the people-nation. Furthermore the revolutionary army becomes a primary instrument of incorporating youth into the revolutionary definition of territoriality. By defending that definition successfully, they necessarily identify with it.

The claim of the revolutionary state to be the bearer of the national identity also depends on how it deals with internal opposition, that is, on its ability to incorporate a large majority of the population into that identity. Thus the state must both be able to mobilize the masses to defend against external threats to the revolutionary people-nation and also be able to build an internal identity that forms the basis of a new kind of society.

The definition of the revolutionary people-nation not only includes various language and regional groups but also determines which class elements are potentially inside the definition and under what circumstances. Stalin defined the kulaks in the Soviet Union as a "class" that was inherently opposed to the revolution and hence outside the revolutionary people-nation. The Cuban revolutionary state nationalized all small farm holdings and small individually owned businesses within ten years of taking power, again defining the owners of such farms and businesses as outside the revolutionary people-nation. Recently, however, in Nicaragua and Mozambique, the necessity of defending the revolution against counterrevolutionary forces, has led the state to reverse itself on incorporating small, private farmers into the revolution—their productivity, and therefore their mobilization, is of primary concern to a hard-pressed economy. If the state is successful in this mobilization and economic output rises significantly, the small peasantry in Mozambique and Nicaragua could become part of the revolutionary vanguard, even if in theoretical terms their revolutionary consciousness is less than that of peasants in cooperatives and nationalized farms.

The revolutionary state bureaucracy has an important advantage over its predecessor in achieving a coherent, inclusive definition of the people-nation. The revolution is not only indigenous but clearly seeks to define itself autarkically and autonomously from its dependent links with the metropole. The style of the revolutionary leaders draws on close identification with local culture rather than foreign consumption styles. The danger to this autonomy comes from having to rely on other nations for arms and aid to defend against external threats and internal dissent; indeed, this new dependency on the Eastern Bloc countries is an important critique by the revolutionary state's opponents.

Whereas the political advantage of the revolutionary movement in creating a national identity is a significant factor in its potential success, its economic advantages are not necessarily greater than those of its conditional predecessor, contrary to what Frank and Amin may claim. The new state inherits the economic problems of the conditioned state—the low level of development of the forces of production and the limited development of the capitalist temporality. Both constrain the possibilities of incorporating the individual into the new people-nation through rapid increases in collective consumption. The advantage for the transition state is in its greater control of surplus and in its ability to use surplus to meet mass needs and to increase collective consumption (public goods). The problematique for the transition state lies in the loss of capital sources and skills because of internal and external opposition to the revolution and in the need to devote such a high fraction of surplus to military spending.

The state's ability to increase collective consumption (basic food needs, education, health care, recreation, economic security, physical security) all contribute to the identification of the individual with the revolutionary territory. Similarly, the development of revolutionary practice among the mass of citizens—incorporation into the literacy campaign, day care centers, health care campaigns, neighborhood organizations for "the defense of the revolution," factory committees, and the revolutionary party itself—also develop this identification.

There is an inherent danger in limiting identification with the people-nation to only those engaged directly in the revolutionary project and those who were previously at such a low level of consumption that the revolutionary state is able to incorporate them through the delivery of low-cost goods and services (literacy, preventive health care, redistributed land). The previous existence of a conditioned people-nation nevertheless provides the basis of legitimate opposition. When such opposition is eliminated by defining it as outside the nation-state (as in four of our case studies), it tends to reduce the pressure on the revolutionary state bureaucracy to complete the project of incorporating the masses into the revolutionary definition of people-nation (in a sense, this is parallel to the failure of the authoritarian, conditioned capitalist bureaucracy to complete its definition). The elimination of legitimate competition also changes the way the revolutionary bureaucracy competes for the political hearts and minds of its constituency: By not subjecting themselves to elections, bureaucratic leaders are more concerned with their position in the revolutionary party than with direct sanction or approval by the citizenry.

Different ideas and programs for development of the people-nation compete within the bureaucracy. Party leadership and the "line" taken by that leadership come to mean more than the overall position of the Party itself (in some ways similar to the role of leaders in the U.S. party system). In the Chinese case, for example, three different development strategies—Maoist, Titoist, and Stalinist—have surfaced over the years, and leadership competition has taken the form of conflicts over which strategy to use and what constitutes it. These are in fact important conflicts and their outcomes profoundly affect the economic conditions of almost everyone in the country—witness the swings in Chinese development strategy and the somewhat less radical shifts in Cuban development strategy and their impact on local life. There also may be considerable participation at the base in discussions about strategies. But the ultimate choice is usually left to a small group, concerned about legitimacy but not subject to direct sanctions for their decision from the mass of the citizenry.

Strategies are important for the leaders associated with them because they serve as a symbol of political-economic views and hence are indirectly related to the amount of legitimacy each leader has with the masses. But leadership style may be even more important for legitimacy, and legitimacy with the masses may be no more important than personal alliances within the Party for maintaining power. Mao changed course several times after 1949, as did Castro after 1959. However, their personal popularity was the principal source of their legitimacy and power and carried them through serious economic errors. The 1989 democracy movement in China required Deng Xiaoping's personal power to convince the People's Army to intervene and prevent a split in Party leadership and perhaps a civil war.

The alternative to a single-party regime (with competition limited to different intraparty lines) is to allow the opposition to continue to exist (as in the Nicaraguan case) under certain rules of the game that effectively allow the revolutionary state to reproduce itself within a previous historical-cultural definition of the nation-state. Until now, therefore, the Sandinistas have been willing to engage opponents of the revolution (primarily the Church hierarchy) openly in a political conflict over the definition of the people-nation and whether the Sandinistas or the opposition are the bearers of national identity. Whether or not the Sandinista-dominated state will continue to allow such competition depends in part on the opposition's willingness to observe the "rules," and in large part on the ability of the Sandinista state to incorporate (through increased collective consumption and revolutionary practice) the population into the revolutionary definition of the people-nation.

However, the Sandinistas' main dilemma in the relationship with their constituency has been whether to include open elections (including counterrevolutionary, opposition parties) as part of these rules, especially in very unfavorable economic conditions. If the Party has succeeded in developing widespread identification with the revolutionary people-nation, such elections will affirm and strengthen Sandinista legitimacy. But the opposite may also occur, if the Nicaraguan populace is convinced that the Sandinistas are inept economic administrators or that the revolution has too high a cost. The results will be different from those in the Soviet Union or Poland, where elections were held but the Party retained considerable control. In Nicaragua, opposition candidates are openly counterrevolutionary and would operate under a completely different set of social rules if allowed to take power.

Knowledge

One of the primary claims of the revolution for legitimacy is the unwillingness of the conditioned state bureaucracy to "nationalize" the system of knowledge and to incorporate the masses into it. The conditioned capitalist state often withholds the most basic knowledge, such as literacy, from a significant portion of the population. It bases its political power on this gap in accessibility to knowledge and uses particularistic, authoritarian political forms to reproduce itself.

Every revolutionary movement in this century has made mass education a principal element of its program. Education is a fundamental means by which the movement extends the revolution to those marginalized by the conditioned capitalist state. Simultaneously, the mobilization developed by revolutionary movements around the delivery of educational services serve to incorporate already schooled youth and adults into the revolutionary project. The literacy campaigns in Cuba and Nicaragua were successful in raising levels of literacy, but were much more significant as political projects. Similarly, Frelimo's more modest literacy program and its rural schools are much more important politically than for the reading skills they developed. China and Tanzania have devoted particular attention to their educational efforts in rural areas for the same political reasons.

At one level, the establishment of mass education in revolutionary societies does not differ greatly from a similar process that took place in advanced capitalist societies, such as the United States, in the last century. In the United States, mass education expanded rapidly at the local level, even before the common school movement of the 1840s. This expansion of primary and secondary education democratized access to knowledge, incorporating the mass of working-class youth and millions of new immigrants into the nation-state as individual Americans conscious of their rights and obligations to the state.

But at another level, there are significant differences. U.S. mass education incorporated youth into a class-based division of labor. It created a class-based division of knowledge as a new system of classifying and standardizing individuals who were already separated from their means of production, and brought individuals to accept expertise (knowledge differences) as a legitimate basis (meritocracy) for such a classification. Mass education in revolutionary societies has as its purpose the elimination of the class structure and the class-based system of knowledge. An additional difference is that revolutionary mass education aims at using knowledge for the enhancement of labor's capacity to produce, not for the profitability of individually owned capital.

The revolutionary movement, even before it takes power, defines knowledge as including revolutionary consciousness. Since such consciousness tends to be inversely related to position in the capitalist class hierarchy, revolutionary knowledge (organic intellectuals, in Gramsci's terms) is concentrated in the masses and is revealed by revolutionary practice. The purpose of mass education, furthermore, is to unify intellectual and manual knowledge (work) and urban and rural knowledge through collective effort, in contrast to capitalist education's objective of separating mental from manual and rural from urban knowledge through individual specialization (expertise) and market competition.

Revolutionary pedagogy also differs from pedagogy in capitalist societies. The latter emphasizes individual performance (skills) and individual rights and responsibilities in a democratic, individual-oriented state. By maximizing individual effort, the individual automatically makes the maximum possible contribution to the society as a whole. The former stresses collective performance and collective responsibility in the form of collective practice. Skills and performance have little meaning outside of their contribution to the society's collective goals. Without revolutionary practice, knowledge is isolated and potentially destructive of the people-nation by placing itself outside the territory of the people-nation.

However, as the revolution passes beyond its early stages, education and knowledge in transition societies take on many of the hierarchical characteristics associated with advanced capitalism. There is no doubt that public education in transition society has created a level of formal skills in the masses that is much greater than in capitalist societies with similar levels of economic development. But the need to develop the material forces of production and to produce higher levels of consumption in the short term, as well as the military exigencies of defending the revolution, move the transition state to emphasize skills rather than revolutionary consciousness as the basis of knowledge and to stress the production of those skills by the educational system. The bureaucracy of the transition state seems to slide into using expertise in the same way as the advanced capitalist bureaucracy does—to separate the working class from participation in decisionmaking. And the transition bureaucracy, also in charge of production and distribution, has much greater control of the production and distribution of new knowledge, particularly over what constitutes such knowledge. The degree to which expertise is used as a mechanism of reproducing the transition state bureaucracy depends on the way the revolutionary party defines its membership and its role as the carrier of revolutionary consciousness. When exclusivity of revolutionary consciousness in a vanguard party is combined with traditional definitions of skill hierarchy, "expertise" in the transition state will be concentrated rather than diffuse. Concentrated expertise easily leads to the development of a new, bureaucratic "class" based on such expertise and the use of the educational system to reproduce that class (Sweezy and Bettelheim 1971). In contrast, a revolutionary party based on Gramsci's view supporting the wide diffusion of expertise, will allow the extensive development of organic intellectuals in mass-based organizations.

Whereas the hierarchization of knowledge and its fundamental role in defining a passive relationship of the worker-citizen to the transition state are characteristic of most transition societies, the definition is a contested one. The Cultural Revolution in China, "schools in the countryside" versus "schools to the countryside" in Cuba, and technocratic planning versus political village organization in Tanzania and Mozambique all represent aspects of this conflict. The struggle over the meaning of knowledge reflects the struggle over the political definition of transition society, to a much greater degree than educational conflicts affect the definition of capitalist society. In the transition society, the relationship of the individual to the state is much less dependent on his or her economic role than in the capitalist state, and much more dependent on his or her political role. Political roles are, in turn, a function of the definition of knowledge and individuals' access to it. The struggle over that definition reveals a great deal about transition development. Knowledge and access to it through education measure both what individuals represent in transition society and how they are re-created by the transition state.

CHAPTER 3

Education and the Transition State

Martin Carnoy

EDUCATION IS A FUNDAMENTAL instrument of change in revolutionary societies. Simultaneously, the way it expands in the postrevolutionary period reflects political conflicts in the transition from conditioned capitalism to some vision of socialist social organization. Educational reform in this period also represents both the dominant, often changing "revolutionary" definition of knowledge and a sense of how the revolution intends to re-create individuals and reintegrate them into the state and the people-nation.

It is logical that the form and content of education should be a fundamental issue of discussion during the formation of the transitional state. This is much more so the case than in capitalist societies where ideological formation and politics are significantly shaped by social relations outside the state, in capitalist production. In the transition from capitalism, however, it is the state where the dynamic of social change is crystallized. As a principal ideological apparatus of the state, the educational system and the definition of knowledge on which that system is based necessarily reveal the shape of social relations and social change.

The primary question before us is *how* and *how much* educational expansion and reform differ in transition societies from their conditioned past—and if the difference is significant, *why* it is so. We argue that such differences do exist and that they reflect the fundamental commitment of the transition state to transforming the basis of the economy and to developing a new sense of nation and history—one that is associated intimately with the new state itself.

THE CONDITIONED CAPITALIST INHERITANCE

Revolutionary movements have, as a rule, inherited from their conditioned capitalist predecessors significant levels of poverty and a population with low levels of skills relevant to a modern economy. Schooling levels were also low. But even in the conditioned capitalist development as it took place in those countries, formal schooling generally played some (and, in several cases, an important) role in defining an individual's position in the division of labor. Relatively few individuals may have had access to more than a smattering of school. In Portugal's three mainland African colonies, for example, illiteracy never fell below 90 percent of the adult population. But formal and nonformal (literacy) education were still symbols of political power and access to resources, precisely because many positions of economic and political power were occupied by those who had education.

In colonized Africa and Asia, schooling symbolized the spread of colonial ideology—including Christianity, attitudes of submission by "natives" to the white colonists (see Memmi 1968; Fanon 1968), the European work ethic, the concept of individual, measurable merit (success or failure in European schools), and capitalist social relations in work—and in language. The fact that this ideology and language were so intertwined with symbols of power helps explain why most countries after independence retained the colonial educational system essentially intact.

Most conditioned capitalist states have difficulty successfully integrating and standardizing the individual into a class-based hierarchy of knowledge for two principal reasons. First, the state is often unwilling or unable to mobilize enough resources to make public education (state-defined knowledge) generally available. Second, even if education is made generally available, the private production sector and the state are often unable to provide sufficient wage employment to absorb those with average education—this tends to make the average level of public schooling and therefore the average level of knowledge insufficient for integration into the regularly employed labor force (Carnoy 1977).

The other side of this coin is that in highly class-structured societies where public education is relatively scarce, such education cannot disguise its class-linked nature. Individuals are differentially schooled, but differential access and success are rather evidently associated with rural/urban location, social class, and region. The hierarchy of knowledge in that education-scarce situation cannot be separated from the unequal social relations in civil society and hence the class nature of the state.[1]

Education and knowledge in conditioned capitalist societies, as in industrialized capitalism, represent mobility and social and political democratization. Education as a symbol of mobility is even more accentu-

[1] In advanced capitalist society (particularly in the United States) and in some rapidly growing newly industrializing economies, to the contrary, the widespread availability of public education, eventually even at the university level, creates a much more convincing image of meritocracy as the basis of the division of knowledge and labor. The more democratic distribution of schooling in the United States and its wider availability makes formal education a less important determinant of economic success than in conditioned capitalist societies (see Jencks 1979, for an example of the U.S. case, and Psacharopoulos 1985, for approximate estimates of the economic returns of schooling in conditioned capitalist countries).

ated, we will argue, in conditioned societies. But unlike the metropolitan state, most conditioned states generally make education and knowledge accessible to the mass of the population only on a limited basis. They do not re-create a "meritocratized" individual and fail to incorporate the separated worker into a state that can use "expertise" as the basis for its reproduction. Obviously, there are a number of counterexamples, such as Argentina, the Philippines, Peru, South Korea, Taiwan, Venezuela, and Mexico, to name several. But even in some of those countries, the average education of the labor force remains very low, and a large portion of the population is bound by "traditional" and personalistic social and economic relations. In most conditioned societies, the masses are so little incorporated into the capitalist knowledge hierarchy (most attend a primary school for only a few years) that they are not subject to the manipulation of "expertise" in the same way that a highly schooled society might be.[2]

We have suggested elsewhere (see Carnoy and Levin 1985) that the tension in capitalist societies between mass education as a democratizing force (social mobility, the equalizing experience of public education, the democratic ideal taught in school) and education as a reproducer of capitalist inequalities (the class, race, or gender division of labor, unequal access to knowledge, the re-creation of the "separated" individual as a citizen identifying with the inequalities of the capitalist people-nation) underlie the expansion and reform of the educational system and the system of knowledge production in those societies. Education as a democratizing force results in the expansion of mass education and more equal access to (the democratization of) knowledge. Education as a capitalist reproductive force requires controls on access and limits educational expansion.

In conditioned capitalism, the tension between these two forces is exacerbated, both from the supply side, through limits on state expansion of public schooling, and on the demand side, through a social demand for schooling, exaggerated by greater material and political inequalities.

On the supply side, the conditioned state is constrained from increasing state social spending (and hence from expanding and universalizing public education) by difficulties of private and state capital accumulation (see Carnoy 1984, ch. 7) and by the nature of the conditioned state itself, which (1) wastes limited state revenues by converting them into the increased consumption of individual bureaucrats and their relatives and

---

[2] Philip Coombs (1985) shows that there will be a larger absolute number of illiterates in the Third World in the year 2000 than today. But what is more significant, many of the poor conditioned capitalist countries, even under the best of economic growth projections, will hardly make a dent in raising the average level of schooling because of the massive numbers of young people who will reach school age in the next 15 years.

friends, and (2) relies on particularistic political relations to reproduce itself, allocating jobs through patronage rather than on the basis of competence. The impact on education of inefficiency and corruption in public bureaucracies (in addition to more limited funding than in the metropoles) cannot be underestimated. Since ministries of education at all levels (federal, state, local) are the largest single public employer in conditioned capitalist economies, these elements are particularly present in public education and limit its expansion. In prerevolutionary Cuba, corruption in the ministry of education was so great that the average amount of schooling per young person fell in the 1950s while budget allocations per pupil rose significantly. The World Bank reported that these increased budget allocations were ending up in the pockets of ministry bureaucrats (Carnoy and Werthein 1980).

Supply-side constraints also result in the provision of such low-quality education to the mass of children that few can hope to reach the higher grades. Rural and marginal urban schools in many conditioned capitalist countries have no textbooks and teachers who only completed primary schooling. Furthermore, what the bureaucracy defines as knowledge (the basis of the meritocracy) is metropole-centered, and hence far from the experience of the average peasant or worker. This knowledge is the basis of the primary and secondary school curriculums. The bureaucracy and the local bourgeoisie therefore systematically convey a message of "impossibility" and "distance" between the knowledge needed for material success and what the masses can learn in their schools. It is probably no surprise to peasants and to the urban poor (themselves only recently peasants or landless agricultural labor) that their children fail in school, even though in many countries, marginal rural and urban communities have shown enormous commitment to their children's education despite such barriers (see Mwiria 1985; Coombs 1985). But failing in school, even in schools where very few succeed, helps to pacify those who might otherwise claim increased access to resources and political power, since such claims are officially restricted to those of proven "merit."

The growing commitment of those with little chance of success reflects the exacerbation of the tension in conditioned society from the demand side. The stakes of success or failure in school are much higher than in the metropole. Schooling was provided by the conditioned state initially for producing "modern" skills required by the state bureaucracy (to mediate its relationship with the metropole) and for incorporating a small "middle class" politically into the conditioned people-nation by giving its children access to university education and the liberal professions. This converted schooling into a very important symbol of escape from marginality, powerlessness, and poverty.

But, more important, the unequal distribution of consumption in conditioned societies accentuates the importance of this symbol. Not only are the highest positions in the society associated with university training (often in foreign universities), but the income associated with these positions are extremely high compared to that of the average worker or peasant. The relative prize awarded for attaining higher levels of schooling is therefore much greater than in industrialized capitalist societies. And schooling appears—much more than in the metropoles—to be the only way to achieve high income and status, especially because such a large proportion of university graduates are state bureaucrats, and the state bureaucracy is an acknowledged road to riches. At the other extreme, the cost of doing poorly in school is usually a denial of access to meaningful political participation and to full membership in the people-nation. Thus, formal education and literacy come to represent the self-authenticity of membership in the modern nation—precisely what the metropole offers to its workers to re-create them as citizens, that is, individual participants in the capitalist state.

This inability or unwillingness to incorporate the individual into a newly defined standardization of differences through schooling has the perverse effect for the conditioned state of creating an "excessive" demand for schooling services and a political conflict with the conditioned state over the lack of such services (Carnoy, et al. 1982; Carnoy and Levin 1985). The state makes years of formal schooling (as a proxy for merit or potential productivity) a condition of material success, but does not sufficiently democratize access to schooling to mask its class role. The importance of education as a symbol of social mobility is accentuated, but so is the reality of its role as a reproducer of great social inequality.

Partly in response to such "excess demand" and the newfound human capital rationale for investing in education for economic growth, the United States and multilateral agencies in the 1960s and 1970s put enormous emphasis on increased schooling in low-income countries as a way of combating poverty and ignorance. As a result, a number of conditioned states have democratized educational access (for example, Costa Rica, which already had relatively high levels of schooling at the beginning of the 1960s, Kenya, Mexico, and Venezuela) through rapid expansion. Even with educational expansion, however, conditioned capitalist economies have had difficulty incorporating the educated into jobs requiring additional education. Expansion reaches into rural and marginal urban areas last, ensuring that the mass of youth in these countries will have lower levels of schooling and education of much poorer quality than do their urban middle- and working-class counterparts. The failure rates at the primary level in rural and marginal urban areas are high, requiring several grade repetitions and resulting in high dropout rates. Thus, in the absence of a policy to equalize income distribution and economic opportunity, increased access to schooling through expansion has a minor effect on overall social equality.

School expansion does, however, make public education available to more people and tends to increase belief in meritocracy (see Mwiria's 1985 study on Kenya, for example). In the absence of expansion, and often even with expansion, the children of peasants, agricultural workers, and marginal urban traders and low-level service workers are excluded from all but a few, often painful, years in low-quality primary schools. The bureaucrats of the conditioned state remain distant from this vast majority of pupils and their parents.

By denying them a new identification, the self-serving bureaucrats inadvertently help a revolutionary movement organize enough of that distanced majority to overthrow the state. Thus, although the conditioned state often is able to reproduce itself through the systematic manipulation of the least-schooled members of the society, any disintegration of the particularistic political relations that form the basis of that manipulation may turn the illiterate and low-schooled against the state. They are the object of the particularistic bureaucracy, not its subject. The object is in no way responsible for the state, or engaged in it, so feels little compulsion to try to prevent its disintegration.

The tension between what schooling promises and what it provides is not the only contradiction in conditioned capitalist education. The apex of these systems—the elite English and French secondary schools in Africa and Asia, the Indian and Chinese universities, the autonomous universities in Latin America—were largely successful in developing local elites who served colonial bureaucracies and conditioned capitalist bureaucracies before independence (and after independence, complemented the bureaucratic structures that were retained and colonial bureaucrats who stayed on). But they were, and continue to be, spawning grounds for revolutionaries. These institutions provided the future revolutionary leaders with certain perspectives and resources that proved critical to their future task. The specifics of this process differed from state to state, especially between Latin America and the areas of Asia and Africa that were colonized much later.

In all cases, however, the institutions of higher education assisted in the development of at least some and perhaps most of the principal revolutionary leaders, who there developed their critical social analysis; learned basic skills (writing, public speaking, critical modes of reasoning); made their first contact with other revolutionaries; and developed more extensive networks of political activists, whom they would mobilize as they began their early stages of protest and action.

The training of such revolutionaries was not these institutions' function as intended by the colonial or conditioned state. Elite secondary schools (in colonial Africa) and universities were and are organized to develop a relatively narrow group of professionals, including educators and state bureaucrats, who would reproduce the conditions needed for the smooth functioning of colonial or conditioned capitalist society. To achieve this, higher education has had to alienate those students not just from the country's previous ruling elite, but—in a much more profound way—from their class or race sense of history and nation. At the same time, they were asked to serve, in the African and Asian cases, a ruling group that they could never enter (the European colonialists) or, in Latin America, a ruling "aristocracy" that they were unlikely to enter. This "betweenness"—between their own, subordinated class or race and the ruling class that they are asked to serve—undoubtedly alienates students and pushes them to revolt against the very conditions that allow them to be relatively successful in the system. Their revolutionary politicization process may also be related to their exposure to the curriculum of the liberal, Western university—with its alleged neutrality in the search for truth and token representation of radical philosophy and social theory—and to the literature and discussion available through student political associations.

Bringing together students into a thinking, relatively creative environment when there exist glaring injustices in the society around them is bound to develop reaction to those conditions. This is an important source of contradiction for the state. But the development of revolutionary leaders in institutions of higher education also raises questions about the nature of revolution. Why is it that the relatively least oppressed members of the dominated groups in colonial or conditioned society tend to become revolutionary leaders? Can the more educated, more privileged revolutionary leaders be expected to turn power over to the masses?

The importance of scarce education as a symbol of social mobility in conditioned capitalist society and the role of education in the formation of the revolution itself has made the expansion of education a fundamental tenet of revolutionary policy. The overthrow of the conditioned capitalist state does not mean the destruction of its symbols, especially those symbols that for generations have come to represent social self-authenticity. Formal education is one of these symbols. Universally, but particularly in societies marked by large differences in material consumption and social status, acquiring formal schooling represents possibilities for individual social mobility, even though relatively few actually achieve such mobility. At an ideological level, capitalist states have promoted the concept that a society with more schooling will be marked by greater income equality and more democracy (see, for example, Kuznets 1955), even though, empirically, the link between expanded schooling and income equality, while positive, is rather weak (Carnoy, et al. 1979). Thus, at both the individual and the societal level, the promise of education for greater equality is strong symbolically despite the absence of a conforming reality.

This symbolic role is not lost on revolutionary movements. They incorporate the symbol of self-authenticity through education near the top of revolutionary reforms. Literacy becomes a revolutionary symbol of equality, and what may be called authentic knowledge—knowledge rooted in the history and culture of the society itself—is posed as a counterforce to the distant, foreign-rooted, metropolitan knowledge represented in the political and material symbols of the conditioned state. Authentic knowledge is both revolutionary and inclusive, and, in that sense, is part of a new definition of the people-nation. The revolutionary movement, in turn, defines itself in terms of educating the mass of peasants and workers into an authentic self-definition that includes worker- and peasant-based knowledge, literacy, participation, and skill development. In China, Cuba, Mozambique, and Nicaragua, where the revolution developed through a long armed struggle, revolutionary guerrilla training included formal schooling. In areas that came under guerilla control, these various movements all set up schools for villagers as part of their definition of "liberated territory."

Revolutionary education obviously has ideological aims.[3] The revolution brings people into schools as a way to reach the population with the revolutionary message. But not only must the revolutionary message have to have some appeal to bring people into these schools, the schooling must also represent a response to an existing demand for the knowledge denied peasants and workers in conditioned capitalist society. By delivering literacy and math skills, revolutionary movements confer a self-identification in terms that had already been partly defined by the preceding capitalist society. School-learned skills are a response to educational demands exacerbated by the gross inequalities of conditioned capitalism.

At the same time, however, there is an attempt to achieve a new self-identification within the context of a new, revolutionary authenticity and definition of people-nation—within what Gramsci (1971) called "counterhegemony" and what Che Guevara called the "new man." Whether this counterhegemony or new person is in fact created in the countries we analyze is open to question. One of the many problems we identify is whether or not schools can carry out this mission if political and economic

---

[3] "One [Cuban] educational leader at the ministry of education, Abel Prieto Morales, said that when he was in Italy, someone at an education conference asked him: 'Is the school in Cuba an instrument of the State?' His answer was, 'Yes, of course, just as it was before the triumph of the Revolution, and as it is in the present day in Italy' " (Leiner 1973, 6).

institutions are not sufficiently transformed themselves both to reflect and to create a new consciousness and new social relations. In a world still dominated by powerful capitalist economies and capitalist values, is it possible to build a work and social ethic that is based on collective goals rather than the aims of individual consumption?

EDUCATION IN THE TRANSITION: REFORMS AND NEW CONTRADICTIONS

The revolutionary movement that overthrows the conditioned capitalist state generally inherits that state's educational bureaucracy, including its teachers and administrators. In two of our case studies, the educational system at independence (Tanzania) or state overthrow (Mozambique) was extremely limited (Tanzania had 80 percent illiteracy in 1962; Mozambique, 90 percent in 1974). Most teachers at the secondary level were Europeans, some of them missionaries, but the vast majority simply colonists. At the primary level, however, most teachers were Africans; indeed, one of the "successes" of the colonial system was to use the educational system to employ African graduates coming up through it as teachers, and thus to mystify the race issue inherent in European colonialism. Many primary schools were in missions, which used a state subsidy to employ African teachers alongside the missionaries.

In Cuba, China, and Nicaragua, the inherited educational system was more extensive and almost entirely indigenous, but characterized by large differences between urban and rural areas, and in decline. China and Nicaragua also had high rates of illiteracy, and Nicaragua a significant element of Church control of the educational system.

The problems faced in developing a new educational system have therefore been somewhat different in each of these cases: In all five countries, existing teachers had to be retrained after independence or revolution, but in Tanzania and Mozambique, a principal issue has been one of replacing runaway European secondary teachers. In addition, the number of African teachers available at the beginning of the transition was very small relative to what was required. A key problem was to train more teachers to permit expansion.

In China, Cuba, and Nicaragua, the main extension of education has been to the peasantry, as in Mozambique and Tanzania (where almost everyone lives in rural areas), but large numbers of urban teachers and university and secondary school students have been available for teaching in rural areas. At the same time, the established teaching force and educational administrators in China and Nicaragua resisted reform. Almost twenty years after the overthrow of the state, the Cultural Revolution in China began as a vehicle to uproot traditional elements in the educational bureaucracy. In Nicaragua, despite a large expansion of the public educational system, the Sandinistas have still not completely overcome significant conservative Church influence in secondary education.

However, these differences should not obscure even more important similarities. All the revolutionary movements analyzed in our case studies, and others (for example, USSR, Vietnam, and North Korea) seem to have undertaken similar reforms and faced similar contradictions in their social and educational development. It is in these similarities that we can find the shape of education in the transition and how it differs from its conditional past.

The Change in the Material Value of Education

The case studies suggest that a fundamental equalization of incomes occurs early in the transition, and that this is characteristic of the process of social transformation in transition societies. These revolutionary states succeed in drastically reducing the income and wealth differences that existed before the revolution. The reduction is achieved in two ways. On one hand, the colonial merchant class or indigenous bourgeoisie/latifundia class and state bureaucracy (as a high-consuming quasi-bourgeoisie) is eliminated, either because they leave on their own (taking all their liquid wealth) or because their wealth is confiscated by nationalization.[4]

On the other hand, the revolutionary state moves to guarantee minimum living standards for those with the lowest material consumption by intervening in agricultural production, pricing, and distribution, as well as controlling the provision of health services and housing. In addition, the wage structure is set so that the ratio of the minimum wage to the salary of a manager or professional is around one to four or five. Nevertheless, as the state bureaucracy develops in the postrevolutionary period, the nonpecuniary rewards that accompany political power begin to distort this ratio considerably.

Finally, the state acts to prevent unemployment. In Cuba, for example, the state even required employment during the 1960s and early 1970s. This eliminates the poverty associated with unemployment. In such countries as Mozambique and Tanzania, where 80 to 90 percent of

---

[4] This general statement is somewhat modified in three of our cases. In Nicaragua, nationalizations concentrated on President Somosa's holdings (about 15 percent of total national wealth) and Somosa-related holdings. This means that many of the merchant and landowning bourgeoisie have been allowed to retain their capital, especially in the export sector. Similarly, in Tanzania, private capital still exists, and in Mozambique, the state has now invited private capital back in as a way of resolving a severe capital accumulation crisis. (China has also recently developed some joint ventures with private foreign transnational companies as a way of getting access to high technology, but on a limited scale.)

labor is in agriculture (and not necessarily in collectivized villages), the guarantee of employment is less meaningful than the ability of the state to guarantee good agricultural yields and reasonable prices for their production. Both, unfortunately, are largely a function of world prices for agricultural output and inputs, such as fertilizers, machinery, and seeds. Neither is controlled by the local state, which appears greatly to reduce state power over minimum income guarantees.

The combination of these actions by the revolutionary state eliminates or sharply reduces private wealth as a source of income. Increasingly, income is derived from work rather than from capital, and the wage structure is greatly equalized. Although in some transition economies, everyone is an employee of the state, in most, private capital (land and commercial inventories) exist. But the state exerts tight controls over prices and wages, and hence sets the income structure.

We suggest that such changes are important in explaining how and why education is different in the transition than in conditioned society. The individual material cost of not doing well in school is greatly reduced, and so is the material payoff of reaching higher levels of schooling. The motivation for high achievement in school comes in part from the continued (but smaller) differences in income, but more from nonmaterial rewards (such as easier, more prestigious jobs and political power) and from pressures of social responsibility (a more productive life and a greater contribution to the people-nation). In other words, more schooling and good performance in school still represent a better life (and greater participation in the nation-state). To this is added the social motivation to do well in school, legitimated and fomented by the revolutionary state: elevating the entire people-nation to higher levels of productivity and creativity through education.

Mass Education and the Creation of the Revolutionary People-Nation

Another reason that education in the transition may be different from education in conditional capitalist societies is the particular use of schooling by the state as a way of incorporating peasants and workers into a new definition of the economy and society—a definition much more associated with the value of labor and work than with capitalists and capital.

At the same time that the revolutionary state reduces the relative private value of education, it greatly expands educational opportunities. These opportunities are extended not only to children but to adults. Opportunities expand through the formal system (traditional schooling grows rapidly) and through the nonformal system (in places of work and the community). On one hand, the state is filling the "excessive" demand for schooling left over from conditioned capitalism, that is, it is supplying a highly valued social good to the population. On the other hand, however, the transition state apparently believes—much more than does even the advanced capitalist state—in "human capital" as the basis of economic and social development.

There appears to be good reason for this. One of the principal differences between capitalism and the transition to some vision of a socialist society is that labor rather than physical capital is the basis of economic, social, and political life in the transition. This difference may become clouded as state bureaucrats or a new state bureaucratic class consider themselves as the owners of the nation's physical capital. Even then, however, labor, not property, underlies the legal structure of the state and political life. In any case, the interest of these bureaucrats is to increase the absolute value of economic output because the greater the absolute value of product, the more options they have to exercise political power. The state's objective is therefore to maximize the return to labor, and a principal means of achieving this is to raise productivity through schooling and training (and also to increase physical capital per worker, but this is not the primary purpose). Since all increased individual productivity increases social output, there is no concern about whether the enterprise or the worker bears the cost or receives the benefits of such training (see Becker 1962 for a definition of specific versus general training, for example) or about private versus public costs of education. All increases in productivity represent an increase in the value of social capital.

Most important, the state bureaucracy depends for its legitimacy almost entirely on reasonably satisfied workers and peasants, not on individual capitalists' willingness to invest their private capital. Increased education no longer competes on the same grounds with subsidies to physical capital as it does when physical capital is owned privately, often by large landowners, import-export merchants, or assembly manufacturers, all of whom have traditionally been primarily interested in low-wage labor, not in an educated highly skilled labor force. Mass education in a labor-oriented, transition society is consistent with the satisfaction of the wage-labor constituency and the long-run increase of social output by the transition economy.[5]

As in capitalist society, public education in the transition is the state's principal ideological apparatus. However, in conditioned capitalist societies, ideological formation and politics are shaped largely in civil society, in capitalist production—and the dynamic of capitalist production (hence,

---

[5] The hypothesis that rapid educational expansion, especially of primary education, may conflict in the short and medium run with increases in output per capita—the material consumption of this same labor constituency—will be examined below as a possible contradiction of transition development.

knowledge and ideological formation) is situated in large part in the metropoles, outside the conditioned capitalist society itself.

In the transition, the case studies suggest, the dynamic of social change is crystallized in the state, although with important caveats when referring to smaller transition economies. Four out of five of our case studies refer to such smaller economies. We will argue that the educational systems of transition states are thus much more important in shaping ideology than was the educational system of the conditioned capitalist state it replaced. The transition state seems to use the schools, nonformal learning centers, and mass media as the means of incorporating the population into a revolutionary, transition conception of social relations and a new definition of a people-nation. Through education, we suggest, the state attempts to give a new meaning to citizenship, one that is largely political and sociocollective rather than economic (the free market) and individualistic.

We hypothesize that mass education serves this ideological objective by bringing all the population into direct contact with the state's ideological apparatus. Especially in societies where the market and private capital continue to exist alongside more collective forms of production and distribution, such exposure to collective, political ideology takes on particular importance. Yet even in almost totally collectivized economies, the continued role of the traditional family and local social hierarchies (China and Tanzania, for example) or the family and the Church (Nicaragua) or a nearby hostile foreign presence (Cuba, Nicaragua, and Mozambique), all appear to make mass education an ideological instrument crucial for legitimizing the transition state.

If enrollment and completion rates increase rapidly, it probably means that families desire their children to attend school, or at least that they do not resist schooling.[6] Despite the reduced material rewards of attending school, mass education has rapidly expanded enrollment and the number of children completing primary school (and, in some cases, secondary school and eventually university) in all the countries we studied.

The greater availability of schools and state-supplied books and uniforms, as well as the better conditions in schools (including, in Cuba, secondary boarding schools) and school-supplied lunches, all reduce the cost to families of sending children to school. Is the reduced cost of sending children to school in transition society one of the principal reasons that the demand for education is not decreased by the reduced material

[6] Off-and-on attendance—which is expected behavior among children of lower social class in conditioned capitalist society—is sharply discouraged by the state and by community organizations in the transition. In the 1960s, the Cuban state gave teenage truants a choice of attending special vocational schools or entering the army (where they would also be trained).

rewards for more education? Indirectly so: As in advanced capitalist society (over a much longer period of time) the combination of free schooling and an increased social wage for low-income parents could significantly change the role of the child. The need for children as present family income sources may be decreased. Increasingly, children (in the eyes of their parents) seem to represent *future* possibilities for the family and the people-nation. In addition, in agricultural areas that have been cooperativized or collectivized, primary (and sometimes secondary) schooling of both children and adults is integrated into the social production process, which, we argue, tends to eliminates the need or possibility of individual family decisions about when and how to attend school. In effect, this suggests that the state in transition societies creates for the masses an attitude toward schooling similar to that held by the middle class in capitalist society: Attendance and success in school becomes an accepted and unquestioned part of a child and adolescent's life.[7]

One of our principal arguments, then, is that the rapid expansion of education in these relatively poor (except relatively well-off and literate Cuba), previously highly illiterate societies can be explained by the labor orientation of the transition state and the primary role of the state in social transformation. Much more than the rhetoric of increased individual equality of opportunity (also used by the conditioned capitalist state in discussing education), it is the elimination of private capital as a political force and the conversion of the local state into the crystallization of the new social dynamic that may explain this expansion. As the locus of transformation, the state uses mass education as the principal element in the creation of the collective/political citizen of a revolutionary nation-state.

These citizens are theoretically (and legally) equal, and, as in capitalist society, should have equal opportunity to succeed. The equalization of access to schooling is certainly part of this process. But, just as the more important inequalities in capitalist society are outside public education in the relations of private production and access to political power, in transition society, the more important *equalities* are outside education in the state's material guarantees and the disjunction between capital ownership and political influence.

Struggles for equality through education in capitalist societies repre-

---

[7] In low-income peasant societies, such as Tanzania and Mozambique, this increase in the social wage is rather minimal. In Mozambique, it may represent only the higher wages available for part-year work on the plantations. Children remain needed as a family income source, even if they also represent a future possibility to a greater degree than in conditioned capitalism. Nevertheless, the greater availability of rural schools and the coordination of schooling with agricultural calendars may reduce the cost of sending a child to school.

sent a struggle of the forces of democratization against the forces of reproduction largely for greater economic equality in civil society (see Carnoy and Levin 1985). In transition society, struggles in the educational system for less hierarchy, greater access to university education for the children of workers and peasants, more participation in shaping curriculum, and so forth, seem to be primarily struggles for greater equality of political power in the state by the forces of democratization against the forces of reproduction. In the transition to some vision of socialist society, the already largely won struggle for economic equality is apparently far less important than the achievement of new kinds of political democracy, including the democratization of knowledge and "expertise."[8]

The case studies suggest, however, that the question of mass education itself is not an issue in the transition. Rather, the questions, conflicts, and contradictions lie in how rapidly that mass education can expand, what levels should expand most rapidly, what its content and process should be, and how knowledge should be articulated into expanded political participation and accountability. We argue that the definition of knowledge, who is to have access to it and how it is to be used, therefore, is central to the discussion of the revolutionary transition.

Increased Material Consumption Versus Increased Education

Is there consensus on state and educational policies in the transition? This is a major question in our analysis. We find a considerable implicit and occasionally explicit conflict over the course of educational expansion and reform, and we argue that this conflict reflects larger conflict in the transformation of transition society. The first of these conflicts is between policies whose objective is to increase material consumption and those that want to focus on the long-term transformation of the economy and society.

In an idealized version of revolutionary society, where political participation has such a high value that material consumption beyond a reason-

---

[8] This argument should not be interpreted at meaning that societies in transition have solved the problem of economic inequality. As we indicated in note 7, the social wage of peasant farmers is still lower than that of urban workers, although the differences are far smaller than in conditioned capitalism. Nevertheless, the issue of the social wage in transition society is less a function of power relations in civil society and more a political issue, that is, a function of relations in the transition state. Economic decisions in the state, however—especially in the four smaller countries we studied—are still conditioned by international economic conditions, as Cuba's failed attempt in the early 1960s to become independent of sugar exports showed. Yet we will show that the Cubans were able, using sophisticated technological innovation, to change conditions in sugar production and raise productivity and the social wage of sugar workers significantly even as sugar prices were stable or falling (see Edquist 1985).

able level of satisfying minimum needs is superfluous, the new state would not have to be overly concerned with accumulating capital. However, the overthrow of the conditioned capitalist state itself is implicitly the result of demands by the mass of population for better material conditions. Furthermore, in countries such as the Soviet Union, China, Nicaragua, and Mozambique, as well as Eastern Europe, North Korea, and Vietnam, the revolutionary state had to rebuild an economy ravaged by civil or world war. And in China, Mozambique, Tanzania, and Nicaragua, the very low material conditions of the mass of the population at the point of revolutionary takeover meant a necessary emphasis by the state on accumulating capital.

The accumulation of capital takes on additional importance for states whose very existence is threatened by outside intervention (China in the 1950s, Cuba in the 1960s, Nicaragua and Mozambique in the 1980s). Capital is necessary for defense as well as for maintaining material conditions.

Beyond military requirements, however, the legitimacy of the revolutionary state hinges in part on its ability to increase mass consumption. State-supplied social services, such as health care, education, day care, and entertainment/recreation are part of this consumption, Increased political participation and a sense of making history, of being an authentic part of history, can also contribute to an overall sense of well-being and to a state's legitimacy. But increases in private consumption—particularly the quality and quantity of food, the availability of housing and transportation, and clothing—are important to most citizens of these societies and enters into the legitimacy accorded revolutionary movements and the transition state.

Because education is a relatively long-term investment in increased productivity (although some studies suggest a significant payoff in higher agricultural productivity from even four years of primary schooling (see Lockheed, Jamison, and Lau 1980) and may require increased physical capital per worker to result in that higher productivity (Sack, Carnoy, and Lecaros 1980), the state is faced by a conflict between spending surplus on rapid establishment of mass education versus spending it on more direct investments in increased output—energy projects, irrigation, agricultural extension, fertilizer, new seeds, agricultural machinery, and so forth. On one hand, education does not compete for foreign exchange (unless textbooks and other educational technology have to be imported); but on the other hand, it competes for scarce skilled labor (teachers), which could be used in more direct productivity-raising investments of time and effort.

We observe that the immediate manifestation of this conflict is reduced emphasis on university expansion for a relatively long period after the revolutionary triumph. Even though many liberal professional and skilled technicians leave the country, creating pressure to fill their ranks with new university graduates, the very dearth of highly trained cadres requires making choices about where to use these scarce resources. Usually, they are brought into the state bureaucracy to organize the economy or sent directly to the field to train technicians for direct production applications, rather than left to teach in the university.

For example, in the two years immediately after the Sandinista victory, the Nicaraguan university system did expand in response to pent-up middle-class demand, but by 1981 a new plan projected drastically slower growth in university enrollment. This plan was implemented, although Nicaragua still spends a relatively large portion of its education budget on university education. Higher education was simply too much of a resource drain to be expanded as rapidly as social demand dictated. Instead, emphasis and resources were shifted from traditional liberal fields to scientific, technical, and medical education. Similarly, in Cuba, the university did not begin to expand enrollment until the early 1970s, almost fourteen years after Batista's overthrow. In China, it is only recently that university education was reestablished after the closing of most universities during the Cultural Revolution. Tanzania expanded its university enrollment in 1962–1967 in order to Africanize its state bureaucracy and its schools and opened a second university in the mid-1980s, but its university population is small and will remain so for the foreseeable future. Mozambique even cut back upper secondary schooling during the first five years of independence, and the very small university enrollment has only recently reached late colonial levels.

The overall conflict between spending on education versus spending on infrastructure more directly related to increases in material output was settled differently in the different cases we studied. At one extreme, Cuba invested a high 4.5–7 percent of gross domestic product—considerably higher than the UNESCO average for member countries—in education throughout the 1960s and 1970s, probably at the expense of increasing housing, agricultural output, and other forms of consumption. In the 1960s, one-third of the Cuban population was in school. The Cuban state consciously attempted to transform Cuba's skill structure and social attitudes through this massive investment.

China also invested heavily in education, especially in rural primary schooling, but relatively much less than Cuba. The Chinese concentrated more of their resources on raising food production at the village level. They succeeded. Tanzania moved very quickly to expand rural primary schools in the 1960s, but did not carry this level of investment on to secondary education. While primary schooling is now universal in Tanzania, secondary schooling is extremely limited. Only about 5 percent of the relevant age cohort attends secondary school. Nicaragua also expanded primary education in response to substantial pent-up demand, but devotes only about 4–5 percent of its gross national product to education. In addition, Cuban teachers play an important role in Nicaraguan rural education, filling in for the extreme shortage of skills in the educational system. Mozambique achieved a massive expansion of formal schooling, doubling primary enrollment in three years and quintupling secondary enrollment, which raised education costs from 2 percent of gross social product in 1971 to 7.5 percent in 1984. But gross social product declined enormously from 1981 to 1986. As a result, Mozambique had to go much more slowly than expected, even in literacy training and primary education, because of its critical shortage of skills and material goods.

All of these countries have also tried to provide education in forms that reduce costs. The models of literacy training in China and Cuba, where students and teachers went into the countryside to teach peasants how to read, have been used in some form in all transition societies. These literacy campaigns are largely a mechanism of political mobilization. Young people from towns and cities are stimulated through the collective, "revolutionary" action of eradicating literacy in the countryside. Those who are illiterate (in all but Cuba, the majority of the population were illiterate at the time of the revolution) are incorporated through such action into the new concept of the people-nation. For both these groups, the literacy campaign is a high-value consumer good that is relatively cheap for the state to produce. It satisfies a primary demand for authentic participation through teaching and learning. It joins young people from cities with older and younger people in the countryside and from marginal urban groups. It gives the new state enormous legitimacy (see, for example, Fagen 1969; Torres 1985).

The supply of low-cost educational services has continued after the literacy campaigns. In Nicaragua, high school students, university students, many teachers, and even the newly literate themselves continue to teach evening postliteracy, primary school–equivalent courses for adults and children. In many rural areas, such courses substitute for formal schooling.

This way of providing schooling saves the state scarce resources. It also tends to democratize knowledge, since the intellectual distance between teacher and student is small, and students can easily visualize themselves as teachers. It enables the state to incorporate far more people into the educational process within the fiscal constraints. It provides many of the more revolutionary aspects of political participation to the population at large, and in that sense is antibureaucratic and challenges the centralization of expertise. But apparently where this popular education does not

grant a degree equivalent to a formal school diploma, it also fails to supply, in the longer run, the consumer satisfaction of formal education. The
prestige hierarchy left over from the conditioned economy is not easily
erased.

In all the countries we studied, there is a more serious problem with
nonformal education: It is marked by much lower success rates than
those of formal schooling, largely because teachers are less well trained
and students spend less time in school. The state itself tends to reduce
the importance of nonformal education by complaining of its inefficiency
and low quality, by cutting its resources, and by trying to bring it into
line with the existing curricula of formal schooling. Strengthening formal
schooling (when it does occur) alongside a deprecated nonformal education only maintains this sense of difference between the value of the two
kinds of education. As we discuss further, below, the state tends to rely
increasingly on formal schooling to supply skills and less on the more
revolutionary and democratic forms of nonformal education.

The Cuban "schools in the countryside" are another example of innovative education that was designed to meet revolutionary (democratizing)
goals while saving scarce resources. These rural secondary boarding
schools were supposed to incorporate urban as well as rural youth into
rural schools that stressed agricultural manual work. They were also designed to increase academic performance in a controlled environment.
Through the students' agricultural labor, the schools were meant to pay
for themselves. The schools in the countryside achieved many of their
goals—especially better academic performance—but the economic value
of the students' work fell far short of schooling costs. Indeed, this turned
out to be a more expensive form of education than building more urban
secondary schools; nevertheless, it was a more democratic form, in that
rural and urban youth shared the agricultural rural work experience (the
development of a shared knowledge in the dominant form of production).

Education for Economic Growth versus Education for Equal Access

The second conflict we observe is over the objectives education should
serve. Which levels and types of education should receive more resources and attention? The revolutionary state generally makes mass basic education its first priority because those peasants and workers and
their children who have been denied access to such schooling are potentially the most important supporters of transition reforms. Above all, the
state needs their backing and is unlikely to get support from professionals
and the petite bourgeoisie (for a countertheory of the potential role of the
petite bourgeoisie in transforming capitalist society, however, see Poulantzas 1975). But investing heavily and primarily in lower levels of

schooling and adult education also may have serious economic and political consequences for the transition state. There always appear to be those in the state bureaucracy and the revolutionary party who favor emphasis on higher technical education, which is much more directly related to capital accumulation and filling short-term needs for administrative cadres.

The literacy campaigns and rural primary school expansions in the five case study countries symbolize the transition state's political commitment to reaching the lower classes with a revolutionary message and to incorporating them into the modern knowledge system. Expanding lower levels of education and reaching out to illiterate peasants and workers with mass mobilization campaigns is consistent with an overall pattern of equalization in the immediate postrevolutionary period. According to some economists, spending on lower levels of schooling is a form of resource transfer from higher- to lower-income groups (Jallade 1976). Even though all schooling is generally traditional and hierarchical, the relative emphasis on the lower levels can be interpreted as the dominance of a "massive democratization" policy in the first years after the overthrow of the conditioned capitalist state. This is apparently a push by the revolutionary party for the masses' increased participation in the economic and social life of the new people-nation. For similar reasons, but in a different historical period and a different political context, primary schooling also first grew almost to universality before secondary schools and universities expanded in the United States (see Carnoy and Levin 1985).

The focus on the expansion of mass education in various forms is generally matched by a deemphasis of higher education. University training is not only expensive, but it necessarily caters to the sons and daughters of professionals and the petite bourgeoisie, generally among the least potentially revolutionary strata of conditioned capitalist society. But holding back university spending also increases urban middle-class opposition to the state. Making it more difficult for their children to attend university reduces the middle class's social wage drastically. In countries such as Tanzania and Mozambique, the political cost of holding back on investment in secondary and higher education is relatively low because members of the prerevolutionary middle class either have left the country or send their children abroad. But in China, Cuba, and Nicaragua the need to save somewhere on education and the ideological bias to make that savings at the university level has significant political impact.[9]

[9] Nicaragua represents a special case of this kind of social demand. There, a significant group of Nicaraguans still relies on private primary and lower secondary schools and public higher secondary and university education to achieve social and economic status for their children. The revolutionary state continues this leftover from conditioned capitalism in order not to raise yet another conflict with the remaining middle class in a difficult period.

The universalization of primary schooling rather than more rapid immediate expansion of secondary and university education may make sense in terms of its relative contribution to economic output, such as rates of return and productivity/cost ratios (Psacharopoulos and Woodhall 1985). For one thing, the costs of primary schooling are very low relative to higher levels because primary school teachers are paid less and physical plant is poorer. But in terms of the absolute contribution of crucial labor services for countries facing critical high-skill shortages, the decision to hold back on secondary and university training may result in serious external diseconomies, lowering general productivity levels because certain skills, such as management ones, are in short supply. In some of our cases, this means that the initial attention to basic mass education shifts rapidly to concerns about increasing educational quality at the primary level, including raising test scores and reducing repetition rates and dropouts, and to increasing enrollment at the secondary level.

Hierarchical Knowledge versus Participative Knowledge

The third conflict in the transition, we suggest, is over the definition of what mass schooling should be. The focus on mass primary schooling is accompanied by other tendencies to democratize access to knowledge. All the societies we studied have invested relatively more in rural education (and rural aspects of the economy) than in urban education and areas. They have reversed the processes of increasing inequality between urban and rural areas characteristic of conditioned capitalism, although the distance between urban and rural life remains large even after many years of rural development and modernization.[10]

They also have placed considerable emphasis on bridging the gap between manual and mental work. Schools generally have some sort of manual labor as part of their regular curriculum, generally beginning with the secondary level. In Cuba, Mozambique, and Tanzania even primary school children do some weekly work activities in school vegetable gardens. In China, Cuba, Mozambique, and Tanzania secondary school students generally do regular manual work while going to school. The purpose of the work programs is largely ideological: Since the traditional

---

[10] With the exception of Nicaragua, modernization generally takes place through forced cooperativization or collectivization. The cost of providing reasonably good social services and increasing the standard of living in rural areas goes down (see Nyerere's arguments about forced resettlement in ujamaa villages in Smith 1986). Building clinics and schools to incorporate rural residents and pupils living in collectives is much more efficient than doing the same for the same numbers living in scattered, individual farms or small settlements. But lowering costs in this way often entails a high price in individual liberty and even human lives.

separation between the working class and the bourgeoisie in conditioned capitalist societies is between manual and mental work, the incorporation of the collectivized individual into the new people-nation requires breaking down these previous classifications.

The participation of rural dwellers and the working class in the political and social life of these societies is therefore much greater in the transition than in the conditioned capitalist state. The poor, the marginalized, and the disadvantaged are much more important socially as a result of the revolution. They are incorporated into the postcapitalist state as collectivized individuals and defined as the makers of the new nation state's history.

But democratizing forces in transition society are caught in serious conflicts. Access to knowledge is rapidly increased for the masses and equalized considerably between rural and urban dwellers and between the children of manual and mental workers. But as long as the definition of knowledge remains in the hands of mental workers and urban dwellers, those in rural areas and those who work with their hands can never participate equally in the social and political decisionmaking that shapes the dynamic of transition society. They can never catch up to those who are doing that defining.[11]

Equalizing, incorporating, and politically legitimizing the expansion of formal and nonformal education in transition society, does not settle the conflict between those who want to democratize knowledge and power and those who want to reproduce the power and knowledge structure. The struggle typically develops in education over the revolutionary definition of knowledge. On one side are those who want to develop concrete, productive skills that include political consciousness and participation and combine mental and manual concepts of work, that is, they see education as developing Gramsci's organic intellectual. On the other side are those who define skill and knowledge as relatively devoid of political consciousness. They tend to separate the mental expertise that directs production and the manual work that actually carries it out. The struggle over knowledge represents, in part, a fundamental conflict in

[11] For years, Poland has awarded bonus points to peasant and workers' children on the university entrance exams in order to compensate for their "disadvantage." Yet even these points have not sufficed to give proportional representation to these two groups in Polish universities (although it has significantly increased the presence of children of workers and peasants), largely because of the continued lower quality of secondary schools in rural areas and in many of Poland's smaller cities (see Tomala, Borowicz, and Kwiecinski 1983). Mozambique has experimented with intensive education programs for the children of party cadres from peasant backgrounds, and has even reduced enrollment in basic education to improve quality and the chances of those from the popular classes who are able to enroll in basic education, but the social classes with urban backgrounds are still much better served by the education system than the peasantry.

transition society—particularly in the transition bureaucracy and in organized popular movements—over forms and strategies for the organization and management of production.

But the struggle also seems to represent a conflict over the control of knowledge-producing institutions themselves. On one hand, academic skills can be developed as part and parcel of popular education—an education that focuses primarily on the incorporation of the masses (peasants and workers and their children) into the revolutionary people-nation. Popular education is mass organization- or community-based, less hierarchical, and emphasizes social and political participation. On the other hand, these same skills can be developed in traditional academic institutions with traditional hierarchical pedagogical methods. Traditional education is organized bureaucratically in ministries of education and thus is usually geared toward pedagogical and bureaucratic objectives, including the wage and working condition objectives of teachers' unions.

The phenomenon to be explained in transition societies is why the tendency over time is toward traditional, hierarchical, bureaucratized, formal schooling and away from popular, participative education as the dominant educational form to impart basic skills. The tendency is particularly important because transition societies emphasize the incorporation of the masses through political and social participation.

In China, these struggles came to be known as "red" versus "expert." During the Cultural Revolution, Mao Zedong and those around him stressed the political consciousness version of skills: Managers were made to work on the assembly line for one month a year; political consciousness rather than academic skills were the most important content in schools; the authority of the teacher in the classroom was challenged by politically conscious students; universities were closed; and professors were sent to "reeducation" camps. The continuing extension of political consciousness was, it is true, advantageous to rural relative to urban workers and to manual over mental workers. The Cultural Revolution stressed the kind of knowledge development that everyone, no matter what their social background, could acquire equally well. Moreover, manual workers and peasants were less suspect of "incorrect" political views than urban intellectuals, technicians, and managers. The period also witnessed an attack on the fundamental authority patterns inherited from ancient China. In both ways, the Cultural Revolution represented a further democratization of Chinese society. But in most other ways, it was highly authoritarian and antidemocratic, largely because the only organization capable of carrying out reforms throughout the country was the army, hardly a democratic institution. Although the Cultural Revolution began in the educational system as a genuine attempt to create a deepening of political development at the local level and to change the knowledge hierarchy, it turned authoritarian and violent because of the institutional structure in which it took place. The hierarchical apparatuses of violence, so important in the original revolution that overthrew the conditioned state, claimed the Cultural Revolution as well. There were no democratic institutions that could contest this claim.

During the first ten years, the Cuban revolution made a similar attempt to develop "socialist man" (these are the words used by the 26th of July Movement) while raising the material standard of living. Cuban leaders rejected the Stalinist interpretation of Marx that required increasing material consumption before political consciousness could be raised. Political development, including manual, agricultural work as part of the school curriculum for both urban and rural youth, the literacy campaign, moral incentives in the workplace, and a deemphasis of university education all formed part of the Cuban attempt to "demarketize" the economy and the school and to form a new, collective Cuban citizen-worker.

Both the Chinese and Cuban attempts to democratize social structures by emphasizing the political definition of knowledge rather than a traditional, academic hierarchy of technological skills were abandoned. Both educational systems turned to emphasizing a more hierarchical definition of skills that divided mental and manual labor and that the state (and Party) felt could increase production in the short run. Production organizations abandoned moral for material incentives and moved to an internal pricing/profit system to increase managerial efficiency and accountability. In China, the change was as sharp and sudden as in the Cultural Revolution. In Cuba, it was gradual—education still retains much of its political emphasis, but is less interested today in the ideological and participative content of knowledge than in the 1960s.

It can be argued that the Cultural Revolution and the long period of ideological reformation in Cuba so overturned previous knowledge and power hierarchies and so inculcated a whole generation with new values and norms that China and Cuba could afford to turn to focusing on developing expertise and increasing "efficiency" within an already highly consciousness-raised setting. The evidence suggests, however, that large gaps in school performance still exist between rural and urban children and between the children of manual and mental workers, just as they do in the Soviet Union and Eastern Europe. Instead of permanently democratizing political structures through deepened political consciousness, these "cultural revolutions" seemed to have convinced those at the top of the existing political hierarchies that economic growth is at least as or more important than political development and that academic skills are more important than skills shaped by social consciousness. That this is a seemingly universal phenomenon in transitional development is borne out by a similar tendency toward a technocratic emphasis in Mozambique and Tanzanian education decisions.

The usual argument against democratizing knowledge through alternative educational processes and mass participation in the definition of knowledge, then, is the cost it implies for economic growth and development in terms of competing in capitalist metropole-dominated world markets, especially in industrial goods and especially if the ultimate goal of the educational system is to find the 3 or 4 percent of university graduates who will compete internationally with their correspondent cadres in the capitalist metropoles.

This suggests that there are constant pressures on the transition state to increase material consumption and that the state interprets this pressure as requiring increased academic efficiency, as measured by traditional criteria, such as test scores in mathematics, language, and sciences. This view translates into traditional pedagogy, emphasizing individual academic competition among students, and deemphasizing other aspects of the school socialization process.

Part of this pressure certainly comes from consumers themselves, who, no matter how socialized into transition collective values and supplied with social goods, including increased education and political participation, still desire increased private consumption. In countries such as Tanzania and especially Mozambique, increasing consumption means raising minimal calorie intake to higher, acceptable levels by making staples regularly available to the mass of the population. In China, it means reaching consumption levels presently associated with middle-income Latin American countries; in Nicaragua, it means restoring consumption for the masses to preearthquake (1970) levels; and in Cuba, it means meeting the competition of television publicity from Miami. The question in all these cases is not only how much to raise consumption but how quickly, and how the knowledge necessary to raise productivity is defined. Focusing on skills through formal schooling is generally the way the state bureaucracy seeks to increase the pace at which productivity might rise, but there is no evidence that productivity does rise more rapidly when children learn basic skills through traditional, hierarchical pedagogy, or even that hierarchical pedagogy is more efficient in teaching children such basic skills (the latter point has also been raised in the United States, for example, in the free schools debate of the late 1960s).

Focusing on traditional academic skills and reducing emphasis on participation and socialization in education is also directly related in the transition society to changes (and struggles) in the bureaucratic leadership's views of how production should be organized and what kind of educational structures, methods, and curricula are set up as a result. In the early days of Mozambique's revolution, for example, potential "soviets" were created in factories and plantations. These were accompanied by the politicization and democratization of schools and an emphasis on increasing primary school and literacy training enrollment. In 1977, the bureaucratic leadership denounced the lack of economic growth and blamed it on "weak" management, too few skills in the labor force, and inefficiency in production (too much participation). By 1980, production decisions were centralized in the hands of the factory or plantation director. The same model was applied in the schools, and based on the same arguments—lack of obedience, discipline, and efficiency. Primary education was cut back, literacy programs lost their priority, academic and formal education were promoted, secondary schools and universities were expanded, the upper secondary level was reinstated at high cost, technical education was expanded at the higher levels, and production as part of the school curriculum was relegated to a low-priority sideline.

The de facto abandonment by the transition state of more cooperative, participative relations in production and education is not necessarily rational in the long run. Gorbachev's efforts at *glasnost* and *perestroika*, *specifically* including the democratization of workplaces, are clear recognition of the negative impact on economic growth and product quality of social bureaucratization. It may be that greater participation combined with increased managerial skills *developed in that context* would eventually produce higher productivity than that possible with capitalist relations of production. With teachers trained to develop and work in the context of such relations, cooperative, participative relations in school might produce much more learning and skills, including those needed for higher productivity. But there is a tendency for hierarchical bureaucracies to believe that hierarchical production and education is more effective in raising productivity, and for the bureaucrats to feel more safely in command with hierarchical management. Since the state bureaucrats, and not the workers, run the production system, it is the outcome of political conflicts in the state that affect how production and the schools are organized and what they emphasize (again, the primarily bureaucratic struggle over perestroika is a good example). Short-run consumption demands by the population will be interpreted by the more hierarchical-oriented groups in the bureaucracy as requiring greater control and less participation throughout the social system, in order to produce greater "efficiency."

Given a choice between popular education and formal, traditional bureaucratic schools, the public appears to opt for the latter, especially when these are more highly valued by those who do best materially and politically in the postrevolutionary society. Public demand for different types of schooling has some impact on the choices made in the kinds of education to be provided. We have already mentioned that the Sandinistas expanded university education rapidly in the first two years after their victory. At certain conjunctures in the transition, the revolutionary leadership may have to give in to the demands of dominant groups, especially the new class that has developed in the state bureaucracy itself or, as in Nicaragua, existing middle classes on whom the regime counts for at least some support. In Tanzania, for example, strong pressure to expand secondary education has led to a state policy of sanctioning private schools for the first time since the Arusha Declaration (1967). Private education in Nicaragua and Tanzania serves to reduce the cost of schooling to the state, but it also prevents (Nicaragua) or undoes (Tanzania) progress toward equalizing opportunity for secondary and higher education for youth from all regions of the country. Private education expands most rapidly in higher-income areas (Unsicker 1987).

Even so, it is not clear that the tendency to define knowledge through traditional, bureaucratic formal schooling is primarily a response by the transition state to popular demand. In the case studies we examine the pressures within the state bureaucracy itself to concentrate on formal schooling as the principal means to provide mass education. We ask whether the new class position of such bureaucratic groups in the transition state gives more democratic relations a chance to develop, especially in the context of the traditional argument for greater and more efficient production and the traditional association of increased productivity with skills developed in bureaucratic, hierarchical schools.

Focusing on skills raises a second, and related, educational process issue: Should schools be primarily vocational, preparing youth and adults for specific, needed occupations, or primarily academic, providing a base for more specific skill acquisition in the workplace? With their emphasis on work as the basis of social fulfillment and on economic planning as the foundation of social production, once shifted from education for ideological socialization and democratization to education for economic growth, revolutionary societies have tended toward schooling for specific skills rather than general academic goals. Yet in the more experimental period of the early revolutionary years and even today in China, in Cuba, and to some extent in Nicaragua, the emphasis on manual labor as an integral part of the curriculum connects secondary schools and universities with production units. Students at those levels work as part of their academic education, and career decisions are developed around such work situations. Many specifically skill-oriented types of secondary education exist in all the countries we studied. These are usually closely related to a production situation, such as a factory or a farm.

Nevertheless, it is telling that transition societies have not demystified what Foster (1965) called the "vocational schooling fallacy." Foster argued convincingly that all schooling is vocational, whether it is academic or specifically vocational, because academic education (the university track) prepares students for vocations as well—in this case, liberal or technical professions. In capitalist society, academic education is separated from vocational education, as if it served a different purpose rather than simply supplying different kinds of knowledge and access to social/material status for different groups (social classes) of youth. In transition societies, all education is defined as vocational, and the state attempts to minimize material and status differences among vocations. For example, in Cuba, the highest status and academically most select secondary schools are called vocational schools. The much lower-status, parallel "workers' and peasants' education" system, primarily geared to adults, today concentrates on upper secondary and university training. It also provides a large number of working adults access to skill-specific knowledge in their off-hours. Unlike the skills learned at the elite vocational schools, these are related to existing jobs rather than to future university-level careers. Everyone is aware of the difference. And, because of the kinds of jobs university students obtain, the skills learned at university, even though tied to the work place through practical training during school, are seen as very different from secondary school skills.

Schooling for specific skills may have very high material payoffs in the short run, especially in the early years of the revolution when such skills are in very short supply. Yet, the population at large recognizes that, despite the ideological and material deemphasis of differences among occupations and types of schooling (knowledge), the best opportunities present themselves for those who are strong academically in formal, traditional schooling. The best vocational education continues to be academic education, even though those students who are interested in more manual occupations do not pay nearly as high a material and status price for such tastes or talents as in conditioned capitalist society.

In this context, the issue of how to evaluate students in the transition becomes critical. The combination of limited places for further education and the traditional testing system focus attention almost entirely on individual achievement in the academic aspect of the curriculum, which rewards what the Cubans call "egoismo"—competitive capitalist attitudes and behavior. As Unsicker (1987) points out in his recent study of the Tanzanian Folk Development Colleges, even if basic education effectively integrates students into the teaching of critical academic skills, the selection of students for postbasic schooling includes a fair representation of girls and of children from rural areas and the popular classes, and secondary and higher education includes a significant component of manual work, traditional examinations will still select for and reinforce capitalist values. The threat that this traditional system of evaluation poses to collective ideals in the transition is apparent: Those who advance in the system will tend to consider themselves more intelligent, harder working, or otherwise more deserving of further schooling and greater material rewards. Manual work in school will tend to be endured as a sacrifice, which only gives individualistic students greater self-justification that they have earned the right to elite status in the transition society, and the right to pass this status down to their children.

Could entire alternative approaches to learning and teaching be created by the state in response to greater demand—approaches that would produce less concentration of expertise and greater emphasis on democratic participation and innovation? We suggest that transition states have democratized education by expanding it greatly at the primary level (and then the secondary level, in China and Cuba). There have been periodic challenges to the knowledge authority in the classroom. In Nicaragua, a brisk debate developed over the "best" way to teach and learn, with a number of important mass organizations arguing against "low-quality" formal schooling and for more socially conscious, pedagogical techniques.

Alternative pedagogical forms are not part of the history of transition societies. These forms developed and were used primarily to break out of the class nature of capitalist schooling.[12] The Soviets attempted to reconstruct Soviet education in the early revolutionary period, on the basis of the ideal of giving all Russian children the possibility of reaching the highest levels of scientific and technological knowledge. They also tried to link school curricula with productive work through student work programs in factories and on farms (King 1986, 156). Krupskaya led this movement in the early 1920s. She insisted on collective study and work as a crucial element in socialist education. Ironically, this was essentially an application of John Dewey's progressive educational philosophy that the norms and values children learn in school will be carried into the workplace.

More recently, in Nicaragua, Paulo Freire's (1970) method was applied

[12] There is an expanding literature on Marxist/socialist pedagogy, although Marx's writings on education are scarce. These writings refer largely to what education should be once there is a change in the mode of production, and so are mainly extensions of Marx's economic and philosophical writing. In some cases, such as the Soviet Union, they also influenced the formal curriculum. The writings can be grouped under experiences in the Soviet revolution (Lenin 1978; Krupskaya 1955; Lunacharsky 1970; and Makarenko 1951, 1961); work in Eastern Europe (Suchodolski 1966, 1967); interpretations and extensions of Gramsci's (1971) theories of education and intellectuals (for example, Lombardi 1969; Broccoli 1977; Adamson 1980; Entwistle 1978, 1979; Borghi 1958, 1974); other work in Western Europe (for example, in contemporary Italy, Manacorda 1966, 1970); studies in Latin America (for example, Gadotti 1987); and work in the United States (Norton and Ollman 1978). A review of this literature is outside the scope of our present study, but it is of interest in considering what the form and content of schooling should be in collectively oriented societies.

in the Nicaraguan literacy campaign and remains the base of popular education pedagogy in that country. That method is based on the development of critical consciousness as an instrument of political organization of the oppressed. Freire insists that education must be redefined from the perspective of the subordinate classes.

However, our research suggests that alternative pedagogical forms generally end up subordinated to the growth of a highly bureaucratized, hierarchicized, formal educational system. That system puts enormous emphasis on acclaim and achievement, and sometimes, as in Cuba, results in a significant increase in "quality" (as measured by test scores on end-of-grade examinations) through the adoption of new technical curricula. In some ways, as unimaginative as the conditioned capitalist education it replaces, especially in social sciences and the humanities—those subjects assumed to be least directly applicable to work and most concerned with the questioning of society and human relations. This apparent absence of critical thinking (the fundamental element of Freire's theory of learning) is one of the most important paradoxes of education in the transition.

Bureaucratization versus Democratization

The conflict over the content of schooling and the corresponding definition of knowledge, as well as the pedagogical models in school (who defines knowledge?), underlie the much greater conflict in the transition state between the democratization and the hierarchization of society. Does transition pedagogy for academic skills come to imply formality? Is it biased in favor of those from homes and wider environments where such skills are already available outside of schools (Bourdieu and Passeron 1977)? Does it reinforce authority structures that impede democratic participation inside and outside the schools? Is knowledge defined primarily as technical expertise, as in the capitalist state?

The case studies suggest that expertise in the transition can become the monopoly of the political bureaucracy. The principal competition for control of the definition of knowledge comes from mass organizations, in those cases where such organizations have some autonomy. Historically, however, vanguard party and state bureaucracy have solidified their political power in the transition state and mass organizations have declined in importance. This corresponds to the formalization of knowledge and the centralization of control over all aspects of political and social life.

The case studies indicate that the ascendancy of the centralized and hierarchical school system, although supported by social demand that was shaped in conditioned capitalist society, is much more directly influenced by the growing ossification of the new political bureaucracy and its tendency to strengthen its political power and reproduce itself through the school. The transition ministry of education bureaucracy has the same interest as its capitalist predecessor in expanding its power and control by building a highly centralized formal school system, teacher training colleges, centralized curriculum, and a system of centralized quality controls (examinations). We suggest, however, that unlike the ministry in conditioned capitalism, this interest coincides rather than conflicts with the overall materialist goals of the state and of the dominant political constituencies, who are now workers and peasants rather than merchant capitalists, landowners, and assembly industrialists.

On one hand, the expansion of formal schooling is potentially a crucial element in the separation of alienated conditioned capitalist individuals from their past (family, religion, individualized materialism), and their re-creation as individuals with collective values and norms, capable of contributing materially and politically to collective goals. Schooling can contribute to the democratization of societies that lack democracy. On the other hand, the growth of a ministerial bureaucracy promotes educational forms and processes that are inherently undemocratic and bureaucratic, because it is precisely such forms that strengthen the control of a centralized bureaucracy over teachers and students. Knowledge in such centralized education is top-down rather than bottom-up. Decisions are made centrally, and control over the process of education and the definition of knowledge is highly centralized. The bureaucracy tends to press for measures of knowledge quality that are consistent with the kinds of knowledge most useful to bureaucracies.

As it becomes better defined, the transition state bureaucracy tends to use the educational system to reproduce itself as a "new class." In the first years and decades after the revolution, this group is diverse and generally unstable, characterized by conflicting strategies and interests. There is also considerable penetration of leadership and managerial positions by workers and peasants, either through adult education and party membership or through the military. But even during these early decades, the children of bureaucrats and professionals closely tied to the state are overrepresented in the elite levels of the reformed and expanded educational system; they are likely to become the next generation of favored bureaucrats, with legitimization provided by their own exam success in the formal school system. The solidification of the bureaucracy also increases the likelihood of increased material benefits accruing to high-level bureaucrats. Higher levels of education gradually come to represent greater material payoffs.

The new class system is founded on meritocracy and closely controlled political power. Expert knowledge is much of the basis of this power. More than in capitalist society, the state has a monopoly over this expertise. Formal education and political party standing are the means by which individuals get access to favored positions. The new class also has a specific relation to the organization of production. One of the first signs that expertise is being concentrated in the bureaucracy is the hierarchization of knowledge on the shop floor and in worker-management relations. Formal education begins to replace experience and political consciousness in job allocation. Political activity is also an important element in social mobility, but as transition societies have matured, all but the highest positions in the state hierarchy become increasingly technocratically influenced.

As long as they represent poles of power alternative to the state or vanguard party hierarchy, mass political organizations may be capable of opposing such technocratic definitions of knowledge and the new class's attempts to centralize power and its reproduction. But prolonged military confrontation with external threats and the apparent tendency for vanguard parties to be highly undemocratic appear to centralize control in the party and the bureaucracy at the expense of mass organizations. Military models tend to dominate in periods of military necessity. It is difficult to escape their consequences.

In capitalism, social movements and important elements of the capitalist class oppose state bureaucratic power. The concentration of political power in the transition state does not have a similar counterweight in the civil society. In the Soviet Union and China, political conflict until now has taken place within the vanguard party itself, particularly between various factions of the new class bureaucracy. Other transition societies have seen opposition come through organized political movements outside the party (Solidarnosc in Poland, for example).

Since the vanguard party hierarchy tends to reproduce itself by reducing popular participation, it is interesting to observe what the implications of expanded mass education and the widening of the knowledge base are for the democratization of political institutions. Can the bureaucracy expand even technocratic forms of knowledge without increasing pressures for greater political participation and the widening of decision-making? Will more general worldwide movements for increased democratization of political institutions play an important role in strengthening mass organizations (and therefore alternative pedagogies) at the expense of centralized bureaucracies (and bureaucratic forms of formal schooling) in revolutionary societies?

What explains this tendency to hierarchize knowledge and to monopolize it gradually in the state bureaucracy? The traditional free market critique of socialism is that all state intervention in the economy ends up creating massive bureaucratic hierarchies, including the hierarchization of knowledge. But this does not explain why socialism has tended to bureaucracy. Does the transition naturally develop structural forms that generate new concentrations of power and attempts to reproduce them, as its critics claim?

The most serious counterexplanation is that the continued hegemony of world capitalism, particularly its domination of technology and of world commodity and financial markets, forces these transition societies to develop their conception of knowledge in ways similar to those of capitalist societies. The failure to do this would retard economic development to an unacceptable degree. It is the state rather than private production units in the civil society, that makes this decision. And it is the state, that develops the expertise to participate in this capitalist world system under favorable terms. According to this view, even transition societies are dependent on the centers of world capitalism, particularly in defining knowledge and expertise, and hence the nature and organization of the educational system.

Both of these explanations are, however, highly restrictive. Politics implies choices. The state and the vanguard party have such choices in the way they define knowledge and access to it. Expertise can be concentrated and mystified in both capitalist and transition societies, or it can be demystified and democratized. The educational system plays a crucial role in the implementation of such choices. When transition states develop a highly stratified notion of knowledge and its production, it is not because they have scientific evidence that this will make their economies more productive or better able to compete in the world system. They may believe that this is the case, but the decision is simultaneously a political decision that is convenient to a new class (or to a segment of that class) interested in solidifying its own position within the society.

In practice, the transition states we studied have actually distributed access to formal knowledge and even expertise much more equitably than capitalist societies at the same or even much higher levels of material development. Nevertheless, education often tends to be highly formalized and knowledge identified with different levels of schooling and degrees, much as in capitalist society. Work relations also tend to become bureaucratized over time as school degrees and job titles replace revolutionary fervor and work experience as the basis of decisionmaking in production. This, we argue, is more a function of local political decisions than of who dominates world technology.

In the case studies that follow, these educational issues are discussed in the context of political struggles that produce revolutions and then consolidate them, shaping new forms of conflict. The bureaucracies that develop in the transition state are modern and knowledge based. They need a highly developed educational system to develop themselves. They try to form that system to reproduce a hierarchy of expertise, but other forces develop—in and through education—that challenge hierarchy. This process, we suggest, is more likely to take place in transition than in capitalist societies, where the most important source of power is not knowledge itself but the capital that knowledge can control. That may be precisely the reason that transition states place so much emphasis on controlling knowledge and ideology. More than in capitalist society, alternative, persuasive ideas in and of themselves can produce alternatives to bureaucratic political control.

PART II

The Case Studies

CHAPTER 4

Introduction to the Case Studies

OUR SELECTION of the five cases to study is based on two principal considerations. First, we chose countries to represent a wide spectrum of social transformations and areas of the Third World. Second, we naturally chose those cases with which we are most familiar. These considerations resulted in the selection of China, Cuba, Mozambique, Nicaragua and Tanzania.

Through the research process, we found that much work remains to be done on analyzing the educational experience of the Soviet Union. It also would have been interesting to have incorporated case studies from Albania, Zimbabwe, and Vietnam, which represent other kinds of models and other ways of dealing with such problems as dependency, foreign intervention, and internal political participation. However, the book is already thick enough as it is, and we felt, after a fairly superficial look at some other cases, that the theoretical model we are developing for the analysis of education in transitional states could equally well be applied to these other countries.

Before the reader takes on the individual case studies, it is useful to chart in brief the prima facie similarities and differences between them. All of the cases are loosely referred to as "Socialist," "Marxist," or "Communist," and certainly the ruling party in each makes reference to the writings of Marx or to its desire to construct a socialist society. In all five cases, the policies pursued by the new governments have been nationalist, anti-imperialist, and suspicious of foreign economic influence. To a large degree, the new governments have looked for their principal base of support in the working classes, and have tried to apply a noncapitalist (or anticapitalist) model of development that is collective and is less exploitative and more equitably redistributive than capitalism.

While some of these revolutions have placed the traditional emphasis upon the proletariat as the leading political force for social transformation, in practice the proletariat was relatively small in the early years of the revolution, even in China and Cuba. All the revolutions therefore had to rely heavily on the peasantry as a driving force for change. This has been problematic. Certainly, to an even greater extent than in the Soviet Union, the five transition states under consideration (and all the other similar cases we can think of) have not followed the pattern of revolution and transformation predicted by Marx: The proletariat has been small to minuscule at the time of the takeover of power, and not particularly prominent in the revolutionary movement as a class or even as individuals.

We also suspect that after the revolution, the proletariat has not yet come to play its leading role either. All five countries were under- or undeveloped to a large degree at the time of the revolution. At least four have had extreme difficulty in building an industrial base, or in changing the structure and relations of production. Four are still very reliant on the export of primary agricultural products, and all are still dependent to a large degree on imports to obtain technology and advanced means of production. It has been extraordinarily difficult to use agriculture as the base of any sustained accumulation, and the transformation of the peasantry has met with severe obstacles. Various collective models have been tried, such as communal villages, cooperative production, and state collectives, but rarely has there been enough surplus available to make sufficient human, material and financial investment for a qualitative transformation of production. Without it, the peasantry has tended to withhold its engagement from collective ventures, or to withdraw, and to put its efforts into individual farming. All agricultural production has been undercut by declining terms of trade.

Western experience shows that agriculture is now easily viable only in three forms, which are largely unavailable to popular-based Third World governments. One is the state subsidization of agriculture. Another is the deliberate creation of shortages to push up the price paid to the producer. The third is the use of primitive techniques, low investment, and extremely low-paid labor. Much of the problem of development in our five cases leads back to the issue of how to deal with this complex situation. In one way or another, on top of various experiments at collectivization, these countries have tried or allowed some combination of the three forms mentioned to be able to accumulate capital. Their efforts have not been aided by the (often justifiable) suspicion of the peasantry, the growth of a parallel black market, and some significant political, technical, and economic errors in the collectivization process.

Whereas the capital accumulation available from agriculture is low, the uses to which it needs to be put are enormous. Both consumption and production goods need to be imported. The state has to pay for its own existence. Social services are necessary, and costly in the short run. On top of this, the (usually justifiable) feeling in the popular state that it is a prime target for attack has led to a large proportion of available surplus being plowed into nonproductive military equipment and personnel.

What is left for investment in industry is hardly spectacular, and the industry that does develop is often undercut by uncompetitive technology, underskilled labor, wastage and plant damage, low-quality final produce, worsening terms of trade, and faulty management. In such a context, it is even more complex to try to reorganize the relations of production, involve the workers in planning and decisionmaking, and democratize the shop floor. As has so often been painfully discovered, the production base of these economies when they were capitalist was enough to make a few rich and leave the many on the margins of subsistence; redistribution under the revolutionary state is morally right, buttresses the state's legitimacy, and makes better margins for the many, but it leaves little surplus for investment, and it mobilizes opposition from previously privileged classes.

The questions of raised consumption and equitable redistribution lie at the base of the new state, and give a special additional meaning to education. Common to our five cases are the rapid expansion and reform of education. In all the cases, before the transfer of power there had been a very limited amount of education available to the population, and a very discriminatory and elitist education system. In all cases, the new state has placed a great deal of emphasis in creating a new system, and looked to it to provide a number of political and economic answers.

First and foremost, as a symbolic mass consumption good and avenue to previously denied participation, basic-level education has been significantly extended. Within a few years of the power shift, primary school enrollment was at least doubled, and mass adult literacy campaigns were undertaken (with varying degrees of success).

This achieved, even if only partially, attention has shifted to the quality of the education provided, and to the higher levels of the system. In all cases, the same sort of conflict has broken out. All this education is (too) expensive—how can it repay itself? Where should investments be made? What kind of education should be given? What are the roles and relations of the teacher and the pupils to be? What kind of production (if any) should the pupils do? How should student success be evaluated—on traditional academic grounds, or on the basis of class origin, or of class consciousness, or of regional equity? Should evaluation be individual at all, if people are being prepared for a collective society? What kinds of skills are necessary—those to make the present (that is, old) economic system function better, or those to change the relations of production entirely and drive through a new collective economic system? "Red and/or expert?" has long been the name of the game.

Unfortunately, it seems that the models of the past have a strong hold on the minds of the present and the future, in the same way as the world capitalist economy has a strong grip on the newly collectivizing small-scale economy. The new state in particular, we argue, reincarnates the old and the new together in its structure and its relations.

The differences among our cases make the similarities discussed above all the more astonishing. Each case is unique.

CHINA

China has been a unified central state with a large bureaucracy for 3,000 years. Its size in itself makes it a case on its own. Its state formation built and fossilized a peasant economy, with the masses subject to extreme poverty. Various imperialist powers dominated the state and pieces of the country in the first half of this century. Nonetheless, China's external dependence has always been very limited, and its indigenous accumulation base enormous.

China is also unique among our cases for having its revolution carried out by a large, experienced, and long-constituted Communist party, which had extensive governing experience in its own areas and in national coalitions. Its revolution was first in time among our cases, and its long history of transition strategies is instructive. The state's latest policy direction toward more individualist and import/export-oriented policies is at one and the same time a powerful challenge to the world capitalist market and a tacit recognition that it is hard to accumulate capital from peasant agriculture and redistributive policies.

CUBA

Given China's particularities, Cuba stands as the "granma" of the other cases—the small transitional economies. At the time of the revolution, the country was more developed than any of the other four, and the peasantry was numerically a much less important force. Of our revolutionary cases, Cuba's revolution was the shortest and least bloody. The specificities behind this produced a particular theory of revolutionary strategy, which has not functioned elsewhere. Cuba's revolutionary movement was not constituted as a political party until sixteen years after the revolution, when it adopted the mantle of the Cuban Communist party. However, Cuba has been supported since the early days of transition by the USSR, against U.S. military threats and economic blockade. This has meant an ability to create a considerable military presence without proportionally deleterious effects on the economy. It has also given Cuba a constant sugar market at prices above the world market norm, which has provided some capital for the development of industry and of very advanced social services.

Tanzania

Somehow, Tanzania never became very important to world capitalism, nor was it cursed with powerful and aggressive capitalist neighbours. The single ruling party, TANU (now Chama Cha Mapinduzi), took power un-challenged in a peaceful transition from British colonialism—only the is-land of Zanzibar, now united with the mainland, underwent a revolution. The party undertook a relatively slow and peaceful transition to its own version of agrarian socialism, using a form of state capitalism for the tiny industrial sector. It never recognized class analysis as a relevant revolu-tionary tool, and some critics charge that capitalism is flourishing under the guise of socialism, in the form of entrepreneurship and a new govern-ment class. Nonetheless, its sweeping collectivizing policies have pro-duced a country rather different from most of those in Africa, and Tan-zania is recognized as a strong progressive voice in international and regional affairs. The country has received a great deal of foreign aid from Western sources, and has built up an impressive record of social services, especially education. The country's model has been described as "revo-lution by education." However, Tanzania has few natural resources, and its drive for self-reliance through agriculture has neglected industry, so that the past decade of international economic depression and instability have taken a heavy toll on its economy and substantially increased its dependence.

Mozambique

Mozambique is by far the poorest and most dependent of the five cases, though in terms of natural resources and development potential, it is far better off than Cuba, Nicaragua, and Tanzania. This disparity arises from the backward nature of the Portuguese colonialism to which it was sub-jected, which made use of the country as a cheap labor reserve for neigh-boring countries, rather than as a site for investment. The Mozambican Liberation Front's (FRELIMO) ten-year war to free the country also uni-fied and "purified" the Front itself. Representatives of antipopular and anticollectivist strategies were exposed by war conditions and expelled. Within a short time after the overthrow of colonialism, Frelimo declared itself a Marxist-Leninist vanguard party dedicated to constructing scien-tific socialism. However, under economic blockade and military aggres-sion from the neighboring South African racist regime, and under the weight of the legacy of underdevelopment, Mozambique's project for so-cial transformation has been severely restricted and damaged and forced onto the defensive.

NICARAGUA

Nicaragua is the smallest economy among our cases, with a reduced accumulation base and one of the lowest per capita income levels in the Americas. Three generations of the Somoza family constituted themselves as both the state and the private sector, governing the country as a private estate. After fifty years of repression, the "three tendencies" in the resistance constituted a common front, the Sandinista National Liberation Front (FSLN), and drove through a popular revolution in two years. Somoza's private police fled across the borders, to return in arms as the core of the U.S.-supported Contras. The FSLN managed to get some support from the USSR against a U.S. economic blockade and military aggression. However, in the face of the pressures, and of different internal tendencies, the FSLN has not proclaimed that its goal is the construction of a socialist society. Indeed, it has worked not only to maintain a mixed economy (even in the face of popular pressure to the contrary) but also to institute a pluralist, multiparty political system (in which the FSLN has won the electoral majority). This strategy has had mixed results, but has not persuaded the U.S. government to leave the country in peace, and so a high proportion of the declining GNP is being spent on military defence.

SCOPE OF STUDIES

Our cases thus cover two African, one Asian, and two Caribbean-American countries; a revolutionary party, three revolutionary movements-turned-party, and one mass single party; four single-party states and one parliamentary state; four dependent small economies and one nearly independent large economy; five largely agricultural economies; and five different models and ideas of socialism and the transition to it. Our five following chapters look at the development of education by each of the five states, using a similar analytical framework but taking due account of national particularities and specificities.

The result is a set of relevant and revealing studies, which show very similar problems coming to the fore and very similar conflicts arising over the strategies to deal with them. One fact stands out: In spite of all the difficulties they have faced, the respective states have tried hard to make education available to everyone, and have tried hard to make it equalizing rather than selective. In many of the countries they have succeeded.

CHAPTER 5

Struggle, Criticism, Transformation: Education in the People's Republic of China

Mary Ann Burris

CHINA'S LEADERS ASSERT that modernization policies begun in the late 1970s will continue to determine the direction of the society far into the next century. These policies have reordered not only education, but the economy and ideology as well. The traditional fear of "confusion" (*luan*), exacerbated by the political upheavals that have disrupted the lives of the Chinese people since 1949, make stability perhaps China's most sought-after innovation. Yet today's swiftly changing China is anything but stable. When current slogans claim that education "holds the key" to success in the Four Modernizations (science and technology, agriculture, defense, and industry), we must look to see what doors that key is to open, how it is to do so, and to whom it shall grant entrance.

As in the other cases presented in this volume, education in China is expected to achieve what are at least in part incompatible goals. On one hand, education is to be central to the drive for modernization. For that, schooling must identify, prepare, and at times indulge the intellectual and skilled elites who are to be the modernizers. That requires an emphasis on education's higher levels and fosters the adoption of imported educational models and pedagogies regarded as critical to modernization elsewhere. On the other hand, education is also to be the primary vehicle for developing a new socialist citizenry. Education is expected as well to reduce inherited social inequalities, to mobilize and politicize the populace, and to promote political participation. For that, schooling must discourage competitive individualism in favor of a cooperative and collective orientation. That requires an emphasis on mass—primary and adult— education and fosters a self-reliant nationalism inclined to reject foreign models and pedagogies. Educational policy is thus forged in the cauldron of this tension between conflicting orientations and expectations. Schools are both the focus and the site of conflict.

China in the last years of the 1980s is a China in transition. The People's Republic, its leaders now claim, is in the "primary stage of socialism." This Chinese interpretation of Marxist theory prescribes as China's single goal for the foreseeable future to ameliorate the contradiction between the material needs of the people and backward production, that is, to make China richer and more advanced. "Modernization" is the way to achieve this. Efficiency is to be the judge, and "scientific criteria, not politics," the modernizers say, are to guide policy. In Deng Xiaoping's often-quoted words, it does not matter what color a cat is—if it catches mice, it is a good cat. But of course this instrumentalism is not neutral science; it is political orientation.

Modernization has brought a certain liberalization to China. There is unprecedented diversity in many aspects of postrevolutionary life, much of it invigorating. Modernization has also brought a tremendous amount of confusion. The collective is being dismantled, and the nature of the social order that will result from the mixed economy is not at all clear. Neither is the political mandate. At the same time that economic relations are taking a drastic turn from the past, the Four Basic Principles are the ideological imperative: adherence to the socialist road, to the dictatorship of the proletariat, to the leadership of the Communist party, and to Marxism-Leninism and Mao Zedong Thought. This odd mix of theory is meant to guide the contradictory policies of the modernizers. Equally important, it is also meant to legitimize the Chinese state, which, after the excesses of the Cultural Revolution and the continuing problems of bureaucratic corruption, sorely needs renewed legitimacy.

This chapter is about education, which in China has always been one of the most powerful legitimizers. We begin with the history and legacy peculiar to China. Traditional educational practices determine the context in which subsequent changes occur, or fail to occur. Next, we see that education in China after its encounters with the West and in the liberated areas before 1949 was characterized by tension and compromise between the past and the possible. The rest of the chapter deals with schooling in the People's Republic of China. First, I discuss the nature of the postrevolutionary Chinese state. Next, I detail the oscillations of postrevolutionary educational change from 1949 to 1987. Third, I present and elaborate three models for socialist educational development evident in China. My central thesis is that educational change in China has been and is the result of struggle. And struggle is a dialectical process.

The revolutionary history of Chinese educational forces, with its conflicts, contradictions, constraints, and traditional continuities is to a considerable degree the history of the People's Republic of China itself. The dynamics of change in Chinese society are reflected in Chinese state apparatuses, such as the army or the Party, but it is in education that political power and policy battles are most obvious. It is there that the civil/state relationship is most exposed, and it is there that China's international relations are rendered explicit. Struggles over the very definition of socialism and the best strategy for facilitating it are the same struggles which have taken place over the goals of education, the curriculum instituted, and the constituency served. Struggles over which borders to protect are the same struggles as those that revolve around whose educational models to adopt. The fact that China has experienced such sweeping educational changes and such divisive educational conflicts speaks in part to the peculiarities of the Chinese context, but also demonstrates the difficulty of defining through practice education's roles in a transitional and socialist society, particularly one with China's developmental needs.

In 1949, China's feudal past still determined the major part of social and productive relations. Confucianism, by legitimating the hierarchical formations in Chinese society and defining the individual's relation to authority and to knowledge, continued to hold tremendous institutional and ideological sway despite the participatory strategies instituted in the revolutionary effort. Hence, in 1949 several educational models existed. Remnants survived from the Qing dynasty's attempt to pattern a modern education system on that of Japan.[1] American models and philosophies of education welcomed during the Republican period served as a foundation for elite tertiary Chinese institutions.[2] Missionary schools and European models of education were still an influence. Experiments in the border regions and in liberated Yenan from 1936 until 1949 had resulted in a distinctive revolutionary philosophy and practice of education. While many Chinese educators felt that this model had limited value for the administration of a school system for the entire nation, it nevertheless had served well the needs of both the revolutionary party and the peasantry, which comprised most of the party's ranks. Lastly, New China in 1949 had but one powerful ally offering hesitant support and its own educational model for emulation: the Union of Soviet Socialist Republics.

It is much too simple to analyze Chinese education, or to analyze Chinese anything, as if it were a monolithic phenomenon. China today has over 1 billion inhabitants—one-fourth of the world's population. It has the largest education system in the world. It has twenty-two provinces, five autonomous regions, and three municipalities that are directly under

---

[1] Between 1902 and 1908, the number of Chinese studying in Japan rose from 271 to 17,000, providing a steady stream of young Chinese who were schooled specifically to form a teaching cohort for the new school system (Hayhoe 1984, 35).

[2] Between 1910 and 1924, the number of Chinese students studying in the United States increased from 600 to 2,200, and many were returning to serve in China's educational system. A whole series of monographs appeared on Chinese education that represented the work of Chinese research students in American universities, such as Teachers College, Columbia University; New York University; and Stanford University. Extended visits to China by such American educators as John Dewey, Paul Monroe, Helen Parkhurst, and George Twiss strengthened the impact of American values and institutions on Chinese education (Hayhoe 1984, 38).

the central government. It has fifty-five national minority groups (though 93 percent of the population is Han Chinese), three languages, and more than fifteen dialects. There are distinctive historical north-south differences and coastal-inland differences. These continue to influence policy formulation and implementation in the present.

Nevertheless, China has been to a large degree a unified polity with an essentially homogeneous culture since the third century B.C. This historical continuity is due to the tenacity and the hegemony of the Chinese state. In the traditional past, as in the modernizing present, it is with the Chinese state and its officials that one must begin an inquiry into the shape of education.

WHENCE IT CAME: TRADITIONAL LEGACIES

Certain historical continuities point to a distinctive conception of education and its connection to the Chinese state. Most obviously, the civil service examination system tied scholarship to the service of the state. Confucian canons set the curriculum, and the three-tiered examination system functioned to locate people in state civil service. Educational practices served to buttress and reproduce state power. The earlier and more common ascriptive system based on lineage did not, in itself, ensure any particular ideological compliance or homogeneity other than parentage, but the system requiring that state officials pass examinations was a meritocratic selection system of sorts that ensured the hegemony of the state ideology.

The Confucian Legacy

The traditional state in China was a hegemonic, patriarchal, bureaucratic state, which paid tremendous homage to a certain kind of learning. The scholar-officials whose class background had everything to do with their inclusion into the Chinese bureaucracy, were nonetheless assured of their posts only through success in the state examinations for which they were "educated."[3]

As early as the first century B.C., "the sage sovereigns used education to get rid of the weeds" (*Li Chi*, in Legge 1885, vol. 3, p. 389). The censure of nonconforming thoughts, tied to the strong reluctance to

---

[3] At certain times, however, some government ranks were inheritable and degrees were in actuality purchased. During most of these periods, there was a considerable degree of corruption and cheating. In fact, during the last decades of the system, scholars would frequent examinations for a long series of years with no view of obtaining a degree for themselves because the profits to be obtained by taking the tests for others was infinitely higher than the salary official position might bring (Smith 1907, 157).

change and the Confucian penchant for culturocentrism, was very much a feature of education in traditional times. This censure met with protest, as one might expect. Almost from the beginnings of the examination system, students resented its rigidity. Criticisms included that the system rewarded only good memory and not deep understanding, that it induced a fever of competition, and that it encouraged learning impractical and useless material (Nivison 1975, 227). Despite the history of protest, the state prevailed and the system continued.

At least one woman protested too. The good scholar-official was like a good wife or a filial son, and the state and society were to function in harmony like a Confucian family.[4] Female subordination was a central feature of the traditional family system and the state that served to protect that system. It was clearly reflected in traditional educational practice. Women were totally excluded from the examination system, and almost always were denied the power that literacy allows. Yet, for those like the poet Yu Hsuan-chi, who managed to become literate, the examination system functioned to keep her in her place—or, at least, out of his. In the mid-ninth century, she wrote this poem on the occasion of seeing the names of the successful examination candidates posted on a temple wall, as was the custom:

Cloud capped peaks fill the eyes
In the spring sunshine
Their names are written in beautiful characters
And posted in order of merit
How I hate this silk dress
That conceals a poet
I lift my head and read their names
in powerless envy.[5]

Erudition in the classics, not specialized or practical training in governance, earned the traditional Chinese bureaucrat his right to office. An official position ensured access to the opportunity for the official's male

[4] It was believed that to keep the state in order was to keep one's family in order. Confucian ethics is essentially the matching of social roles with prescribed behaviors. The family-state connection had a practical place in the material context whereby early Chinese states were actually run by families and, therefore, to a large degree, to keep one's family in order was literally to order one's state. In later times, the scholar-official was to serve the emperor as a good wife, sometimes as a filial son. Traditional Chinese poetry uses the husband-wife simile to allude to the emperor-official tie. This family-nation connection is reflected in the Chinese term for "state," *guojia*, literally meaning "state family."

[5] Yu Hsuan-chi, "On a Visit to Ch'ung Chen Taoist Temple I See in the South Hall the List of Successful Candidates in the Imperial Examinations," in Kenneth Rexroth and Ling Chung, eds. and trans., *The Orchid Boat: Women Poets of China* (New York: Seabury Press, 1972), 19.

progeny to become literate, thereby reproducing family and state power in male hands. The scholar-officials constituted a social, political, and cultural ruling class for over 2,000 years. The ideology and pedagogy of "schooling" that this system engendered, the power of the educated literati, and the power of the state were lasting and interrelated. Those slips of bamboo that were the earliest textbooks have long since turned to dust, but the state that funded their copying endures.

Not only did this traditional preoccupation with the family as the symbol of order determine who might and who might not be taught, but it also had everything to do with how knowledge was conceived and what learning was believed to be. The Chinese word that is usually translated as "to teach," *jiao*, tells us about the philosophical conception of learning and helps explain Chinese educational methodology even today. The first part of the character means "filiality," and the second means "to tap." The modern term for education, *jiaoyu*, adds a character which means "to nourish," leaving the first character unchanged. Traditional learning methodology largely consisted of imitation, recitation, and model emulation. Part of this can be explained by the nonphonetic nature of the Chinese language; other aspects were determined by the Chinese worldview. Model emulation did not begin with Lei Feng, the selfless proletarian of the 1960s. It began with the sage emperors.

The traditional role of the teacher posits Confucian ideology against social practice, which is to posit myth against reality. Confucian orthodoxy proclaims a tremendous amount of respect for the teacher. Initially proxies for fathers, the teachers in traditional times tended to be failed examination candidates hired by wealthy families with the express purpose of seeing to it that their sons were not similarly unsuccessful. Their pay and living conditions were often abysmal and the respect they garnered limited. The classical and nonspecialized training of the teacher/scholar did not prepare him to be of much use to society if he could not serve in the state ranks. Within the confines of the classroom, he might be the unquestioned authority, but in society the teacher was often of lower status than his students, certainly of lower status than a state bureaucrat (Smith 1907, 66).

Traditional schooling was never to function as a neutral site of free thought and debate. Confucian orthodoxy made politics and morality synonymous with education as the interlocutor. The curriculum monopolized by classical canons stressing discipline, authority, and morality produced what most historians agree was a narrow and conforming (though in some senses, erudite) elite who served as the embodiment of the state. It also produced a select group of "men of literature" (*wen-ren*), who devoted themselves to artistic pursuits and whose legacy includes the rich poetry, prose, calligraphy, and painting of traditional high culture known to us today. Sometimes the government official himself was also a man of unquestionable literary or artistic prowess. Traditional literature and art, even landscape poetry and bird and flower paintings, were, in more ways than meets the untrained eye, political.[6] There is precedent for the fact that Mao Zedong and Zhou Enlai were poets as well as politicians.

Still, like any other state, the traditional Chinese state was concerned with its legitimacy. Each traditional dynasty codified its hegemonic ideological vision through the practice of engaging its literati to rewrite history in agreement with its interpretation of the world. The state, therefore, had control over the production of knowledge, not merely the evaluation of the schooled. Furthermore, the need to teach the people a system of moral beliefs that would publicly sanction state actions and power and ensure a certain stability to the social system was met by what might be termed the "informal" aspects of the traditional educational agenda. This informal "schooling" was instrumental to the continuance of the traditional Chinese state. Mo Tzu, a Chinese functionalist born in 470 B.C., pointed to the importance to the state of a consensual ideology: "If it is inquired, how is it that the emperor is able to govern the whole realm? The answer is, it is only because he can unify all ideas of the whole realm. And the rule of the realm depends on all minds being unified with that of the emperor and so in harmony with heaven also" (Mo Tzu, Chuan 3, Section 12 in Galt 1951, 114).

This effort had to reach more than those destined for elite civil service status. Though Buddhism and Taoism exerted varying influences, particularly as the basis for popular religion, Confucianism held the reins as the ideology of statecraft and set the "curriculum" for this informal schooling of the masses just as it set the content of the exams. On a very basic level, never approaching the nuances of the debates of the few who were literate, what the masses needed to know was the philosophy of the five relationships (father/son, ruler/subject, old/young, husband/wife, friend/friend) that gave each person his or her rules of acceptable conduct in Confucian society and legitimated unquestioned power in the hands of the state. The accepted worldview determined the role of the individual in traditional China. Since the state was viewed as a large family, the virtue of obedience defined the relationship between the ruler and his subjects. It was not a rule of law, but a rule of relations. Law was unimportant to the Confucian political outlook. What was important was that the state possess a good ruler who would instruct the people by his own

---

[6] From the very beginning in the Lun Yu (Analects) and then the commentaries to the Book of Odes and Ch'u Tz'u (Songs of the South), there was a moralizing and political principle to poetry, as to art in general. Nearly every character or brush stroke was imbued with a further meaning through allusion: the mountain was an emperor, the courtesan a minister, the shrike a calculating miscreant.

example (Rubin 1976, 18). What was also important in practice was the poverty and repression, which served alongside education and example to keep the masses in their places.

Mencius, who lived from about 372 to about 289 B.C. and is regarded as the second sage after the grand teacher Confucius, wrote of the relative relationship between governing and educating: "In gaining the good will of the people, good government is not the equal of good education. The people may fear good government, but they love good education. Good government gains the people's wealth; good education gains the people's hearts" (Mencius, in Legge 1865, vol. 2, 240).

Here we have set out for us 2,000 years ago the same basic challenge faced by contemporary Chinese state modernizers: the need to capture the people's wealth while also winning people's hearts, or, in the words of radical education theory, accumulation and legitimacy. While Mencius saw accumulation to be the responsibility of "government," and legitimacy to be that of "education," we see that education played such a central role in determining who would govern and how, that education was really at the heart of both.

Western Influence; The Dynastic Cycle Collapses: The Republic Fails

By the mid-nineteenth century, the traditional Chinese order was close to collapse and national self-confidence was at an unprecedented low. The Unequal Treaties forced on the Chinese by Western imperialist powers after repeated defeat and the national disintegration brought about by the Taiping Rebellion forced a reformulation on the part of Chinese intellectuals and educators about the direction of their nation. These years witnessed the beginning of a monumental effort to discover an amalgam of foreign and Chinese institutions and techniques that would allow China a self-respecting place in the world, an effort that continues to this day. Isolationist attitudes were reevaluated. The T'ung Chih restoration attempted to create a modern state with modern institutions peopled by a very different kind of bureaucrat from the traditional Confucian scholar-official (see cartoon). The fact that it failed to do so is the result not only of the tenacity of tradition, but of the world context in which it was being attempted.

Adapting China's highly developed educational system to the needs dictated by the new world order was a basic problem of the restoration.[7]

---

[7] National survival was the struggle of this century. By the end of the nineteenth century, China had lost territory to the British, French, Russians, Japanese, and Americans. The salient features of these educational adaptations to Western power and Western influence can be found in Appendix 5–1.

"The traditionally dressed figures to the right carry plaques identifying their achievements in the old educational system. After passing under a gateway labeled 'Intensive Course' surmounted by a cloud of 'electricity,' they emerge dressed in modern student uniforms holding flags proclaiming their degrees in botany, mining, and economics" (Borthwick 1983, 142) *Xingqi huabao*, no. 46 [1907], reprinted in Sally Borthwick, *Education and Social Change in China* (Stanford, Cal.: Hoover Institution Press, 1983).

Chang Chihtung's answer to the dilemma, "Chinese learning for the foundation; Western learning for utility" (*Zhongxue wei ti; xixue wei yong*), carried tremendous intellectual and policy weight then and continues to do so today.

The establishment of a functioning republic between 1911 and 1949 was thwarted by warlord factionalism, world wars, civil strife, and continuing poverty. Still, in the midst of the chaos and defeat of the first two decades of this century, there was tremendous intellectual fervor. The May Fourth movement in 1919 is heralded as a high point in China's cultural revolution, and many of the philosophical and literary innovations of this movement had an impact on Chinese views toward education. During these years, Western philosophers and educators[8] were in-

[8] John Dewey, who visited China between 1919 and 1921 and whose students had great influence in educational circles, and Bertrand Russell, who was in China in 1921, were among the more instrumental in bringing Western ideas about schooling to China.

vited to China, modern universities were set up, some women were given formal schooling, and textbooks were written in the vernacular for the first time.

In the early 1920s, May Fourth radicals turned to the countryside for answers to changing China. In 1921, not only were the Chinese Communist Party and the Chinese Socialist Party founded, but the first Peasant Associations as well. In 1927, the always-uneasy Nationalist-Communist alliance disintegrated as Chiang Kaishek's troops murdered hundreds of CCP members and sympathizers in the cities, further forcing the locus of organization and of struggle into the countryside, where innovations in education and governance were carried out and where the fight to defeat Japanese imperialists was combined with a struggle for liberation. From the beginning of the Sino-Japanese War in 1937, through Japan's surrender in 1945 and until the Communist victory in 1949, the country was divided and at war over its future. The West by and large sided with the losers.

The Yenan Era, 1937–1949

On the night of October 15, 1934, a hundred thousand men and fifty women left Kiangsi after defeat at the hands of the foreign-assisted Kuomintang and began the twelve-month 6,000-mile Long March to Shensi province in northwest China. Eight thousand of them survived to follow Mao Zedong, by then the unquestioned leader,[9] into one of China's poorest and most backward areas. There, they laid the foundations for the Communist victory fifteen years later. The Long March experience set the tone for what was to become the "Yenan spirit" of sacrifice, diligence, pragmatism, and faith in the human spirit.

The Party's educational work in the border regions was based on the Maoist faith in schooling to transform consciousness and on the Party's need to mobilize participants in the anti-Japanese war and in the revolutionary struggle. Tens of thousands of peasants participated in mass education sessions during the war years. The curricula of these sessions included practical information about agriculture and health[10] as well as war

[9] Leadership in the Chinese Communist party was in contention before this time. What are referred to as the "Twenty-eight Bolsheviks," a group of Moscow-trained Chinese Communists, did not lose their bid for power until January of 1935, when Mao managed to institute his strategy of revolution despite Stalin's disapproval (Meisner 1977, 33–41).

[10] In 1937, the infant mortality rate was 50%. The communists' medical care and health education campaigns played a large part in winning the allegiance of the peasantry. One analysis of primary school textbooks in the border regions revealed that references to hygiene, cooperation, and courteousness were third most prominent after glorification of labor and abolition of feudal practices (Karen Minden, "The Development of Early Chinese Com-

strategy and politics. The border regions had an estimated literacy rate of 1 percent, and the fact that the 1942 winter mass education campaign took as its motto "political understanding first, literacy second" (Chauncey 1982, 247) shows that "transforming consciousness" was a primary goal.

During the two Yenan rectification campaigns in 1942 and 1945, some educators resisted radicalizing formal schooling. They questioned the ability of the mass education/mobilization model to meet the needs of the new society and worried that the educational quality of New China might suffer if Western models were abandoned. The Chinese Communist party emerged from the war years, one scholar claims, "with an educational system awkwardly poised between pre-war Westernized pedagogy and communist political ideals" (Chauncey 1982, viii). Many would say it is still poised there.

From the beginning, the Chinese Communist party was a heterogeneous vanguard with vying concepts of how to proceed to build the New China and educate the New Chinese. After the victory, the ministry of education declared at its first National Work Conference that "the education of new China should use the new educational experience of the old Liberated areas [Yenan model], should absorb the useful experience of the old education [Nationalist model—an amalgam of Japanese, American, and European elements], and should make use of the experience of the Soviet Union" (Seybolt 1973, 7). This was, as we shall see, an extremely tall order.

NEW CHINA: A STATE IN CONTENTION

From the outset, one important fact stands out in analyzing the last four decades in Chinese history: The postrevolutionary Chinese state is a state in contention. It always has been. Leadership struggles are a feature of the landscape. The Chinese revolutionaries, like the revolutionaries in Nicaragua, Mozambique, and Cuba, promised a better future for the common people. Like the state nurtured in the liberation, liberated education is to "serve the people." In China, there has been disagreement over who they are and how to serve them.

The current regime has a developmental agenda, and education must serve that agenda. Economic growth is the focus. In this fundamental way, it is no different from developing nonsocialist states. Schools in postrevolutionary China, as in capitalist nations, have contradictory roles.[11] Even though China's economy has been socialized, the socialization of political power or consciousness has not consistently followed.

munist Health Policy: Health Care in the Border Region, 1936–1949," *American Journal of Chinese Medicine* 7 [1979]: 299–315).

[11] For a more thorough analysis of these contradictory roles, see Chapter 7.

Land reform and the nationalization of industry do not automatically create socialist persons and empowered citizens.

Education is supposed to help do that, but now that the economy is being reorganized, education's role as mediator between economics and politics is made even more complicated. In 1940, Mao wrote:

> Thus, a given economy first determines a given politics, and after this determines a given education. Education is thus derivative of and secondary to politics. Therefore, education is determined not only by economics but by politics as well. On the other hand, education performs a definite service to economics and to politics (regardless of its subjective content or of its intentions). That is to say, the political ideals of a given society are its educational ideals, and its political mission is its educational mission.   (Mao Zedong [1940] 1961)

Today's political mission is a nationalist developmental mission. As the stated objective of education is to serve the Chinese nation in its competition in the international economic order, the individual is also to be schooled to that national end. Vestiges remain of the traditional notion that the individual's main responsibility to the state is obedience. Mao wrote that political ideals set the educational mission and that they should determine the individual's role in society, the economy, and schooling. They should define what is knowledge and what is praxis. The bind is that today's political ideas are not as clear as they once were. The economic persona has center stage. Party decisions, claims Zhao Ziyang, are not to be based on politics, but on science. This modernization orientation demands a certain entrepreneurial (individualistic) ethic. But too much individualism undermines the collective orientation of socialism and may threaten a socialist leadership's security of tenure. Individualism in Mao's sense, as in Lenin's, was seen to lead to a decay in discipline in Party ranks. Thus, contemporary Chinese life is not characterized by a division between areas where political factors are predominant and another, the "private life," where the needs and interests of the individual are paramount.[12] Daily life is political and public.

When we ask who the state is composed of, we must include the Party and the bureaucrats at all levels who help make it function. When we ask what the educational contingent of the state is, we find intellectuals, teachers, and cadres. It is important to distinguish between the power of the Chinese state and the power of the officials who staff it, particularly when we are seeking to understand education. The interests of middle- and upper-level Chinese bureaucrats (as well as of teachers) have tended to favor hierarchical and restrictive educational models, which do not

---

[12] See Andrew J. Watson (1973, 291–330), for an analysis of behavioral and social patterns in contemporary China as they relate to tradition, to family, and to political life.

necessarily serve best the interests of the transitional Chinese socialist state in particular, and certainly do not ensure the success of the construction of socialist relations in general.[13] This distinguishes most of the postrevolutionary years from traditional times, when the interests of the Confucian literati were in concert with the state's protection of the hierarchical status quo through educational practice. Julia Kwong claims that Party members have tended to dominate the decisionmaking levels in educational policy circles but that noncommunists or "traditional elites" have occupied the implementation levels (Kwong 1979). Efforts in China to radicalize education have often been fended off by educators and educated officials themselves.

But the situation today may be changing. The "traditional elites" may be assuming policy power. Of those on the current Central Committee, 209 (73.3 percent) have at least a college diploma, which is an increase of 37.9 percentage points compared with the previous committee. The Political Bureau Standing Committee membership now boasts 80 percent with college educations, up from 33.3 percent for the previous Standing Committee (*The 13th Party Congress and China's Reforms* 1987). At implementation levels, professionals are to be given power over all administrative affairs; Party cadres are to limit themselves to ideological work. Older intellectuals and professionals have joined the Party in unprecedented numbers during the last five years, though party membership is eschewed by many who were educated after the Cultural Revolution. In all things Chinese today, the generation gap is evident and compelling. One of the modernization reform's most profound proclamations is that it will separate the functions of the Party from those of administration, that is, separate politics from policy as it is to be put into practice. Of course,

[13] Richard Kraus and Reeve Vanneman (1984) in their monograph, *Bureaucrats, Peasants and the Paradox of State-Building in the Third World*, detail the ways in which education engages the most vital interests of bureaucrats, particularly in Asian societies, and outline the conflicts between the bureaucrats and the peasants over the former's monopoly of higher education. They write: "Conflicts develop over two issues in particular. First, measures to undermine educational credentialism as a basis for assigning state positions strike at a major source of bureaucrats' privileges and promise increased influence for degreeless peasants. Second, the rapid expansion of education threatens bureaucrats' monopoly of scarce degrees and opens up opportunities for the children of the wealthy peasantry, at the expense of offspring of officials." (A revised version of this monograph is Kraus and Vanneman 1985.) Chinese bureaucrats have been either individuals with formal schooling themselves or those promoted during times when "redness" and poor class background were credentials enough for cadredom and who later see that access to higher education for their children is likely to maintain the standing of the family. Most parents want the best for their children; Chinese bureaucrats are no exception. This does not preclude the possibility that huge numbers of Chinese cadres are steadfastly and altruistically committed to the construction of some version of socialism; it simply brings the question of shared interest into the analysis.

this affects education. The new models for university administration range from the former "everything under the leadership of the Party secretary" to "separate but equal powers" to "everything under the leadership of the college president." In most schools, the power of academic committees is increasing as that of Party committees decreases. There is no more talk of allowing the uneducated masses to judge what is best for education at the higher levels of formal schooling. Yet, decollectivization does transfer more of the costs of education to the individual, as it has with other social services, such as medicine.

The "contract responsibility system" (chenbao), first introduced in farming and industry, has also entered the educational arena. Its effects could be no less far reaching in schooling than they have been in the rice paddies and in the textile plants. Scores of educational policy documents call for institutional autonomy, and diversified educational finance schemes are likely to ensure that it will be at least partly realized. Schools, or even departments within schools, are to take responsibility for their own finances as well as their own administration. Educational units are supposed to "chenbao" their own educational quality, and many of them do. But economic criteria sometimes prevail, and a preoccupation with profit overshadows other concerns. Since many returns to education are not purely economic,[14] some aspects of schooling may suffer at the same time that others may indeed benefit from this increased incentive and decentralized locus of control.

Things are not, as was noted at the beginning of this chapter, stable and settled, however. For much of the nearly forty years since liberation, the Chinese themselves placed class struggle at the center of their theory of social change. Today, the Party has discarded what it views as its erroneous policy of "taking class struggle as the key link." Education is now the "key link" to progress. In what has been declared the "primary stage of socialism" that China is now in, reformers claim that the principal contradiction is between the material needs of the people and backward production. Not unlike the earlier literati who redefined fundamental terms as they rewrote their histories to legitimate the political present, China's current leadership maintains that class enemies are those who would un-

[14] Department leaders at the tertiary level, for example, now have the added responsibility of finding ways to increase the salaries of their staffs. For some departments, this means facilitating sideline teaching, research, or even unrelated but recompensed activities. In many schools, departments compete with one another to do this. Sometimes the primary task of teachers, to work together to teach the students assigned to them, is pushed into the background as the shorter-term concern for economic advancement takes precedence. Such a system differentially affects disciplines because all knowledge is not equally marketable. And, while it may mean that more innovative teaching methods are given space in which to develop, it also means that some of the longer-term social returns to education are no longer guiding educational practice.

dermine socialist modernization and therefore get in the way of meeting those material needs.

As the description of educational practice in China from 1949 to 1987 illustrates, change has been the only constant. No single set of reforms has been thorough, and power in a single line has never been consolidated. In part, the complex dialectics of social change make this so; in part, the contradictory ideas about socialism held by those with state power determine it.

Not only has the content and constituency of Chinese education been subject to revision during political upheavals, but the theoretical location of education in socialist society itself has been challenged and reformulated. In the current scheme, education, like science, is touted as part of the productive forces, not primarily part of the superstructure, as has at previous times been claimed. One Chinese educational theorist and policymaker claims that any part of education that is directly related to productive forces is of a nonclass nature and does not belong to the superstructure (Li Kejing 1980, 19). Mao believed that natural science has no class nature but that its study and application has. Skills training to Mao would be different in socialist and capitalist societies. To the modernizers who locate education primarily in the productive forces, it would be much the same. A skill is a skill. Education is a technical process. Economic efficiency and productive rationality cross the political chasm between capitalism and socialism; the "science" that drives policy of which Zhao spoke is neutral. In fact, however, this fundamental question about the function of education in society and its role in development is a political question. It is as theoretical as it is practical. What is taking place today under the Four Modernizations is not simply "the replacement of utopianism by rationalism" (Bastid 1984, 191). Rather, it is evidence of the contending political struggle within the state and the complex social realities which it reflects.

CHANGE IN EDUCATION, 1949–1987

The People's Republic of China has the world's largest educational system. Its total enrollment comprises about 40 percent of all students in the developing world (World Bank 1981, 18). One-fifth of the Chinese population is in school. In postliberation China, 46% of all graduates from specialized schools have been teachers (King 1984, 178). In 1984, the Chinese education system enrolled 213,850,000 students and employed 11,800,000 people. While the Chinese population has roughly doubled since 1949, in 1983 there were 4.6 times the elementary school students that there were at the time of Liberation, 41.3 times the students in regular junior and senior middle schools in 1949, 9.4 times the university students, and 58 times the graduate students (*Sanshiwu Nian Lai Wo Guo Jiaoyu Shiye de Juda Chengjiu* 1984). China has developed substantial adult education and vocational programs at all levels. Nonformal education has attempted to bridge the gap between school and the world of work through night schools, correspondence courses, spare-time university programs, television courses, and training given in the workplace. Two out of three adult Chinese are now literate, where 1949 estimates suggest that at least 85 percent of the population were illiterate (World Bank 1981, 5).[15] By any standards, the development of education in postrevolutionary China has been impressive. It has also been tumultuous.

The shape of China's educational tumult is a recognizable one. It is the amplified dialectic of change. Mao Zedong's strategy for continuing revolutionary progress was threefold: struggle, criticize, transform. We see it repeated again and again in the history reviewed below. There is struggle over educational policy. Policies are instituted, criticized, and changed. Then, there is again struggle, criticism, and transformation. What we find is not a pure Hegelian thesis-antithesis-synthesis. New policy is often in opposition to what directly preceded it, and subsequent reform in some ways synthesizes what has come before.

What determines the reality of Chinese education is not only the scope and breadth of these waves of change, but their frequency as well. Change has been swift. Every cohort in postrevolutionary Chinese schools has taken leave of a system with different priorities from those with which it began. Resources are limited, and even if there were consensus, everything could not be emphasized at once. But there has not been consensus; the balancing act is conflictual. Often the shortcomings of a particular educational strategy are its undoing before its strengths can bear fruit.

State Consolidation and National Reconstruction, 1949–1952

The first priority of the new government was national reconstruction. The country had been devastated by four decades of war. The people were poor, and the economy was in a shambles. The general program for development was gradually to nationalize industry and to collectivize agriculture. On September 29, 1949, the People's Political Consultative Conference passed the Common Program, outlining the general principles for socialist development. It claimed that education should be "new dem-

---

[15] Estimates of literacy in China are particularly problematic because of the nature of the language and the problems it presents for assessment. Estimates based on the traditional definition of literacy (ability to read the Classics) are between 1 and 2%. Using a more functional definition of literacy, estimates for Qing dynasty China range as high as 30 to 45% of men and from 2 to 10% for women. See Rawski (1979).

ocratic"—that is, national, scientific, and popular, and that it should foster the ideology of serving the people.

In 1950, specific reforms were adopted, including curriculum revision, the institution of new primary, middle, and spare-time schools, the reorganization of educational leadership, the restructuring of higher education, and the nationalization of private schools. Emphasis was placed on nonformal education. By 1952, 2.3 million workers and 27 million peasants had attended short-term schools for workers and peasants, and more than 48 million peasants had been to the winter schools set up to teach elementary literacy skills during the off-season (Löfstedt 1980, 76). Despite the fact that implementation of many of the educational policies was hampered by financial constraints (culture, education, and public health received only 4 percent of the national budget during these years, when national defense was a priority), the government created worker-peasant schools in many areas, established minban (people-run) schools, expanded teacher-training institutes, nationalized private schools, carried out a literacy drive,[16] awarded university stipends, built twenty polytechnics, and inaugurated twenty-six new technological institutes. Tertiary schooling was reorganized, with all institutions made into specialized technical institutes, polytechnics, or general universities (Löfstedt 1980, 72, 74). As Table 5–1 indicates, student enrollment at all levels increased dramatically between 1949 and 1952, more than doubling for both primary and secondary schools.

One of the more pressing problems immediately following the revolution was the question of intellectuals and teachers. The Communists found themselves having to rely on frequently unsympathetic intellectuals to administer higher education and on untrained, if enthusiastic, peasant cadres to oversee schooling in the countryside. In 1951, Zhou Enlai outlined a program to reform the thinking of intellectuals and teachers by subjecting them to criticism and self-criticism conducted against "bourgeois individualist ideology and revisionist education." This became the Thought Reform movement—the first of many to come.

The First Five-Year Plan and Soviet Influence, 1953–1957

The First Five-Year Plan for education stressed improved quality. The state leadership announced that for 1953, educational work should follow

[16] The campaign started with teacher training and special organizations were set up all over the country—including women's organizations, trade unions, Party branch committees, and the Youth League. Final figures for 1952 claim that more than 2.3 million workers and 27 million peasants had attended short-term schools, and more than 40 million peasants had been to the Winter Schools. More than 7 million people had attended courses during the drive to promote the "quick method" of learning to read and write (Sheringham 1984, 75).

TABLE 5–1
China: Student Enrollment by Level of Schools, 1949–1985 ('000)

| Year | Total[a] | Institutions of Higher Learning | Secondary Schools[b] | | | Primary Schools |
			Subtotal	Secondary Specialized Schools	Regular Secondary Schools	
1949	25,776	117	1,268	229	1,039	24,391
1952	54,436	191	3,145	636	2,490	51,100
1955	57,887	288	4,473	537	3,900	53,126
1958	99,061	660	11,998	1,470	8,520	86,403
1961	87,077	947	10,344	1,203	8,518	75,786
1964	103,825	685	10,195	531	8,541	92,945
1967	115,397	409	12,545	308	12,237	102,443
1970	131,811	48	26,483	64	26,419	105,280
1973	170,965	314	34,947	482	34,465	135,704
1976	209,675	565	59,055	690	58,365	150,055
1979	207,898	1,020	60,249	1,199	59,050	146,629
1982	187,902	1,154	47,028	1,039	45,285	139,720
1985	201,252	1,703	50,933	1,571	47,060	133,702

[a] Excludes schools for adults; similarly hereinafter.
[b] Excludes workers' training schools. Subtotal includes students in agricultural middle schools and vocational middle schools. In 1949 and 1967–79, these students are included in the regular secondary schools figure.

the major policy of "readjustment and consolidation, development of the important points, qualitative improvement, and steady advance." One of the ministry of education's self-criticisms about its performance to date was that educational efforts suffered from a lack of planning, uniformity, and leadership, especially in the field of higher education. (Hu and Seifman 1976, 41). Heavy Industry was the development priority of the day, so education focused on technical and tertiary schooling. No further expansion was planned for primary education, but additional senior secondary and short-term secondary schools for workers and peasants were to be set up. Tertiary enrollment was targeted to increase by 10 percent. (Löfstedt 1980, 81.) The earlier emphasis placed on popularization was not abandoned, but the urban sector was slated for more financial and priority attention.

There was increasing Soviet assistance and influence in education during this period, including scientific research exchanges and the issuing of thousands of new textbooks and teaching guides translated directly from Russian into Chinese. There was a drive to centralize power under the control of the Chinese Communist party. Political contradictions surfaced within the Party over the pace and direction of change. Liu Shaochi's favored direction entailed more emulation of the Soviet model and an emphasis on the expertise needed for economic development; Mao Ze-dong's favored the utilization of the Yenan model and popularization of teaching methods that would raise political consciousness. Liu's strategy held sway as the First Five-Year Plan was formulated and initially implemented, but Mao's concern that a heavily centralized bureaucratic state would preempt the institution of socialism came to the policy fore in its last years of implementation.

Beginning in 1954, all college students had to study Russian, and the teaching of English was suspended. Middle school hours, instead of being reduced so that more emphasis could be given to productive labor, were actually increased so that many students attended 33 hours per week. Political study was curtailed in favor of more traditional courses of study, particularly science and mathematics. For women, the Five Goods campaign enjoined devotion to the role of "socialist housewife."

A collectivization movement in the countryside in 1955 increased enrollments, which had begun to fall off (see Table 5–1). In 1954, about 49 percent of the primary school age cohort were enrolled in school and about 3.5 percent of that group were subsequently enrolled in general middle schools (Löfstedt 1980, 81). Efforts to provide normal schooling to produce the needed teachers were accelerated. Participation in literacy drives increased; this time, the official connection was made between economic underdevelopment and illiteracy, and learning to read took on strategic significance in the development strategy of the state. Enrollment at all levels continued to grow. In general during this period, however, there was a slowdown in the growth of the number of primary schools (see Table 5–2), secondary specialized schools (see Table 5–3), and universities (see Table 5–4). Regular secondary school enrollment increased (see Table 5–5), and there was a high social demand for the right to regular middle schooling throughout China. Transition rates in 1957 dropped by half, demonstrating that there would be an increasing number of senior middle school graduates who could not be accommodated in tertiary schooling, whereas before then practically all students who finished senior middle school could go to college.

The role of intellectuals continued to be contentious. In May of 1956 Mao launched the movement to "let a hundred flowers bloom, and a hundred schools of thought contend." Deep and acerbic criticism by intellectuals of the state of affairs brought persecution of those who had been most critical during the Anti-Rightist Campaign of 1957. The mass of crit-

TABLE 5–2
China: Primary Schooling, 1949–1985 ('000)

Year	Number of Schools	New Students Enrolled	Graduates	Total Students Enrolled	Full-time Teachers	Annex: Children in Kindergarten
1949	347	6,800	650	24,390	836	
1952	527	11,490	1,490	51,100	1,435	420
1957	547	12,490	4,980	64,280	1,884	1,090
1962	668	15,860	5,590	69,240	2,511	1,450
1965	1,682	32,960	6,680	116,210	3,857	1,710
1970	961	28,320	16,530	105,280	3,612	
1975	1,093	33,520	19,990	150,940	5,203	6,200
1976	1,044	31,610	24,900	150,060	5,288	13,960
1977	982	31,120	24,740	146,180	5,226	8,970
1978	949	33,150	22,880	146,240	5,226	7,880
1979	924	31,020	20,880	146,630	5,382	8,790
1980	917	29,420	20,530	146,270	5,499	11,510
1981	894	27,490	20,760	143,330	5,580	10,560
1982	881	26,720	20,690	139,720	5,505	11,130
1983	862	25,440	19,810	135,780	5,425	11,400
1984	853	24,730	19,950	135,570	5,370	12,950
1985	832	22,980	20,000	133,700	5,377	14,800

icisms indicated that the educational system, which had been built on the Soviet model, displeased not only the old school "bourgeois reactionaries" but also the young students, who joined in with harsh cries against the system. Protesting students of 1957 were revolting against both the new and the old. It was the unfortunate position of the Chinese Communist party to be identified by its critics with what was objectionable in both.

The Great Leap Forward, 1958–1960

A new program for economic development was adopted in May 1958, by the Chinese Communist party, known as the "General Line for Socialist

TABLE 5–3
China: Secondary Specialized Schooling, 1949–1985

Year	Number of Schools (units)	New Students Enrolled ('000)	Graduates ('000)	Total Students Enrolled ('000)	Full-Time Teachers ('000)	Annex: Workers' Training School Graduates ('000)
1949	1,171	98	72	229	16	
1952	1,710	351	68	636	35	3
1957	1,320	123	146	778	58	69
1962	1,514	39	305	535	61	11
1965	1,265	208	91	547	55	48
1970	1,037	54	28	64	39	
1975	2,213	344	248	707	73	67
1976	2,443	348	339	690	80	54
1977	2,485	366	340	689	87	103
1978	2,760	447	232	889	99	89
1979	3,033	491	181	1,199	113	97
1980	3,069	468	410	1,243	129	255
1981	3,132	433	605	1,069	136	353
1982	3,076	419	446	1,039	149	323
1983	3,090	478	375	1,143	156	269
1984	3,301	546	376	1,323	161	
1985	3,557	668	429	1,571	174	284

Note: Includes technical schools and secondary teacher's training schools; excludes worker's training schools.

Construction." It was meant to be a mass mobilization campaign combining self-reliance and "walking on two legs"—that is, developing industry as well as agriculture, large as well as small enterprise, modern as well as indigenous methods. Many sinologists point to the Great Leap Forward policies as the line of demarcation between the Soviet model and attempts to forge a distinctively Chinese model of socialist development. In January of 1958, Mao presented the "Sixty Articles on Work Methods," which would help set the direction for the Great Leap Forward. In it, he underscored the need to unify the "two opposite things"—being "red" and being "expert." It was education that was to unify these opposites.

TABLE 5-4
China: Institutions of Higher Learning, 1949–1985

Year	Number of Schools (units)	New Students Enrolled ('000)	Graduates ('000)	Total Students Enrolled ('000)	Full-Time Teachers ('000)	Annex: Graduated Postgraduates (units)
1949	205	31	21	117	16	107
1952	201	79	32	191	27	627
1957	229	106	56	441	70	1,723
1962	610	107	177	830	144	1,019
1965	434	164	186	675	138	1,665
1970	434	42	103	48	129	
1975	387	191	119	501	156	
1976	392	217	149	565	167	
1977	404	273	194	625	186	
1978	598	402	165	856	206	9
1979	633	275	85	1,020	237	140
1980	675	281	147	1,144	247	476
1981	704	279	140	1,279	250	11,669
1982	715	315	457	1,154	287	3,178
1983	805	391	335	1,207	303	4,572
1984	902	475	287	1,396	315	
1985	1,016	619	316	1,703	344	13,900

Note: Includes those trained in institutes under the Chinese Academy of Sciences and in other institutions.

Under Mao's impetus the Great Leap Forward set out to break the monopoly of schools and universities and the privileges of degree-holding intellectuals. The two outstanding features of this educational revolution were the implementation of the policy of coordinating education with productive labor and implementation of the mass line for organizing schools. People's communes were set up, and minban schools run by the masses enrolled increasing numbers of children in the countryside. Agricultural middle schools were established. Earlier emphasis on quality and higher education was reversed, and stress was placed on proletarian education and equal access. Elementary enrollment, while continuing to

TABLE 5–5
China: Regular Secondary Schooling, 1949–1985

Year	Number of Schools[a] (units)	New Students Enrolled ('000)	Graduates ('000)	Total Students Enrolled[b] ('000)	Full-Time Teachers ('000)
1949	4,045	412	280	1,039	67
1952	4,298	1,383	221	2,490	94
1957	11,096	2,493	1,299	6,281	234
1962	19,521	2,800	2,025	7,528	399
1965	18,102	3,457	2,098	9,338	457
1970	104,954	14,153	6,865	26,419	1,174
1975	123,505	24,436	14,947	44,661	2,092
1976	192,152	32,054	17,232	58,365	2,725
1977	201,268	33,608	21,444	67,799	3,187
1978	162,345	26,989	23,753	65,483	3,182
1979	144,233	23,419	23,844	59,050	3,078
1980	118,377	19,343	15,810	55,081	3,020
1981	106,718	17,405	16,403	48,596	2,844
1982	101,649	16,424	11,954		2,597
1983	96,474	15,769	11,954	43,977	2,597
1984	93,714	15,649	11,402	45,542	2,557
1985	93,221	16,069	11,949	47,050	2,652

[a] 1979 figure includes 2,107 agricultural schools and 31 vocational middle schools.

[b] 1979 figure includes 226,500 students in agricultural middle schools and 8,400 in vocational middle schools.

be higher in urban than in rural areas, reached a peak in 1959. The ministry of higher education was merged into the ministry of education, and the percentage of working-class students in tertiary schooling was increased. "Red and expert" universities were set up; some of these were full-time comprehensive colleges and others were spare-time universities for peasants. Students and intellectuals were sent to the countryside in the "xiafang movement" designed to help them learn from the common people. Nonproletarian teachers were criticized.

Eradicating illiteracy was set as a goal for the Second Five-Year Plan

(1958–1962). Official statistics for 1960 show that more than 5 million illiterates learned to read and write in that year. The claim was made that the proportion of illiterates among the industrial workers had dropped from about 80 percent in 1949 to 15 percent in 1960.[17] Women entered the work force and the schools during the Great Leap Forward in greater numbers, and communal kitchens and day care were founded.[18] Barefoot doctors by the thousands were trained for service in rural areas. Most accounts by Chinese themselves mark 1958 as a year of tremendous optimism and enthusiasm.

On the eve of the Soviet abandonment of China and recall of China's debt in 1960, the Chinese leadership recognized a need to pay attention to quality in schooling again, noting the connection between schooling and economic development. The poor harvests resulting from bad weather and the chaos of rapid collectivization, coupled with the repayment schedule of the Soviet debt, created an economic crisis throughout China, known as the Three Bitter Years (1959–1961). Furthermore, Chinese technicians now had to accomplish what had previously been done with the help of Soviet technical advisors. As a result, the two-systems approach to schooling favored by Liu Shaochi came into favor, and the mass mobilization of the Great Leap Forward was judged a failure.

Retrenchment under the New Economic Program, 1961–1965

Leaders in the field of education found that the rapid expansion of primary and proletarian education as well as the emphasis on "redness" over expertise during the Great Leap Forward had caused problems concerning the quality of schooling. Teachers were overworked and poorly trained. The Soviet withdrawal of technical assistance continued to exacerbate the problems created by the urgency of economic concerns. Both these factors greatly shaped educational priorities. There was a renewed emphasis on productivity in all levels of society, and those educational innovations conducive to raising productivity (such as the minban and agricultural middle schools) were restructured. Literacy continued to be considered essential, but the Party placed increased emphasis on higher education. The leadership relied on intellectuals and professional teach-

[17] The target for full literacy was to be able to read and write 1,500 characters (Sheringham 1984, 75).

[18] Elisabeth Croll reports a sixfold rise in female contribution to social production between 1955 and 1956 (Croll 1979, 17). Although collectivization dramatically increased women's contribution to what was recognized as social production, women earned only 25% of the work points awarded by all cooperatives in 1956 (Davin 1976, 148). The communal kitchens in particular met with resistance from men and were short-lived, as were the early day care centers in the countryside after the Great Leap Forward was declared a failure.

ers to solve China's schooling problems. They increased research activity and officially accepted the disparity between rural and urban schooling. Part-work, part-study education suffered setbacks. As of 1962, workers and peasants were no longer given priority in entrance to higher education (Seybolt 1976, 49). The curriculum was streamlined, and the study of English received official encouragement. Keypoint schools[19] were officially sanctioned and China attempted to "build on the best," which meant disproportionate attention given to coastal areas and northeastern cities. Such schools were clearly elitist, designed to identify early the academically outstanding students who were to be groomed for higher secondary and university education.

A return to the empowerment of central ministries took place and planning returned to pre-1957 centralized authority. Antagonism between contending development strategies grew. Liu Shaochi, named president in April of 1959, launched reforms calling for monetary incentives, private plots, output quotas on the basis of households, and excellence in education. In 1961, the Socialist Education Campaign, in many ways in direct contradiction to Liuist strategies, was launched by Mao and his followers. Its aim was "to break the encirclement of the spontaneous tendencies toward capitalism." Urban universities and middle schools sent students to communes to perform productive labor. Cadres went to the country to follow the "four withs" among the peasants—eating with, living with, working with, and discussing with (Chesneaux 1979, 117, 118). The "Emulate Lei Feng Campaign" became a nationwide obsession in 1963. Still, the cry of the day was for improved quality in schooling.

There was a severe conflict between Mao and other Party leaders favoring revolutionary educational policies and their adversaries, who held the policymaking power. The Liuist reforms were barely in place as the political scene was set for the coming Cultural Revolution, which would claim those reforms were "revisionist" and their supporters "capitalist roaders" or "bourgeois elements."

The Great Proletarian Cultural Revolution, 1966–1969

In a letter to Defense Minister Lin Biao, Mao Zedong wrote on May 7, 1966: "While the students' main task is to study, they should also learn

---

[19] Keypoint schools are primary, secondary, and tertiary institutions targeted for disproportionately high funding based on an assessment of their superior quality. They are controlled directly by the ministry of education. Admission is by examination. These schools tend to have both the best teachers and the most advanced materials. They all tend to be located in urban areas and have student bodies disproportionately composed of the children of intellectuals and cadres.

other things, that is to say, they should not only learn book knowledge, they should also learn industrial production, agricultural production, and military affairs. They should also criticize and repudiate the bourgeoisie. The length of schooling should be shortened, education should be revolutionized, and the domination of our schools and colleges by bourgeois intellectuals should not be tolerated any longer" (*Beijing Review*, January 1976).

In June of 1966, a new method of enrollment in universities was announced, which would put proletarian politics first. Educational leaders were dismissed; Liu Shaochi and Deng Xiaoping were formally criticized as "capitalist roaders." The Central Committee of the Chinese Communist party appointed a Cultural Revolution Group to study the question of the nature of art and literature in socialist culture, and intensified censure resulted. Work teams were sent into the universities to facilitate the "continuing revolution" there. The old two-track system of schooling was criticized for its inequality, and the two-line struggle assessment gained favor. No regular teaching occurred in Chinese schools in the autumn of 1966. From 1967 to 1974, there was no functioning ministry of education. Red Guard organizations were set up, many of them armed. Examinations were abolished. The number of school years was reduced. Manual labor was required of all students. Most universities were closed between 1966 and 1970. Workers' universities and reeducation colleges with a political curriculum and a strong labor requirement for retraining intellectuals were set up. Many intellectuals were persecuted; more than a few died. Nonformal education received priority attention. All schools were directed to apply Mao's policy of "education serving proletarian politics and education being combined with productive labor" (Hu and Seifman 1976, 192).

By 1968, most primary and secondary schools had resumed their teaching, but the Red Guard factions continued to be disruptive. Workers' propaganda teams entered the schools to oversee the tasks of "struggle-criticism-transformation." Increasing numbers of students were sent to the countryside to "learn from the peasants." In 1969 alone, an estimated 2.7 million educated young people went to the countryside (*Beijing Review*, February 1976).

The massive uprisings of the Cultural Revolution raised very real questions as to the role of a people's army, the function of education, the definition of "the people," and the legitimacy of and degree of unity within the state. It raised the questions that eventually must be faced by all successful postrevolutionary states: how to continue the revolution with a generation of people who have no concrete experience with revolutionary struggle, how to consolidate collective consciousness, how to ensure that the superstructure facilitates a continuous transition and regeneration of socialism. "It is right to rebel" was the slogan that carried the tide. But today, when it is more right to modernize, the Cultural Revolution is referred to as the Ten Wasted Years for education because an entire generation of experts is said to have been lost.

Mao's Last Years—the Waning Cultural Revolution, 1970–1976

In education, the Cultural Revolution lasted well into the 1970s, though China was beginning to pose basic questions of policy and open to the outside world in the early 1970s. (Richard Nixon's visit took place in 1972.) In the first years of the 1970s, the government continued to stress universalizing primary education and cautioned the provinces against stressing secondary education at the expense of primary education. When universities did reopen in 1970, admission was by recommendation from work units; in practice, this often meant that children of cadres entered "through the back door." In the following five years, several compromises were reached in education between those who still favored the previous "revolution in education" and those who did not. Some degree of testing, for example, was allowed as a criterion for university entrance in some places. Questions were raised about the practicality of "politics in command" strategies in education; curricula were rewritten. The "Criticize Lin Biao and Confucius" campaign, which linked traditional Confucian conservatism, with a new conservatism dominated political life for over a year.[20] In 1975, the ministry of education was reinstated. Great debates over education's role in socialist construction took place. Deng's short-lived rehabilitation ended in 1976, when he was again criticized for denying class struggle as the key link, but he was soon to rise to power again.

Mao Zedong died on September 9, 1976 (Chu De and Zhou Enlai also died in 1976, the year of the Tangshan earthquake), and during the next month, nationwide demonstrations took place to celebrate the fall of the Gang of Four who had essentially engineered the most radical changes during the Cultural Revolution period. Hua Guafeng was elected chairman of the Central Committee and change was everywhere in the air. The instability of the Chinese political balance in 1972–1976 reflected a vacillation between a rejection of the ultraleft, which favored highly po-

---

[20] The Criticize Lin Biao and Confucius campaign was very complex. Lin had been attacked both as an ultrarightist and as an ultraleftist, and then as a two-faced renegade. The debate dealt with the traditional Confucian and Legalist schools, which were contending during the Qin Dynasty (221 B.C.). In essence, a contradiction was underlined between tradition and modernization (the Legalists were the modernizers here). Confucianism was attacked for its elitism and revisionism; the Legalists were presented as progressives who gained power by creating a centralized state.

防 止 "个 人 突 出"

刘 痒

Liu Yung, "Preventing 'individual prominence,' " *Feng Ci Yu Yo Muo* (Satire and Humor), *Renmin Ribao* (People's Daily), August 20, 1979.

liticized and proletarianized education, and a rightist current, which favored elitist schooling.

Turning Away from the Past and Preparing for Modernization, 1976–1980

These early post-Mao years witnessed a continuing power struggle between the remnants of the Left, who had not yet been totally discredited by the Cultural Revolution, and the moderates, whose main spokesperson was Deng Xiaoping. Just as schools had been among the first institutions to feel the effects of earlier social upheavals, so were they one of the first arenas of reaction against previous policies judged to have "wasted" years and nearly destroyed the system of schooling. Liu Yung's cartoon is only one example of the criticism leveled against what came to be called "excessive concern with egalitarianism" in education. Entitled "Preventing Individual Prominence," it depicts an official holding a baton that forces all runners to stay at the same pace.[21] Others criticized the

[21] Lin Yun, "Preventing Individual Prominence," *Renmin Ribao* (People's Daily), August 20, 1979. Reprinted in Ralph Crozier, "The Thorny Flowers of 1979, Political Cartoons and

political content of schooling, the "back door" favoritism of admission policies, and the low quality of instruction during Cultural Revolution years. Since 1976 there has been at least a partial denial of the Maoist idea that social and political demands go hand in hand with the economic returns of education.

The National Education Conference of 1978 set policies and made projections designed to recover the quality of post-Great Leap Forward education and then build on it. The Conference resurrected the keypoint schools associated with the early 1960s New Economic Program. Curriculum was standardized. The revolutionary committees that had overseen education were abolished in 1978. A new enrollment system was instituted for tertiary schooling, and examinations were reinstituted. Again, as in the past, illiteracy was judged to be a detriment to development and strategies were discussed for lessening it. Educators began to institute tracking at all levels. Discipline and excellence were stressed. Professorial ranks were reestablished. A "small pagoda" approach[22] to access to levels of schooling was judged to be the most appropriate for China's particular level of development. Growing numbers of Chinese students went to the industrialized capitalist countries to study, and the yardstick for measuring the success or failure of the "backward" Chinese education system was stretched to the measure of the industrialized and capitalist West.

In "Respect Knowledge, Respect Trained Personnel" (May 24, 1977), Deng Xiaoping, then beginning his latest ascent to political power, spoke clearly and strongly about his priorities for modern education: "The key to achieving modernization is the development of science and technology. And unless we pay special attention to education, it will be impossible to develop science and technology. Empty talk will get our modernization programme nowhere; we must have knowledge and trained personnel. Without them, how can we develop our science and technology? And if we are backward in those areas, how can we advance? We must recognize our backwardness, because only such recognition offers hope" (Deng Xiaoping [1979] 1984, 53).

A Communist Party Congress in August of 1977 officially declared the close of the Cultural Revolution and the inauguration of the new period of Great Unity. The Party now blamed the setbacks in China's development on the Gang of Four, and an empowered Deng Xiaoping urged the

---

Liberalization in China," in Bruce Cummings, ed., *China from Mao to Deng* (New York: M.E. Sharp, 1983), 35.

[22] The "small pagoda" is an educational concept first put into practice in the Soviet models of the 1950s in China. This approach to education has schools selectively reducing the size of the student pool as one goes up the pagoda from elementary to graduate training on the basis of quality and competence.

Chinese on to the path of the Four Modernizations, which would propel China into the modern age. At a national science conference in 1978, Deng attempted to reassure intellectuals that they would no longer face discrimination. As "mental laborers," they were members of the working class. The promises in the new constitution and the very real problems of the day brought critiques from students and intellectuals in what came to be known as the Democracy Wall period.[23] In March of 1979, as the Democracy Wall movement was crushed, Deng Xiaoping laid out the four guiding principles for the Four Modernizations: staying on the socialist road, upholding the leadership of the Communist party, adhering to Marxism-Leninism-Mao Zedong Thought, and upholding the dictatorship of the proletariat.

Testing Four Modernization Strategies, 1980–1985

The reformulation that had charactered education as a productive force in 1979 and 1980 justified educational policies that had been criticized in more radical periods of the past. Rather than a wholesale return to former Liuist line strategies, however, a third line came into evidence. Emphasis on quality and specialization continued, but with a centrifugal force of decentralization at work. Keypoint schools gained favor, but not without controversy and compromise. As the power of Deng Xiaoping and his supporters was secured, educational policies were formulated and tested that would serve the Four Modernizations and its new economy. There was continuing discussion about the place of ideological training in education, with the notion of "spiritual civilization" (*jingshen wenming*) being touted as the ideological aim of current reforms.[24] There was disagreement over the wisdom of a market economy, but amendments to school policies did begin to allow for a certain marketlike flexibility. Day students were enrolled who could pay their own tuition; private schools were allowed. Experimentation took place in the decentralization of educational policy. For example, Shanghai began to administer its own examinations. International agencies entered China and began to influence educational policy choices.

The leadership began to pay particular attention to vocational training

[23] Discussions and wall posters addressed many issues. Democracy, called "the fifth modernization" by activist Wei Jingsheng (now in prison serving a fifteen-year sentence), was among the more vociferous demands. Inspiration was again found in nineteenth-century Chinese and Western philosophers, and social critics and journals championing human rights and equality, and attacking spiritual enslavement and artistic censorship, were legion.

[24] This phrase, introduced in the autumn of 1979 by Ye Jianying during a speech on the thirtieth anniversary of the founding of the PRC, has become the modern version of a collective "red and expert socialist persons" in current propaganda.

and the need for middle-level technicians to work in modernizing industry. The 1982 census estimated that 10 percent of the population had the educational level of a senior middle school student or higher. Approximately 23 percent of the population was believed to be illiterate[25] (*Guangming Ribao*, April 20, 1983). The ratio of Chinese college, middle, and primary school students in 1983 was 1:50:128[26] (*Gongren Ribao*, November 13, 1983). In 1984, there were only 3.7 million vocational and technical school students, compared to 45.54 million in regular middle schools. These findings have been analyzed by Chinese policymakers as unsatisfactory for meeting China's strategies for economic and technical development. One of the most difficult mandates of the new human resource needs approach to educational planning, therefore, is successfully convincing both individuals and local-level bureaus to concentrate their support and funds on expanding secondary vocational schooling.

University-level schooling was also targeted for its contributions to modernization efforts. During this period, there was a change in the leadership in many universities. The academic ranking system abolished during the Cultural Revolution was completely restored in 1980; appointments were to be determined by academic quality and seniority, not political criteria (Rosen 1985). University enrollments increased—instead of the less than 4 percent of secondary school graduates who could anticipate going to college in the late 1970s, by 1984 about 10 percent could get in. This is partly attributable to dropping secondary school enrollments, but it is also a result of the more flexible system, which admits a number of fee-paying college students (Whyte 1985, 59). There is a call for universities to work with enterprises on joint research/manufacturing ventures. The responsibility system in universities aims at eliminating overstaffing problems[27] and at creating "four modern" faculty—revolutionary, young, knowledgeable, and specialized. Universities are to be responsible for balancing their own budgets. Intellectuals have the right to engage in sideline teaching, writing, and research for profit. Disciplines once deemed bourgeois (such as psychology and law) are finding their way back into university curricula. New masters' degrees and doctorate programs have been established. To emphasize the importance of the occasion to the state and to the nation, on May 27, 1983, Premier Zhao Ziyang awarded the first eighteen doctorates (seventeen males and one female) in the Great Hall of the People (King 1984, 179).

A diversified system of education separating various elements in soci-

---

[25] A peasant must know 1,500 characters to be considered literate; a worker must know 2,000.

[26] In the United States, the ratio is 1:1:2.

[27] In 1982, there were 249,900 full-time faculty members and 298,000 students. In some universities the teacher-student ratio was 3–4:1.

ety (for example, peasants from workers, urban from rural) has been part of the drive toward specialization and efficiency. The Chinese people and policymakers alike are conscious that such policies will increase inequalities in society, including gender inequality. Women's and girl's participation in schooling appears to be on the decline.[28] At the present time, males are about three times as likely as females to get a higher education. The number of females getting tertiary schooling is about 3 per 1000. While females represent up to 50 percent of students at some of the low-status teachers colleges, they constitute only 16.5 percent of students at the nation's top technological institution, Qinghua University, in 1985. The differences seem to be greater at the graduate level. In late 1982, the prestigious China University for Science and Technology, training ground for the Chinese Academy of Sciences, sent seventy-two students to the United States for their Ph.D.s. Three were female (Hooper 1985, 97). Newly decentralized job placement schemes have meant that women graduates face discrimination in finding work because profit-maximizing enterprises find it in their interests to hire men. A slogan pronouncing the "three special strengths" of women as manual dexterity, special expertise in household matters, and a civil nature, make Chinese women and Western scholars of China understandably concerned about just how the role of the "modern" woman in modernizing China will differ from that of "modern" man and the "socialist person" of earlier times.

As Table 5–1 indicates, total enrollment in schooling was on the decline in the mid-1980s, particularly enrollment in secondary schooling. Apparently, this is due to declines in attendance in rural areas, prompted by current economic policies which make family farming potentially extremely profitable and encourage the practice of keeping children at home to contribute to family enterprises (Whyte 1985, 48). The number of regular secondary schools is also dropping, but the number of institutions of higher education is on the rise. Vocational secondary schools are also increasing in number, but are not yet meeting projected personnel needs for industry. In 1983, still less than 3 percent of the total secondary enrollment was in vocational or specialized secondary institutions (Ministry of Education [PRC] 1984, 22). All are geared to "learn from the pacesetters," and education is to be "directed towards modernization, towards the world, and towards the future."

[28] The responsibility system in the countryside has encouraged families to keep their female children home to work on family plots or in family cottage industries. In higher education, the trend began in the early post-Mao years. For example, between 1976 and 1979, the percentage of female freshmen dropped from 39.91% of the total to 22.53% at Jilin University; from 36.80% to 26.02% at Wuhan University; and from 31.61% to 19.57% at Nanjing University (Pepper 1984, 142).

Consolidating the Four Modernizations and Looking to the Future,
1985–1987

The ministry of education, elevated to a state council education commission in 1985,[29] has been given more power and autonomy to set the agenda for education. Analyses by Chinese educational policymakers[30] and by outside advisors have contributed to the tremendous changes being made to ensure the strength of the educational "key link" to modernization. Policies tested during the previous two periods to accomplish this are becoming institutionalized. In a 1986 country report prepared by the state education commission, the new educational objectives not only underline education's link to modernization, but also reflect a distinctly new approach to knowledge:

> Education must serve the nation's socialist construction and the socialist construction must rely on education. This is the basic guiding principle in developing China's education in the new historical period. According to this principle, the common task for all types of schools at different levels in China is to be geared to the needs of the nation's modernization drive and the competition in the world and to the needs of future development. . . . They [schools] should also enable their students to develop morally, intellectually and physically and to become discipline-abiding; to love their socialist motherland and the socialist cause; to take up the hardship in order to devote themselves to the growth of the nation and the prosperity of its people; and to develop a permanent aspiration to pursue new knowledge, to think independently and to create. (State Education Commission [PRC] 1986, 4)

In the Decision of the Central Committee of the Communist Party of China on the reform of the educational structure in May 1985, guidelines were set for the development of schooling for the next decade. This decision outlines greater institutional autonomy for tertiary institutions, articulates policy on the unevenness of development in different regions, decentralizes the administration of primary schools, places more emphasis on credentialing and vocational training, reinforces tracking students into parallel educational subsystems, and reforms personnel and job

[29] The position of the minister in charge of the commission is concurrently held by a vice-premier of the State Council, ensuring a close tie between economic and social policymaking and education. The minister has eight deputies and many of its members are concurrently vice-ministers or deputy chiefs of the state planning commission, the state economic commission, the state science and technology commission, the ministry of finance, and the ministry of labor and personnel.

[30] Articles in numerous Chinese journals attest to the centrality of this issue and to the depth of self-criticism and domestic analysis which is taking place. See, for example, Wu Wei (1986) and Zhao Li (1986), as well as a number of articles by Chinese educators and policymakers regularly translated into English in the journal *Social Sciences in China*.

placement systems. Educational projections are differentiated by region, that is, targets for universal schooling are higher and sooner for cities and coastal areas than for inland and rural ones. In China's April 1986 passage of the "Law of Compulsory Education" and the Seventh Five-Year Plan (1986–1990), it was announced that nine-year compulsory schooling will be gradually introduced. During the first six years, junior middle school education will become universal in cities and coastal areas, and within ten years it will become universal in the countryside. A national wage adjustment for primary and secondary teachers aimed at correcting their underpaid status has been carried out. There is a simultaneous promotion of disproportionate investment in higher education and in compulsory basic schooling, both measures in line with development needs.

Also in line with perceived development needs has been a drastic increase in academic exchanges with the outside, particularly with the United States, Europe, and Japan. From 1978 to 1984 over 26,800 Chinese students and visiting scholars were sent to sixty-three countries for over six months.[31] Since 1984, institutional links between Chinese and foreign universities and the number of Chinese students going abroad to study have greatly increased. By far, the majority of students leaving China for advanced training are in the natural sciences and engineering. This is consistent with Deng's earlier assessment of the "backwardness" of Chinese science and technology and with the priority that popular notions of modernization place on advancing them.

More of the national budget now goes toward education than in the postrevolutionary past. Public expenditure on education had consistently been around 5 percent of the national budget from the 1950s through the 1970s, but in 1982 it reached 10 percent.[32]

In late 1985 the state education commission developed a three-stage fifteen-year plan designed to retrain existing teachers, readjust specialties, and achieve "professional quality" (State Education Commission [PRC] 1986, 15). Since that time, retraining and continuation schools have been set up, and the serious shortages of teachers in vocational and technical schools has provoked the creation of special teachers colleges to train teachers of vocational subjects. A plethora of educational research organizations have been founded to inform and test policy and special courses have been instituted to train educational administrators. Normal schools have been given the added bonus of having a higher priority than other types of universities in recruiting and admitting new students.

[31] Of these, 12,022 went to the United States, 3,847 to Japan, 2,489 to Germany, 1,833 to Britain, 1,452 to Canada, 1,299 to France, and 30 to the Soviet Union (Huang Shiqi 1987, 230).

[32] Local levels provide a substantial portion of schooling costs in China, and there is growing financial support for education from international agencies.

Hence, as the modernizing strategy suggests, much support has been given to the development of postsecondary schooling. The number of students and the number of schools have grown. More than one hundred new universities were founded between 1984 and 1985 (see Tables 5–1 through 5–5).

University student protests in December of 1986 brought ideology into the forefront of discussions of educational goals in China once again. The dismissal of Hu Yaobang from his post as Party leader and the changing of the leadership of the National Academy of Sciences in January 1987, as well as the criticism and dismissal of intellectuals accused of "bourgeois liberalism" and support of "wholesale Westernization," all point to the tension between growing individualism and decentralization and the efforts of the Party to maintain control of the modernization processes (*Renmin Ribao*, January 12, 1987). What began in December of 1986 as university student demonstrations concerning local issues[33] rather quickly accelerated into national issues of concern and of perceived potential threat to the Chinese state. In response, the state education commission has issued provisional regulations stressing that special attention should be paid to political, ideological, and moral qualities of candidates wishing to enter universities who might be called upon to demonstrate their compliance with what is called the "five loves"—love of socialism, of the Communist party, of labor, of science and technology, and of the motherland.

Also in reply to the student movements, there was an official announcement that the policy to "let a hundred flowers bloom and a hundred schools of thought contend" was to continue in science and the arts, while controls were to be tightened against "bourgeois liberalism" in the domains of politics and ideology (*Renmin Ribao*, February 1, 1987). Once again, the challenge is posed of how to keep the baby of Western technological development and the sometimes energizing changes a mixed economy brings while throwing out the bath water of individualism, cultural penetration, and political liberalization.

CONTENDING MODELS OF SOCIALIST DEVELOPMENT

Some speak of each socialist experiment as a particular model of socialist development: They speak of the "Cuban model" or the "Tanzanian

---

[33] Students in Hefei, where the demonstrations began, were protesting the local elections, which they felt excluded them; students in Shanghai were primarily concerned with their living conditions; students in Shenzhen were protesting a new tuition scheme designed to tie tuition to grades (that is, the better the grades a student received for one term, the lower his/her tuition for the next). Students in Beijing did, it seems, address freedom of the press issues as well as student living conditions.

model" or the "Mozambican model." Certainly, the peculiarities of historical context give some truth to this approach. But, if what we are about is trying to understand the dynamics of change in one location in such a way that it may offer insight into other locations, a more distilled conception of contending models better serves our needs.

The Chinese themselves in the early days of the Cultural Revolution spoke of the conflict between two development models, or two "lines." In education, these lines are most commonly referred to as the "red" and the "expert" line. In both education and in other aspects of society, this dichotomous conceptualization has provided Western social scientists with a scheme upon which to hang many an analysis of postrevolutionary political upheavals. Simply stated, the Great Leap Forward and the Great Proletarian Cultural Revolution are the times when the "red," or politics-in-command, line was strongest. The early 1950s, early 1960s, and the early 1980s are times when the "expert" line has been on the ascendant.

Limited by this two-line conception, one could claim that the current policies in education have simply reverted back to the Liuist strategy, which placed paramount importance on expertise and excellence, even at the expense of equality. But Chinese postrevolutionary history has not been simply a lateral pendulum swing between repeating "red" and "expert" lines. The dialectical confrontations of politics and ideology in education has engendered forward motion as well.

Current modernization strategies point to a third current—one that in some ways is a synthesis of the other two, but in others is very much distinct from either. The Maoist line aimed to decentralize certain governmental prerogatives through mass line strategies, while the Liuist line worked to institute a highly centralized and empowered top-down state bureaucracy. What we find today in China is a combination of centralized and decentralized systems of governance, of economics, and of schooling. The current development agenda calls for a mixed economy. This calls, in turn, for a mixed education scheme. In this context, education plays its role in the productive forces and enters the market as a private consumption good, continuing all the while to meet the socialist state's superstructural need to produce "socialist persons" by inculcating a particular ideology and producing and reproducing a specific structure of knowledge. Today, the development agenda is a technocratic one, and the empowered knowledge is that which is seen to further the advancement of science, technology, industry, and defense. The modern economic mandate requires an individualism not called for in the earlier "expert" line.

We cannot extricate education from a broader vision of the goals of socialist construction or from the means set out to achieve those ends. The three trajectories distilled as models in Table 5–6 are three broad socialist visions. Each sets out particular means, implying correspondingly disparate ends. In practice, these strategy packages are neither mutually exclusive nor pure. The Titoism in this model is not simply Yugoslavia or a Yugoslavian model; Stalinism is not the Soviet model, and Maoism is not simply the Chinese model. Rather, any Leninist party-state is over time "a synthesis of these three trajectories" (Friedman 1984, 15). In China today, as yesterday—and indeed in the countries discussed elsewhere in this volume—the nature of the synthesis is in dispute.

Dorothy Solinger, Richard Kraus, and Peter Van Ness have used these three trajectories to analyze Chinese commerce, art, and foreign relations (Solinger 1984). To their outline, I have added a sketch of educational policies as they would fall into the Maoist, Stalinist, and Titoist categories. The tabular format makes explicit the connections between policies in education and policies in other areas. As conceptual frameworks distilled from reality rather than reflecting it, the models are more distinguishable from one another on paper than they have been in practice. As each model dictates a particular role for education, this conceptualization allows us to consider the various ways in which education and state relations are formulated and educational policy is set to ensure the fundamental social, political, and economic changes mandated by the postrevolutionary context.

While this analysis is drawn primarily from observations of the People's Republic of China, these trajectories are visible in other contexts. Anton Johnston, writing of Mozambique in this volume, speaks of "direct democratic," "centralized technocratic," and "decentralized functionalist" approaches to socialist development; these correspond to the Maoist, Stalinist, and Titoist models. The chapters on Cuba, Nicaragua, and Tanzania also point to similar contending models for education. Each of these approaches grows out of real social and political needs. Each has a proposal for removing the obstacles it perceives to be hampering a successful transition and institutionalization of socialism. And each has a distinct educational agenda.

In China, education in the Maoist path prioritizes the elimination of inequality and the raising of collective socialist consciousness. There is an emphasis on the connection between work and study, particularly for its ability to erase the rural/urban and the manual/mental distinctions in Chinese society. Economic development is to occur contemporaneously with social and political transformation. Education in the Stalinist trajectory reinforces the centralized power of the state vanguard, places importance on the training of experts, and allows teachers their more traditionally defined positions of authority. Development needs are to be met through the enforcement of state plans. With its priority of productivity, the Titoist strategy seeks to train experts. It emphasizes squarely

TABLE 5–6
Maoist, Stalinist, and Titoist Models of Policy, Art, and Education

	Maoist	Stalinist	Titoist
THE POLICY PROCESS			
Point of policy initiative	Mass line—from the commune up	Center	Center/enterprise
Sector emphasis	Industry and agriculture	Heavy industry	Agriculture and light industry
Strategy of implementation	Social mobilization	Central plan	Plan/market
Strategy focus	Individual "socialist person"	Social system, national infrastructure	Enterprise, individual "expert"
State concern for women's status	State initiated, mobilize for equality, emphasis on women's role in production	State managed, bureaucratic, emphasis on women's role in reproduction	State unconcerned, market emphasis on efficiency
Legal norms	Rule by politics	Rule by Party/state	Rule by law/science
International economic relations	Self-reliance	Integration with socialist camp	Integration with capitalist camp
Free trade	Bad, causes capitalism, class division	Cautionist, must be properly managed by state organs	Good, increases productivity
ART			
Management	Political, grassroots mobilization	Bureaucratically managed, professional	Supply and demand, laissez-faire politically

TABLE 5-6 (*Continued*)

	Maoist	Stalinist	Titoist
Aim of art	To mobilize, incorporate, and politically educate	To nurture uncultivated masses	To entertain
Audience	Politically active	Politically receptive	Politically passive
EDUCATION			
Primary theoretical position	Part of the superstructure	Part of the productive forces	Part of the productive forces
Rationale	Education for class struggle	Education for economic development	Education for economic development
Administration	Decentralized, semi-autonomous	Centralized	Bifurcated: centralized/autonomous
Financing	Egalitarian, community/state	Planned, community/state	Diversified, individual/enterprise/province
Access to schooling	Political and social criteria—aim at an egalitarian outcome (*minban*)	Centrally monitored examinations—aim at excellence (keypoint)	Decentralized—aim at meeting market need, diverse criteria
Teacher role	Participatory	Authoritarian	Combination of two
Curriculum	Politics and work, practical	Traditional, quality-oriented, research	Specialized, technical, practical
Key sectors	Primary, adult study/work	College track, tertiary	Vocational/technical, tertiary

technical and vocational training as meeting the human resource needs of economic development. Connections made through joint projects and research cooperation between enterprises and schools aim at the development of new consumer products or technological advances, rather than focusing on their ideological benefits or their likelihood of eliminating social inequalities. In the Titoist strategy, what serves the educational enhancement of the individual serves the modernization efforts of the state. In the Stalinist strategy, what serves the state dictates what constitutes the development of the individual. In the Maoist strategy, what serves the collective serves the state. Education is fundamental to the success of any of these strategies or any synthesis of them because it must produce its participants, help produce and then reproduce its social formations, and thereby create its present and ensure its future.

CONCLUSIONS

Paulo Freire speaks of education as the midwife of liberation. Deng Xiaoping calls it the key to modernization. Fidel Castro claims that revolution and education are the same thing. As the studies here document, schooling—both formal and nonformal—plays a pivotal role in the transition to socialism. But it is not as if the postrevolutionary ministers of education have a tabula rasa on which to engrave the policies most likely to usher in the new society. Neither is it a given that what is engraved will be implemented. Instead, all ministers of education and the states of which they are empowered members can be actors only as they are also and simultaneously reactors. In China, they are constrained not only by the inherited level of development but also by the lack of consensus in the leadership. In none of post-1949 policy struggles were all the victories consummated or all the futures set. Rather, the transition of a vanguard from a collective whose purpose was to defeat past injustice to a state whose mandate is to ensure a better future is by definition a process of struggle.

Our analysis suggests the extent and complexity of the interconnections between traditional legacy and contemporary policy in China. The state implants a self-protective and self-reproductive ideological agenda in educational practice. Morality combines with politics to circumscribe individual autonomy. Access to a meritocratic system is limited. Earlier notions of model emulation, leader worship, pedagogy, student protest, and the nation as "family" remain powerful. Teachers' status, incomes, and influence, then and now, have not reflected the importance ostensibly assigned to education, a gap that is one of the central failings of modern educational practice. Then and now, China has looked to education to help it compete with foreign powers. Both before and after the revolution, the Chinese have been preoccupied with the need both to win the people's hearts and to fill the people's stomachs.

The People's Republic of China was established on particularly denuded land and under particularly disagreeable conditions. The China of 1949 was a very poor nation. Instituting socialism was not simply a matter of redistributing wealth but one of creating it. Education was not concerned merely with redistributing existing knowledge but with creating it as well.

The process of "struggle, criticism, and transformation" is a continuing one. Some would argue that it must be ongoing if the goal is to construct a society responsive to the needs of its members. We have catalogued here the struggles over the direction for Chinese education; we have seen how the criticism of past shortcomings has been used as a springboard for subsequent reform. But we cannot say we have witnessed the transformation to socialism as if it were complete, the endpoint in a linear and accomplished progression. This construction we seek to understand is, rather, a dialectical process, only to be once and again restruggled, recriticized, and retransformed.

There is no single blueprint for success. The three models for socialist development presented in this chapter characterize different strategies for transition and define distinct relations between domestic and international policy, between the people and the state, between education and production, and between the individual and the collective. They also presage very different societies.

Is each of the models, or each set of actual state strategies, equally likely to facilitate the construction of socialism? This depends, of course, on how we choose to define that term. If we are satisfied that any state is socialist if it owns the means of production and outlaws particular private relationships to capital and to labor, it would be simpler to conclude that "socialism" could unilaterally result. If we focus on socialism's promise to advance the forces of production, our answer is also more easily reachable. If, on the other hand, we agree with Nicos Poulantzas (1980) that there is no socialism without democracy, or if we agree with Rosa Luxemburg ([1905] 1961) that there is no socialism without the equal empowerment of all of "the people," our prognosis is a more difficult one. Clearly the recent student protests calling for "democracy" underline the fact that this is an issue of timely concern in China.

Mao was fond of saying that the Party is the seed and the people are the soil. As the tiller of this transition, the state/Party can best accomplish its harvest through dialogical relations with the people. Education provides the hoes and the nutrients necessary to bring from this soil the bread of justice, the realization of a society based on collective participation and shared reward. But the best of harvests is still many seasons in the working.

CHRONOLOGY OF EDUCATION AND MAJOR POLICY CHANGES IN CHINA

	Politics, Economy, Society	Education
1850–1911	Qing dynasty collapses	1850: Classics still content of civil service exams; missionary influence increases
		1862: Foreigners allowed to train Chinese palace officials
		1867: Western science included in official curriculum
		1872: First Chinese students go abroad to study
		1897: First modern primary school set up; normal schools follow
		1902: Court orders that foreign languages be studied in China
		1905: Civil Service examination system abolished
1911–1949	Republican era Revolution fought	1919–1926: Chaos; twenty different ministers of education
		1921: John Dewey and Bertrand Russell visit China to lecture
		1922: School reform decrees that texts be written in vernacular
		1929: Beijing Normal University established
		1931: League of Nations team argues against reliance on U.S. model of schooling
		1935: Peasant and cadre education set up in base areas

(Continued on next page)

EDUCATION AND MAJOR POLICY CHANGES IN CHINA—*Continued*

	Politics, Economy, Society	*Education*
1949–1952[34]	State consolidation National reconstruction	Nationalization of private schools Teachers the target of thought reform Comprehensive curricular reform Reorganization of tertiary education Literacy campaign (land reform) Ministry of higher education established Stipends awarded to university students Reduction of school time Minban schools set up
1953–1957	First Five-Year Plan Soviet influence	Reliance on professionalism for teachers Soviet texts and teaching guides translated into Chinese Universities remolded along lines of Soviet technical academies Introduction of academic degrees Expansion of rural education Teachers' wages raised and training upgraded Two-track system set in place separating rural from urban schooling Antirightist campaigns Accelerated literary drive Secondary graduates exceed tertiary enrollees (1957)

(*Continued on next page*)

[34] The 1949–1977 years in this chronology draw heavily on Löfstedt 1980.

EDUCATION AND MAJOR POLICY CHANGES IN CHINA—*Continued*

	Politics, Economy, Society	*Education*
1958–1959	Great Leap Forward	Abolition of ministry of higher education
		Workshops in schools and schools in factories
		Part work/part study schools
		Number of working-class students increases
		Criticism of nonproletarian teachers
		Collectivization drastically accelerated
		Movement to send intellectuals to countryside
		Popularization of curriculum
1961–1965	Retrenchment New economic program	Stress on quality
		Promotion of keypoint schools and return to two-track system
		State investment going to urban schools while rural schools financed locally
		Revival of ministry of higher education
		Reduction of primary enrollment
		Resistance to work
		Study schools
		Continued literacy drive
		Reliance on specialists
		Increased educational differentiation (two education systems and two labor systems)

(*Continued on next page*)

EDUCATION AND MAJOR POLICY CHANGES IN CHINA—*Continued*

	Politics, Economy, Society	*Education*
1966–1969	Great Proletarian Cultural Revolution	Struggle at universities Persecution of intellectuals Elimination of two-track system Length of schooling reduced Examinations abolished Army sent in to schools Schools close Ministry of education closed down Student-centered educational methods endorsed Manual labor required of all students Stress on political education and correct ideology Denigration of book learning Promotion of equality as educational goal Revolutionary committees brought in to run schools
1970–1976	Mao's last years Cultural Revolution wanes	Education's role in the superstructure emphasized Continuing confusion and hesitance Entrance to schools determined by work units "Three-in-one" system of unifying teaching, scientific research, and production Question of deteriorated academic standards addressed Entrance examinations reestablished (1976)

(*Continued on next page*)

EDUCATION AND MAJOR POLICY CHANGES IN CHINA—*Continued*

	Politics, Economy, Society	*Education*
1977–1980	Four Modernizations begin	Chinese students sent abroad to study
		Target to double number of university students
		New textbooks and curricula written
		Resumed literacy drive
		Education stresses discipline and excellence
		Restructuring of secondary education
		Keypoint schools reinstituted
		Professorial ranks restored
		Teacher-centered education returns
		"Small pagoda" system reinstituted
		Removal of class designations
		A responsibility system patterned on the rural decollectivization drive introduced in schools
		"Respect knowledge, respect talent" becomes the slogan
1981–1987	Strengthening of the struggle over new policies	Education proclaimed the key to the Four Modernizations
		Education characterized as part of the productive forces
		Emphasis on higher education and quality
		Worker-peasant-soldier students reexamined

(*Continued on next page*)

EDUCATION AND MAJOR POLICY CHANGES IN CHINA—*Continued*

Politics, Economy, Society	Education
1981–1987 (*cont.*)	Tertiary enrollment increases (including a substantial increase in the number of students going, and staying, abroad)
	Primary enrollment decreases
	Faculty allowed to make contracts with enterprises
	Decentralization
	Teachers get pay raise
	Ministry of Education raised in status to commission
	Nine-year compulsory schooling plan
	Autonomy of universities increased
	Link between Party leadership and academics weakened
	Increasing scientific exchange
	Policies introduced to control brain drain
	Questions raised about "wholesale Westernization"
	Student protests
	Foreign assistance to education increased

THE BEIJING SUMMER, 1989

This chapter was written before the Beijing events of June 1989 demonstrated to the world the volatile nature of change in today's China. Those events do reflect, however, a theme I have developed throughout this analysis: Even before the tanks advanced down the Avenue of Eternal Peace, modernization was a contentious matter. The heavy-handed state intervention not only bluntly demonstrated the power of the postrevolutionary Chinese state and continuing strife within it, but also painfully underscored the contradictory roles of schooling and of students in modernizing China. In China, educational struggle is political struggle.

There is much to say about the summer of 1989 in China and much to wonder about the kind of state that will emerge from its ashes. As I indicated at the beginning of this chapter, modernization policies have reordered not only education, but the economy and ideology as well. As the summer of 1989 painfully showed us, the changes that modernization has called for in one sphere have not found workable reflections in others. Students are not the sole victims of this inconsistency, but their leadership role in what the Western press calls the "democracy movement" and the Chinese press calls "counterrevolutionary insurgency" brings into stark relief the difficulty of redefining national mission without redefining political power. Throughout this chapter I have stressed the Chinese state's decaying legitimacy. Beijing's "la noche triste" has surely intensified that decay.

Students have always been important to the Chinese state. The 1989 rift between student activists and the state will have far-reaching consequences. As I have argued here, change in Chinese education has been the result of struggle, and those struggles have been and continue to be political. Modernization in China is founded on contradictions in which schools are often enmeshed. University students left their schools before final examinations in 1989. It is impossible to predict whether or not those who return to their campuses will be able to reap the potentially bountiful dialogical harvest I foresaw. What is certain is that we have not seen the end of the struggle.

CHAPTER 6

Educational Reform and Social Transformation in Cuba, 1959–1989

Martin Carnoy

IN 1959, CUBA BEGAN a process of revolutionary change that transformed virtually all its institutions. Educational expansion and reform played a vital role in this transformation. The Cuban revolution made education a synonym for incorporation into the revolutionary process. It also has relied on the educational system to develop the skills needed for economic growth and industrialization. Today, Cuba has the highest level of education in Latin America. All children, even those from the humblest families, get at least ten years of high quality schooling. There are enough well-trained teachers for Cuba to export them to Nicaragua and Angola. This was a costly achievement, especially under the conditions of a U.S. embargo and military confrontation. It also involved a number of errors and assumed too much about the power of education to create a new kind of person, especially with Cuba in earshot of the world's most successful consumer culture.

We will make five principal claims about Cuban education after 1959. First, despite many conflicts in the revolutionary leadership about economic development strategies, the revolutionary state has maintained an underlying socialist vision of Cuba's transformation—in particular, a conception of a future Cuban society where people organize their work and politics around collective rather than individual interests—the reform of educational content has consistently included a strong ideological component based on collective work and moral incentives. Second, because revolutionary leaders have been committed to the redistribution of resources, to the transformation of Cuban agriculture and rural life, and to independence from U.S. economic power, the revolution changed the objectives, pace of expansion, and clientele of the educational system drastically. Third, because the revolutionary state viewed education as a key element in the society's transformation, changes in the shape of the educational system are directly related to changes in economic and social policy. Fourth, changes in Cuban society—and hence in Cuban education—took place within the context of a counterrevolutionary reaction aided and often directed by the United States, which entailed high economic and social costs. Fifth, the failure of the educational system (and the revolutionary process itself) to create the level of socialist consciousness desired and expected by Cuba's leaders has, in turn, shaped changes in economic policy—essentially, a move away from reliance on moral incentives towards material incentives, in both work and consumption—and has kept pressure on the political leadership itself to keep defining and enforcing socialist morality.

More than in other transition states, we argue, Cuba could afford to invest heavily in education, both because the revolutionary state inherited a well-educated population (and a relatively high income per capita)—by Latin American standards of the time—and because the Cuban economy was subsidized by the Soviet Union to a greater degree than other transition societies were.[1]

Even so, Cuban educational policy set a standard for educational expansion and reform in other Third World countries, particularly in Latin America. The threat of Cuban-style revolutions elsewhere induced conditioned capitalist states to meet the Cuban challenge of making educational expansion (and improved health care) a litmus test of democratic reform and human rights, in countries where capital, not labor, was the state's dominant constituency. We will suggest that despite the possible conflict of rapid educational expansion with capital accumulation in Cuba, this conflict was organically different from the inherent contradictions of similar educational policies in conditioned capitalist societies. Therefore, although economic growth was almost zero in the 1960s, Cuba continued to spend heavily on education; in contrast, similar slowdowns in conditioned capitalist societies in the 1970s and 1980s have led to cutbacks in total social spending (Coombs 1985).

Like the other countries we studied, Cuba also expanded education steadily and in "classic" fashion, from the bottom up. Secondary education grew rapidly only when primary schooling had reached most Cuban children, and university expansion did not even begin until the early 1970s, when bottlenecks in secondary education were on the way to being solved. Whereas shifts occurred in the type of education that was emphasized and in various programs at the secondary level, the emphasis

[1] According to a report made to the U.S. Congress in 1982 (cited in Brundenius 1984, 66), the total accumulated Soviet assistance to Cuba from 1961 to 1979 was $16.7 billion, of which no less than $11.0 billion was in direct subsidies on commodities traded with the USSR (exports of sugar and nickel and imports of petroleum). This amounted to approximately 20 percent of Cuba's GDP in that period. There is, however, some controversy over the meaning of "subsidy" in these commodity agreements among centrally planned economies. The "subsidy" calculation is based on world market price, but it could be argued that the price paid by the Soviet Union to Cuba for sugar and nickel is a "fair" price in terms of the value of the work that goes into their production, and is also a wise investment by the Soviets in Cuban development.

on *more* schooling was constant throughout the revolutionary period. Nonetheless, the leadership's choice not to expand university education in the 1960s (despite the immense loss of professionals through emigration) was less for educational-technical reasons (for example, educators' standard claim that good primary and secondary education is needed before university education) than for ideological reasons—the decision was primarily influenced by a national policy to develop socialist consciousness concurrent with economic growth and to increase schooling first for disadvantaged (rural and urban marginal) groups.

The expansion of education was, from the very beginning, driven primarily by ideological goals, as the Cubans freely admit (see Leiner 1973, 6). The education process was supposed to redefine citizenship in collective terms and nationalism in international revolutionary terms. Schooling was to develop a motivation for collective rather than individual material success, and a sense of belonging to Cuba as a revolutionary society. In part the goal was to extra-nationalize those Cubans who fled to Miami (they are no longer "Cubans") and to build solidarity with and commitment to other revolutionary societies, such as Nicaragua and Angola.

PREREVOLUTIONARY CONDITIONS

Until 1959, Cuba had been an economy and society dominated by U.S. trade, investment, and culture. The United States virtually controlled the island's economic and political institutions; they were organized to develop the society within the U.S. sphere of influence. According to Mesa-Lago, "United States investment in Cuba by 1958 was possibly the second largest in Latin America, and in the period 1949–58, an average of two-thirds of Cuba's foreign trade was with the United States" (Mesa-Lago 1981, 8). Much of this investment (about 20 percent) was in sugar mills, but U.S. business had penetrated every corner of the economy, including public utilities and communications, banks and financial institutions, mining, and petroleum refining (Brundenius 1984, 11–12). Although only about 40 percent of Cuban sugar mills were owned by U.S. firms, these mills, as well as other plants owned by foreigners, represented the bulk of the technologically modern production facilities (Ritter 1974, 5). In addition, U.S. capital controlled 90 percent of telephone and electric light and power services, and 50 percent of the public railways (Ritter 1974).

In many ways, Cuba in the 1950s was like other Latin American conditioned economies, pursuing a narrow concept of development, sometimes successfully (during sugar booms) but mostly unsuccessfully for the mass of Cubans. It is true that Cuba was an extreme case of conditioned development: extremely closely tied to the United States and extremely dependent on a single crop, but relatively rich because it could produce that crop at low cost, because of its preferred position in U.S. markets, and because of its large sugar crops, nickel supplies, and, in the 1950s, tourism and gambling.

Yet Cuba also differed from most conditioned capitalist societies. Because of the dominance of sugar in agriculture and the plantation cultivation of that crop, a typical rural laborer in prerevolutionary Cuba was a wage-earner rather than a peon or subsistence farmer. In 1952, paid workers comprised 63.6 percent of the total agricultural labor force. The thirst for land characteristic of the peasant was subordinate in the rural proletariat to demands for better living and working conditions, higher wages, job security, and better educational opportunities for children (Manitzas 1973). Furthermore, the nature of Cuban history was such that a Spanish landed aristocracy was displaced rather late (by the 1898 war of independence) and, because of rapid capitalist penetration into sugar cultivation, was never replaced by any politically important criollo aristocracy. Cuban owners of sugar and tobacco plantations were almost entirely urban based. The hacienda system was—relative to the rest of Latin America—essentially nonexistent in twentieth-century Cuba (Manitzas 1973).

A relatively fluid social order in this conditioned capitalist economic structure gave rise to an important contradiction: Organized labor expanded and flourished; in fact, more than one-fifth of the entire Cuban population were in unions (Manitzas 1973, 9–10). Labor unions were not confined to just cities and mining communities, but extended directly into the countryside, "where industrial workers and agricultural labor comingled in the large sugar complexes. Unionization, the admixture of industrial and agricultural wage workers, and, finally, a highly active Communist Party in union leadership for many years, gave a coloration to the Cuban lower classes that was largely lacking in most other Latin American countries. In essence, it exposed them to values and norms of behavior that were secular, rationalistic, and fundamentally modern in stamp" (Manitzas 1973, 10).[2]

---

[2] Because of subsequent events, it is worth remarking on the prehistory of the Cuban Communist party. The Party, founded in 1925, followed a popular front strategy beginning in 1935. Under Cuban conditions, this meant cooperating with the Batista dictatorship. Batista, in turn, allowed the Party to operate openly and achieve legality. To understand why Cuban unions were well-established and had considerable Communist influence, we have to go back to the Batista regime of the late 1930s and 1940s. That regime was reformist and heavily influenced by the New Deal. It regarded itself as a form of social democracy. The constitution of 1940 enlarged the sphere in which the unions could operate and even promised land reform. Communists secured most of the key positions in the Cuban Union

These economic and social conditions were reflected in the Cuban educational system. As in the case of GNP per capita, the average level of education in the Cuban population was relatively high by Latin American standards. In 1953, only 20 percent of 20 to 29-year-olds (educated in the 1930s and 1940s) had no schooling, 72 percent had some primary education, 6 percent had some secondary education, and 2 percent had some university education (Carnoy and Werthein 1977). Actual enrollment in public schools as a percentage of the relevant age group was 58 percent in primary schools, 19 percent in secondary schools, and 5.5 percent in universities (Mesa-Lago 1981, 165). All of these figures were among the highest in Latin America, equivalent to educational levels in Central America (aside from Costa Rica) almost twenty years later. The illiteracy rate among all adults had declined to 23.6 percent by 1953 (Mesa-Lago 1981, 164).

However, education was very unequally distributed and the educational system was stagnant in the years before the revolution. In 1953, urban illiteracy was 12 percent, and rural illiteracy, 42 percent (Mesa-Lago 1981, 164); and a much smaller percentage of rural than of urban children went to school at all (Carnoy and Werthein 1980). Access to secondary school and university was limited to children of higher-income families, and the university turned out primarily general professionals who had majored in law and economics, subjects most likely to get students jobs with the U.S. companies operating in Cuba or often entry to professions that depended on foreign investment. Of the 17,000 students in the University of Havana in 1953–1954, only 1,500 were in the school of science. Of these, 409 studied civil engineering; 463, electrical engineering; 404, agricultural and sugar studies; and 226, pure science and mathematics. "Attendance was often half-hearted, standards, in many cases, were low among faculty and so among students" (Jolly 1964, 253–54).

Cuba on the eve of the revolution had a relatively small proportion of illiterates, a well-organized labor force with a reasonably high amount of

---

Congress, and two Communists had cabinet posts.

Political conditions changed sharply with the Cold War and the 1952 coup—changes that show how closely the Batista regime was ideologically bound to fluctuations in the U.S. political climate rather than to conditions in Cuba. The Communists were suppressed (as they were in the United States), but even then, leaders such as Blas Roca, Juan Marinello, and Carlos Rafael Rodriguez could live undisturbed in Havana. The dictatorship's plan was apparently to keep the Communists in reserve in case they were needed to blackmail the Americans. At the same time, Communists were purged from the unions and political life. The Communists, in turn, for rather good ideological reasons (as well as their survival), maintained an ambiguous attitude toward Castro's armed struggle against the dictatorship. This attitude poisoned the relationship between the 26th of July movement and the Communist party for more than a decade after the revolution (see Enzenberger 1976).

schooling (about 75 percent had completed some primary school or more), a proletarianized rural labor force, who were relatively interested in increasing their children's education, a relatively large number of teachers, and high educational spending (although much was being siphoned off into graft)—in short, a relatively well-educated population already well integrated in a conditioned capitalist wage-labor system.

ECONOMIC AND POLITICAL CHANGE AFTER THE REVOLUTION

The entrance of the 26th of July movement guerrillas into Havana on January 1, 1959, marked a new era in Cuban history. The Batista regime had collapsed under pressure not only from the growing strength of the guerilla army, but from bourgeois opposition to the regime's corruption and brutality. Very early, it became clear that the new government was going to make radical changes in Cuban society: In the first six months of 1959, Castro seized the U.S.-owned Cuban Electric Company; reduced electricity rates for rural areas by one-half; and announced a new law reducing housing rents by as much as 50 percent (for the lowest rent payers), a Vacant Lot Law, which wiped out any appreciation of market value of urban real estate in excess of 15 percent, and an Agrarian Reform Law, which set limits to the amount of land an individual could own and expropriated the rest for redistribution and the formation of "people's farms" and cooperatives (Brundenius 1984).

The revolution also quickly set out to change Cuba's relationship with the United States. Reaction and counterreaction in the second half of 1960 resulted in the confiscation of all U.S. properties in Cuba, the breaking of economic and political ties with Cuba by the United States, and a U.S. trade embargo. Although the nationalizations began as retaliation against the United States, other foreign and Cuban properties were also affected. By early 1961, 75 percent of Cuban industry and 30 percent of Cuban land were collectivized (Brundenius 1984, 44).

The reconstruction of the state through much of the first two revolutionary decades was—and even today is—based largely on the ideological aims of a small group of leaders, who held complete power through the legitimacy of the revolution itself, reinforced by the threat of U.S. intervention. These leaders sought, through their legitimacy and the power of the revolutionary state, to change human interrelations in Cuban society. Thus, economic and social goals were set in a dominant ideological framework. Mass organizations rooted in the 26th of July movement, such as the Committees for the Defense of the Revolution (CDRs), carried out the policies at the local level.

The social and economic transformation reflected four principal aims: (1) a much more equitable distribution of consumption and the provision of minimal levels of health services, education, and nutrition to everyone in the Cuban population; (2) the elimination of unemployment; (3) rapid economic growth to increase the standard of living of the Cuban population; and (4) the elimination of the market mechanism as an allocator of resources and its replacement by an administratively run economy in which people responded to moral incentives rather than economic rewards.

Cuba went through a series of distinct phases between 1959 and the mid-1970s. These can be characterized as *initial transition* (1959–1961), in which the new leadership redistributed Cuba's national product, mobilized the population, and nationalized industry; *agricultural diversification and rapid industrialization* (1961–1963), in which the leadership tried to move the economy into Soviet-style development and away from sugar production; *economic growth through export expansion and the development of "socialist man"* (1964–1970), in which sugar production was accepted as the lead sector and emphasis was placed on agriculture and the creation of socialist attitudes and values as the basis of work incentives; and *material incentives, rationalization, and economic growth* (1970–present), in which the leadership implemented a central planning model combined with greater decentralization of decisionmaking at the plant and municipal level, and in which the emphasis was placed on economic growth through increased efficiency, industrialization, mechanization of agriculture, and material incentives.

These changes between 1959 and the early 1970s reflect several important features of the Cuban revolution (some of which it shares with other revolutions)—features that are crucial to understanding Cuban educational change in the last three decades. These features may be briefly characterized as (1) ideological struggle over conflicting models of socialism; (2) evolution of the revolutionary states's political structures over an unusually long time period; (3) trade-offs between the goals of developing collective consciousness and increasing production and consumption; (4) enormous success in reducing unemployment; and (5) the conflict with the United States.

First, there was an ongoing struggle in the leadership between proponents of various concepts of the "correct road to socialism." The struggle was primarily ideological, but it also hinged on the economic success each model enjoyed. There were three ideological positions represented in these first years of the revolution: reformism, which argued for a social democratic model of development (the modernization and nationalization of Cuban capitalism and the construction of a democratic, modern, redistributive welfare state); Guevarism, which argued for a change in social consciousness *preceding* development of the material base; and Libermanism, which argued for a pragmatic market socialism similar to that in the Soviet Union.

After the first economic successes of 1959–1961 (gross material production grew 4.3 percent in 1959, 1.5 percent in 1960, and 2.8 percent in 1961 [Brundenius 1984, tab. 2.8]) resulting from economic reform and the greater use of existing capacity (reformism), the attempt to industrialize under a Stalinist model failed (1962–1963). That failure prompted the leadership to look for alternative paths of development for its insular, plantation economy. Heavy industrialization was postponed, and sugar was reluctantly accepted as the engine for development (1964–1966). At the same time, there was an ideological struggle in the leadership between the two nonreformist alternatives of Guevarism and Libermanism.

According to Mesa-Lago (1981), "Guevara believed that the 'subjective conditions' (ideas, consciousness, willingness; all belonging to the superstructure in Marxist terms) could decisively influence the 'objective conditions,' that is, the material base, the forces of production, the structure which in the conventional interpretation of Marxism determines the superstructure. Guevara and others argued that the successful development of consciousness ahead of material-base development could enable a country to skip the transitional socialist stage between capitalism and communism or to build socialism and communism simultaneously" (Mesa-Lago 1981, 19).

The Liberman model was being pushed by a "moderate, pragmatist group" (Mesa-Lago 1981, 20), composed primarily of members of the prerevolutionary pro-Soviet communist party. This group favored market socialism—the application of selected market mechanisms within the framework of a socialist economy—and argued that objective conditions had to be developed first and consciousness would follow. The Libermanists believed that "to ignore the law of supply and demand and cut down material incentives would have a negative effect on production and the development of the material base" (Mesa-Lago 1981, 21).

In 1964–1966, the two models competed, with the Guevarist model dominating in industry and the Liberman model dominating in agriculture and domestic and foreign trade. In 1966, Castro announced the push toward Guevarism with new collectivizations in agriculture. By 1968, all small business was also placed under state control. The Guevarist model's shortcomings resulted in low economic growth and a general failure to put the Cuban economy on a solid economic footing (Mesa-Lago 1981). After the dislocation caused by the 1970 effort to produce 10 million tons of sugar, Castro moved away from the "idealism" of reforming Cubans' consciousness toward building the economy more on the then current Soviet socialist methods. Since the early 1970s, Cuba has followed the more Libermanist approach, even to the point, in the early 1980s, of allowing private consumer markets in agricultural products to develop in urban areas and permitting individual artisans to provide services privately.[3] Central planning is the main organizational element of the economy, and profit, interest, taxes, depreciation, and cost analysis, which were considered "bourgeois economics," in the Guevarist phase, are now accepted as key economic instruments of socialist planning (Mesa-Lago 1981, 29).

A second important feature of the revolution was the long gestation period of the present organization of the Cuban state. The 26th of July movement that overthrew the Batista regime and took state power in January 1959 was not a political party and had little political structure. This was a guerrilla group around which had mobilized a loose coalition of urban groups intent on getting rid of Batista. Many of those in the movement simply wanted to replace the dictatorship with a democratic capitalist state that was more independent of the United States. But, as we have shown, Castro and his closest associates were from the very beginning committed, at the least, to a major restructuring of income and wealth in Cuba. This restructuring favored the poor over the rich, rural dwellers over urban residents, renters over property owners, and Cuban over foreign ownership of productive capital. By late 1960, it was already clear that the restructuring was going far beyond any mere reform of Cuban capitalism, and in April 1961, Castro announced that Cuba's revolution was socialist (Brundenius 1984, 43–44).

The centralized leadership of the movement depended on mass organizations and mobilizations to carry out policies decided at the top. The key mass organizations were the Committees for the Defense of the Revolution, which were (and still are) organized on a block-by-block basis in the urban centers and over wider physical areas in the rural zones. Today, about 70 percent of the population participates (to various degrees) in the CDRs. The CDRs were and still are in charge of mobilizing for volunteer work, community projects, delivering social services (vaccinating the population, collecting garbage, and settling domestic disputes, for example), and also—as their name implies—monitoring "antirevolutionary" activity (which gave them the reputation among those opposed to the State of being a political police). Other mass organizations also served to mobilize the community: the women's federation (FMC), labor unions (which were very weak until 1970), the farmers' organization, youth or-

---

[3] Nevertheless, Fidel's commitment to socialist consciousness as a foundation of Cuban development continues even until today. In 1986, the state (in this case, it seems to have been Fidel himself) closed the private agricultural markets, arguing that certain Cuban farmers were accumulating large amounts of money and this was contrary to socialist aims (*New York Times*, February 6, 1987, sec. F). We will discuss this commitment in detail below.

ganizations, and so forth. The Communist party, therefore, was not a key factor in Cuba's state structure until much later, when it replaced the mass organizations—particularly the CDRs—as the principal link between the population and the state's central leadership.

The new state, organized under the leadership of the 26th of July movement and working through the mass organizations, had advantages and disadvantages. On one hand, there was a very loose organizational structure to make decisions shaped by information from the base, and little organizational ideology to carry out a systematic program for the island's transition from capitalism. On the other hand, the loose organization made it difficult for a "new class" with special privileges or special power to develop. And since the Cuban Communist Party (CCP) was not playing a vanguard role in the 1960s, the Party was generally more democratic and open than in Eastern Europe or the Soviet Union. It gradually grew to include about 10 percent of Cuba's adult population. Further, the long period of being without a vanguard party allowed the state leadership in the 1970s to develop parallel political organizations even as it gave increasing power to the CCP (more about this below).

At the same time, decisionmaking power centralized in the hands of a few at the top produced decisions about economic policy in the 1960s that resulted in successes or mistakes so great that they affected the whole island. Good examples of successes in the 1960s were the fishing industry and pork production; one of the biggest failures was the 10 million-ton sugar goal in 1970. Mistakes were admitted and policy changed. Personalized decisionmaking and the political legitimacy to mobilize the masses (Castro's popularity with the Cuban people has been high continuously during his almost three decades in power) have allowed Cuba to make rapid and rather sudden changes in policy.[4]

Besides the personalistic and centralized ideological and political decisionmaking of the reconstituted Cuban state, the essence of politics in Cuba was, until the early 1970s, and to a lesser extent even until today, mass mobilization. One of the principal objectives of the new government when it assumed power in 1959 was to incorporate the mass of Cubans into the mainstream of economic and social activity. Two organizations played a key role in this process: the CDRs and the educational system, including the 1961 literacy campaign. The CDRs already had 1 million members by September 1961 (Fagen 1969, 69–103). The educational system served as the base for the literacy campaign of 1961—a campaign in which all teachers and many students participated, going for

---

[4] Nevertheless, MacEwan (1981) argues that the top-down process in the 1960s made the mass organizations into *implementors* of centralized decisions, and this ultimately separated most Cubans from the revolution, reducing the legitimacy of the state and leading to economic problems and to the reforms of the 1970s.

nine months into the countryside to teach almost one million illiterates how to read (Fagen 1969; Carnoy and Werthein 1980). But even after the literacy campaign, schools were organized to serve adults almost as much as they did children. After the campaign, formal education was viewed as the principal means to bring the population into full participation (high productivity) in the economy.

Since the end of 1975, with the First Communist Party Congress and the official recognition of the Party as the major administrative and mobilizational organ of the state, the Cuban state has moved toward a political structure closer to those in Eastern European socialist countries. The Party became the principal organizer of political and economic activities at the local and national levels. But there are important differences between Cuba and Eastern Europe—Cuba gave mass organizations some voice in decisionmaking and created elected local assemblies years before such organizations gained any voice in Eastern European countries.

In the 1970s, the mass organizations were given more decision-influencing power in addition to their traditional role of carrying out decisions made at the top. Castro acknowledged in 1970 "that the trade union movement was in poor shape and should be revitalized through democratization (free election); it also should be allowed to defend the workers' rights" (Mesa-Lago 1974; Fidel Castro, September 1970, quoted in Ritter 1974, 330). The mass organization of women (FMC) has been much more active and influential than women's organizations in Eastern Europe, despite the legendary "machismo" of Cuban men (Molyneux 1982). Cuba has enacted a Family Law which officially gives increased rights to women as women in their relations with men (the law mandates shared responsibility for raising children and for home work), as well as promoting the development of child care—making Cuba the most progressive society in the socialist world with regard to women's rights. According to the FMC's leaders it enjoys autonomy and supports itself with contributions from its members, but receives "guidance" from the Party. The organization maintains close links with the state commission in work (which determines occupational definitions, criteria for job qualifications, and salaries) and with the ministries of education and higher education (Stromquist 1984).[5]

In 1974, a completely new political organization was created—Poder Popular—which consists of popular assemblies whose members are elected at the local level. The government's experiment in popular power began in July 1974, with secret elections in Matanzas province for district

[5] One of the most important impacts on family life, however, has come from the expansion of health care: Cuba has the lowest child mortality rate in Latin America and 98 percent of deliveries take place in hospitals.

representatives to the People's Municipal Assemblies: each CDR nominated a candidate. Fifty-four percent of the elected delegates were not Party members (Zimbalist 1975, 23). The local assemblies of Poder Popular have authority over local enterprises; the district assemblies (elected by the local assemblies) have power over district enterprises, and so forth. The operation of Poder Popular is also integrated with the activities of the mass organizations. Thus, the parallel political organizations have been given considerable say over economic policies in the 1970s and 1980s—a distinct shift from the centralized power of the 1960s—even while the Communist party has hegemony over political affairs (MacEwan 1981, 176–79). In a real sense, Poder Popular and the mass organizations act as alternative sources of advice and information for the leadership and, if those organizations are seen by local constituencies as having power, as sources of government legitimacy.

The third important feature of the Cuban revolution is that its different phases are marked by a trade-off between the attempt to develop collective consciousness and the attempt to develop the forces of production (to accumulate capital and increase consumption). Economic growth was low under the Guevarist model of economic organization, with its emphasis on creating "socialist man" simultaneously with increasing the productive forces. Table 6–1, based on Brundenius's estimates, shows that gross domestic product per capita fell during the 1960s, especially during 1964–1970. Cuba also faced other problems in this period, including sabotage from the United States and the impact of the trade embargo. Nevertheless, most analysts agree that moral incentives were not successful and that the turn to material incentives and more rational, centralized, technically and economically based planning with decentralized accounting systems and managerial decisionmaking was largely responsible for higher growth after 1971.

Perhaps the biggest turnaround came in 1980, when the leadership decided to allow small private artisan businesses to start up again as a way of alleviating the pressure for home repairs and other consumer services. The artisans worked from their homes after doing state jobs. Shortly afterwards, the state opened the first of the farmers' markets, where farmers were allowed to sell 20 percent of their output at prices that they set themselves without government control. The prices were high "but farm production rose and the shortages [of foodstuffs] nearly disappeared" (*New York Times*, February 8, 1987, sec. F, p. 1). In mid-1985, the economic liberalization continued: Cubans were permitted to buy their homes and sell them rather than turning them back to the state.

But this process of economic liberalization ended quickly in May 1986, when Fidel Castro discovered that a number of Cubans were using the liberalization to make fortunes. The peasant markets gave rise to a new breed of intermediaries and to hoarding, speculation, and price gouging (Black 1988, 374). In addition, according to Castro's own statements (*New York Times*, February 8, 1987), Cuban society seemed to be riddled with corruption. There was considerable resentment of this new prosperity among the "quasi-lumpen" sectors who got rich "without this bearing any relation to the contribution of their labor to the collectivity" (Black 1988, 376). Castro shut down the farmers' markets and halted the private ownership that had produced a construction boom. Confronting a steep economic downturn, which has severely reduced foreign exchange earnings, he appears to have turned back to the values of the 1960s without actually reinstituting moral incentives per se: "His revolution, now in its 28th year, was being deformed he said. Cuban Communists were behaving like 'capitalists in disguise.' A new wealthy class was developing in a country where classes had been eradicated" (Black 1988, 376).

This abrupt policy reversal highlights three important features of the Cuban state—(i) centralized political power; (ii) emphasis on ideology and distribution rather than growth; and (iii) problems of not having material incentives. (i) Despite the considerable decentralization of economic decisionmaking in the 1970s, Castro's political power is still dominant, particularly in setting the moral and political agenda. (ii) Although there are economic efficiency implications of the new moralistic policy—especially since government spending has been cut back sharply—the overriding considerations are ideological and distributional, two features of Cuban policy that have always entered into economic decisionmaking with as much weight as that of economic growth. In this case, it would have been difficult for the state to move to an austerity policy without simultaneously eliminating the possibility of some Cubans making large incomes. In an important sense, from a political and ideological standpoint, the necessary "efficiency" cutbacks of government spending required what from a purely materialistic standpoint might be considered an "inefficient" move to cut back private production. The Cuban state, and especially the dominant force in that state, Fidel Castro, regards this egalitarianism as the fundamental morality of revolutionary Cuban society. Castro now derides the technocrats of the 1970s as "tribal witch doctors," who had created nothing but "impotence, a parody of socialism" (Black 1988,74). (iii) Even after thirty years of revolutionary socialization, the rewards of socialist behavior (in contrast to the rewards of individual materialism) are not evident enough to produce such behavior without a heavy dose of state-led and -enforced morality. Worse, it appears that the revolutionary principles of self-sacrifice and communal effort are visibly eroding: "At a Havana party meeting last December, Fidel singled out one electronics factory where, 'out of 1,900 men, only one volunteered

TABLE 6–1
Cuba: Economic Performance, 1958–1985 ('000,000 of pesos and dollars)

Year	Global Social Product (GSP) (pesos)	Gross Material Product (GMP) (pesos)[a]	Nonmaterial Spending (pesos)[b]	GDP (pesos)[c]	GDP/cap. (U.S. $)[d]
1958	n.a.	3,480	678	4,158	866
1959	n.a.	3,628	737	4,365	891
1960	n.a.	3,658	742	4,427	887
1961	n.a.	3,787	819	4,606	909
1962	6,082	3,698	843	4,541	882
1963	6,013	3,737	880	4,617	877
1964	6,455	4,075	982	5,057	936
1965	6,771	4,138	967	5,105	921
1966	6,709	3,986	1,020	5,006	883
1967	7,212	4,083	1,032	5,115	885
1968	7,331	4,377	1,058	5,435	924
1969	7,236	4,181	1,107	5,288	884
1970	8,356	4,204	1,060	5,264	867
1971	8,936	4,127	1,099	5,226	847
1972	10,349	4,405	1,261	5,666	901
1973	11,910	4,902	1,490	6,392	996
1974	13,424	5,241	1,708	6,949	1,065
1975	14,063	5,708	1,967	7,675	1,158
1976	14,458	5,959	2,355	8,314	1,236
1977	14,772	6,409	2,644	9,053	1,329
1978	16,458	6,844	2,760	9,604	1,395
1979	16,987	6,988	2,834	9,822	1,417
1980	17,606	7,179	2,874	0,053	1,455
1981	22,172	8,328	2,949	11,277	1,620
1982	23,113	8,653	3,065	11,718	1,676
1983	24,337	9,077	3,012	12,089	1,712

TABLE 6–1 (*Continued*)

Year	Global Social Product (GSP) (pesos)	Gross Material Product (GMP) (pesos)[a]	Nonmaterial Spending (pesos)[b]	GDP (pesos)[c]	GDP/cap. (U.S. $)[d]
1984	26,053	9,730	n.a.	12,742	1,787
1985	26,904	10,178	n.a.	13,190	1,830

Sources: Global Social Product, 1958–1974: Brundenius 1984, tab. 2.1 (1962–1966 figures are in constant 1965 prices; all others are in current prices. Global Social Product, 1975–1985: *Anuario Estadístico de Cuba 1985*, tab. III.1. Gross Material Product, Nonmaterial Spending, GDP, and GDP/capita, 1958–1981: Brundenius 1984, tab. 2.7 (all in 1965 prices).

[a] Values for 1981 through 1985 were estimated by multiplying by the growth rate of GSP in real terms (1981 prices), from *Anuario Estadístico de Cuba 1985*, tab. III.1—this was 16%, 3.9%, 4.9%, 7.2%, and 4.6% in 1981, 1982, 1983, 1984, and 1985, respectively.

[b] Values for 1982 and 1983 were estimated by multiplying 1981 figure by the growth rate of educational spending from UNESCO, *Statistical Yearbook 1986*, tab. 4.1.

[c] Values for 1984 and 1985 assume that NMS was constant in 1984 and 1985.

[d] Equivalent to U.S. dollars in 1980 (= 0.71 pesos).

to cut cane in the sugar harvest. . . . Voluntary work had languished, it had become something of a pastime, a formality' " (Black 1988, 76).

As regards the trade-off between income distribution and growth, Brundenius makes the case that income distribution became somewhat more equal over the whole period between 1962 and 1978, and even between 1973 and 1978, when the growth rate was high. Thus, even with material incentives, income distribution did not become more unequal, in large part because education was equalized and because lower wages were allowed to rise somewhat more rapidly than higher wages in the 1970s (Brundenius 1984, ch. 5). This means that the low 4:1 wage ratio between managers/physicians/high-level professionals and unskilled workers still obtains. It is important to add that this equalization of income distribution emerged from an ideological commitment to revolutionary change, not only in economic terms but in racial, cultural, and sexual terms. As the white upper class left for the United States after 1959, mulattoes and blacks occupied many of the vacant power positions. The enormous growth of women in the labor force brought many of them into higher-paid and more prestigious occupations. New social differences have emerged but not nearly to the degree as in Eastern Europe. Education is important in determining status and relative salary, but income and consumption differences are small. The emphasis on economic equality has therefore had a great impact on reducing racial and sexual divisions in Cuban society (Stromquist 1984).

In sum, the Cuban leadership abandoned moral incentives and reliance on voluntary labor in the early 1970s to increase capital accumulation and economic growth, but did not abandon its ideological stance regarding equality and the ideological foundations of a society that should be built on socialist consciousness. The economic growth strategy was successful. Brundenius's estimates suggest that Cuba's GDP per capita almost doubled between 1971 and 1981. More recent statistics indicate that the reasonably rapid rate of growth continued until 1985 (see Table 6–1), although the fall in oil prices (Cuba processes and exports a significant amount of Soviet oil) and sugar prices have caused a major downturn in 1986 (*New York Times*, February 8, 1987, sec. F, p. 1). Industrial growth has far outpaced agricultural growth in the 1970s, but even agriculture has more than kept pace with population growth since 1971 (Brundenius 1984, tab. 3.10). No doubt, Soviet aid has helped produce this increase in production and consumption, but so has mechanization of sugar cane harvesting and sound economic investment. All in all, Cuba's economic performance in the last decade and a half has probably been the best in Latin America.

A fourth feature of the revolution has been its enormous success in reducing unemployment drastically during a period of slow growth, and then mechanizing agriculture, quadrupling the number of women in the labor force, and gradually shifting labor from agriculture to industry, all while keeping the economy at reasonably full employment.

Although unemployment data is sparse, the new state was apparently able to reduce the unemployment rate from 13.6 percent in 1959 to 1.3 percent in 1970 (Brundenius 1984, 127). In part this was achieved by keeping labor force growth lower than population growth, probably by bringing large numbers of Cubans into full-time schooling and into the army. In addition, women did not enter the labor force in the large numbers that they did in the 1970s (women were about 14 percent of the labor force in 1960 and remained at only 18 percent in 1970 [Brundenius 1984, tab. A1.3]). Unemployment grew in the 1970s to about 5 percent, almost entirely in the female labor force, which increased rapidly as child care and more consumer goods became available (Brundenius 1984, tabs. A1.4 and A1.5). Overall employment grew by more than 2.3 percent annually in the 1970s, so that by 1979, 33.3 percent of the total Cuban population were employed, up from 28 percent in 1960.

The remarkable aspect of Cuban development in the 1960s is that the low-growth economy was, in effect, faced by labor shortages. Through its full employment policy and the vast commitment to educational expansion, the state encountered difficulties in finding enough Cubans to cut cane during the harvest and to expand industrial production.[6] At the

---

[6] Nevertheless, in April 1971, there were approximately 300,000 school-age (4 to 16 years

same time, many Cubans were employed in low-productivity work, and the labor force tended to be rigidly immobile. This situation changed drastically in the 1970s, as large numbers of young women, armed with primary and secondary school degrees, entered the labor force. Later in the decade, the first effects of the baby boom of the early sixties began being felt; this increase in the labor force combined with Cuba's achievements in mechanizing sugar harvesting in the 1970s eliminated a drastic shortage of cane cutters that had developed early in the postrevolutionary period.

The fifth relevant feature of Cuban development in this period is the conflict with the United States and the flight of emigrants from Cuba to the U.S. The Bay of Pigs invasion in April 1961, and the continuing sabotage during the 1960s, pushed Cuba to build a large (and expensive) military, which drained resources from other investments. Sabotage by Cuban exiles supported by the CIA definitely disrupted Cuban economic development during that decade. In addition, the U.S. trade embargo, in place since 1961, forced Cuba to make severe adjustments to changes in her normal trade pattern, particularly since most of the machines and equipment in Cuban factories and on farms had been made in the United States.

U.S. hostility also led to its definition of Cuban immigrants as political refugees, which meant that the United States was willing to accept Cubans in numbers not affected by normal visa requirements. This stimulated the flight of the hard-hit middle and upper classes to the U.S. Since a high proportion of the emigrants were university educated, this immigration took its toll of the technically capable, even though many of the emigrants were lawyers, trained to serve the intermediary service and commercial sectors in the pre-Revolutionary economy (Fagen 1964, 391–92; Jolly 1971, 216).

These features of the Cuban state and its economic development policies suggest that Cuban state decisionmaking processes have always been highly centralized in a small group of people around the person of Fidel Castro. The major change in these processes came in the early 1970s when serious economic errors forced Castro and that group to become more sensitive to political and social demands as transmitted through the

---

old) young people who neither studied nor worked. This figure was equivalent to only 12 percent of the student population, but the percentage increased with age: 23 percent among those 14 years old, 44 percent of the 15-year-olds, and 60 percent of the 16-year-olds (Mesa-Lago 1974, 93). To combat this problem, a law was passed in 1971 against loafing, which made it a crime to be neither studying or working. About 100,000 teenage dropouts were drafted into the military over the next two years. For the rest, compulsory education was extended beyond the sixth grade, requiring dropouts to attend workshop schools which combined work and study (Leiner 1975, 70).

mass organizations and other political structures. Indeed, they handed over local, day-to-day decisionmaking to the Cuban Communist party, the Committees for the Defense of the Revolution, Poder Popular, and plant and farm managers. To that extent, decisionmaking power became decentralized. But political and ideological decisions, as well as decisions determining the general course of Cuban economic policy, although more influenced by the Party, the mass organizations, and Poder Popular after the early 1970s, remained in the hands of the few at the top.

This raises important questions about the relationship between decentralization and democracy in transition societies. Those who concentrate on free markets as the basis of individual freedom and democracy would argue that the existence of such markets are the sine qua non of a democratic state. But in transition societies, where the link between individual economic power and state power has been broken, free markets can exist, and individuals can accumulate capital without having much or even any access to political power. Excessive capital accumulation in such markets can even result in a state reaction that destroys markets, as the recent policy reversal in Cuba suggests. Increasing economic power in the hands of individuals confronts the inherently anticapitalist ideology of the state.

With the separation of individual (and capitalist class) economic power from state power, the meaning of democracy changes. For one thing, the distribution of income and wealth is more equal than in most capitalist societies. From Rousseau's or Jefferson's point of view, this has an important impact on the possibilities for political democracy, since greater equality in civil society makes it more likely that the state will govern in the name of the general will rather than for particular economic interests. Yet, in transition societies, the argument that this equalization alone is equivalent to democratization is incorrect, as the Cuban case makes very clear. The equalization of income and wealth in Cuba in the 1960s and 1970s did not make Cuba more politically democratic in terms of the development of institutions that formalize dissent, even within the ideological framework of the revolution. The decentralization of decisionmaking in the 1970s did increase democratic possibilities in that it increased participation in local economic decisions and indirectly brought opinions to the ears of higher-ups. And in the sense that the Cuban Communist party has a broader membership than that of most vanguard parties, the local decisionmaking process is more open than in Eastern Europe or China. But there is little doubt that mechanisms for political sanctions of leaders and their decisions, which are crucial to a democratic state, simply do not exist in Cuban political society. Neither does the possibility exist for political players to criticize decisions and still stay in the game. The key political, social, and economic decisions are made by a small group, un-sanctionable by the people themselves. Policy discussions in that group are closed and not subject to public scrutiny. This group, it is true, is widely supported because it is willing to admit errors and change policy. It has also been very successful in its transformation of Cuban society and in delivering the basic necessities to all Cubans. Nevertheless, it does not allow a competitive agenda to be openly discussed through a competitive political process—not even an agenda within the fundamental ideology of the present leadership:

> [I]t would be unjust to reproach Fidel for lacking the capacity for self-criticism; he is, as Cubans often say with irony, the revolution's only dissident and its only investigative reporter. He has accepted responsibility for the planning failures of the 1970's and the "hustlerish mentality" bred by the market reforms in the early 1980s. But self-criticism goes only so far. Then as now, no one beyond a narrow circle of trusted advisors was willing, or able, to question the wisdom of policies before they were adopted. Acclaim still too often replaces debate, and "dialogue with the crowd is not the best form of democracy," as Rene Dumont, an early advisor to Fidel, put it back in 1963. (Black 1988, 77)

EDUCATIONAL EXPANSION AND REFORM IN THE REVOLUTIONARY PERIOD

It is in this context that educational reform took place after the revolution. Whereas before 1959 the educational program was stagnant, serving to maintain a well-defined class structure and providing only a relatively small percentage of Cubans with access to the dynamic, foreign-dominated sector, the revolution's educational reform was geared to develop all Cubans into a skilled labor force and to create a generalized socialist consciousness. Education and educational change in revolutionary Cuba became a symbol of the revolution itself; mass education became a means to mass economic participation and mobilization. Both of these were the very essence of the revolution and were intimately connected to the educational reform. Whereas before 1959 the schools had remained unaltered for a generation, the revolution made the educational system into an institution of constant change and experimentation.

For our purposes of analyzing educational reforms, the chronology of state policies is important, especially the period 1959–1960 (the economic and social reform period), which coincided with a simple expansion of formal schooling (liberal reform); the period 1961–1963, in which the Cuban leadership attempted to turn away from sugar production and toward Stalinist-type industrialization, but which was also a period of mass mobilization, coinciding with the literacy campaign and rapid expansion of rural and adult education; the 1964–1970 period of first partial and then total Guevarist economic policy, characterized by moral incentives and personalized (under Fidel Castro) direction of economic and social change, coinciding with the unification of schooling and work and the development of secondary education "to the countryside" and "in the countryside"; and finally the period from 1970 to the present, a period of emphasis on efficiency and economic growth, the reconstitution of the Cuban state as a more traditional state bureaucracy run by the vanguard party (the Communist party was officially recognized as the organizational base of the state in 1975), coinciding with improving the "quality" of youth education at all levels, increasing university education, specialized, elite vocational education at the secondary level, and a gradual slowdown in the emphasis on basic secondary schools in the countryside. Educational changes are therefore closely related to much broader changes in state policies.

Among the most important specific aspects of educational change beginning in 1960 was a massive program of adult education, including (1) a nine-month, all-encompassing literacy campaign; and (2) a rapid move to meet basic educational needs in school, which meant a shift in emphasis in education from urban children to rural children and adults, from universities to primary and secondary schooling, and from academic to vocational training. Important shifts in curriculum also occurred, with increased focus on the school as a place where students learn to work collectively and get early preparation in vocational skills. For the higher educated, this meant part-time employment while attending university; for primary and secondary pupils, it meant that manual work was an integral part of the school curriculum. By the late 1960s, however, the quality of intellectual work also became an issue, and the curriculum was reformed to increase the technical level achieved by all schoolchildren.

Such changes required changes in the form of schooling as well as in its substance. Vocational training required workshops, so factories were built as part of the schools or schools were built next to factories. Boarding schools increase the time a student spends in the learning and socializing environment, so young people were moved from urban areas into rural boarding schools.

Providing schooling for one-third of the population and providing much of it in the form of a total environment (boarding) or in terms of special vocational training is expensive. It demands massive financial and human resources. The 1961 literacy campaign alone, for example, involved closing schools for 9 months and maintaining 250,000 teachers and university students in the countryside. Masses of new teachers had to be trained, not only in the subject matter to be taught but in facing the particularly difficult conditions of the rural areas where most were sent.

Special teacher training schools were established. This was all very expensive: During the 1960s, Cuba devoted about 4.2 percent of its national product to education. In the 1970s, this climbed to 7 percent (in 1979), almost twice the average 4 percent that UNESCO set as a goal for developing countries. This focus on mass education, the redistribution of educational spending from the urban to the rural population, and the improvement of the general level of human potential, not only through increased education, but through improved health care and the reduction of psychological stress through guaranteed income and work, may have conflicted, at least in the short and medium run, with the goal of an improved level of individual consumption.

In Cuba, because of its proximity to the United States and the presence of a politically active exile Cuban community, the slow economic growth of the 1960s and the resultant food and housing shortages had a particularly high political price: Cuba was forced to defend the revolution against critiques of its economic "failures." The ideological successes of the educational system, both in raising Cubans' view of their own capabilities and in raising their revolutionary consciousness, were confronted by the ideological costs of long food lines, poor housing, and lack of those consumer durables associated with U.S. capitalist culture.

These costs of concentrating more on building socialist consciousness and a classless society through mass, production-oriented education and moral incentives and less on accumulating capital had their impact on education. Ultimately, the world capitalist consumption culture *and* Soviet concepts of socialist capital accumulation (material incentives, decentralized and accountable decisionmaking, socialist pricing, and industrialization) forced Cuba to move gradually away from a policy of having all secondary students attend expensive boarding schools in the countryside and toward a more "normal" emphasis on developing skills in cheaper urban day schools for students who lived in urban areas. Furthermore, much more emphasis was placed on university education, beginning in the early 1970s.

Educational expansion in Cuba was crucial to rationalizing and legitimizing a fundamental change already taking place in the economic and social structure. Cuban educational reforms and expansion corresponded to new relations in production under Cuba's brand of revolutionary socialism. Fundamental to these new relations is an ideology of equality among all members of Cuban society. Schooling even before the revolution was linked to equality in the sense that more schooling meant greater access to all institutions in the society, as well as more income. With the revolution, the expansion of education was an expression of a new democratization of Cuban society, where democracy was defined very differently than in capitalist societies: Rather than focusing on individual (or even mass) political rights, the Cuban leadership viewed democratization primarily in terms of economic equality—that is, in terms of the masses' access to the society's resources, and the relatively much more equal distribution of those resources. Such an interpretation obviously rationalizes the lack of political opposition and individual political rights, with the potential costs this implies for greater voluntary participation, identification with the state, and legitimacy of the state's social and economic policies.

At the same time, Cuban schools, along with other, political institutions, are responsible for developing a particular social consciousness that corresponds to a socialist ideal, an ideal derived from discussions and struggles in the Cuban political hierarchy. This ideal also reflected in part previous discussions and failures in the revolutionary process. Thus, expanded schooling was and continues to be a response to demands from below for greater equality (an ideal inherited from the prerevolutionary era) and also attempts to develop new ideals and new relationships in Cuban society, reflecting the norms and values of a political elite.

The major Cuban educational reforms fall into four categories—adult education, expansion of the formal school system, development of skilled rural labor and social consciousness, and, later, focus on technical proficiency and higher education. First, we show that the immediate ideological and legitimation needs of the revolution (particularly the redefinition of the nation as a revolutionary nation) required mass mobilization of the total population and the incorporation of that population into the labor force and a new political culture. The fact that the leadership of the 26th of July movement decided to mobilize the Cuban poor characterized the reforms of 1959–1961 as revolutionary rather than just reformist. Much of the mobilization was achieved through extensive adult education programs. The adult education programs promoted under the revolution were neither avocational courses for interested hobbyists, nor continuation courses for an ambitious few; rather they were part of the leadership's project for incorporating everyone into the revolutionary definition of the new Cuban nation. Second, the new government expanded the formal school system, emphasizing, almost from the beginning, primary and secondary education and especially rural school expansion. Third, the nature of formal schools was changed, incorporating a socialist view of work and adapting the schools to the changing needs of the Cuban economy. The problem of developing a skilled rural labor force and creating a new social consciousness became key factors affecting school reform in the 1960s and early 1970s. Fourth, the pressure for capital accumulation ultimately shifted emphasis in the economy toward greater efficiency, and with that shift, school expansion became more traditional in the mid-1970s, focusing on higher education and raising students' technical proficiency.

In societies in radical transition from one economic system to another, education can act to condition people into the new system. Therefore, the schooling process intends to develop new attitudes and values to contribute to the development of a new system of production rather than the reproduction of an existing system. In a radically changing society, institutions outside the production system, such as the schools, apparently are called upon to transmit these new attitudes and values toward the process of radical change itself. In Cuba, the formal school system, including schools for workers and peasants, was reorganized to carry the day-to-day responsibilities for changing values in this manner.

The radical reforms in the Cuban educational system corresponded to the transformation of the country's economic and social structure, a logical and necessary means of carrying out the revolution's objectives of mobilization and incorporation. Once the initial phase of this transformation was completed, further educational reforms corresponded to changes in labor force needs and changes in the Cuban leadership's view of how to increase productivity within a socialist economic and social framework. After the mid-1960s, the productivity problem was seen (in the long term) as a problem of both skills and consciousness. Gradually, moral incentives were replaced by more direct incentives (for the most part, collective ones, but also some individual ones) designed to improve efficiency in the economy and the educational system. Productivity had to be increased because of labor shortages, and socialization into collective consciousness just was not working well enough to do the job. Cuban planners shifted not only to material incentives but to a strategy of steadily increasing physical capital per worker and focusing education on developing worker skills needed to work that capital. These later changes reflected the various attempts to solve the economic growth problem within the constraints of the egalitarian and mass mobilization goals set by the revolution. The Cuban government continuously adapted the educational system to fit its strategies for increasing output per capita and making the transition economy viable.

At the same time, the underlying earlier revolutionary theme that education was a right and thus must be available to everyone also continued as a foundation of educational policy. This democratization of Cuban society—in large part, through the expansion of social services—was in itself an important legitimation of the socialist state and an ever-growing accomplishment of revolutionary Cuba that set it apart from other, capitalist Latin American countries. But it meant that education had to keep expanding at a rapid rate in order for the state to fulfill its democratization mandate to the Cuban people.

EDUCATIONAL REFORMS UNDER THE REVOLUTION

The principal educational reforms in postrevolutionary Cuba revolved around mobilizing the entire Cuban population into productive activities and transforming the ideological base through which these productive activities functioned. At the same time, reforms also responded to the need for more highly skilled labor in both rural and urban areas for economic growth and the development of particular skills as defined by the overall shift in Cuban economic policy toward technical self-sufficiency and particular shifts in policy as described above.

Literacy Campaign

In 1961, designated by Fidel Castro as the "Year of Education," the whole population was mobilized over a nine-month period into a teaching force to eradicate illiteracy on the island. More than 250,000 men and women and schoolboys and schoolgirls were transported all over the island and supplied with 3 million books and more than 100,000 paraffin lamps. At the beginning of the year, the official illiteracy rate was 21 percent; by December, the government claimed that it was 3.9 percent, the lowest in Latin America (Jolly 1964, 192).

The cost of the campaign was high: "When the costs, both direct and indirect, of organizing, training, and supplying, and at times, paying those who participated in the campaign are measured against the tangible results, it is easy to conclude that the campaign was far less than the smashing success the revolutionaries claimed" (Fagen 1969, 54). But Fagen goes on to argue that although the campaign was not an "overwhelming and unquestionable triumph from a scholastic point of view," this is not the principal criterion on which to evaluate it because the campaign was intended to mobilize and to change Cuban political culture. In those terms it was "seminally important in the evolution of the institutional and political culture of the revolution . . . even those who were most cynical about the pedagogical achievements of the campaign would probably admit that the widespread cultural and psychological barriers inhibiting adult education in Cuba were broken in 1961, even if functional literacy were not achieved for very many of the so-called new literates" (Fagen 1969, 55). The literacy campaign not only brought the revolution to the most physically isolated members of Cuban society but also brought the more urban, more educated groups (particularly youth) into contact with the rural poor and illiterate. The campaign was therefore a means to connect elements in Cuban society that had been successfully separated by conditioned capitalist development. Bringing urban youth to the countryside through the educational system became a dominant theme in education from 1961 on, and the breakdown of barriers between urban and rural areas (both in production/distribution and values) has been an integral part of the Cuban development process.

Adult Education

With the successful completion of the literacy campaign, attention was turned to those adults who had just been taught to read and write, as well as those who had not completed primary school. Several kinds of adult education were developed, and all were concerned with raising adults' cognitive skills and incorporating them into the new ideology. Formal education classes began in early 1962 for adults 14 years old and older who had become literate during the campaign and for those who had never finished primary school. In addition, there were special worker-peasant improvement classes for adults who had completed three or more years of primary school but not the sixth. Often preuniversity and university students taught in these classes to earn money for their own studies.

Of the approximately 450,000 adults enrolled in these continuation courses in 1962 (see Table 6–2), about half were new literates who had graduated during the recent literacy campaign (Jolly 1964, 211). After very high enrollment in the mid-1960s, the number of students in worker-peasant education began to drop, as would be expected—many adults became literate through basic education; about 350,000 graduated from the sixth grade by 1967; and the low-schooled adult population grew progressively older, slowly moving out of the labor force.

Two new types of adult education began to develop in the late 1960s as part of this same trend: lower secondary school for adults, and the worker-peasant faculties to prepare adults for entering university. The faculties are crash university preparatory courses and are open to members of trade unions, armed forces, those in the ministry of education, and members of mass organizations. The time schedule of the faculties is coordinated with work shifts, and classes are usually held at the place of work. The experience of these courses led Castro to predict, "In the future, practically every plant, agricultural zone, hospital, and school will become a university" (Castro, in Read 1975, 217). By 1976/77 (the peak year) about 111,000 people were enrolled in the faculties, and by 1978/79, 12,000 were graduating annually.

It could be argued that if the economic growth rate had not been so high in 1959–1960 and if the Cuban leaders realized in 1961 the economic difficulties they would face by 1962 and 1963, they might not have invested so much effort and resources in the literacy campaign and adult education programs. But the complete commitment of the revolutionary

TABLE 6–2
Cuba: Educational Enrollment by Level of Schooling, 1958–1986 ('000)

Year	Basic Primary[a]	Secondary	Pre-University	Other Secondary[b]	University	Adult
1958	6,257	263	372	25.4	256	—
1962	12,073	1,076	155	43.7	173	4,684
1965	12,422	1,252	241	112.0	262	5,742
1970	15,304	1,712	155	97.6	351	3,166
1972	18,527	2,004	220	n.a.	487	2,787
1975	17,958	3,826	377	262.7	847	5,946
1980	14,685	6,776	1,597	375.4	1,517	2,770
1982	13,631	6,102	1,642	413.9	1,734	3,929
1986	1,001.0	622.5	178.2	387.5	256.6	173.3

Source: *Anuario Estadístico de Cuba 1986*, tab. XIII.8. (1962 and 1972 are taken from Carnoy and Werthein 1980).

[a] Does not include preprimary education, except in 1962 and 1972.

[b] Includes teacher training, postprimary and postbasic secondary technical/professional education, and postprimary skilled worker education.

government to a strategy of using education (in all its forms) to create a new concept of the people-nation to which all workers and peasants would belong (and feel that they belonged) made the literacy campaign and adult education logical political necessities at the time they were implemented.

Formal School Expansion

Before and after the literacy campaign, there was a very rapid expansion of formal schooling, for both adults and youth, especially at the primary level. In 1958/59 there were about 7,500 primary schools, with an enrollment of 717,000 pupils. In the first year of the revolution, this figure had increased by more than 40 percent, to over 1 million pupils enrolled, with the greatest increase in rural primary schools. Rural primary enrollment continued to grow rapidly from 1959 to 1962, at about 7 percent annually, but then the growth tapered off, increasing again after 1967. By 1974/75, there were almost 13,000 rural primary schools and 2,800 urban ones, with a total of 1.8 million pupils enrolled. Enrollment stayed approximately level until the year 1976/77 and then began to decline (1.55

million in 1980/81 and 1.08 million in 1985/86). Less than twenty years after the revolution, essentially every child in Cuba was graduating from primary school, whereas in 1956/57, only 50 percent were enrolled.

Secondary school enrollment also increased rapidly, but this growth slowed down in the late 1960s to about 5 percent yearly. Almost all the growth was at the basic secondary level (seventh through ninth grades). From 1971/72 on, however, the growth of enrollment at this and the preuniversity levels was very rapid, from 186,000 pupils at the basic secondary level in 1971/72 to 690,000 in 1979/80 (an 18 percent annual increase) and from 16,000 to 135,000 at the preuniversity level (a 30 percent annual increase). By 1980/81 172,000 pupils were graduating from basic secondary school, and 33,000 were graduating from the preuniversity level. From 1980 through 1985, the number of pupils graduating from basic secondary school remained constant despite declining enrollment, suggesting that the attrition rate was declining. In the mid-1980s, preuniversity schools were graduating more than 42,000 youth.

The figures in Table 6–2 and Table 6–3 indicate that Cuban education expanded from the bottom up—first primary education, then lower secondary education, then preuniversity education, and finally university education, which grew slowly until the early 1970s and then exploded

TABLE 6–3
Cuba: Distribution of Population and Labor Force by Level of Schooling Completed, 1953, 1979, and 1986 (percent)

Level of Schooling Completed	Population over Age 14		Labor Force			
			1979		1986[a]	
	1953	1979	Male	Female	Male	Female
Less than primary	74.6	34.7	31.9	19.1	—	—
Primary	19.4	23.9	24.7	20.2	26.5	18.5
Basic secondary	2.4	22.7	25.7	29.4	54.2	52.4
Preuniversity	2.2	15.4	13.7	25.6	12.0	17.5
University	1.4	3.3	4.0	5.7	7.4	11.5

Sources: 1953 and 1979: Brundenius 1984, tab. A1.7. 1984: Anuario Estadístico de Cuba 1986, tab. IV.16.

[a] The 1986 data are not strictly comparable with those for 1979 except at the university level. Since we did not include any of the "technical and professional" category listed in the Anuario in the preuniversity level, we underestimate that level and overestimate the basic secondary one. Also, it is not clear from the Anuario whether those in the primary and basic secondary categories have actually finished those levels. But the 1984 figures do suggest a continued upward trend in the amount of education in the labor force.

from an enrollment of only 49,000 in 1972/73 to 257,000 in 1986/87. The relatively large investment in lower levels of schooling reflects the mass-base approach of the government's educational program in the early years of the revolution, which included the use of education as a means to fulfill the revolution's goals of equalizing income and services. Despite the tremendous effort devoted to school expansion and teacher training to fill the new schools, school expansion ran into difficulties in the late 1960s: There was a recognized teacher shortage at the secondary level; and partly as a result of the low qualifications of many rural primary school teachers and the shortage in the secondary schools, dropouts became a serious problem.

Educational spending as a percentage of GDP increased rapidly in the 1970s, that is, as Cuban material growth increased, social—including educational—spending increased even more rapidly. It was during this period that massive increases in secondary and higher enrollment took place. In the 1980s, economic growth continued, but spending on education slowed down, largely because enrollment growth tailed off, especially at the secondary level. Table 6–4 suggests that spending per student in the twenty-two years between 1961 and 1983 increased more rapidly at the primary than at the secondary level, and that even in the 1980s, spending on primary school pupils has continued to increase only slightly less rapidly than at the secondary level (per pupil). There is little question, however, that in the 1980s, university students have been an increasing focus of budgetary allocations, rising rapidly from 7 to more than 12 percent of the educational budget. Spending per university student has also increased much more rapidly than at lower levels.

Technical Education

As an alternative to the general studies program at the secondary level, students in Cuba may pass from basic secondary education directly into vocational training. In the 1960s, before the universalization of lower secondary school, students could make this choice at the end of primary school. Right after the revolution, there was an initial enrollment increase in industrial and administration schools, but this increase was small compared to what followed, once a skilled labor shortage developed in the economy after 1961. With the commitment to industrialization in 1961–1963, the enrollment in industrial schools increased rapidly, more than tripling the 1959 figure by 1963. Similarly, with the advent of planning and centralized administration of production there was an enormous increase in the number of administration students. But under the emphasis on personal direction of the economy in the late 1960s, the number of economic and administration students (and schools to train them)

TABLE 6–4

Cuba: Educational Spending per Student by Level of Schooling, 1961–1983 (current pesos)

Year	Primary	Basic Secondary	Total Secondary	University
1961	54	n.a.	177	n.a.
1965	69[a]	n.a.	278/318[b]	n.a.
1966	65[c]	n.a.	305[d]	n.a.
1980	210	535	451	576
1982	244	671	565	891
1983	274	660	610	923

Sources: UNESCO, Statistical Yearbook 1970, tab. 219; Statistical Yearbook 1975, tab. 6.1; Statistical Yearbook 1980; tab. 4.1; Statistical Yearbook 1984, tab. 4.1, for educational spending figures. These were divided by the number of students in each category to obtain spending per student.

[a] Expenditures per student were estimated by UNESCO as 65 pesos in 1965 (Yearbook 1970, tab. 2.21).

[b] Expenditures per student were estimated by UNESCO as 294 pesos in 1965 (Yearbook 1970, tab. 2.21). The first figure shown (278 pesos) is estimated from the spending figure shown in Table 2.19 of the 1970 Yearbook, and the second figure (318 pesos) is from the 1975 Yearbook.

[c] Estimated by UNESCO as 66 pesos (Yearbook 1970, tab. 2.21).

[d] Estimated by UNESCO as 295 pesos (Yearbook 1970, tab. 2.21).

declined markedly. Castro noted this decline in his December 1975 speech at the First Communist Party Congress, considering the decline in administrative cadres one of the major errors of the previous decade (Castro 1976, 109).

The technical schools represented only the tip of the iceberg in terms of the technification of all education in the Cuban system. Philip Foster (1965) has argued that all schools in every society represent vocational education but that academic schools prepare students for different vocations than do so-called vocational schools. In postrevolutionary Cuba, the differentiation between academic secondary schools and technical schools continued, but the status differential between them became much smaller than in capitalist society, particularly in the early years of the revolution, when there was little expansion of university education. Indeed, there was tremendous pressure at that time for university students to train to become secondary school teachers, and there was additional pressure by the government on secondary graduates to perform "vocational" tasks as a prerequisite to taking higher education. This was part of the emphasis on decreasing the cultural gap between workers and professionals. In addition to this particular facet of the relationship between education and work, in the post-1962 period, Cuba began to be faced by a labor shortage, and thus people with technical training were essentially guaranteed skilled jobs in industry or agriculture.

Schools to the Countryside

In the context of the pressing need for rural labor and the emphasis on agricultural production, the turn toward moral incentives and the development of socialist consciousness, beginning in 1966, was translated into increased emphasis on collective work rather than individual achievement. Although the concept of "socialist emulation" had been present in the revolution's ideology since 1961, with the advent of moral incentives, school curricula focused increasingly on the relation of schools to work and on teaching young people in schools to behave in a collective, unselfish, and altruistic manner.

The educational reform that combined the need for agricultural labor and the development of the new "socialist man" was "schools to the countryside." The first experiment of moving a school to the countryside took place in 1966. The objectives were to eliminate the differences between city and country, establishing close bonds between the school and daily rural life, to educate the new generation in and for work, and to provide additional labor for the sugar harvest and other agricultural activities. Teachers and students would live and work together in the countryside for approximately seven weeks. During this period, they would be introduced to the mechanics of group organization and self-government based on cooperation and group work. Working side by side with cane cutters and peasants probably contributed to the reduction of class distinctions, especially those rooted in the separation of mental and manual work.[7]

The schools to the countryside reform also met at least part of the need for additional agricultural labor. In the 1972–1973 school year, almost 200,000 students were still involved in part-year production through the program. Students did almost 20 million hours of farm work, representing about 3 million student days. Working on 160,000 hectares of land, they harvested 2.5 million quintals of vegetables and small fruit and 800 million pounds of cane, and sowed 19,000 hectares of land. Mesa-Lago (1974) argues that even though the productivity of these students was much lower than that of the professional cane cutters, their net contri-

---

[7] As Bowles points out, because the "leadership of the camp often goes to those who work well, not to the monitors or to others who excel at intellectual tasks . . . the occasional inversion of the hierarchy of the school's system itself teaches an additional lesson for equality" (Bowles 1972, 296).

bution to output (after the costs of feeding and housing them), was probably positive. Thus, the program was consistent with both the development of collective consciousness and the need to overcome shortages—at least in the short term—of agricultural labor.

Schools to the countryside are still a feature of secondary schooling in Cuba. Students from urban areas continue to go to into rural areas for thirty to forty-five days a year to do agricultural work. By the late 1970s, however, such urban youth work was primarily for consciousness-raising purposes rather than for their contribution to the agricultural plan.

Schools in the Countryside

Despite students' volunteer work in the 1960s, agricultural output rose less than 20 percent between the low year of 1963 and 1969, barely recovering to 1961 levels (see Brundenius 1984, tabs. A2.7 and A2.9), and nonsugar agricultural output fell slightly between 1963 and 1969 (I have used 1969 for this comparison because of the unusual nature of the 10 million-ton sugar goal in 1970). The failure of agricultural growth in the 1960s and the continued need for agricultural productivity increase so that the rest of the Cuban economy could develop brought out the fundamental economic difficulties faced by the Cuban leadership: The almost complete elimination of open unemployment and reliance on moral incentives seemed to have reduced productivity in rural areas. Even before the problems of the unachieved 10 million-ton 1970 sugar harvest, Cuban leaders were beginning to reject the concept of moral incentives as a path to economic development and were looking for other solutions.

In addition, low growth created another dilemma: The rapid increase in schooling—particularly secondary schooling—in the context of low economic growth was becoming difficult to maintain. According to Brundenius's (1984, tab. 2.7) estimates, the sum of educational and health spending hardly rose between 1964 and 1970, remaining at about 20 percent of gross domestic product. The large increase in secondary school students in this period, with relatively few resources to staff the secondary schools adequately, led to teacher shortages. Combined with the loss of days in the countryside, all this also resulted in low academic performance.

Corresponding to the attempt to solve these difficulties, the schools to the countryside began to be deemphasized after 1970 for three reasons: (1) It became clear that the voluntary system of labor in rural areas would not solve production problems; (2) even though the camps seemed to be increasing social consciousness, students were losing an average of 45 days per year working in the countryside, and although they were supposed to be studying at the same time they were working, "by nearly everyone's admission, not much serious study goes on in the work camps or other non-classroom activities" (Bowles 1972, 302);[8] and (3) during the rest of the year, the schools were largely traditional in their mode of operation and their cost.

To solve these difficulties, the schools to the countryside were replaced by the "schools in the countryside." The schools in the countryside were boarding junior high schools (seventh, eighth, ninth, and tenth grades) catering to primarily urban but also rural students and combining work and study in the countryside on a yearround basis. Most important, these schools were seen as a solution to the resource drain that secondary schooling posed to the Cuban social budget. The program was also intended to raise collective consciousness in students through the combination of study and group work. In this sense, the school in the countryside was no different from its predecessors and maintained the underlying ideology of the revolution, attempting to socialize young Cubans into a socialist vision of society. The schools had their own distinct organizational characteristics: Most of the students came from urban areas, boarded at the school, and maintained contact with their families by spending weekends at home. But unlike other schooling concepts, this type of educational institution was built around plans for agricultural production (citrus, coffee, vegetables) and was made part of the agricultural plan. The schools systematically combined work and study during the entire school year. The schools were expected, through this production, to finance themselves by producing goods with as much value as the schools cost to operate. Also, this type of school was organized to train young people who would stay in agricultural careers. Finally, because the students boarded at the schools and were supervised by monitors, academic performance was expected to rise.

In many ways, the schools in the countryside were successful. Academic performance did apparently increase, and dropouts decreased. Although we have no data on test performance, we do know that promotion rates went up rapidly in secondary schools in the early 1970s: 85.6 percent in 1972–1973, compared with 79 percent in 1971–1972 and 66 percent in 1970–1971 (Gallo, et al. 1975, 52). Collective consciousness was probably raised as well (Leiner 1975; Zimbalist 1975).

But the schools did not come close to financing themselves. The estimates of how much the students produced during the twenty hours they

[8] In 1971, delegates representing teachers, educators, scientists, and cultural agencies and institutes participated in the First National Congress on Education and Culture. Among other recommendations, they criticized the "escuelas al campo" on the grounds that the time lost from formal schooling was having negative effects on the academic work of students and that the activities of the program had been poorly integrated into the formal school system.

worked weekly in the fields was revised downward considerably. At the time that the schools in the countryside were first being built, it was estimated that the work of 500 students boarding at the school would essentially repay its current operating costs and even leave some output for paying off the rather high capital costs of building such a school. These estimates proved impossible to achieve. The value of student agricultural output turned out to be as low as one-fifth the original projection (this estimate is derived from my conversations with teachers at schools in the countryside and should not be interpreted as official). Thus, student work while in school failed to solve education's large financial requirements; indeed, schools in the countryside ended up being a rather expensive solution to the secondary education problem.

Although it was intended to have all Cuban lower (basic) secondary students in such schools by the end of the 1970s, less than 450 schools were built, and the highest percentage of secondary students attending was 36 percent in 1976. Thereafter, the percentage declined to 32 percent by 1980. The failure of self-financing, the increased economic growth beginning in 1972 (which made self-financing less of an issue), the solution to the shortage of rural labor through mechanization of sugar harvesting, and the new emphasis on industrial growth, all contributed to a reduced government focus on basic secondary schools in the countryside. Instead, urban secondary school students increasingly tended to stay in urban basic secondary schools as the decade progressed.

Yet the concept of bringing urban students in contact with rural work continues to be an important one in Cuba, and the Cuban leadership has not at all abandoned the fundamental ideology of combining agricultural labor with learning and of developing collective consciousness through the schools. Cuban young people do some kind of work in every level of schooling—this is part and parcel of their educational program. In addition, although the construction of basic secondary schools in the countryside has slowed down, the next level of schooling—preparatory secondary schools—has increasingly gone into the countryside: In 1973, there were only five such schools in the countryside, but by 1984, there were 209, with 113,000 students, or 48 percent of the total at this level (1984 was the high point in the proportion of preuniversity students in such schools).

Vocational Schools

Perhaps the most evident educational manifestation of the shift in policy from building socialist consciousness to focusing on immediate development of the structure of production and capital accumulation are the academically elite secondary schools (seventh to eleventh grade) constructed in various Cuban cities in the early 1970s. These schools, called "vocational schools," address the goals of economic growth and development of higher-level management and technical capability as a primary concern.

Whereas the overall emphasis in Cuba's educational resource allocation has always reflected a strong commitment to equality, and perhaps even the desire to thwart the development of a technocratic elite, the vocational school policy seems to run against that commitment. The revolution has also always stressed rapid scientific and technical advance, and this has also always posed a temptation to give special educational opportunities to especially talented students. The Vento Vocational School had already been created in Havana in 1966–1967. This became the Lenin Vocational School in 1972–1973, one of seven such selective high schools in Cuba, training a total of about 25,000 students.

The Lenin School was the prototype of such schools: It has a capacity of 4,500 students, is very well equipped, and employs highly skilled teachers, focusing mainly on scientific and technical subjects. The selection process for any of the vocational schools is very restrictive, with the Lenin School the most restrictive of all. In 1980, when I visited it, the average grade in the last three years of primary school for those students entering was 97 out of 100. But the average even in the other six schools was over 95 out of 100. Dropouts in the early 1970s were only 2 percent of the cohort (*Granma*, special issue on the Lenin School, February 1974). Not surprisingly, rural students are very underrepresented in the vocational schools, and the children of professionals and government functionaries, overrepresented.[9] To a large extent, the schools guarantee the reproduction of a "new class" of bureaucrats, many of whose parents already occupy top positions in the urban-led state.

As in all of the other countries we studied, there is a fundamental conflict between egalitarianism and the reproduction of an elite through a merit-based school system designed to select the best and the brightest. The underlying organization of Cuban schools is virtually no different than in Europe and the United States. They are highly competitive at an individual level, culminating in the tough requirements to enter the elite vocational schools. The types of students who do well in this system are not very different from those who do well in all Western-type schools. They are also the ones who can master the technological complexities of modern production. Cuba has given in to elitism on the one hand, but attempts to control it through a highly equalized distribution of wages and

---

[9] Even so, these "elite" students do industrial and agricultural work twenty hours per week at the vocational schools as part of their curriculum. The Lenin School, for example, is associated with an electronics factory nearby, which produces radios and computers.

salaries and through the state's (as personalized in Fidel Castro) commitment to collective goals and egalitarian morality, even to the extent of giving up economic growth.

Higher Education

After 1959, the university also became a school of higher technical training, preparing people for specific kinds of work in short supply. It is significant that the egalitarian aims of the revolution were so predominant in its early years that expenditures on university education, which before 1959 catered to upper-class needs for educational legitimation and to middle-class demands for upward mobility, were curtailed relative to the heavy emphasis on primary and lower secondary schooling. In part, this also served a political function. Huteau and Loutrey (1973, 70–72) note that the university was not very radicalized in the 1960s and was basically a hotbed of bourgeois liberalism. University containment served, therefore, to keep it from becoming a focus of opposition to the regime.

Enrollment in higher education declined in 1960–1961 (partly because of the mass mobilizations for the army and the literacy campaign), and did not reach 1958 levels again until 1965. The number of graduates from the universities did not begin to increase rapidly until 1966–1967, but then climbed steeply, especially after 1971. University enrollment more than doubled between 1970 and 1975, and has continued to increase rapidly into the early 1980s, suggesting a dramatic shift in policy (see Table 6–2). Two reasons such an increase was possible were the vastly greater numbers of secondary graduates by the late 1960s, and the greater financial resources available as the economy began to grow rapidly in the early 1970s.

Fundamentally, however, university expansion was part of the shift in economic strategy. The focus of that strategy after 1970 was on centralized, technocratic planning, with decentralized decisionmaking at the factory level—economic growth was based on a greatly increased number of highly trained decisionmakers.

Yet even before this expansion of higher education, the need for technical personnel to carry out the revolution's growth aims had, by the early 1960s, already caused a drastic shift in the enrollment patterns for different university careers. Although university enrollment in 1967 was only slightly higher than that in 1958, the number of engineering graduates had increased sevenfold. The same is true for agricultural science, although both increased even more rapidly in the 1970s. Enrollment in medicine also increased markedly after 1961, as the Cuban government attempted to replace the large number of physicians who had emigrated to the United States and simultaneously create a new breed of physician who would work in rural areas.

Entrance to the university is set by quotas in each given specialty, based on the needs of the economy as determined by the plan. The high school graduate selects and ranks five specialties. In high schools, students are counseled into such career choices through *Circulos de interes* (career interest groups), which focus on a particular university-level professional training course (e.g., medicine, veterinary medicine, agronomy); the students learn about the profession in the interest groups. In addition, each high school prepares a list of students in order of merit. Finally, each student must take an entrance exam at the university of his or her choosing. Those with the best performances are given their first choices. In addition, about 50 percent of the more than 200,000 students at university are workers selected from priority lists drawn up by enterprises, usually in the fields most related to the jobs they perform (Stromquist 1984). In line with the emphasis on manual work as part of the student's schooling experience at the primary and secondary level, the university curriculum has been designed to include student work practice within production enterprises.

THE CONSEQUENCES AND PROBLEMS OF CUBAN EDUCATION

There are certain clear characteristics of and themes in Cuban education after 1959. First, educational reform in Cuba has been marked throughout the revolutionary period by a constancy of ideological practice. This practice is rooted in the revolutionary state ideology, which is based, in turn, on a vision of socialism, socialist society, and human behavior in such a society. It is the Cuban state that has defined that vision and the practices that follow from it. State decisions, in turn, were and continue to be made by a relatively small group of individuals—in the broadest decisions, perhaps only *one* individual, Fidel Castro himself. The different models of how to achieve a high rate of material growth within the context of broad ideological objectives (greater equality, high levels of education and health services, collective consciousness, Third World leadership) appear to be the principal source of conflict in the leadership circle. Policy changed often in the 1960s. There was also a great deal of educational innovation in that period, some of it relying on mass mobilizations and most on directives from the top carried out by the growing corps of teachers and educational administrators.

The difficulty of achieving the state's socialist vision has altered economic strategies over time, but the underlying ideology has not changed. Fidel's goal since the mid-1960s has been a "synthesis, a search for the ever-elusive balance between moral and material incentives to unglue an inefficient economy" (Black 1988, 76). It is this goal and the underlying ideology that has been constantly translated into educational practice in the schools.

From 1961 until today, Cuban education has stressed volunteer work and collective rather than individual identity. Since the early 1960s, students have done physical labor as part of their school curriculum. Many urban students spend some of their school years in a rural boarding school, even though the shortages of agricultural labor that characterized the Cuban economy in the 1960s have now been solved through the mechanization of sugar harvesting. Those who do not board in schools in the countryside work more than a month of the year in schools to the countryside. Students in the elite vocational schools work in factories twenty hours a week. University education also makes work experience a part of the academic curriculum. Even though there has been a shift after 1970 to greater individual competition in schools for higher individual grades (as part of the shift to material incentives), "socialist emulation"—that is, correct collective political behavior—is still very much part and parcel of the Cuban educational experience.

Whether the collective aspect of education sinks in is another matter. It is unclear whether the typical young Cuban, brought up under the revolutionary regime from day care center to school to workplace, is primarily motivated in his or her behavior by collective aims or by the same material and personal goals characteristic of individuals living in capitalist societies. Cubans are definitely interested in buying color television sets and other appliances—there are long waiting lists for these high priced items and they are used to reward high-productivity workers. But there was also significant public reaction against the capitalist behavior of private farmers and small business people in recent years. Cubans may want more material goods, but they also resent those who cheat the system.

Second, Cuban education has been characterized by a rapid and steady expansion, beginning with expansion of adult and primary education, followed by expansion of secondary education and, in the 1970s, by a continued rapid growth of secondary schooling and an exponential growth of university enrollment and graduates. This commitment to and pattern of educational expansion is consistent with (1) the revolutionary leadership's emphasis on improving labor productivity as the basis of economic growth in Cuba; (2) its emphasis on equalizing access to resources among all sectors of the population, especially through increasing access for the rural population; and (3) its reliance on education as the key institution for incorporating the mass of the population into the revolutionary people-nation—this is particularly evident in the expansion of adult education, the universal enrollment of children into elementary and lower secondary school, and the special education programs for the handicapped, the marginal, and juvenile delinquents (for example, the large number of youth in the 1960s who neither worked nor attended school).

The results of the expansion, at least in quantitative terms, are impressive. By 1979, the average level of educational attainment in the population over 14 years old was 7.5 years (compared to 3.6 years in 1953); in the labor force, 8 years; and in the female labor force, 9.2 years, all figures among the highest in Latin America (Brundenius 1984, tab. A1.7, 137). There is also reason to believe that the average academic quality of Cuban education improved significantly after 1970 (see Carnoy and Werthein 1980).

The third characteristic of educational expansion in Cuba is that it is both indirectly and directly tied to economic policies and that these economic policies, at least in the 1960s, were the product of conflicts among a small group of decisionmakers (and hence often did not reflect the reality of Cuban organizational possibilities). The indirect tie is the relationship between the shift to developing "socialist man" as the basis for Cuban economic policy in 1964–1966, the slowdown in economic growth, and the subsequent slowdown in educational expansion. The reliance on education to raise collective consciousness, to mobilize the Cuban population into the revolutionary project, and to equalize access to resources for the most marginal groups in Cuban society made for an extraordinarily rapid growth of spending on education between 1959 and 1964. It is evident in retrospect that collective consciousness was not raised adequately to make moral incentives a viable basis for increased productivity and economic growth. The slower growth that resulted from the Guevarist policy (and probably, in addition, from an "overinvestment" in education during the first years of the 1960s) combined with teacher shortages at the secondary level to slow the increase in spending on education in the second half of the decade. Furthermore, the squeeze on available resources for educational spending caused the leadership to begin looking for new ways to provide secondary education—in particular, the schools in the countryside were designed as a financial and pedagogic alternative to the traditional urban secondary school. Once the shift back to material incentives and the reorganization of economic decisionmaking produced higher economic growth in the 1970s, the squeeze on educational spending was reduced, and secondary school expansion continued at the pace of the early 1960s. Also, by the 1970s, the teacher shortage had been solved. Even so, productivity is still low, and the tendency is not to work very hard.[10]

[10] According to George Black, writing in *The Nation* in 1988, Fidel "gives the impression these days of fighting a frustrating uphill battle against workers who would rather be consumers than *hombres nuevos* . . ." (Black 1988, 76). How, Fidel has asked, was Cuba supposed to achieve economic development "working seven, six, five hours a day?"

The direct effect of the shifts in economic policy are found in two aspects of educational change: (1) The emphasis on socialization and greater equality during the 1960s placed correspondingly more emphasis in education on consciousness-raising, adult incorporation, rural primary schooling, and basic education. Beginning in the late 1960s and early 1970s, the shift in economic policy toward economic growth, more technocratic decisionmaking, and material incentives was matched by a distinct change toward raising academic excellence (increasing test scores and reducing dropout rates) and developing cadres of scientific and technical personnel (the development of the elite technical schools). (2) The shift in economic policies throughout the 1960s and early 1970s (1959–1961, 1962–1963, 1964–1966, 1966–1970, and 1970 onwards) were all matched by distinct changes in the offerings of technical schools—the education most directly tied to the direct demands of the economy. Similarly, but less evidently, the shifts in economic policy were related to university careers, both in the early years of the revolution, when the university shifted toward training students for technical careers, and in the 1970s, when students could no longer choose faculties of study on their own, but had to conform to enrollment patterns planned for higher education.

It was crucial for the Cuban state to increase Cuba's material base at some point. Otherwise, it could not continue to expand public services, including education. Social spending growth slowed down greatly in the late 1960s, largely because material growth had been low for years. Cuba continued to expand education and health care in these years, but, as Table 6–2 suggests, secondary education growth—which should have been more rapid in the late 1960s—could not increase because of lack of material growth. This led to the concept of the schools in the countryside to allow expansion without large budget increases and explains the rapid expansion of the secondary and university level in the early 1970s, when the higher material growth rates beginning at that time increased the base for state social spending.

The question remains whether a somewhat different strategy in the early and mid-1960s that placed less emphasis on rural primary and adult education—both aimed at incorporating rural workers and peasants into the revolutionary project and consistent with the redistributional objectives of the revolutionary leadership—and placed greater weight on urban secondary and university schooling would have resulted in higher material growth rates in the later 1960s. Castro alluded to this possible error in the "overemphasis" on rural primary education in his 1975 speech to the First Communist Party Congress. But other analysts (see Carnoy and Werthein 1980) have concluded that the need to define the revolutionary nation in the 1960s was much more important for consolidating state power than material growth, especially with the threat of U.S. invasion.

The significant ideological emphasis on manual work and collective consciousness appears primarily outside the classroom, in the work activities of students while in school. The classrooms and learning processes in Cuban schools are otherwise no different from those in European education. The academic side of education is also highly competitive, with the coveted entrance into vocational schools based, above all, on individual academic performance, and university entrance also influenced heavily by individual academic "merit" (however, it is also a function of which university and field of study the individual student chooses). At the same time, it is possible for workers to get into university directly from places of production, and the collective, volunteer work experience that is such an important part of a pupil's overall educational experience cannot be discounted in terms of influencing the values and norms with which a young person leaves school. The unanswered question is whether the status associated with higher individual academic performance and the better jobs that follow from individual achievement dominate social motivation and behavior in what Cuban leaders would like to transform into a socialist, collectively oriented society.

Part of the problem in this transformation is, it appears, that although the collective has a strong and positive sense of its revolutionary role in the Third World and its economic and social achievements (for example, that it has stood up to the hostility of its giant neighbor, that it has one of the world's better educational systems, that it has achieved a significant level of economic growth, and that it sends physicians and teachers to many other Third World countries), that same collective gets to participate relatively little in the larger political decisions that affect its present and future. This does not mean that there is no political participation at all. But the serious questioning of policy and bottom-up influence on political leaders is relatively absent, so much so that there is little motivation to exert undue energy in being innovative and highly productive, not only in politics, but in other aspects of daily life. Without such openness in the larger political system, the influence of collective socialization in Cuban schools is necessarily muted, or at least made much less observable. Collective behavior is likely to be political behavior as soon as it gets beyond being cooperative in carrying out volunteer tasks willingly at work or in the neighborhood. Collective consciousness should be expressed through mass organizations, but in order to do that, mass organizations must have genuine political power. Neither does collective consciousness imply continual consensus. We have little idea how school socialization in Cuba affects the expression of dissent, because dissent is not generally expressed openly and institutionally.

It appears that in the forms that this socialization was supposed to have an impact—primarily through economic action—it has not been very successful. This, in turn, led the leadership to shift to other forms of raising economic output, rather than opening up the political system. To some extent the policy was successful: Investment in human capital and more decentralized economic decisionmaking in the 1970s and early 1980s did pay off in higher economic growth until the conditions in international markets turned against Cuba in 1986. But even such growth was achieved under conditions of tremendous inefficiency, according to Castro himself (Black 1988). And in terms of building socialist values and motivation, the ideological cost of the 1970s' mindless technocracy and the 1980s' venture into capitalism was high. Perhaps more than in any other socialist state, Cuba's leadership has held on to its revolutionary socialist ideals in the 1980s. It has used those ideals to bring the population to an extraordinarily high level of education—an education steeped in consciousness-raising. Productive capacity has been raised to much higher levels, and so has productivity. Yet the economy is still inefficient, and workers do not work hard. *How* to develop economically on the basis of a collectively motivated, collectively conscious labor force is still an unanswered question.

CHRONOLOGY OF ECONOMIC CHANGE AND EDUCATIONAL POLICY IN REVOLUTIONARY CUBA

	Goal Priorities	Growth Strategy	Institutional Strategy	Mobilization Strategy	Economic Performance[a]	Educational Policy
1959	Income redistribution (land reform; urban reform; automatic rapid growth)		Business as Usual / Redistributive reforms	Material incentive structure	1959–1960 Growth: exceptionally rapid / Income redistribution: made more equitable / Unemployment: significant reduction	Expansion of formal schooling (liberal reform)
1960	Reduction of dependence on the U.S.		-------- Nationalizations		Dependence: all relations with the U.S. severed	
1961	Growth and structural diversification	1st Growth Strategy	Freewheeling	Some volunteer work	1961–1963 Growth: negative	Literacy campaign

Note: For clarity, the column on economic performance has been divided into discrete time periods. Solid lines indicate pronounced changes in strategy. Dashed lines indicate less pronounced, more gradual changes in goal priorities and strategies.

[a] In terms of growth, income distribution, full employment, and reduced dependence.

		Central Planning Soviet-style		
1962	Instant industrialization	Material incentives; some moral incentives	Income distribution: more equitable Unemployment: further reduced (labor shortage in agriculture; covert unemployment)	Rapid expansion of rural and adult education, technical education
1963	Agricultural diversification	Emulation Voluntary work	Dependence: greatly increased dependence on the USSR	

(*Continued on next page*)

	Goal Priorities	*Growth Strategy*	*Institutional Strategy* (The Great Debate)	*Mobilization Strategy*	*Economic Performance*[a] 1964–mid-1970	*Educational Policy*
1964	Growth without structural diversification	2d Growth Strategy Export-oriented Sugar-centered			Income distribution: more equitable (because of intense rationing); emergence of privileges in late 1960s	Emphasis on expanding rural primary schooling
1965	Reduction of dependence deemphasized	Industry serves the needs of agriculture Massive investment effort		Increased emphasis on moral incentives Political religion	Unemployment: overt unemployment eliminated; covert unemployment remains serious	

1966	The "new man" becomes overriding objective but is also the means to achieve growth	Growth: stagnant in aggregate terms; success in some sectors (nickel, rice, fishing); 1970: success in sugar at expense of nonsugar economy	Schools to the countryside; attempt to develop the "new man" by combining work and school
1967		Dependence: profound dependence on the USSR continues	

(Continued on next page)

ECONOMIC CHANGE AND EDUCATIONAL POLICY IN REVOLUTIONARY CUBA—*Continued*

	Goal Priorities	Growth Strategy	Institutional Strategy	Mobilization Strategy	Economic Performance[a]	Educational Policy
1968			*Revolutionary Offense* High degree of centralization	Deemphasis on material incentives		Lower secondary school for adults; worker-peasant faculties
1969			Administering role for armed forces	Mass mobilization by moral suasion and military methods		

1970 ---------

Deemphasis
on
schools to
the coun-
tryside;
establish-
ment of
schools in
the coun-
tryside

(Continued on next page)

ECONOMIC CHANGE AND EDUCATIONAL POLICY IN REVOLUTIONARY CUBA—*Continued*

	Goal Priorities	Growth Strategy	Institutional Strategy	Mobilization Strategy	Economic Performance[a]	Educational Policy
					Mid-1970–1972	
1971	Growth continues as key objective Reduction of dependence further deemphasized	Modification of 2d Growth Strategy Diversified investment allocation Reduced investment effort	Democratization Some administrative decentralization; minibrigades	Democratization Reduced role for the party Reemphasis on material incentives	Growth: recovery of the nonsugar economy; problems with sugar sector, 1971–1972 Dependence: profound dependence on the USSR continues Income distribution: emphasis on material incentives reduces equality but increases equity of income distribution	Rapid expansion of university level begins Construction of elite secondary vocational schools

Year				
1972	Democratization becomes ultimate as well	High priority to investment in housing	Depersonalization of economic administration	Selective coercion (antiloafing law)	Unemployment: 101,081 loafers go to work (1971); productivity reduces covert unemployment
1973					
1974					Emphasis on raising educational quality

(Continued on next page)

ECONOMIC CHANGE AND EDUCATIONAL POLICY IN REVOLUTIONARY CUBA—*Continued*

	Goal Priorities	Growth Strategy	Institutional Strategy	Mobilization Strategy	Economic Performance[a] 1971–1975	Educational Policy
1975	Growth continues as key objective, with major emphasis on production for export and industries not using imported materials		Continued depersonalization of economic administration Centralized planning with decentralized decisionmaking at factory level	Experiment with local elections (Podor Popular) in province of Matanzas	Approximately 9% growth rate Continued dependence on USSR Direct support of African and Nicaraguan liberation movements Inequalities in income distribution somewhat reduced, but higher-educated get increased benefits, such as access to car	

| 1976 | First Five-Year Plan (1976–1980) Somewhat lower planned growth rate (6% annually); continued diversification and investment; continued mechanization—increased industrialization | Strengthening of Communist party Collective material incentives Elections for local delegates to National Assembly Podor Popular to administer local areas |

(Continued on next page)

ECONOMIC CHANGE AND EDUCATIONAL POLICY IN REVOLUTIONARY CUBA—*Continued*

Goal Priorities	Growth Strategy	Institutional Strategy	Mobilization Strategy	Economic Performance[a] 1975–1980	Educational Policy
1977 Growth key objective		Increased technocracy	More power to the Communist party.	Continued relatively high growth (4.6% annual increase in per capita income) Continued support of Sandinistas and Angolan liberation front Cuba alllows 120,000 Cubans to emigrate to U.S.	Growth of higher secondary schooling in the countryside

1978

1979			Deemphasis of lower secondary schools in the countryside
1980	Small artisan business allowed to operate to alleviate pressure for home repairs and other services		*1980–1985* Continued 5% per capita growth rate Increased agricultural output Increased inequalities in income

(Continued on next page)

	Goal Priorities	Growth Strategy	Institutional Strategy	Mobilization Strategy	Economic Performance[a]	Educational Policy
1981	Growth continues on key objective	Second Five-Year Plan Farmers' markets opened Prices free of government control.		Greater market freedom; profit motive allowed Material incentives strengthened		Emphasis on urban secondary schools
1982						
1983						Continued expansion of higher education

1984	Economic efficiency				
1985	Individuals allowed to buy and sell homes				Universalization of secondary education
1986	Restoration of morality in economic development.	*Third Five-Year Plan* Free markets closed; private ownership ended Austerity measures	Increased centralization of economic decisionmaking	Return to communist principles Appeal to collective goals	*1986–1989* Lower sugar and petroleum prices cause steep economic downturn Underemployment and some unemployment

(*Continued on next page*)

ECONOMIC CHANGE AND EDUCATIONAL POLICY IN REVOLUTIONARY CUBA—Continued

	Goal Priorities	Growth Strategy	Institutional Strategy	Mobilization Strategy	Economic Performance[a]	Educational Policy
1987						
1988						
1989	Anticorruption campaign Rejection of perestroika					

CHAPTER 7

"Modernizing" a Socialist Vision: Education in Tanzania

Joel Samoff

TANZANIA SEEMS TO OFFER a success story of educational reform. In a brief period, a very poor country has introduced institutional changes that reach nearly all its citizens. Primary education is essentially universal. Initial instruction uses a language and draws on experiences and materials that are familiar to everyone. Tanzania and Africa feature prominently in the curriculum at all levels. A national board sets and marks examinations. Tanzania's adult literacy is now among the highest in Africa. Although affluence clearly enhances the likelihood of academic success, poverty does not preclude it.

These accomplishments in turn provide the foundations for other programs. Nutritional and prenatal information can be disseminated much more widely. Agricultural improvement programs can reach remote farmers. Members of cooperatives and unions can monitor their leaders more effectively. Tanzanian citizens evince a pride in their language and their country that derives neither from chauvinistic propaganda nor from xenophobia, but rather—notwithstanding their relative poverty—from a sense of accomplishment and self-confidence. In the two decades since the end of European rule, these are major achievements.

Yet, many of the problems that stimulated the educational reforms of the first quarter-century of Tanzania's independence persist. Although the gap between the most and the least affluent Tanzanian citizens has been narrowed, stratification has not become unimportant. Some people lead more comfortable lives than others, and, more important, their children and children's children are more likely to lead comfortable lives than are the children of today's lower strata. Notwithstanding successive efforts to create and maintain a school system in which individual achievement and merit determine admission and progress, and despite attempts to redress regional imbalances, parents' occupation, income, social status, and class remain highly correlated with school success. While some Tanzanians finish school with a deep sense of national service and community obligation, others continue to regard themselves as a privileged elite, to disdain productive labor, to avoid posts in remote rural areas, and to rely heavily on external models and assistance. Tanzania is now much more integrated into the capitalist world system than it was at independence. The Tanzanian economy struggles to produce enough to feed its citizens and to export to pay for its petroleum and other imports. In recent years, it has been unable to weather significant environmental or market stresses without recourse to external aid. Education intended to lay the foundation for socialist construction seems to have generated only sporadic, partial, and frequently frustrated socialist initiatives.

The primary explanation for this combination of sustained educational reform and halting, perhaps stymied, socialist construction, lies in the complex intersection of external and internal dynamics, and especially in Tanzania's unique mix of socialist vision and peripheral capitalist practice. Development in Tanzania has been characterized as "revolution by education." Tanzania's guiding and widely cited educational policy document, *Education for Self Reliance*, has provided inspiration and guidance in many other countries. Yet in practice Tanzania has followed an inconsistent educational strategy. The simultaneous pursuit of apparently incompatible policies reflects the shifting alliances and vacillating directions in its politics.

Tanzania offers us, therefore, a particularly useful case study for precisely these reasons: The Tanzanian experience suggests both the potential and the limits for nonrevolutionary noncapitalist development and its accompanying educational reform.

Social Transformation: The Contexts

Fundamental social transformation—what we have called earlier organizing the transition—is an extraordinarily complex and difficult process, whose central events are more likely to be characterized by struggle than by planning. There are few comparable experiences elsewhere from which to learn. The transitional process, whatever its forms, must envision a society in which the economy is oriented toward meeting basic human needs (with production decisions guided by mass demand rather than private profit), the patterns of social interaction do not attach wealth, privilege, and status to differences of race, ethnicity, gender, religion, or class, and citizens are active participants in setting goals, implementing policies, and evaluating results. (Fagen, et al. 1986, 10).

In schematic terms, the transition in Tanzania involves (1) reorganizing the economy to make it far less dependent on market forces, which remain largely externally controlled and (2) to find alternatives to market prices for valuing labor; (3) establishing rules for access to social services (and other desired goods) that do not function largely to reproduce existing inequalities; (4) developing patterns of distribution and redistribution oriented toward collective rather than individual consumption; (5) creating participatory politics in which the units of participation are something other than atomized individuals; and (6) fostering incentive and reward structures not dominated by competitive individualism. This transitional process must also (7) be able to meet—in the short term—basic human needs and support a visibly improving standard of living, which requires (8) continually and rapidly increasing production and thus productivity and (9) integrating dispersed and largely disconnected private producers into a coherent national economy, while (10) reducing the political power of the largest of the private producers. Finally, this transition process must also (11) work toward fundamental alterations of social relations within the family, which are necessary both to achieve the goals noted above and to eliminate gender inequalities. For Tanzania, all of this must occur in a setting where the production system is highly dependent on the world economy, the proletariat is undeveloped, and the peasantry remains semiautonomous.

The end of British rule in 1961 created the possibility for the transition.[1] Yet, as in much of Africa, the end of European rule in Tanzania was not in itself a revolution.[2] The Africanization of political power and administrative office was of course important and dramatic. Perhaps less dramatic—at least at the time—but equally or even more important were the maintenance of the basic structure of the Tanzanian economy, the persisting external orientation of production and consumption decisions, and the expanding role of international capital. Nor did the transition from British to local rule foster a prolonged mass mobilization and participation in an active struggle. Indeed, the major anticolonial armed conflict in Tanzania had been waged at the beginning of this century. In the mid-twentieth century, rooted in myriad local grievances and led (though that may overstate the power of national leaders to control the direction of events) by a relatively better educated elite, the nationalist party provided a framework for linking elite discontent with mass resistance and for confronting the British. Although it may not have been clear at the

---

[1] At the creation of the League of Nations, England assumed mandatory responsibility for Tanganyika, a former German colony; that mandate was subsequently converted into a United Nations trusteeship. Hence, for most of this century Tanzania had European administration but not direct colonial rule. In practice, the differences between trusteeship and colonial rule were few (Chidzero 1961; Taylor 1963). For the modern history of Tanzania, see Iliffe 1979; Kaniki 1980; Kimambo and Temu 1969; McCarthy 1982.

[2] For convenience, I use here the current term, Tanzania, to refer both to the contemporary United Republic of Tanzania and to Tanganyika prior to its union with Zanzibar in 1964. For the period since its independence in 1961, I am concerned here with mainland Tanzania. Education in Zanzibar, which has remained a sphere of local authority throughout the union, is less well documented and is most often not included in national educational statistics.

time, both the violence against European institutions and authority and the British harassment of nationalists were relatively mild. Successful negotiators, more than victorious guerrillas, orchestrated the assumption of sovereignty.

Having secured power largely nonviolently, the new leadership envisioned a similar process of broad social transformation whose revolutionary character would be manifested in its spirit and in its consequences, not in the blood spilled to achieve it. The positive response to the nationalist movement throughout the country, the apparently rapid collapse of British control, and the sweeping victories in the national elections of the late 1950s encouraged observers, both within and outside Tanzania, to blend rhetoric and reality. In fact, organizational and institutional capacities were far more limited than they seemed. In the terms employed in this volume, Tanzania was certainly a conditioned state, but it had not yet become a transition state.

Ujamaa

Tanzania's[3] articulated policy orientation is summarized in the term *ujamaa*, a Swahili word literally translated as "familyhood" and generally used to mean "socialism" or "Tanzanian socialism." The ambiguities in that range of reasonable translations mirror the ambiguities in its meanings. Although it is beyond the scope of this discussion to explore fully the complexities of ideology in Tanzania, it is useful to map the terrain of ujamaa.[4]

The imperialist and colonialist incorporation of Tanzania into an expanding world system spawned forces that were ultimately severely constrained by that incorporation process. The nationalist movement that coalesced in the aftermath of World War II, more a broad front than a

---

[3] Note here a persisting terminological problem: to refer to "Tanzania's" experiences is either to assert that those experiences are common to Tanzania's diverse populace or to treat the experiences of one set of Tanzanians as the experiences of the populace as a whole. Students of Africa far too often obscure the importance of the social location of ideas and interests in this way. To the extent that "Tanzania" acts, or is acted upon, it is usually only some of the people who are involved. Yet the expansion of the world capitalist system led to the identification of nation-states as major actors, and thus the global arrangement made the territorially defined entity labeled "Tanzania" an arena for conflict and a focus for action. The global system thus affected what Tanzanians did, or could do, in part by shaping their field of action. It is in this sense that "Tanzania" is used here.

[4] Most authors are primarily descriptive in their discussions of Tanzanian political ideology. Among those who have addressed ujamaa more analytically (from very different perspectives) are Coulson 1979; Mohiddin 1981; Nellis 1972; Pratt 1976; Saul 1979; Shivji 1976; Siddiqui 1984; and Smith 1971. I draw here on Samoff 1981.

party, was dominated by the small, or petty (petite), bourgeoisie.[5] This included both the would-be exporters, importers, factory owners, large farmers—who were restrained by the rules preventing Africans from becoming large-scale capitalists—and the small bourgeoisie proper of artisans, shopkeepers, traders, teachers, and civil servants. It was with this class, which claimed to represent the anticolonial front and thus all Tanzanians, that decolonization was negotiated.[6] What resulted was an independent state ruled by an alliance of classes, increasingly clearly differentiated. The dominant class in that alliance was external: capital based overseas, operating through both transnational corporations and the governments of the major capitalist states. That class was dominant but not omnipotent; it could rule only through an alliance with internal classes. Within Tanzania, where there were not yet industrial or financial capitalists, the immediate struggle within the ruling class alliance was between two intermediary classes, one rooted in commercial enterprise and the other in administration.

In that setting, there were two distinct sources of socialism in Tanzania. One came from a relatively few socialist militants, or perhaps anticapitalist revolutionary democrats (Thomas 1978), both within and outside the small bourgeoisie. They believed that overcoming poverty required a socialist organization of production, and they initiated and supported cooperative production long before ujamaa became an official policy. The second and more visible and politically influential source of attention to socialism stemmed from what has been termed a defensive radicalism (Ake 1976, 1984). A combination of anticolonialism, antiimperialism, nationalism, rejection of the extreme inequalities of the capitalist world, and a preference for planned change found expression as socialism. Although this ideology used Marxist terminology, it was more critical of the bourgeois life-style than supportive of socialist construction. To the extent that there was outlined a socialist program, it emphasized nationalization of major economic institutions, planning, equality of income, improved social services, and democratic participation, with inter-

---

[5] This usage risks several terminological confusions. Many commentators have described the leaders of African anticolonial movements as "middle class." They were "middle" only because colonial rule prevented them from being "upper"; in fact, they constituted the uppermost stratum of Africans. In addition to the misleading labeling, that characterization makes "class" a relatively static description of stratification, rather than a dynamic construct for investigating the sources of change in society. As "class" is used here, it is defined by both *role in production* and *opposition to another class*. See Samoff 1982a, 1982b.

[6] I prefer the commonsense use of the term "class" at different levels of analysis to the logically more precise, but generally more opaque, use of "segment," "fraction," and "subclass." Thus, in my usage here, "class" can refer (at the global level) to workers and owners and (at a smaller scale) to industrial and commercial capitalists, or to rural landowners and urban workers.

mittent concern for agrarian reform (Cliffe 1978). In other words, a nationalist critique of imperialism, and thus capitalism, led a portion of the leadership to espouse a largely undefined socialism to defend the liberal policies they supported.

The lack of definition was quite purposeful. As Nyerere later pointed out, challenging British rule required a broad national alliance. To have specified that alliance's ideology more precisely would have risked excluding potential powerful allies and would have assisted the British in their efforts to exploit divisions within the nationalist movement to maintain European control.

The Liberal Hope

The 1960s began with a romantic optimism about development in Tanzania. With the fetters of European rule removed, the imagination and energies of Tanzania's citizens could be unleashed to fashion the new society. The initial optimism was jarred by successive political crises: an army mutiny, a sharp drop in the world price for a major export crop (sisal), diplomatic ruptures with England and West Germany, sharp disagreements with the United States, and university students' dramatic protest against conscription into the National Service and more generally against policies aimed at curbing elitism among the small educated elite.

The liberal hope had failed. The liberal development strategy—a relatively open economy, emphasis on export production to generate foreign exchange, encouragement and support for successful farmers, concentration of resources in pilot projects expected to have a broad impact, an increasing but still limited state role, and the maintenance of friendly relations with the major powers[7]—had not produced the desired results and seemed to be moving in the opposite direction. The analysis of this failure appeared in the Arusha Declaration of 1967 and the series of position papers that followed.[8] Presented in a style accessible to the citizenry, these papers identified the major problem as external dependence. The remedy outlined was to be a commitment to self-reliance in all spheres. There was, finally, a serious effort to define the content and

[7] For this characterization and periodization of Tanzania's development policies, see Samoff 1981. Among other sources on development policies, see Green 1977, 1979; Hydén 1980; International Labour Organization [ILO] 1978, 1982; Lofchie 1978; Saul 1979.

[8] The *Arusha Declaration* and related papers, including *Socialism and Rural Development* and *Education for Self Reliance*, are collected in Nyerere 1968a and 1968b. These papers had several purposes. In addition to the analysis of the failure of the liberal development strategy, there was also an effort to define more clearly the content of Tanzanian socialism, the announcement of the nationalization of major economic enterprises, the imposition of sharp income and consumption restrictions on leaders (defined broadly), and the beginning of the reorganization of the school system.

form of Tanzanian socialism, as well as a clearer recognition of the significance of inequalities within Tanzania.

The end of the liberal hope was also marked by a new assertion of party supremacy.[9] The forms varied. The 1965 Interim Constitution provided for a single-party state. Lethargic party branches were rejuvenated, and new party branches were created in workplaces. In 1968, nine leaders were expelled from the party. Although the cases differed somewhat, each of the expelled individuals had been an outspoken critic of the party. Several had been forceful advocates of their local constituencies, challenging both national policies and the national officials responsible for implementing them. The expulsions were in part an act of political communication. While there were important local elements in each case, the general message was clear: The party was supreme, and criticism was to be both restrained and largely confined to appropriate institutional settings. The expulsions also had a symbolic character. There was a limit to tolerable criticism, and when that criticism was in a public forum, the limit did not stretch very far. As well, the center, whether as the party headquarters, as the president, or as the regional and area commissioners (who served as representatives of the president and as party secretaries), wielded far greater power than did local representatives, even those whose local base was apparently quite strong.

A New Optimism: The Radical Development Strategy

The end of the 1960s saw the creation of a new development strategy, with the reduction of external dependence through increased self reliance at its core. The government's direct role in the economy was substantially increased. The nationalized companies were organized as parastatal corporations, with directors responsible to the national leadership rather than to stockholders. The open economy was increasingly closed: license and tariff restrictions on imports, controlled foreign exchange transactions, and government partnership for most foreign investors, who were to be limited to specified economic sectors. Individual accumulation and consumption were severely restricted. Cooperatives and socialist villages were encouraged, both rhetorically and through preferential treatment in allocating credit, awarding government and parastatal contracts, and providing technical assistance. Industrialization was to focus on basic industries, those whose products were critical to local agriculture, provided inputs to other basic industries, and sought to meet con-

[9] The Tanganyika African National Union (TANU) became Tanganyika's sole official party in the 1965 interim constitution. It merged in 1977 with its Zanzibari counterpart, the Afro-Shirazi Party (ASP), to form a single national party, the Chama Cha Mapinduzi (Party of the Revolution) (CCM).

sumer needs. Indigenization of skilled positions was to be accelerated; where expatriates were needed, they were to be recruited from more diversified sources, especially from socialist and smaller European countries. Foreign policy became more sharply critical of imperialism and international capitalism and more Africa-oriented (Nnoli 1978; Mushi and Mathews 1981).

Socialist construction figured more prominently on the political agenda. The Arusha Declaration and related papers sought to provide a clearer specification of the content of Tanzanian socialism. They also marked an effort to weaken the grip of foreign capital and to displace the largely Asian commercial class. There were new encouragements to the formation of socialist villages, both practical and symbolic. MPs, for example, were expected to live in ujamaa villages.[10]

Apparently prompted by the coup in Uganda, in 1971 the party issued guidelines that included a strong statement on the central role of workers and a critique of the arrogance and self-aggrandizing behavior of party and other leaders (Tanganyika African National Union [TANU] 1971). Those guidelines, and in particular the clause specifying limits on leaders' authority, were widely cited by workers who sought to exercise greater control over the work place. An additional set of party resolutions in 1974 (the Musoma Resolutions) addressed elitism among students and led to the acceleration of the achievement of universal primary education and the requirement that university applicants have at least two years of successful work experience and party activity (TANU 1974).

This socialist thrust had its origins in the center. Workers were not the primary source of the new initiatives. Rather, they were to be protected by directives from the national party leadership. After a period of worker militancy, the political machinery began once again to favor management, focusing more on disruption of production than on workers' grievances. Registration increased but voting declined in the 1970 elections. Those elections reflected an effort to realign political forces in Tanzania, an initiative originating largely in the center, not at the local level. The efforts to block the consolidation of an African bourgeoisie were serious but structurally impeded by their limited links with a mass base.

The early 1970s were in fact the time of a new assertion of central control. Ironically, the policy was termed decentralization. From the perspective of the national leadership, decentralization was intended to address both too much and too little local autonomy. Local government had become increasingly problematic, both administratively and politically. Some local councils were essentially bankrupt, unable to meet their basic responsibilities even with substantial subventions from the national

[10] For an overview of national elections in Tanzania, see Samoff 1987b.

treasury. At the same time, other local councils were rallying points for opposition to national policies. The key decision, apparently heavily influenced by the recommendations of an expatriate survey mission, largely organized by a U.S. management advisory firm, and later regretted by Nyerere, was to eliminate councils at the district level, effectively undermining what had been the primary elected center of local power. The elimination of cooperatives followed in 1976. Earlier regarded as the appropriate model for introducing socialism to Tanzania's farmers, cooperatives too came to be criticized as inefficient and occasionally corrupt. Like the local councils, they were deemed to cost too much for too little benefit. Also like the local councils, they were increasingly dominated by local interests, in this case, the larger farmers, resistant to the socialist development strategy. As local farmers became customers rather than owner-members, they lost control of the remaining institution likely to be directly responsive to local concerns.

Decentralization thus meant the assertion of increased central control and direction at the expense of local power bases. It did, however, permit a series of national campaigns, including villagization and adult literacy, and an incipient effort to transform the organization of rural agriculture that surely would have been more difficult to institute, more troublesome to manage, and much slower paced in a setting where local interests had more secure and more legitimate power bases. Yet, as decentralization undermined locally responsive political institutions it both contributed to increased local disaffection and reduced Tanzania's ability to cope with the crises that were to follow.

The restored optimism of the radical development strategy, eroded by decentralization, was corroded by two dramatic events in the mid-1970s: a sharp rise in oil prices and a severe drought. For these and other reasons, agricultural production stagnated, foreign reserves were quickly depleted, and industrial expansion slowed, forcing the Tanzanian government to seek extensive foreign assistance.[11]

The end of the 1970s was marked by war.[12] In late October, 1978, the Ugandan army invaded and occupied northwestern Tanzania. Primarily based in the southern and central parts of the country, Tanzanian soldiers made their way across the country—much of it on foot—to confront the Ugandan army. Although ostensibly no match for the relatively well-supplied army of a state under military rule, the Tanzanian armed forces

---

[11] It is not possible here to explore in detail the alternative explanations for the agricultural crisis of the mid-1970s, or to enumerate fully its consequences. The range of the debate on that period, and on the assessment of Tanzanian development more broadly, is reflected in Bienefeld 1982; Green, 1981a, 1981b, 1983; Green et al. 1980; Hydén 1980; ILO 1982; Lofchie 1978; Tanzania, Ministry of Agriculture 1982.

[12] The literature here is sparse; see Avirgan and Honey 1983.

prevailed, expelling the Ugandans from Tanzanian territory within a few days and then driving the retreating Ugandans across Uganda to the north. The Tanzania Peoples Defense Forces remained in Uganda—from one perspective, to restore democratic government, from another, as an occupation force—until mid-1981. Far more than has generally been recognized, the war with Uganda imposed a heavy strain on the Tanzanian economy. An indirect cost at home seems to have been an increase in armed crime, smuggling and other marketing outside official channels, and illegal currency transactions.

The late 1970s were also a period of apparent economic recovery.[13] The production of key crops improved. That increased output, coupled with a shift from crops intended for export to foodstuffs to be consumed locally, reduced the need for food imports and thus freed some foreign exchange. The recovery in foreign exchange reserves, fueled especially by the sharp rise in world coffee prices, was apparently deemed sufficiently secure to ease import restrictions.

The apparent economic recovery was to prove short lived. After a few years of more regular rains, drought returned. Agricultural production, still below early 1970s levels, again stagnated. Foreign exchange reserves were again quickly depleted. This time, however, international assistance was far less forthcoming than it had been only a few years earlier. Several external donors took their cue from the International Monetary Fund (IMF), whose insistence on sharp cuts in public spending, especially on social services, and on a substantial devaluation was rejected by the Tanzanian government. Indeed, the disagreements between the IMF and the government of Tanzania were not resolved until 1986, despite devaluations in 1983 and 1984. Although some foreign assistance, especially from the Scandinavian countries, continued to be available, the occasional shortages of consumer goods, and at times of foodstuffs, of the 1970s became endemic. Petroleum product imports consumed half the limited foreign exchange available, with severe impacts throughout the economy.

---

[13] See Green, et al. 1980, especially ch. 6, for details of the policy response to the crisis of the mid-1970s and the subsequent apparent recovery. They conclude, "By the end of 1977 the [recovery] strategy had been substantially successful and the results were positive. Overall output and agricultural production were again expanding at rates similar to those achieved before the crisis, net external reserves were at record levels, and constant price output per capita was about 8 percent above the 1973 level" (p. viii). It was also the case, they point out, that "the coffee boom of 1976–77 had concealed the size of the underlying structural deficit and contributed to the accumulation of record foreign-exchange reserves" (p. viii). It is striking that this period of partial recovery, and the economic strategy employed to produce it, are scarcely noted and rarely discussed in the general, and generally critical, reviews of the Tanzanian economy during this period.

"Modernization" without Modernization

In sum, influenced by theories of modernization and still heavily reliant on external sources of capital, skills, and technology, independent Tanzania's leaders initially sought and largely followed foreign development advice. By the mid-1960s, however, their initial optimism had been tempered by frustration. Rapid modernization, social harmony, and international cooperation all seemed in jeopardy.[14] On the agenda but hardly secure, socialist construction proceeded at best spasmodically. Or rather, in practice socialist initiatives and the consolidation of peripheral capitalism coexisted, with neither definitively victorious. Tanzania's marginal situation in global terms both imposed constraints and created possibilities (Wallerstein 1974). Its leaders gained some maneuvering room from the former British administration's and international capital's relative disinterest. At the same time, the process of underdevelopment left little foundation—neither a dynamic economic sector with a self-sustaining increase in productivity nor an organized and increasingly self-conscious subordinate class—on which socialism could be built.

EDUCATIONAL REFORM: THE SETTING

Thus, a combination of optimism and frustration provided the setting for the extensive educational reforms since Tanzania's independence in 1961. In the tension between consolidating peripheral capitalism and organizing a socialist transition, three major political trajectories can be discerned.[15] One envisions a rather more independent state firmly entrenched in a capitalist world system (what I have been calling the consolidation of peripheral capitalism). Tanzania's mid-1980s economic "liberalization" marks the reinvigoration of this orientation, with re-

[14] For a brief overview and periodization, see Samoff 1981. Recent general political histories include Coulson 1982; Iliffe 1979; and Yeager 1982.

[15] A detailed review of Tanzanian politics and its extensive literature is beyond the scope of this discussion. On Tanzania as a peripheral capitalist state there are both advocates (Lofchie 1978; Kahama, Maliyamkono, and Wells 1986) and critics (Shivji 1976; Mueller 1980; Coulson 1982). On Tanzania as a state in transition, some authors find sluggish but significant progress toward what might be termed social democracy (Pratt 1976; Green et al. 1980; Resnick 1981), while others regard the apparent transition as a short-lived and inherently insecure moment of class alignment, conflict, and realignment (Samoff 1981; Saul 1979). Although the case for socialist development has been argued (Shivji 1976), the politics of its implementation—beyond general critique and ringing calls for sweeping change—have been less well addressed (but see the contributions to Othman 1980; Shivji 1985; and Tandon 1982). In this assessment it is important to distinguish between rhetoric and policy (for example, programs that are announced as socialist initiatives but that clearly reduce popular participation and/or increase stratification).

newed attention to the standard of living of the upper strata, greater receptivity to foreign investment and development advice, and a willingness to slow, or postpone, social transformation. A second political current seeks a noncapitalist development strategy (Thomas 1978; Cliffe 1978). Here, the language of socialist construction functions to elaborate a critique of capitalism and to rally support under a nationalist, anticapitalist banner. The task is to transform Tanzanian society without alienating any of the powerful states. The resulting policies alternate between asserting national autonomy and establishing state control over production and distribution on one hand and placating international capital and providing incentives and rewards for the national elite on the other. A third political orientation asserts unequivocally that societal progress requires social transformation—that people's standard of living is a function of the progress of socialist construction.

The three images thus projected—of a peripheral capitalist state, a state in transition, and a nascent socialist state—are not simply images, or goals, or even primarily ideologies. They are the products of the contest for the control of state power in independent Tanzania. The successor to the conditioned state remains at issue. It is that contest for the control of state power, combined with efforts to maintain the legitimacy of the state and of its dominant classes, that has generated ostensibly inconsistent educational policies. It is useful, therefore, to characterize those policies in terms of their political roots.

Patterns of Educational Policy

The primary educational concerns of the early years of independence were rooted in the creation of a nationalist leadership that was both a protege and a critic of the departing Europeans. Like their predecessors, the new leaders firmly believed that the lack of high-level skills was a major obstacle to development goals. With a very small pool of adults who had completed secondary school and an even smaller number of university graduates, Tanganyika had, it seemed, to assign its highest educational priority to human resource development, especially at the upper levels. For the new leadership, the political imperative to replace Europeans with Tanzanians reinforced that priority. At the same time, expanded access to school had been a central plank in the nationalist platform. Initial educational policy in independent Tanganyika, therefore, emphasized high-level skills and more schools (in that order).

In the tension between these two goals, educational expansion had different meanings for citizens and leaders. The popular pressure was for access to primary schools, which in the earlier era promised upward social mobility. In the human resource orientation of the national leadership, however, the critical educational task was to develop high level skills. Primary school expansion would come later. Hence, although many new schools were opened and the enrollment increased rapidly, after an initial spurt, school expansion roughly matched the growth of the population.[16] By 1973, still fewer than half the school-age children were attending school (TANU 1974, 106).

As the developmental nationalism of the early 1960s was succeeded by the radical populism of the late 1960s, educational goals were modified. Education was no longer to be considered an elite privilege or even primarily an investment in human capital. Rather, education was to be a fundamental right of citizenship (Nyerere 1985, 45, 52). These two themes—that education was a basic right of all citizens and that effective popular participation required literate citizens—reflected a revised education agenda. The development of high-level skills remained important, but providing a basic education to all Tanzanian citizens and developing adult literacy were now also high priorities.

Notwithstanding the terminology of underdevelopment and dependence it frequently employed, the leadership's conception of development continued to reflect a sense of development as modernization and of education as an investment in human capital; that is, there persisted a deep-seated and powerful understanding of education as a vehicle for transmitting to the new generation the skills deemed necessary for economic growth. The logic seemed clear. If a critical obstacle to development is the shortage of skills and if skills are essentially the property of individuals, then it makes sense to expect schools to have training as their core mission, to organize schooling around the progressively more demanding selection of the most skilled students, and to assess both programs and individuals in those terms.

Not infrequently, the persistence of this understanding has undermined educational reform efforts. Indeed, efforts to define education for Tanzanian socialism are continually evaluated in terms of education for modernization. Advocates of education as the development of human potential, of schools as the breeders of cooperative and collectivist self reliance, and of the closer integration of schools and their communities have all been assailed for proposing deviations from the ostensibly objec-

---

[16] Unfortunately, there are many inconsistencies in the educational statistics for Tanzania, even within the data provided by a single source (a problem, of course, not unique to Tanzania). Additionally, frequently data on schools and enrollments in Tanzania in fact pertain only to government (or government-assisted) schools and their students. The data presented in this chapter are drawn from an extensive review of Tanzanian educational statistics from diverse sources and thus portray reasonably accurately the situations discussed. Where discrepancies could not be resolved, and where the margin of error was too large to draw clear inferences, the data have been excluded.

tive process of training and selection by individual achievement that is assumed to be essential. The importance of noncognitive school activities is debated in many countries. In Tanzania, however, that debate is not simply about educational priorities. Rather, it has to do with the specification of the political agenda. Although socialism remains on that agenda, modernization has dominated the practice.

But not completely. A fundamental premise underlying national policy over the past two decades—a premise shared by the other countries discussed in this volume—is that social transformation must precede economic growth. The modernizationists assume that the reduction of inequalities and the expansion of participation can, in general, be accomplished only at the cost of economic growth. From that perspective they argue that addressing inequality and encouraging participation must wait until after the initial economic growth, or, at best, that social transformation may occur as a by-product of growth strategies. Notwithstanding disagreements over direction within it, however, the Tanzanian leadership has maintained its sense that remaking society must precede, or perhaps accompany, rather than follow economic growth. Unlike the modernizationists, their assumption is that social transformation is required to promote political participation, which in turn is a prerequisite for economic growth.

In part, then, educational policy has reflected the tension between these two pressures. On one hand, understanding social transformation as the foundation for economic growth calls for schools that organize learning around principles of equality and participation, that reduce the gap between the rewards attached to intellectual and manual work, and that develop close ties with their communities. On the other hand, the emphasis on academic mastery and individual achievement in the schools manifests the deeply embedded and persisting assumption that economic growth requires skills more than it requires participation and equality.[17]

By the late 1960s and early 1970s there had also begun to emerge a more explicitly socialist agenda for education (Hirji 1973; Mbilinyi 1972, 1973a, 1973b). In part, the socialists offered a critique: Expanded access, community schools, and adult literacy would change little if the reward structure continued to favor academic achievement and individual success. To achieve equality and democracy required not only universal education but also specific attention to the role of education in reaching the

---

[17] These comments refer primarily to school-based educational activities. Thus far, the impressive successes in reducing adult illiteracy have not been integrated into a strategy for political mobilization or into a program for continuing educational programs outside the schools. Although educators speak in terms of continuing education, their practice suggests that they, and perhaps the political leadership, regard adult education as a transitional program addressed to unschooled adults that is rendered unnecessary by its own success and by universal access to basic education.

educationally (and politically) most disadvantaged parts of the population. Education, therefore, had to become a vehicle for mobilization, for class organization, and for constraining elites.

By the end of the 1970s, the progress was impressive. Essentially all Tanzanian children could find a place in school. Literacy was widespread. That progress, however, had at best lukewarm support from many educational administrators, who criticized spreading limited resources so thinly and who pointed to the apparently declining quality of education. The renewed assertiveness of the technical-managerial perspective on Tanzanian development of the early 1980s was accompanied, therefore, by an effort to refocus the educational agenda on academic achievement and vocational training. Human resource development, with some effort to respond to popular pressure by permitting school expansion and by ensuring employment for at least some school graduates, had again become the order of the day. The educational agenda of the bureaucratic governing class and its allies seemed, at least for the moment, to have swamped the socialist initiative.

Educational Policies: The Process

Educational policymaking and implementation in Tanzania manifest conflicting, and at times incompatible, policy styles (Hyden 1979, 1984). Efforts to plan, to accomplish major changes rapidly, to maintain central control, and to encourage local participation are all in tension with one another. Indeed, the attempt to fashion a noncapitalist state may have left Tanzania with some of the least desirable characteristics of each of the systems used as models.

Policy introduction and implementation by "campaign" is common in Tanzania (Hyden 1979). With great publicity, a sweeping new policy is announced and optimistic goals are set. Initial implementation often precedes detailed analysis and planning. The new policy becomes a national crusade, demanding energetic support and selfless dedication.

Mass campaigns of this sort have several advantages. They can mobilize resources and energize popular participation and support. They can extend communication and widen the political and administrative reach of party and government. Policy by campaign is also self-limiting. After an initial flurry of activity, attention wanes, pronouncements become less frequent, and actual policy may revert to what it had been earlier. Equally or perhaps more important, since the initial unrealistic targets are rarely met, all goal-setting efforts come to be regarded as statements of intention and hope rather than as guides to practical action. Where it is evident that the national campaign has resulted in little change, the legitimacy of the political process itself erodes. An inherently political policy process of this sort, where political education and mobilization are far more important than technical expertise and rationalized resource use, simply cannot be sustained in Tanzania's vacillation between technical-administrative and political-mobilizational perspectives on development.

A second characteristic of the educational policy process, supported by both modernizationists and socialists, is centralized decisionmaking. For the modernizationists, avoiding the divisive demands of region, religion, and ethnicity, and rationalizing and maximizing scarce resources require that planning be dominated by an even more scarce resource, expertise. To this perspective the socialists add a concern with redistribution, which is unlikely to occur in the absence of strong central authority. Consequently, notwithstanding the rhetoric of participation and bottom-up planning, public policy in general, and especially educational policy, has been highly centralized. Precisely because expertise is scarce, however, and because communication channels are often circuitous and unreliable, the degree of centralization in policymaking exceeds central capacities to make policies. Pronouncements proliferate, but follow-up, evaluation, and adjustment are weak, driven more by crises than by systematic monitoring.

At the same time, at least some leaders are seriously committed to popular participation. There have been several waves of institutional reform, all intended to increase the leverage of local citizens in specifying goals, programs, and practice. More than in many other African countries, Tanzanians do speak out on policies that concern them and are able to influence both the policies and their implementation. Indeed, in important respects, centralization in Tanzania requires local participation. Although there has legally been one political party since 1965, and despite occasional heavy-handed exercises of central authority, Tanzania is not a totalitarian state. Even were that the leaders' intention, the infrastructure could not support the nationwide imposition of an authoritarian order. To secure compliance with central directives, therefore, the Tanzanian government requires popular support. The existence and intensity of that popular support are in turn dependent on popular participation. Hence, effective centralization is necessarily a function of effective local participation, which is necessarily often corrosive of central direction. I shall return subsequently to this tension between central direction and local autonomy, which is neither avoidable nor ephemeral. My concern here is to note that patterns of both centralization and local participation in Tanzania have often been counterproductive. The centralized policy process adopted in Tanzania regularly collides with limited managerial and communication capabilities. At the same time, within a hierarchical and bureaucratic administrative structure, to encourage local participation by asserting that key decisions will be initiated and made locally must eventually generate frustration, opposition, and cynicism.

Put somewhat differently, institutional forms designed for a highly politicized setting where informed and politically conscious local citizens
participate regularly in making policies and implementing decisions have
regularly been overwhelmed in Tanzania by a deep-seated ethos of modernization: Decisions require expertise, which means that the popular
role must be severely constrained; energized local participation is more
likely to be divisive than constructive, and therefore to be avoided rather
than encouraged. Formal policy vacillates between reliance on mass support and distrust of mass participation. Ostensibly politicizing institutions
become vehicles for depoliticization.

A third characteristic of the educational policy process in Tanzania is
its structural susceptibility to external influences. Like their colleagues
elsewhere in Africa, Tanzanian educational policymakers look to the
North Atlantic for models, analyses, and diagnoses, and for approval. Often subtle, this deference to external authority conditions policies—from
specifying what is problematic to designing intervention strategies to
evaluating outcomes (Fuenzalida 1983). Even more important, most new
projects in education, and a significant portion of the recurrent budget,
rely on externally provided finance (see Tables 7–1 and 7–2).

I am not here suggesting a conspiracy among donors or between donors and Tanzanian leaders, or that donors set educational policy in Tanzania, or that Tanzanian educators do only what donors will support. Tanzanian educators have shown remarkable independence in a very
constrained situation and surely will continue to do so. Expectations
about what can be funded do, however, influence what is proposed and
what is attempted—for example, Folk Development Colleges with a
Swedish heritage, vocational schools in the Cuban style, functional adult
literacy programs with UNESCO's underlying assumptions, among others.

This reliance on foreign finance has another indirect impact. Success
in securing foreign assistance becomes itself a source of power and influence within Tanzania. The tendencies toward self-protection and self-ag-
grandizement that characterize administrative structures everywhere are
in Tanzania in part played out within a web of international connections.
Increasing the resources within one educational subsector, for example,
may depend as much on building an alliance with, say, Swedish educational advisers as on constructing a supportive political coalition within
Tanzania.

EDUCATIONAL REFORM IN TANZANIA, 1961–1986

Since it is not possible here to discuss each of the many educational reforms in Tanzania over the two and a half decades of independence, it is
useful to outline their salient elements. (See the Chronology of Education and Politics in Tanzania for a sequential presentation and Table 7–3

TABLE 7–1

Tanzania: Foreign Contributions to Educational Development Expenditures, 1962/63–1981 82 (TSh '000 000)

Year	Tanzanian Share		Foreign Loans		Foreign Grants		Total Educational Development Expenditure		Total Foreign Share	
	TSh	%	TSh	%	TSh	%	TSh	%	TSh	%
1962/63	41	35.3	64	55.2	11	9.5	116	100.0	75	64.7
1963/64	58	34.9	92	55.4	16	9.6	166	100.0	108	65.1
1964/65	112	32.9	197	57.9	31	9.1	340	100.0	228	67.1
1965/66	63	23.9	169	64.0	32	12.1	264	100.0	201	76.1
1966/67	95	34.1	137	49.1	47	16.8	279	100.0	184	65.9
1967/68	142	86.1	n.a.	—	n.a.	—	165	100.0	23	13.9
1968/69	80	30.0	00	0.0	187	70.0	267	100.0	187	70.0
1969/70	136	36.8	135	36.5	99	26.8	370	100.0	234	63.2
1970/71	206	49.0	136	32.4	78	18.6	420	100.0	214	51.0
1971/72	150	30.0	131	26.2	219	43.8	500	100.0	350	70.0
1972/73	171	29.1	180	30.6	237	40.3	588	100.0	417	70.9
1973/74	125	23.2	112	20.8	301	55.9	538	100.0	413	76.8
1974/75	256	40.4	161	25.4	216	34.1	633	100.0	377	59.6
1975/76	218	15.3	253	17.8	954	66.9	1,425	100.0	1,207	84.7
1976/77	263	12.9	374	18.3	1,402	68.8	2,039	100.0	1,776	87.1
1977/78	366	20.4	275	15.3	1,154	64.3	1,795	100.0	1,429	79.6
1978/79	379	19.2	168	8.5	1,431	72.3	1,978	100.0	1,599	80.8
1979/80	883	30.2	298	10.2	1,739	59.6	2,920	100.0	2,037	69.8
1980/81	716	22.6	179	5.6	2,274	71.8	3,169	100.0	2,453	77.4
1981/82	614	20.4	n.a.	—	n.a.	—	3,008	100.0	2,394	79.6
TOTAL	5,074	24.2		—		—	20,980	100.0	15,906	75.8

Source: Tanzania, *Mfumo wa Elimu ya Tanzania 1981–2000*, vol. 2, p. 17. Data refer to budget esti-mates for education development expenditures.

Notes: Original source includes discrepant figures (corrected here). Beginning in budget year 1972/73, funds for primary education (approximately 42% of the total education sector budget) were disbursed through regional government.

It is important to note that development expenditures constitute a small portion of total expenditures on education: approximately 13% of Ministry of National Education expenditures in 1983/84 and an even smaller portion of total government expenditures on education.

TABLE 7–2

Tanzania: Sources of Finance for Ministry of National Education's Development Budget, 1980/81, 1982/83, and 1983/84

	1980/81		1982/83		1983/84	
Source	TSh ('000,000)	% Total Dev. Budget	TSh ('000,000)	% Total Dev. Budget	TSh ('000,000)	% Total Dev. Budget
Sweden	838	34.2	568	23.2	674	19.5
Tanzania	703	28.7	865	35.3	1,436	41.6
Denmark	255	10.4	326	13.3	403	11.7
World Bank	123	5.0	421	17.2	657	19.0
Norway	100	4.1	25	1.0	35	1.0
F.R. Germany	88	3.6	110	4.5	51	1.5
UNICEF	25	1.0	44	1.8	63	1.8
Af. Dev Fund					45	1.3
Netherlands					35	1.0
Finland					35	1.0
EEC					20	0.6
Other	19	13.0	91	3.7		
TOTAL	2,450	100.0	2,850	100.0	3,455	100.0

Sources: 1980/81 and 1982/83: Roy Carr-Hill, Primary Education in Tanzania: A Review of the Research (Stockholm: SIDA, September 1984) (Education Division Documents No. 16), p. 19. Original source: SIDA/TAN Sector Reviews, 1980 and 1982. 1983/84: Annual Joint Review of the Swedish Support to Education and Vocational Training 1983, app. 3.3.

for summary statistics.) Each of the major educational policy initiatives was prompted by a sense that Tanzania's schools were not serving adequately their development tasks, and, to varying degrees, all have been implemented. Thus, burdened by the institutional legacies of European rule and operating in an external environment that was simultaneously hostile to major national policies and supportive of many educational reforms, Tanzanians sought to conduct their revolution by education.[18] In

[18] The enthusiasm of that perspective is reflected in Resnick 1968. For overviews of education and development in Tanzania, see also Gillette 1976; Hinzen and Hunsdorfer 1979; King 1984; Mbilinyi 1979; Morrison 1976; and Msekwa and Maliyamkono 1978. Recent research and commentaries on education in Tanzania that touch on some of the themes discussed here include Carr-Hill 1984; Cooksey and Ishumi 1986; Ishumi 1981; King 1983; Malekela 1983; Maliyamkono 1983; Maliyamkono, Ishumi, and Wells 1982; Mosha 1982;

TABLE 7–3
Tanzania: Summary Education Statistics, 1985

Type of Institution	Number of Institutions	Number of Learners	Number of Teachers	Teacher:Pupil Ratio
Primary (all)	10,173	3,169,759	92,586	1:34
Primary (government)	10,147	3,160,145		
Primary (private)	26	9,614		
Secondary (all)	190	83,098	4,329	1:19
Secondary (government)	86	42,323	2,726	1:16
Secondary (private)	104	40,775	1,603	1:25
Teachers' training				
Teachers colleges	39	12,311	958	1:13
Technical colleges	2	1,449	204	1:7
Arusha	1	392	76	1:5
Dar es Salaam	1	1,057	128	1:8
University[a]	2	3,414	1,025	1:3
Dar es Salaam	1	2,989		
Morogoro	1	425		
Foreign		1,006		
Adult education centers (1982)	9,928	4,912,511	148,108	1:33
Adult literacy classes		4,079,531		
Functional literacy		2,493,234		
postliteracy		1,586,297		
Folk Development Colleges		16,419	374	1:44
Short courses		13,922		
Long courses		2,497		

Sources: Tanzania, *Basic Education Statistics in Tanzania (BEST) 1981–1985* (Dar es Salaam: Ministry of Education, 1986); Tanzania, *Basic Facts about Education in Tanzania*, rev. ed. (Dar es Salaam: Ministry of Education, 1984).

[a] Excluding Tanzanian students studying abroad.

the view of President Nyerere, socialism—the declared national goal—was a state of mind.[19] To achieve the transformation of individual consciousness that socialist construction required and to prepare its architects and work crews, radical educational reforms were essential. Hence, the reforms noted here were both responses to specific problems within

Omari, et al. 1983; Psacharopoulos and Loxley 1985; and Unsicker 1987. Nyerere's initial paper, *Education for Self Reliance* (1967), has been reprinted many times, including in Resnick 1968 and Hinzen and Hundsorfer 1979. See also Nyerere's retrospective overview (1985) and the official report of the Presidential Commission on Education (Tanzania 1984).

[19] Although commentators on Tanzania frequently quote President Nyerere's statements

the educational system and at the same time basic elements of a broad strategy of socialist transition.

The Trajectory of Educational Policy

Schools in Tanzania are expected to accomplish the tasks assigned to schools everywhere: teaching young people to read, write, and manipulate numbers; instilling the discipline of social order and of workplace routine; inculcating a sense of pride in the nation, the people, and their history; and for a select group of students, developing their imagination, creativity, and ingenuity as far as possible. Since independence, however, developing skills has been considered schools' most important task, reflecting the initial focus on *education for modernization*.

As I have noted, the expansion of the skills pool is deemed necessary to achieve economic growth and thus to improve the standard of living. In addition, an expanded skills pool is presumed necessary to assert public control over and manage large-scale economic enterprises and to staff the civil service of a government committed to planning, to regulating the economy, and to providing extensive public services. School-based training is also expected to improve the employability of the youth and to reduce the need for, and the length of, postschool training programs. By the mid-1960s, however, in both development strategy and educational policy, expectations had not been fulfilled. The flow of events highlighted the inadequacies of the modernization perspective.

Among the 1967 policy papers that addressed these problems was *Education for Self Reliance*, which offered a broad indictment of Tanzanian education and announced several major reforms. The principal goal was to reduce dependence by promoting *education for self reliance*. Primary schooling was to become a basic education: a shift from emphasis on the preparation of those few students who would advance to postprimary institutions—an arrangement in which a majority of those enrolled failed—to a curriculum primarily intended to equip young Tanzanians for adult roles. School-based productive projects were to integrate each school more fully into its local community, to involve the educated elite in manual labor, and to provide some resources to support the school. Since their education was provided from the public treasury, higher-level students had a national obligation of community service. In short, schools

---

of the 1960s as evidence for his current thinking, it would be a serious error to fail to recognize changes in understanding that have emerged over the past two decades and an injustice to Nyerere himself to reject a priori the possibility that he has revised his own thinking. It impossible within the confines of this paper to explore the understandings of socialism in Tanzania of the 1980s, but it is important to note that socialism is taken to involve contradiction and conflict in the society and not simply an attitude of mind. (See, among other sources, Chama cha Mapinduzi 1981.)

were to be development institutions, oriented toward national needs and goals. Although major educational resources were still to be devoted to high-level skills development, the school system as a whole was expected to upgrade the competencies of the entire populace, to promote a broader sense of community, to nurture attitudes of cooperation and patterns of collective effort, and to foster a sense of self-confidence. For Tanzania to be self-reliant, its schools had to construct the foundation.

The 1967 policy papers also indicated an increasing concern with the apparent intensification of social differentiation. What had been assumed to have been an egalitarian social order began to show the marks of stratification. A second goal for schooling, therefore, was to reduce inequality across society. Education was expected to contribute to this goal, most directly by reducing inherited inequalities in recruitment to high-level positions. The education sector was also expected to reduce inequalities by affirmative action: special allocations to districts and regions deemed to be disadvantaged, preferential selection and promotion, increased rewards for manual labor and community service.

As the elaboration of Tanzanian socialism proceeded into the 1970s, the leadership recognized that an expanded skills pool, a literate citizenry, and reduced political dependence provided a necessary, but far from sufficient, base for creating and then managing the egalitarian, non-exploitive society that was envisioned. To overcome peripheral capitalist underdevelopment required socialist construction.

Schooling was to become *education for Tanzanian socialism.* The task was to lay the foundation for expanded citizen participation and democratic practice. Citizens had to learn not only how to manage their local councils and cooperatives, but, beyond that, how to govern. If public institutions were to be accountable to the populace, people had to be taught to expect that accountability, to routinize it, and to protect it from both attack and erosion. Especially after it was decided to accelerate the achievement of universal primary education, the schools seemed the obvious site for this sort of educational practice.

Of these three major educational policy directions—modernization (skills development), self reliance, and Tanzanian socialism—the last has been the least well analyzed, articulated, and elaborated. In part, that is because among policymakers the three policy goals are presumed to be sequential. Greater self reliance depends on successfully meeting skills needs. Nurturing a mobilized citizenry and maintaining participatory political institutions, in turn, is assumed to depend on both generating needed skills and achieving significant self reliance. From this perspective, it was straightforward to conclude that assigning the highest priority to skills development required delaying attention to politicization and popular mobilization.

In part, the priority assigned to skills development, and to schools as recruitment filters for most of the wage labor force, reflects the persistence of an understanding of development as modernization rather than as social transformation and of the political dominance of the modernizers over the socialists. Indeed, the tension between these orientations, and the regular reassertion of modernization as the dominant perspective, have been enduring features of Tanzanian educational policy.

EDUCATIONAL EXPANSION

Much of the resources and human energy allocated to education in Tanzania have been directed toward expansion. As I have noted, expansion has been regarded both as a widespread popular demand and as an independence promise of the nationalist movement. Expansion is considered critical to self reliant economic growth, to the political mobilization of the citizenry, and to establishing and maintaining a democratic political order. In addition to these collective concerns, expansion is widely perceived by individual Tanzanians as the critical requisite for improving their access to jobs, power, wealth, and prestige.

Expansion of access to schooling has followed several paths. The elimination of the Standard IV examination, first in urban schools and then nationwide, permitted those who found primary school places to remain in school throughout the primary cycle. Similarly, the elimination of the Form 2 examination made secondary school a four-year program for those selected.[20] The nationalization of all private primary schools at the end of the 1960s and then the achievement of universal primary education by the late 1970s have made basic education available to all young Tanzanians. Although the policy contours have been somewhat erratic, tolerance for and periodic encouragement of private (that is, nongovernmental) secondary schools had by the mid-1980s doubled secondary enrollment. Adult literacy programs, whose emphases and forms have in part mirrored the changing priorities in educational policy more generally, have reached widely across the society, reducing illiteracy from an estimated 67 percent in 1967 to 15 percent in 1983.

In addition to the logic that relates schooling to development, the role of schools as a prominent social service has fueled this expansion. Experiences throughout Africa underlined the fragility of postcolonial political institutions. New leaders needed to provide visible and rapid benefits to the populace. Although they might lack trained teachers, curriculum materials, and even stationery, there could be new schools nearly every-

---

[20] The Form 2 examination was restored in the mid-1980s. Improving the quality of instruction, and perhaps exercising tighter control over teachers, had again become more important than expanding access and reducing inequality.

where in a relatively short period, especially when local communities were willing to donate materials and labor. Even the most rural areas could thus see the fruits of the new order. Providing clean water, or rural medical facilities, or paved roads, or electrification, or functioning agricultural extension centers was likely to take much longer. Hence, rapid expansion of schooling was commonly understood—by both leaders and the mass public—as a central element in the legitimization of the new government, and of the structure of the state itself.

CURRICULUM REFORM

Over the twenty-five years of Tanzanian independence there have been successive curricular reforms. Syllabi and texts have been nationalized, with continuing attention to studying Tanzania, East Africa, Africa, and the Third World from a Tanzanian perspective. Kiswahili has become the language of instruction in primary schools (with the indirect consequence of effectively eliminating expatriate teachers from those schools). Setting and marking national examinations is now done within Tanzania. Political education has been introduced at all levels.

There have also been efforts to shape the curriculum to nurture the worldview, values, orientation, and style deemed appropriate for the new Tanzanian: inquiring and self reliant, an active participant in community affairs with a preference for cooperative and collective activity, and concerned more with public service than with individual rewards. The introduction of basic education—primary schooling to be available to all young Tanzanians and to be complete in itself—brought a more rural and community-oriented focus to the curriculum. The new curriculum also seeks to demystify expertise, or, rather, reject the disjunction between mental and manual labor. The evidence here, largely impressionistic, is mixed. On one hand, some young Tanzanians do finish their schooling with a sense of political direction, an orientation toward public service, and a degree of confidence in themselves and their society. On the other hand, many do not. Teacher-student relationships, classroom organization, and approved patterns of student behavior reflect the focus on skills development (schools as places where knowledge is transmitted, students are processed, and graduates are produced) far more than they incorporate the practices of education for liberation (schools as sites of critical consciousness, learner-centered dialogues, and cooperative communal initiatives) (Hirji 1973; Mbilinyi 1977, 1979).

Although there are now productive projects at all schools, initially intended to develop skills, to institutionalize the school-community links, and to offset some school operating costs, the results are mixed (Adams 1982; Baume 1983). Not infrequently, the children labor and the teachers supervise. Systematic attention to agricultural strategies is minimal;

farming practices tend to be those of the surrounding community. Since additional work in the fields continues to be used as a sanction for school infractions, and since students come to school in part to escape the farm, everyone tries to avoid manual work. Additions to the school treasury are modest, occasionally disappearing entirely before they can be spent on the school. There are, however, striking exceptions. Some secondary schools function as quasi-autonomous villages, generating sufficient funds to support capital improvements.

These reforms of educational content have moved toward several divergent goals simultaneously. Like the other dimensions of the educational system, they are themselves contradictory, and they reflect tensions in the larger political system. One push is toward localization and nationalization. At the same time, external expertise is more highly valued than knowledge developed locally. Both academic programs and individual results require periodic external certification. A second push is toward reducing the psychic gap between mental and manual activities. Clearly, however, intellectual labor is rewarded more highly, a pattern unlikely to affirm to youth that farming is a valued endeavor or to encourage them to look forward to life in the village. A third push is toward closer links between schools and their communities. That, too, is undermined by the fundamental assumptions that schools are primarily for developing knowledge and expertise, that knowledge and expertise are qualitatively different and necessarily detached from farming and other productive activities, that knowledge and expertise are fundamentally properties of individuals, not collectivities, and that, therefore, the isolation of the schools serves both students and communities well.

EDUCATION AND SOCIETY

A major challenge to the integration of schools into their communities has been the difficulty in combining rapid educational expansion with the commitment to reducing inequalities, usually expressed in regional terms. Both school fees and private primary schools expanded educational opportunities in the relatively affluent regions (the cities and those rural areas where farmers produced a high-value export crop). The elimination of school fees and the nationalization of private primary schools was, therefore, expected to narrow the gap between the more affluent and the less affluent regions. The achievement of universal primary education further reduced differentiation at the primary level. By then, however, the terrain had already begun to shift. Inequalities in the number of primary schools were succeeded by unevenness in the distribution of high-quality primary education. And the struggle to expand access moved from the primary to the postprimary level (for details on a striking case in point, see Samoff 1987a). At the same time, the rate of school expansion overwhelmed available funds, leading to a restoration of school fees.[21]

Successive efforts to reduce university students' elitism through curriculum modification seemed to leave students' sense of their unique status and their expectation of privileges largely unchanged. Consequently, the focus of those efforts was broadened to include preuniversity selection and preparation. Party policy adopted in the early 1970s required university applicants to present evidence of two years' successful productive and party activity along with their grades. The expectation was that sending students to work between secondary school and the university, largely in their home villages, would reduce their alienation from family and community. Ultimately, however, other concerns prevailed. When the enrollment of women at the university plummeted precipitously, the two years' work requirement was waived for female secondary students. Apparent shortages of qualified applicants led to similar waivers for students in geography and subsequently engineering. Eventually academic schooling proved more powerful than education for social transformation. At the urging of university faculty and educational administrators more generally, the government and party accepted the recommendation of the Presidential Commission on Education to abolish the work requirement for university admission.

As Nyerere has repeatedly stressed, Tanzanian development could not await the education of a new generation. Education had to focus on adults as well as children. Literate farmers were expected to adopt new agricultural practices more readily and to apply inputs more effectively. Moreover, literacy was deemed necessary for effective citizen participation. Since the late 1960s, adult literacy programs have played a major role in Tanzanian educational policy (Hall 1975; Hinzen and Hunsdorfer 1979, ch. 5; Kassam 1978). An initial pilot functional literacy program in the UNESCO pattern was rapidly expanded, with impressive results (Malya 1979).

Literacy programs were expected to be community based and to have substantial party involvement. Local adult education coordinators were deployed throughout the country, and funds were allocated for village libraries. Folk Development Colleges (FDCs), in part modeled on the Scandinavian pattern and largely installed in what had previously been

[21] Initially small and termed "contributions," school fees figured prominently in the deliberations of the Presidential Commission on Education, whose recommendations led to the establishment of the principle that parents should share the costs of educating their children. In practice, school fees are probably less regressive than they might seem. Though not insignificant, required fees are not high enough, in themselves, to exclude many children from school. Since nearly all parents want their children to go to school, such fees are much more collectible than other sorts of taxes.

agricultural training institutes, were created to provide post-literacy-program learning centers (Mosha 1982, 1983; Unsicker 1987). The FDC students were to become village animators, energizing opportunities for villagers to use their newly developed literacy. Yet, although the language of Paulo Freire's (1970) education for critical consciousness was occasionally employed, the literacy campaigns were not organized as efforts at political mobilization. Here, too, modernization prevailed over social transformation. As a consequence, newly literate peasants did not become an organized political base for establishing and extending their incorporation into the political system or even for protecting the FDCs and maintaining them as institutions primarily responsive to village needs and interests.

Ironically, defending expanded education largely in terms of the need for skills has reinforced the public's expectation that schooling is the primary route to an improved individual (and thus family) standard of living. That in turn has intensified the frustration of the young people who complete their basic education with little prospect for employment other than returning to the family farm. The skills focus has also reinforced credentialism—employers' demand for increasingly higher levels of certification—in the workplace (Dore 1976).

The skills focus for education in general, public and private concern with unfulfilled employment aspirations of primary school completers, and diploma-driven employment practices combined to create pressure for increased vocationalization in schools at all levels. Educated unemployment could be addressed by more relevant education. Within a brief period, all secondary schools were required to create vocational specializations for all students, modifying their curricula accordingly.[22] The expectations were that students who completed secondary school would make better farmers (agriculture is by far the largest specialization) and that little or no postsecondary vocational training would be required for urban sector employment. The initial results have been disappointing (Psacharopoulos and Loxley 1985), though perhaps predictable. At least in the early years, vocational education in what the leadership and the populace expected to remain largely academic secondary schools was limited, and often perfunctory. Like their parents, students regarded schooling as the route off the farm, not back to it. In practice, students' secondary school preferences and official placements were little influenced by the vocational biases. That the vocationalization of the secondary schools did not reduce unemployment among their graduates is not surprising. The unattractiveness of farming had largely to do with the unavailability

[22] Each school was required to offer one or more of the four specializations (termed "biases"): agriculture, commerce, home economics (for female students), and technology.

of start-up capital and tools (and, in some areas, of land), producer prices, expected long-term returns from agriculture, and the apparent sparkle of urban areas, not with the lack of requisite skills. Unemployment too had more to do with the relatively slow rate of job creation than with the youth's skills. Notwithstanding the disappointing results,[23] vocationalized schooling is attractive to educators and the public and is likely to continue. "Irrelevant education" is, after all, a comfortable explanation for educated unemployment and its accompanying social dislocation. The remedy appears feasible and need not be politically disruptive. Transforming rural agriculture, accelerating job creation, reducing urban-rural differentiation, and politically educating young people all seem much less manageable and much more politically threatening. Now implemented in all secondary schools throughout the country, vocationalization has begun to develop a momentum of its own.

Educational Expenditures

Educational spending has constituted a major portion of total government expenditures during 1960–1981 (see Table 7–4), drawing on both local and foreign sources.[24] For a poor country with a small educated cadre

[23] In fact, the preliminary assessments are not particularly persuasive. Since the vocationalization had barely begun, its limited impact is primarily a function of its slow start-up and does not reveal much about its longer-term consequences. In addition, confidence in these initial findings is undermined by the major study's inadequate differentiation among school types, severely flawed outcome measures (especially, the likelihood that most examinations assess English-language competence rather than the content being tested), and inattention to both the choice criteria for student preferences and the match (or rather, lack of match) between those preferences and ultimate placement (King 1986).

[24] The data here are far more problematic than is immediately apparent, even though the Tanzanian government has been rather more systematic in maintaining and keeping accounts than have governments in many other peripheral countries. Those data problems include the following: (1) Figures given are inconsistent among sources and over time; (2) data categories are not always adequately specified and may in fact change over time (for example, in many sources, the expenditure data for "Tanzanian schools" may refer in fact to *all* schools, or to *government-assisted* schools, or to *government* schools); (3) what many sources present as "expenditures" are in fact budgeted expenditures (which are rarely identical to and may be quite different from actual expenditures); (4) where actual expenditures are presented, the data are normally taken from the annual accounts, which are often prepared prior to approved supplementary allocations (that is, the data may refer to the actual expenditure of funds allocated at the beginning of the fiscal year and at the same time not include additional allocations made during, or, more commonly, after, the fiscal year; (5) commonly, data on educational expenditures refer to expenditures by the ministry of education, and do not include either expenditures on education by other ministries or agencies (for example, primary schooling financed by local government, or factory-based evening classes supported by employers) or expenditures essential to schooling but not directly instructional (for example, roads, vehicles, electrical service, and piped water); (6) expendi-

and high illiteracy at its independence and an ethos of citizen mobilization and participation, how could it be otherwise? It is widely accepted in Tanzania that the populace's limited education is a major obstacle to development, that more schooling is needed to end international dependence, and that schools should be responsible for selection as well as for education and training. All of those understandings further increase the pressure to expand educational expenditures.[25] The challenge, therefore, has been to balance the demand for expanded schooling with the need to fund other sectors and at the same time to reduce the inequalities (especially regional disparities) inherited from European rule. That balance has been sought through several related policies.

One strategy has been to reduce the expenditure per pupil. In practice, that requires reducing the expenditure on personnel, by far the major component of educational costs. There has been a good deal of success in this regard in adult education, through the use of volunteer teachers and educational radio programming and by organizing some literacy programs to rely on recent literates for the bulk of the instruction. The acceleration of the achievement of universal primary education required increased and rapid teacher training, much of it conducted through distant learning and in-service programs.[26]

At the same time, the cost of education at the upper levels has remained high (see Table 7–5). With few exceptions, the products and income derived from school self-help projects have not significantly reduced school expenditures. Although the average income generated per student has increased, its absolute magnitude remains far below the ini-

---

tures are commonly expressed in current shillings, thus ignoring changes in the value of the currency over time, which may have been substantial and which are rarely linear. Cross-national comparisons are even more problematic, since the problems listed above are compounded by differing definitions of key categories and measures. Consequently, we must assume that the margin of error for these data is wide, and we should be cautious in attaching much significance to small differences, either within countries over time or among countries.

[25] Although the effort to restrain school expansion in the 1960s was justified in part by characterizing education as expenditure on consumption rather than an investment in production, that orientation served more to rationalize than to influence policy.

[26] Distant learning (training) involved a brief residential program prior to assuming teaching responsibilities, followed by correspondence courses, periodic visits by teacher-educators, and occasional seminars at school sites. Omari, et al., assert that "if traditional training programs had been used, it would have taken 11 years and TShs. 1.2 billion to produce 40,000 teachers, whereas this program took 6 years and TShs. 242 million" (1983, 44). Note that both Tanzanian and external evaluators have concluded that primary school quality (assessed largely through results on the Standard VII examination) fell as a result of this accelerated teacher training and have recommended that distant-trained teachers be sent to upgrading programs in teachers colleges (thus eliminating some of the initial cost reduction).

TABLE 7–4

Tanzania: Expenditures on Education Compared to Total Public Expenditures and GNP, 1960–1981

	Public Expenditures on Education as Percentage of:				
				GNP	
Year	All Govt. Recurrent Expend.	All Govt. Dev. Expend.	Total Govt. Expend.	Recurrent Educ. Expend.	Total Educ. Expend.
1960		6.96			2.90
1961	15.51	13.81	15.23		
1962	15.25	18.70	16.87		2.80
1963	15.12	14.53	14.91		
1964	17.15	22.32	19.64		
1965	15.76	12.32	16.86		3.00
1966	14.24	10.48	13.69		
1967	13.77	7.89	12.71		
1968	13.40	1.86	13.80		3.15
1969	13.54	6.10	12.21		
1970	17.79	8.47	16.00	3.70	4.50
1971	10.92	15.41	14.65		4.10
1972	13.29	15.28	17.30		
1973	12.28	8.50	15.70	4.04	
1974	12.23	7.21	12.23		
1975	19.08	7.06	15.29		5.20
1976	14.49	6.50	14.53	5.32	
1977	15.73	6.31	15.86		
1978	12.44	6.12	13.20	4.26	4.90
1979	17.81	5.11	11.71		
1980	15.76	3.68	14.54		5.65
1981	17.01	4.35	12.10	4.40	

TABLE 7–4 (*Continued*)

Sources: Annual Joint Review of the Swedish Support to Education and Vocational Training, 1983, app. 3.2; Bank of Tanzania, *Tanzania: Twenty Years of Independence* (data for fiscal years 1963/64–1980/81; 1980/81 is an estimate); Carr-Hill, *Primary Education in Tanzania* (data from UNESCO, *Statistical Yearbook 1983*, tab. 4.1); Eicher, *Educational Costing and Financing in Developing Countries*, 1984 (data from UNESCO, *Statistical Yearbook*); Legum, "United Republic of Tanzania: The Economics of Disintegration," *Africa Contemporary Record 1982–83* (London: 1983), B289; Morrison, *Education and Politics in Africa: The Tanzanian Case* (data at factor cost; GDP/capita); Omari, et al., *Universal Primary Education in Tanzania*, 50; Tanzania, *The Economic Survey, 1971–1972* (Dar es Salaam: Ministry of Finance and Planning, 1973); Tanzania, *National Accounts*, various years; Tanzania, *National Accounts of Tanzania, 1966–74* (Dar es Salaam: Ministry of Finance and Planning, 1987); Tanzania, *Public Expenditure, Consolidated Fund Services and Supply Votes* (Dar es Salaam: Government Printer, 1986); Tanzania, *Statistical Abstract 1966* (for Central Government expenditures, for fiscal years 1960/61–1965/66); Tanzania, *Statistical Abstract 1970* (for Central Government expenditures, for fiscal years 1963/64–1969/70); Tanzania, *Statistical Abstract 1973–1979* (for Central Government expenditures, for fiscal years 1973/74–1978/79); UNESCO, *Statistical Yearbook 1973, 1975, 1983, 1985*; Wolff, *Controlling the Costs of Education in Eastern Africa*, 1984 (data from *UNESCO Statistical Yearbook*; World Bank Appraisal Reports, Sector Studies); World Bank, *African Education and Socioeconomic Indicators: An Annex to Education Policies in Sub-Saharan Africa* (Washington: October 1986), tab. 14; World Bank, *World Development Report, 1984, 1987*, tab. 23.

Note: Available sources provide widely discrepant figures. Where I have not been able to resolve the discrepancies, I have listed here the mean of the available data. Empty cells reflect missing or especially unreliable data. In using these data, it is important to recognize that the margin of error for particular figures is often greater than the apparent variation between years.

TABLE 7–5
Tanzania: Estimated per Student Expenditure, 1982

	TSh	Ratio
Primary pupil	780	1.0
Secondary pupil	8,078	10.4
Teachers' college student	14,320	18.4
Technical college student	19,218	24.6
University student	85,524	109.6

Source: Tanzania, Ministry of Education, *Basic Facts about Education in Tanzania* (Dar es Salaam: Ministry of Education, revised 1984), 16.

tial expectation of 25 percent of school operating costs (see Table 7–6). Each of the cost-cutting measures adopted, however, has other, perhaps undesirable, consequences. For example, current policy calls for new secondary schools to be day, rather than boarding, schools. Transferring from the public treasury to students' families the costs associated with housing and feeding their children and supervising their leisure time is expected to permit very rapid expansion, projected to double govern-

TABLE 7–6

Tanzania: Economic Production Activities of Government Secondary Schools, 1981–1985 (Tanzanian shillings)

	1981	1982	1983	1984	1985
Investment (production costs)	12,605,497	14,413,571	17,038,005	24,044,689	21,136,280
% Change	53.0%	14.3%	18.2%	41.1%	−12.1%
Income	15,855,817	20,704,561	25,587,432	37,234,910	36,323,300
% Change	43.4%	30.6%	23.6%	45.5%	−2.4%
Profit/loss	3,250,320	6,290,990	8,549,427	13,190,220	15,187,020
% Change	15.3%	93.5%	35.9%	54.3%	15.1%
Unit profit per student	85.60	161.60	215.15	322.50	415.70
% Change	16.8%	88.8%	33.1%	49.9%	28.9%

Source: Tanzania, *Basic Education Statistics in Tanzania (BEST) 1981–1985* (Dar es Salaam: Ministry of Education, 1986), 11.

ment secondary schools in less than a decade. At the same time, the day school arrangement is likely to favor urban children, since few rural areas are sufficiently densely populated to support many (or any) secondary schools and since such schools will in general recruit more heavily from their immediate areas. Day schools also make it more difficult to distribute secondary school students throughout the country, both equalizing the selection across the regions and giving students experiences in other than their home area. Similarly, although the evening secondary schools operated by the Institute of Adult Education do operate at a lower expenditure per pupil (essentially, the cost of training and maintaining their teachers is borne by the government school system, whose teachers moonlight in the evening schools), they, too, favor urban over rural residents and more affluent over less affluent areas. Thus, some of the apparent inefficiency in secondary and tertiary education is in fact indirect expenditure to reduce inequalities. What is called increased educational efficiency, therefore, is likely to have its own price: exacerbated inequalities.

As I have noted above, a substantial portion of the development (capital) expenditure on education has been provided by foreign donors, another strategy for expanding schooling more rapidly without an equally rapid increase in expenditures on education.[27] Although the figures

[27] Note that these data both overstate and understate the significance of the foreign contribution. On one hand, education development expenditures are a small portion of total spending on education—for example, approximately 13% for 1983–1984 (Carr-Hill 1984, 13). Hence, the large foreign contribution is relatively small in terms of overall spending. At the same time, although foreign donors normally support new projects and not contin-

themselves are dramatic, the patterns of foreign influence are more complex and subtle than the data suggest. Indeed, Tanzania's leaders are quite sensitive to the possibility of the external determination of national development goals and strategies. Any initiative that could be clearly labeled as the consequence of foreign pressure would encounter staunch opposition. Yet, external agendas are influential. That influence operates in several forms. Internationally set priorities (for example, attention to gender inequalities in access to schooling) become a context within which educational planning is carried out. Since funds for schooling are chronically tight, proponents of new programs commonly look to external assistance. In doing so, they must find a match between their own goals and those of potential donors. Clearly, those programs that fit best within foreign assistance agency priorities are most likely to be funded and thus to be carried out. As that occurs, those Tanzanians who are most successful in negotiating foreign support acquire increased status and often authority. They also become candidates for donor-financed overseas travel. Those visits, in turn, influence subsequent thinking about policy directions. External agencies normally require systematic reporting and evaluation. Consequently, those projects most amenable to the required recordkeeping tend to be favored. Projects for which recordkeeping and evaluation are inherently more difficult (for example, locally based adult education groups) are correspondingly more difficult to fund with foreign assistance. In sum, although foreign assistance has been critical to the rapid expansion of schooling in Tanzania, it has not been free. Difficult to measure precisely, its costs are not unimportant, especially over the longer term.

Yet another strategy for reducing educational expenditures is to raise funds directly and indirectly from the citizenry. It has long been common in Tanzania to expect local residents to donate labor and materials for the construction of school buildings. Impossible to quantify or even estimate accurately, the value of those contributions has been enormous, accounting for a significant proportion of school facilities throughout the country, including teachers' houses and auxiliary buildings, especially at the primary level. The current secondary school expansion plans presume that school construction will be a local responsibility. In most areas that is assumed to mean labor and materials contributed by residents.

With support from the Presidential Commission on Education,[28] sec-

---

uing programs, in practice that is at times an accounting sleight of hand. Swedish assistance, for example, has provided paper and thus exercise books to the primary schools (*Annual Joint Review 1983*).

[28] Tanzania's leadership has periodically created a national commission charged with investigating a highly visible troubled situation and making appropriate recommendations. Constituted to include representatives of institutions deemed politically important, such

ondary school fees were restored in 1985. Primary school fees dated from the era of European rule and continued into independence. Collected by the local education authority, primary school fees were an important source of revenue, especially since they were far more easily collected than local personal taxes.[29] Abolished in 1973 as part of the effort to reduce regional inequalities, primary school fees were effectively restored in the 1984, now termed a "development levy" (Tan 1985).

Postprimary schooling, however, had a different history. The British administration maintained separate school systems for Europeans, Asians, and Africans in Tanganyika and initially discouraged postprimary academic education for Africans. The British had provided, however, limited secondary education for the sons of the colonized elite, seeking in Tanganyika as elsewhere to socialize a new leadership and to nurture a class whose political identification would reach more to colonial and other European-dominated institutions than to anticolonial nationalism. The educated African elite was schooled, equipped, housed, fed, and transported at government expense, though fees were charged at some of the initially European and Asian schools. Independence saw the integration of the racially distinct secondary schools and the control over and then, in 1964, the elimination of secondary school fees.

That secondary education should be rapidly expanded and free made sense in an era when the critical development need was understood to be high-level skills. From the societal perspective, postprimary education was intended to groom leaders. In an egalitarian and democratic ethos, it would be inappropriate to pay a fee to enter the public service. Selection by merit for limited leadership positions made postprimary schooling a public, not private, investment. Yet substantial private benefits clearly accrued to those who proceeded beyond primary school. That advantage became even more important as the high priority assigned to universal primary education and adult literacy in the early 1970s severely limited the expansion of postprimary education, with the result that a smaller and smaller percentage of those who entered school could proceed beyond the seventh year. With a small educational establishment at independence, 36 percent of the students who completed

commissions often become a major site for political conflict and for reconciling conflicting orientations among the political elite. The Presidential Commission on Education was created in 1980 and reported in 1982 (Tanzania Ministry of Education 1982a, 1982b). Another two years were to pass before formal consideration of all of its major recommendations (Tanzania 1984) was completed. The Commission's chairman, an influential member of parliament who was publicly chastised for releasing the Commission's report to the press prior to formal party action, was subsequently appointed Minister of National Education.

[29] For a discussion of school fees and financing primary education in an area of Tanzania with a very dense school network, see Samoff 1974, 40–51.

primary school were admitted to secondary school. After the very rapid expansion of primary education in the 1970s, by 1981 only some 2 percent could proceed to government secondary schools (see Table 7–7). Of those who began their schooling in 1971, barely 4 percent were selected for secondary school in 1978, and only 0.2 percent entered the University of Dar es Salaam in 1984 (see Table 7–8).

Private secondary schools, which had earlier seemed a major threat to Tanzania's egalitarian goals, were by the late 1970s seen as a partial solution to the combination of insatiable demand for expanded access with available funds insufficient to finance that expansion. Now encouraged, private secondary schools,[30] though required to be formally registered, were permitted to charge fees at officially approved rates. Stressing the chronic lack of funds and pointing both to the value of secondary schooling and to parents' apparent ability to pay the fees, educators successfully lobbied for the introduction of school fees in government secondary schools. Although the fee established was only a quarter of what had been

TABLE 7–7

Tanzania: Selection to Secondary Schools as Proportion of Students Completing Primary School, 1961–1986 (selected years)

Year	Students Completing Primary School (N)	Students Selected for Form I from Those Completing Standard VII/VIII in:					
		Govt. Schools		Private Schools		Govt. and Private Schools	
		N	%	N	%	N	%
1961	11,732	4,196	35.8	n.a.	n.a.	n.a.	n.a.
1965	29,367	5,942	20.2	458	1.6	6,400	21.8
1970	64,630	7,350	11.4	3,021	4.7	10,371	16.0
1975	137,559	8,680	6.3	5,114	3.7	13,794	10.0
1980	212,446	8,913	4.2	6,677	3.1	15,590	7.3
1985	429,194	10,881	2.5	11,745	2.7	22,626	5.3

Source: United Republic of Tanzania, Ministry of Education, *Basic Education Statistics in Tanzania (BEST) 1981–1985* (Dar es Salaam: Ministry of Education, 1986), 7.

Note: For the data presented here, Tanzania = mainland Tanzania.

[30] In the political ethos of contemporary Tanzania, and in contrast to the situation elsewhere in Africa, private secondary schools must be owned and managed by approved voluntary agencies (including churches and the YMCA), community organizations, or local governments. Formal rules and community sentiment bar both schools intended to make a profit and schools run by individual private entrepreneurs.

TABLE 7–8
Tanzania: Academic Education of the 1971 Cohort Year in School, 1984

Year	School	Grade	Number of Students	% of Previous Year	% of 1971 Cohort
1984	University	1st Year	1,176	42.0	0.2
1983	Secondary[a]	Form 6	2,801	96.7	0.5
1982		Form 5	2,896	16.8	0.6
1981		Form 4	17,200	88.1	3.3
1980		Form 3	19,515	99.5	3.7
1979		Form 2	19,608	93.1	3.7
1978		Form 1	21,057	5.0	4.0
1977	Primary[b]	Standard VII	422,803	105.1	80.5
1976		Standard VI	402,247	95.9	76.6
1975		Standard V	419,324	97.1	79.9
1974		Standard IV	432,048	90.5	82.3
1973		Standard III	477,404	99.2	90.9
1972		Standard II	481,308	91.7	91.7
1971		Standard I	525,011	—	100.0

Source: Tanzania, *Basic Education Statistics in Tanzania (BEST) 1981–1985* (Dar es Salaam: Ministry of Education, 1986).

[a] Government and private secondary schools.

[b] Government schools (private primary schools enrolled 9,614 students in 1986, 0.3% of the total primary school enrollment).

proposed, the principle was established: There would be a direct charge for postprimary education.

Concomitantly, obstacles to the registration of private secondary schools were eased. In the egalitarian emphasis of the late 1960s and early 1970s, such schools served less than one-quarter of the secondary school population. By the mid-1980s, private secondary schools and students outnumbered their government counterparts in Tanzania (see Table 7–9) (Samoff 1987a).

Here, too, there is a dual edge. Relying on parents' contributions of labor and materials and taxing families to educate their children have certainly permitted a more rapid educational expansion than would otherwise have been possible. In addition, the creation of private schools reflects popular demand and local political initiatives, both of which seem quite consistent with a philosophy of self reliance. At the same time, it is the most affluent areas that have been most able to take advantage of this privatization, thus increasing regional disparities. For example, by 1984 one-fourth of all the secondary schools and fully 42 percent of all the private secondary schools in the country were in Kilimanjaro Region, whose residents were 5.3 percent of the total mainland Tanzanian population. Kilimanjaro students constituted 28.7 percent of all of the Form 5 students in Tanzania in 1982; in ethnic terms, the Chagga, 3.7 percent of the national population, provided 20.5 percent of those Form 5 students (Cooksey and Ishumi 1986, 17 and 28, quoting Malekela 1983, 154 and 160).

As high as they are, the tuition and fees of a private secondary education probably keep few children out of school. Since so few students are ultimately admitted, and since access is so highly valued, parents whose children are selected will make extraordinary efforts to find the necessary funds, drawing on relatives, friends, neighbors, and other networks.

While children from poorer families who are selected may manage to enter secondary school, it does seem likely that differences in parents' wealth manifest themselves long before secondary school selection: progress in school is related to parents' socioeconomic status.[31] Affluent parents are less likely to require their children to devote many hours to tending the fields or herding animals. They can also purchase private instruction during the primary school years and provide a home environment that is more supportive of educational achievement. Children of affluent parents are likely to have traveled more and to have more frequent opportunities to hear and speak English (emphasized in the selection examinations and the secondary school language of instruction). Affluent parents are better able to establish residences elsewhere in the country where their children can repeat or have reduced competition. Finally, affluent parents are better situated—in terms of both available funds and political efficacy—to increase the number of private secondary schools in their community and improve their quality.

---

[31] Studies of African education provide conflicting findings on the relationship between socioeconomic status and access to and success in school. It has often proved difficult to distinguish the independent significance of socioeconomic status from the impact of differences in ethnicity, race, gender, urban residence, and other factors. That is probably especially problematic in countries like Tanzania, where most students come from peasant background and very few are selected to proceed: There is so little variation in both independent and dependent variables that the consequences of status differences are overwhelmed. The evidence in Tanzania does suggest, however, that the rate of school success is higher for elite children. For an overview, see Blakemore and Cooksey 1981, ch. 3; and Court and Kinyanjui 1980.

TABLE 7–9
Tanzania: Government and Private Secondary Schools and Enrollment, 1961–1986

Year	Government (N)		Private (N)		Total (N)		% Private	
	Schools	Students	Schools	Students	Schools	Students	Schools	Students
1961		11,832						
1962	61	14,175	1		62		1.6	
1963	61	17,275	1		62		1.6	
1964	63	19,897	5		68		7.4	
1965	69	21,795	7	1,065	76	22,860	9.2	4.7
1966	70	23,836	17	3,792	87	27,628	19.5	13.7
1967	72	25,557	30	8,565	102	34,122	29.4	25.1
1968	73	28,043	35	7,571	108	35,614	32.4	21.3
1969	74	29,958	37	8,092	111	38,050	33.3	21.3
1970	74	31,217	40	9,961	114	41,178	35.1	24.2
1971	75	32,603	41	10,749	116	43,352	35.3	24.8
1972	76	33,288	40	10,503	116	43,791	34.5	24.0
1973	80	34,502	44	12,623	124	47,125	35.5	26.8
1974	81	35,926	53	14,366	134	50,292	39.6	28.6
1975	81	38,327		15,038		53,365		28.2
1976	81	39,947	61	17,196	142	57,143	43.0	30.1
1977	81	41,965		19,213		61,178		31.4
1978	84	41,792	71	22,400	155	64,192	45.8	34.9
1979	83	40,298	69	28,003	152	68,301	45.4	41.0
1980	83	38,830	71	28,466	154	67,296	46.1	42.3
1981	83	38,292	75	29,310	158	67,602	47.5	43.4
1982	85	38,983	81	30,162	166	69,145	48.8	43.6
1983	85	39,737	82	31,536	167	71,273	49.1	44.2
1984	85	40,617	84	33,591	169	74,208	49.7	45.3
1985	85	42,892	96	36,633	181	79,525	53.0	46.1
1986	95	43,911	107	45,703	202	89,614	53.0	51.0

Source: Ministry of (National) Education.
Note: Statistics provided by different sources do not fully agree. I have listed what I regard as the most accurate figure. (In many sources, school and enrollment data refer in fact only to government schools.)

Thus, Tanzanian educators are expected both to expand schools rapidly and to reduce inequalities in access to schooling. Yet each of the strategies pursued to secure additional resources for education—increasing internal efficiency (that is, reducing the expenditure per pupil), securing foreign assistance, requiring local contributions, and instituting school fees—puts other national policy goals at risk. In the tension between expansion and equality the current balance has shifted toward the former. In the contemporary alignment of political forces, school expansion has priority over reducing inequalities.

Persisting Problems

Many of the specific goals envisaged in educational reform policies in Tanzania have been achieved. Nearly all young Tanzanians will enter school, and most will complete the basic seven-year primary program.[32] That in itself is an extraordinary accomplishment. Curriculum revision—focusing educational content more directly on Tanzania's experiences and concerns—has been extensive. Examinations are constructed and graded within Tanzania. Although there is wide variation in practice, almost all schools do maintain productive projects, and in some schools there are important lessons in production techniques, cooperative labor, and marketing strategies. Many formerly illiterate adults have gained access to the world of writing; new institutions—Folk Development Colleges, village libraries—have been created to nurture and extend their new competence. All students at the University of Dar es Salaam focus some attention on Tanzanian and East African society and environment. In many respects, educational reform has been quite successful.

In other respects, however, and especially in its role in laying the foundation for socialist development, it has been far less successful. I want here to review briefly what are regarded in Tanzania as the persisting problems—issues of economic, political, and social organization and of ideological content—which the educational system is expected to address. In doing so, it is important to note that the specification of critical social problems is itself a function of political conflict—that is, not only the priorities assigned to public policies, but also the ostensibly objective definition of the problems to which those policies are addressed, result

---

[32] Since children enter school at different ages, several measures of enrollment are relevant. The 1984 data suggest that there are enough school places for nearly all children (enrollment: 95%), that approximately two-thirds of the school-age children are actually in school (enrollment: 68%), and that 80–90% of the children will eventually enter school (Ministry of National Education (Tanzania) 1981; Carr-Hill 1984).

from conflict among contending forces within and outside Tanzania. This is not simply a matter of semantics, such as labeling the study of the party constitution "political education" or "civics" or "indoctrination." A good deal of public discourse involves the exchange of political symbols (Edelman 1964, 1971). To be able to define the symbols themselves is to influence the terrain on which policy debate is conducted, to delimit what can be legitimately expressed, and to assign value (positive or negative) to particular expressions. To define the symbols is also to specify *whose* problems will receive public attention and from which perspective that attention will be oriented.

Consider, for example, the common view that "educated unemployment" is a serious problem in contemporary Africa. That many of the young people who finish school do not find the jobs they expected seems obvious. Since the "problem" seems self-evident, discourse can turn to proposed remedies: more school-based vocational training, postschool vocational courses, stronger socialization to reduce students' expectation of wage employment, slower school expansion, and so on. In this way, debate is effectively limited to a range of alternative policies bounded by largely unchallenged assumptions about the nature of the problem itself and about the types of solutions appropriate to problems of that sort. Yet *whose* problem are the frustrated aspirations of those who complete primary school? Would those young people be better off if they were unemployed *and* illiterate? Would society benefit from less education and reduced aspirations? What in the history of education in Africa (or elsewhere) leads us to believe that the level of unemployment (and underemployment) among school graduates can be effectively addressed by reforming school patterns?[33] It seems reasonable to infer that the concern with "educated unemployment" stems largely from apprehension about the difficulties in meeting the political demands of a potentially very powerful segment of society. "Educated unemployment" is more problematic than, say, gender inequalities in access to education because in the contemporary setting it is more likely to threaten those in power and the political order itself. To understand "educated unemployment" as a problem of job creation rather than schooling is itself threatening, since unlike misdirected schooling, the failure of development policies points directly to the leadership.[34]

[33] Foster's (1965) early cautionary note seems to be both widely cited and widely ignored. Perhaps that, too, reflects the politics of educational policy: It is less threatening to dominant political coalitions to locate problems in the schools and attempt to reform schooling than to identify the organization of production as problematic and suggest transforming the economy.

[34] I do not mean here to raise, let alone resolve, the complex issues involved in the

Educational administrators see one set of problems. Parents see another. Teachers see a third. Modernizationists and socialists have very different sets of priorities, not only because their politics differ, but also because their political differences lead them to experience a different world.

Too Much Demand and Too Little Money

The education establishment in Tanzania locates the major problems in the tension between insatiable demand and insufficient funds. Even though schools have been expanded much more rapidly than anyone had thought possible, even though universal primary education was accomplished several years ahead of the original schedule, and even though most adult Tanzanians have acquired basic literacy, still the public pressure for more schooling persists. As I have noted here, and as others have noted elsewhere, the persistence of that pressure is not surprising. What educators regard as a means for achieving a specific social goal (schooling to generate needed skills), the public sees much more broadly as the path of advance toward multiple goals (from security against drought and other environmental disasters to an improved standard of living to stable and supportive political communities, and more). Providing primary education to everyone has thus not reduced the demand, but rather shifted it toward the level of education that is not universally available. From the educators' perspective, that demand simply cannot be met, either now or in the foreseeable future. Acutely aware of both the high cost of schooling and the limited funds available, educators have often been the voice of caution, protesting the technical impossibility of expansion policies promoted by the political leadership.

From the educators' perspective, since demand escalates even faster than schools can be increased, the major consequence of very rapid expansion has been declining quality (among others, see Omari, et al. 1983, 38–50, 65–80). For example, at the time of the 1974 decision to achieve universal primary education by 1977, the primary schools already had a deficit of approximately 10,000 teachers (Omari, et al. 1983, 44). Accel-

---

relationships between education and work. Rather, my concern is simply to stress that the specification of problems worthy of public policy attention is a function of analytic perspective, and therefore ultimately of political conflict. In that, I am pointing to what Bachrach and Baratz (1962, 1963, 1970) have termed the politics of nondecisions and what those influenced by Gramsci characterize as hegemony (see Carnoy 1984, 65–88, for a discussion and references).

erated enrollment would require an 80 percent increase in the teacher corps—40,000 new teachers—within the next three years (Stabler 1979). The teacher training institutions, themselves short of staff with a total enrollment of 9,978 in 1974 (Tanzania 1981, 375), could not possibly meet the new demand. Although in principle, effective teacher preparation could be accomplished through the distant learning and in-service programs that were established, in practice, program development barely preceded, and at times followed, the enrollment of teacher trainees. The predictable result, educators point out, has been a decline in the quality of instruction. What else could one expect, they stress, in schools where classes can have a hundred pupils sitting at thirty desks and sharing ten books?

Measuring the quality of instruction in Tanzanian primary schools is a complex task. In addition to developing students' basic reading, composition, and arithmetic skills, primary schools are expected to introduce basic concepts and procedures in science and social studies, to foster familiarity with commonality and diversity in Tanzanian history and society, to prepare a small group for postprimary education, to socialize and politicize young people, to engender values and attitudes consonant with Tanzanian socialism (for example, cooperative labor rather than ego-centered individualism), to integrate their programs with the local communities they serve, and to teach and model self-reliance. How does one measure high-quality learning in self-reliance or in political mobilization? In practice, many of those enunciated goals have never been fully incorporated into the reward system for either teachers or students. As elsewhere, teachers teach to the exam, in this case, the Standard VII examination, which governs selection for further education and is thus formally the major determinant of an individual's life chances. Since that examination is organized around the basic academic work, it is academic achievement that is generally taken as the standard for assessing both individual progress and the quality of instruction more broadly. By that measure, the quality of instruction did decline in Tanzanian primary schools.[35] Based on that conclusion, plans have been developed to upgrade the distant-learning teachers.

[35] The major study compared examination results of students from schools with residential college-trained teachers and those from schools with distant-trained teachers. The causal link was presumed in the design of the study: that the source of declining quality was the inadequate training teachers had received. There was little or no attention to the wide range of other possible explanations—for example, that doubling the primary school enrollment had recruited many students who had previously selected themselves out and who would have done less well on an academic examination irrespective of teachers; that declining exam scores were to a significant extent a function of lower competence in English, which may have stemmed from less well prepared teachers but which was not wholly undesirable, since a smaller percentage of primary school students would proceed to the sec-

Note that the political leadership resisted the complaints about declining quality. Nyerere argued that the attention to falling standards was in practice an effort to protect bourgeois advantage: "We cannot protect the excellence of education for the few by neglecting the education for the majority. In Tanzania, it is a sin to do so" (quoted in Omari, et al. 1983, 41).

In the educators' view, this and other problems are compounded by the political content of Tanzanian education policy. From their perspective, operating an effective educational system requires not only securing additional foreign assistance and decreasing the burden on the public treasury by encouraging private schools but also reducing the priority assigned to schools' extraeducational concerns (inequality, participation, political education).[36]

Too Few Schools

For the majority of Tanzania's citizens, the central educational problem is that schools have expanded too slowly. As universal primary education was achieved, the focus of that demand shifted from primary to postprimary education. Put somewhat differently, twenty-five years after independence, still only a small elite has access to the schooling that matters. From this perspective, efforts to increase the links between schools and their local communities, to introduce more vocational training into the school curriculum, and to eschew preparing students to proceed to higher levels (for example, intensive instruction in English) all function to deflect peasants' aspirations. What leaders describe as an education relevant to a poor Third World country and supportive of a broad social transformation, Tanzania's citizenry regards as the creation of a two-tier educational system: an elite level that leads through postprimary education to a comfortable life-style resting on a mass level that is self-limiting and returns its graduates to the countryside. Hence, although peasant families might seem to benefit most from a ruralized and vocationalized pattern of schooling, in practice they are often its most outspoken critics.

---

ondary schools, where English is the language of instruction; that the accelerated teacher training and the ethos of universal primary education led new teachers to pay more attention to self-reliance and political education (that is, a higher quality of instruction in subjects not measured by the examination); and more.

[36] Many educational researchers and evaluators share this aversion to the broader conception of educational goals. Cooksey and Ishumi, for example, conclude that "the attempt to further ethnic balance through regional quotas has meant (1) a substantial diminution of the average quality of secondary school entrants. . . . It is arguably the case that the gains . . . cannot be justified in view of the high price which is paid in terms of educational quality and efficiency." Hence, they argue, quotas should be abolished (Cooksey and Ishumi 1986, 30, 32–37).

Why, they insist, should our children be excluded at the outset from the main recruitment channel? Why should they be denied a chance to learn English and the other subjects needed to proceed to secondary education and better jobs? Why should our children not have the same curriculum as the children of the bureaucrats? In sum, if schools are to be the primary path toward a better life for anyone, they should be open equally to everyone.

At the same time, parents often complain that their children complete school without marketable skills, or with skills whose marketability depends on start-up capital and/or tools and equipment that are unavailable. This critique also points to frustrated aspirations. The problem is not that their children have not learned farming techniques, which parents expect them to learn at home, but rather that they have not mastered the sorts of skills that will enable them to leave the farm.[37]

For the Tanzanian populace, then, it is elitism and bureaucracy that are problematic, not funding. Indeed, as the experience with private secondary school shows, when opportunities are available, the needed funds materialize. This populist perspective has remained for the most part unfocused and only occasionally clearly articulated. In part, that has to do with the history of the parents' auxiliary of the party, formerly TAPA (Tanganyika African Parents Association) and now Wazazi.[38] The organization was founded to open and manage primary schools in an earlier era (Morrison 1976; Omari 1968). Even then it had difficulty in bringing its schools up to the required standards. Once primary schools were nationalized and universal primary education in government schools was accelerated, TAPA's primary purpose disappeared, and the organization, which had always been characterized by a few strong local branches and a weak national center, decayed. Since for most of the past decade government policy has been to discourage, or restrain, the creation of private secondary schools, it made little sense for the party to try to revitalize TAPA. Consequently, while Wazazi can provide an umbrella to protect and legitimize some local school creation initiatives, and although occasionally Nyerere and other Tanzanian leaders address it as the representative of

[37] Commentators often deride these expectations. After all, most peasants' children will become farmers. Like their higher-status fellow citizens, however, rural farmers hope for a significant generational improvement in the standard of living. Especially where social transformation and equality of opportunity are frequently articulated goals, it makes little sense to expect peasants' children to be content to pick up their parents' hoes. The educational challenge thus far unmet, therefore, is to develop an educational system that is less costly and more responsive to the local situation and that at the same time does not in its operation become a major impediment to social mobility for most of the population.

[38] Literally, Swahili for "parents," Wazazi is a short form for the Jumuiya ya Wazazi wa Tanzania (Tanzanian Parents Association), which succeeded the Tanganyika African Parents Association (TAPA) at the 1977 creation of the CCM.

the parents, Wazazi has not functioned as the major articulator of the interests of Tanzanians as parents.

Schooling for Whom, in Whose Interest?

Neither the educators' concerns with insufficient funds and declining quality nor the populace's demand for more rapid expansion fully captures the underlying premise of Tanzanian educational policy. Even though political education is a part of the curriculum in all Tanzanian educational institutions, most Tanzanians—both leaders and populace—continue to understand education largely as a technical process. Managing schooling and learning is like running a complex machine: Well-informed leaders can organize the scarce available resources, understand when to lubricate the bearings and change the gearing, and thus manufacture high-quality products. Put somewhat differently, although social transformation is prominent in the rhetoric and announced goals of educational reform, schooling in Tanzania continues to be primarily concerned with skills and selection and continues to be organized around modernizationist assumptions and criteria. Expected to guide development, those modernization assumptions generate policies in and around schooling that themselves become obstacles to change and thus the focus of political conflict.

It seems clear that as long as schooling remains the principal path to the good life—or, rather, as long as access to a higher standard of living, influence, and status depend on sequential progress along a linear schooling track—popular demand for more schools will persist, escalate, and remain unmet, and perhaps unmeetable. Concomitantly, when schools are dominated by their selection role, both learning and social transformation are sidetracked.

BASIC EDUCATION AND SCHOOLS AS SELECTORS

In this setting, primary schooling can never become the basic education, universally available and complete in itself, envisioned in the official statements of educational philosophy and goals. Educators, parents, and students themselves all insist that primary schools continue to prepare students to proceed to secondary school even though currently only some 5 percent of those who complete primary school are selected for government and private secondary schools. Primary schools and teachers are assessed on this measure. As a result, primary schools necessarily provide a curriculum that is neither adequate nor complete for the majority of their students. The perception of primary education as neither adequate nor complete is captured symbolically in the designation of those who master successfully the primary school curriculum: primary school "leavers." Not "completers" or "certificate holders" or "diplomates" or "graduates," or another term coined specifically for this purpose, they are "leavers," people who have not successfully completed their education. The resilience of that designation suggests its symbolic importance in preserving the central focus of primary schooling: preparation and selection.

As long as the educational program available to all citizens (currently, primary schooling) reveres the expertise it does not provide, it fosters a continuing reliance on expatriate technology, skills, and personnel. It also reinforces the deference to education elsewhere, and therefore to foreign educators and their criteria of value. Although there are powerful extraeducational determinants of elite selection in Tanzania, as schools function to recruit the future elite, much of their practice promotes continued dependence, undermining efforts to teach self reliance. More generally, educational programs orchestrated to nurture a fragile peripheral capitalism are inhospitable to the requisites of fundamental social transformation.

Although what I have been calling the modernization perspective expects schools to be sites of elite selection, it also expects that process to work best when it is least visible. Asserting that there is no fundamental incompatibility between selection and learning, it glorifies learning to permit selection to continue relatively undisturbed. Such subtleties are probably impossible in Tanzania and perhaps much of the Third World. The route to the top is simply too narrow to be disguised. And where governance is more bureaucratic and centralized than liberal and democratic, it is essential to distinguish those who have followed that route from those who have not.

SCHOOLS AND OTHER NATIONAL POLICY GOALS

To the extent that schools remain focused on skills and selection, they remain distant from other articulated national policy goals. Even the human resource expectations (commonly termed "manpower planning") of schooling remain unfulfilled. At first glance, it would seem straightforward for Tanzania's centralized educational system to meet specific skills goals. If the planners project the need for, say, electricians, then the school authorities, who have final say over curriculum, selection, and student assignment, ought to be able to ensure that there are regularly trained an appropriate number of people with the requisite skills. Yet both educators and planners decry the schools' failure to provide technical and other intermediate-level training. In other words, the very authorities responsible for achieving the outcome they say is desirable complain that the goal remains as distant as ever. This apparent inability of the school managers to focus the schools on what they say they regard as the high-priority tasks reflects the pervasiveness and the power of the modernization agenda. For the school managers, the larger goal (preparing technicians) is sidetracked by a variety of smaller decisions. The day-to-day business of managing schools has to do with widening access and narrowing selection. Sorting out conflicting claims on scarce resources and trying to cope with the crises of overcrowded and underequipped classrooms and overtaxed and underprepared teachers demand priority attention. At the same time, parents' complaints about the low success rate on the Standard VII examination ring louder than calls for more technical education.

Human Resource Development: A Stunted Hybrid

The "manpower planning" orientation itself is a hybrid whose components are drawn from the expectation in both capitalist and socialist educational philosophies that schooling will concentrate heavily on skills development.[39] But Tanzanian educators have appropriated the emphasis on the link between schools and skills while ignoring the corresponding importance of modifying the structure of social rewards to support this pattern of schooling. Rurally focused (and not simply located) secondary schools, for example, have not been favored in resource allocation and political recruitment as they have in Cuba. Consequently, they remain second-level and second-choice.

The other part of the hybrid, appropriated from the modernizationists, has also involved borrowing form and process while ignoring context and underlying relationships. Notions of efficiency, developed out of analyses of comparative costs and benefits which are constructed from a very narrow sense of human capital and returns on investment, serve primarily to hide the politics of a very uneven distribution of resources and to disguise the identity of the primary beneficiaries of that distribution. Ostensibly objective in its operation, promotion by examination largely favors the already advantaged. The insistence on objectivity becomes a rationale for excluding from the promotion criteria both teachers' evaluations (deemed too subjective) and accomplishments outside the academic subjects (deemed impossible to quantify adequately). It is not surprising, then, that teachers, parents, and students all focus their attention and

---

[39] Acknowledging the popular pressure for expanded access, the approved recommendations of the Presidential Commission on Education included public demand as a criterion for secondary school expansion, but at the same time retained the prior emphasis on human resource development: "Both the 'Social Demand' and 'Manpower Needs' approaches will be used in development plans aimed at meeting the country's manpower requirements in different fields and levels of expertise" (Tanzania 1984, 10).

energy on mathematics, English, and history, grudgingly devoting the required time (and perhaps not even that) to farming, technology, and self reliance projects. The rewards for individual achievement in a highly competitive environment render distinctly unattractive efforts devoted to developing attitudes of cooperation, reciprocity, and national service. Mastering the syllabus is simply more important than developing a critical consciousness, and memorizing official facts prevails over analyzing underdevelopment.

Self reliance thus becomes a form without a critical function, serving neither the modernization nor the social transformation agenda. Forms detached from their economic, political, and social roots produce unfertilized and unirrigated hybrids that either wilt before they flower or succumb to the combined assault of multiple challenges they are too weak to resist. The societal soil itself is probably too poor to nurture this hybrid. That is, even were it better nourished, the human resource orientation is probably unworkable in a setting where the infrastructure is weak, data generation and collection are limited and inconsistent, and external influences on the economy as a whole, and thus on job creation, remain dominant.

Notwithstanding the schools' focus on skills and selection, vocationalization efforts at all levels are unlikely to have much impact on overall outcomes. On the one hand, vocationalization will be resisted within the schools as a distraction from the academic activities that matter. Similarly, peasants will resist vocationalization, regarding it as a strategy for relegating their children to an inferior educational track. On the other hand, since the vocationalization programs are largely disconnected from the forces that create jobs—forces that to a large extent still derive their impetus outside of Tanzania—they are unlikely to increase significantly the employability of young people once they have left school.

The obstacles to the human resource orientation and to effective vocationalization are compounded by the concentration of certification at the highest levels of schooling. With few clearly defined employment opportunities or career paths at middle and lower levels, employers cannot incorporate success at those levels into their credentialist practices. That is, in the absence of more differentiated and/or vocationally specific certification at the lower level, general success in primary school will remain more important than the acquisition of particular competencies. Hence, once again, the institutional arrangements incline students, parents, and teachers toward success in the Standard VII examination as the only measure that matters. Where nearly everyone goes to primary school and nearly everyone is not selected to proceed, even that examination may not matter much.

Recall that schools were to prepare the new people need to conceive, design, and then create the new society. More prosaically, the assumption was that the worldview and values implanted during the period of European rule fostered the behaviors that were to be eliminated from the new society: selfish individualism, aggressive competition, and exploitation. As in the other countries discussed in this volume, Tanzanian schools were to be the major site for both the combat against the old values and the gestation of their successors. The evidence of the first quarter-century of independence suggests that Tanzanian schools are not incubating socialists. Indeed, as I have stressed, the schools themselves are institutions of social differentiation. That differentiation is reinforced by distinctions of reward, influence, and status, which in turn are formally certified by promotion and selection procedures. Similarly, schools reinforce rather than reduce the differentiation between mental and manual labor, and by their practices support students' expectations of a more secure and more comfortable life-style, both during their schooling and after it.

Notwithstanding the reiterated commitments to schools as community institutions intended to stimulate and foster the new society, the underlying ideology embedded in the curriculum and organization of Tanzanian schools retain their role as midwives to the reproduction of the old society. Skills, achievement, and political participation, for example, continue to be understood in individual terms and measured and assessed individually. The authoritarianism and hierarchy—rather than participation and democracy—of classroom, school, and school system are zealously defended. It is not surprising, therefore, that those who are successful in the educational system evince a career preference for security over innovation and responsibility (Barkan 1971). They have mastered the schools' lessons well: Stability is in general preferable to the risks of innovation, and personal and family benefits outweigh collective rewards.

This set of values is also reflected in adult education. Although there have been critiques of functional literacy programs on just these grounds, in general, literacy education in Tanzania is primarily oriented toward the acquisition of basic communication skills and only secondarily concerned with political mobilization.[40]

Schooling and Inequality

Focused on skills and selection, schools are unlikely to have much impact on reducing inequalities or elitism. On this, the evidence is quite consis-

[40] One striking consequence of this is that rural adults, and even the most active participants in literacy programs, have rarely been consulted in the bureaucratic battles for control over the institutions of adult education (Unsicker 1987). There is little evidence that newly literate adults have become a mobilized constituency to articulate and defend their interests in the political arena.

tent. Notwithstanding several different strategies for reducing regional inequalities in access to education and in standard of living more generally, differentiation by region and district, and thus by ethnicity, persists—indeed, has increased (Malekela 1983 presents systematic and detailed evidence).

It is striking that the inequality commonly deemed most important is regional, and thus in the popular perception tribal, differentiation. There is far less attention to inequalities of gender, religion, race, or class, which are at least as dramatic in quantitative terms as the differences among regions.

Regional inequalities in access to schooling have far-reaching societal consequences. Schooling, after all, is the major recruitment mechanism for wage employment in general, and especially for high-level positions. Those regions with more schools, and with more children in school, will be better represented in decisionmaking throughout the society. Although ethnic inequalities may become in themselves an important political issue, perhaps even more important is a much less visible consequence of the regional disparities in access to education: the institutionalization of a particular worldview.

Kilimanjaro Region provides an informative illustration. Most (though, of course, not all) Kilimanjaro residents share a distinctly unsocialist ideology, nurtured by the local links to the world coffee market. Begun in Kilimanjaro early in this century, coffee production flourished. Coffee sales became one of the major sources of foreign exchange for Tanganyika, as it remains for contemporary Tanzania. Kilimanjaro thus became a gateway between Tanganyika and the world economy. Coffee beans were shipped out, and buyers, cash, consumer goods, and ideas flowed in. Capital could be accumulated to expand coffee production, to send local youth out for education, to develop the regional infrastructure, and to invest elsewhere. The coffee economy has also had dramatic political impacts both within the region (for example, facilitating the commoners' displacement of the chiefs) and outside it (greatly enhanced leverage in national politics).

During this process, a particular understanding of development, and therefore of desirable national policies and of Tanzania's global role, was elaborated. Put simply, development required the integration of Tanzania into the world system. Kilimanjaro residents were quite receptive to the development advice proffered by a World Bank mission to Tanzania at its independence: Emphasize export production; maintain good relations with traditional trading partners; encourage individual entrepreneurs; support the most successful farmers; aim at growth now and equality when the level of growth makes that feasible. That perspective continues to be articulated energetically.

As that ideology is institutionalized, it entrenches the myth of meritocracy. If Tanzania desperately needs the skills of its most competent citizens, then schools and examinations should be organized around advancement by competence. In this view, evidence of status inequalities (regional, class, or other) points to aberrations to be corrected, not the inadequacy of the selection system itself. Similarly, in this view, where socialism is rhetoric to be tolerated and managed, and where school farm projects and vocationalized secondary education are appropriate for the less successful students, it is desirable—indeed, necessary—that academic examinations determine promotion and that those who complete the basic educational program be regarded as school leavers. What matters is quality, of students and of schools, and quality has to do with academic accomplishment, not equality or socialist militancy. Consequently, the national significance of regional inequality—Kilimanjaro's relative advantage in access to schooling—is not simply a matter of ethnic imbalance. It is as well one dimension of the institutionalization of an ideology (Ake 1984).

The other inequalities noted above receive far less policy attention. Gender is perhaps a partial exception. Several policy changes have addressed the education of females. At entry into primary school, girls and boys are admitted in equal numbers, no small accomplishment. The percentage of girls has increased at all levels (see Table 7–10). Major educational policies, for example, the 1974 requirement that secondary school students have two years of work experience prior to university admission, have been modified because they were found to depress female enrollment. The Presidential Commission on Education proposed as a policy goal the elimination of gender inequalities in secondary and higher education (Tanzania 1984, 11). Yet it remains the case both that the percentage of female students declines dramatically beyond primary school and that the equalization policies implemented thus far are primarily concerned with regional origin, not gender. Efforts to reduce gender inequality have yet to address the discriminatory consequences of the large number of sexually segregated boarding government secondary schools and the gender specification of one of the four vocational specializations, home economics.

Though not well documented formally, religion is associated with access to and success in school. Indirect evidence suggests that Muslims are a smaller proportion of the total school enrollment than of the total population. This differentiation is rarely addressed directly, and there are not, to my knowledge, formal policies designed to increase the proportion of Muslim students. Similarly, although data on students' race have not been reported consistently, there is indirect evidence that higher proportions of Asian and European (both very small populations in Tan-

TABLE 7–10
Tanzania: Education for Women—Female Enrollment as Percentage of Total Enrollment, 1981–1985

	% of Female Students				
Educational Level	1981	1982	1983	1984	1985
Primary education					
Standard I	49.8	50.1	50.0	50.4	49.5
Standard VII	43.3	44.5	45.5	47.0	48.5
Standard I–VII	47.7	48.3	48.9	49.4	49.9
Secondary education: Forms 1, 4, 5, and 6					
Form 1	35.7	36.8	36.9	38.3	38.6
Government	33.6	33.8	33.4	34.3	34.4
Private	38.3	40.1	40.9	42.5	42.8
Form 4	33.7	33.3	34.8	35.3	36.7
Government	31.3	31.1	32.2	32.8	32.9
Private	36.6	35.8	38.0	38.0	40.5
Form 5	22.4	22.2	21.0	22.3	22.7
Government	23.1	22.7	21.7	22.1	22.2
Private	19.1	18.8	15.3	22.9	23.2
Form 6	22.3	23.2	22.2	20.9	21.2
Government	22.9	23.2	22.8	20.9	22.4
Private	14.3	24.3	16.6	21.3	20.0
Forms 1–6	34.0	34.5	35.0	35.8	36.9
Government	31.9	31.7	31.9	32.2	32.4
Private	37.3	38.0	38.9	40.1	41.4
Teachers colleges	42.4	36.7	37.9	38.5	41.1
Technical colleges	10.0	10.9	10.7	10.7	11.8
University (under-graduates)	24.0	21.2	19.6	18.9	16.0

Source: Tanzania, *Basic Education Statistics in Tanzania (BEST) 1981–1985* (Dar es Salaam: Ministry of Education, 1986), 215 tab. 7.

zania) than of African children are in school. Africanization of high-level jobs has been a major national policy commitment, defined, and with occasional exceptions implemented, in terms of citizenship rather than race. There is no comparable Africanization or Tanzanianization policy for schooling.

Schools do not maintain records of students' social strata. As I have noted, although income stratification is only a partial indicator of class differences, it seems clear that children from the middle and upper classes are more likely to get more and better schooling than workers' and peasants' children. In short, while region (ethnicity) is regarded as an important and appropriate focus and organizing unit of public policy and political activity, religion, race, class, and perhaps gender are not. Put somewhat differently, regional (ethnic) differences are highly politicized, while the other social cleavages are deemed politically less significant.

The small size of the European and Indian populations and their apparent political insignificance may make their educational advantage seem unimportant. Religious differences have thus far not been highly divisive in Tanzania, even during the 1985 presidential election campaign, when a Zanzibari Muslim succeeded the Catholic founding father, Julius Nyerere. Koranic and other Muslim schools have never been a serious academic alternative to secular (that is, Western and at least unofficially Christian) education. And the Tanzanian leadership has regularly sought to constrain social differentiation, both within and outside schools.

From one perspective, then, regional (ethnic) inequalities are the primary focus of policy attention because other social cleavages seem politically less threatening. That explanation, however, begs the question by assuming that ethnic identities are in some way inherently more powerful and more incompatible than other identities. A more fruitful analytic perspective, I think, sets out to explore which identities have been politicized, why, and how, and to examine the intersections among the different identity patterns (Samoff 1982–1983; Saul 1979, 391–423). The politicization of ethnicity (as opposed to the inherently political character of ethnic identities) has strong roots in Africa.[41] More important, it continues to be nurtured in the present, in part precisely by policies that reinforce ethnic identities in an effort to reduce regional inequalities. Why? Perhaps these other social cleavages are perceived by policymakers as inherently more threatening and thus to be excluded from policy attention for fear of generating or exacerbating unmanageable hostili-

[41] As does the politicization of racial identities, which have not received comparable educational policy attention in Tanzania.

ties.[42] Ethnic conflict may seem more immediately divisive and at the same time more tractable than class conflict, or, rather, the management of ethnic conflict need not threaten the political order, while the intensification of class conflict surely will. That leaves unexplained, however, why citizens themselves do not regard these inequalities as both politically salient and a focus for political action. It is not possible here to undertake a broad analysis of lines of cleavage and their political salience in the Tanzanian political economy. But it is important to note that the educational policy concerns of a leadership that has announced its commitment to socialist construction are focused more on ethnicity than on class.

SOCIALIST VISION AND CAPITALIST PRACTICE

Why have educational reform policies and programs not been more successful in laying the foundation for and nurturing Tanzanian socialism? With apparently unchallenged national power, with a strong commitment to socialist development, with an openness to assessment and a willingness to modify programs, and with broad mass support, why have Tanzania's leaders found the educational system so institutionally malleable and at the same time so structurally intractable? What do we learn from these efforts at educational reform, about Tanzania and about the role of education in social transformation more generally?

Several preliminary comments are in order here. One is that observers must be sensitive to time horizons. Far too often do researchers expect programs to result in broad changes scarcely months after their inception. In the absence of traumatic events, social change is likely to be a long, and certainly not linear, process. Reverses will succeed advances. Each will be important but transitory. The situation at any particular moment may or may not indicate the direction of change, but it surely does not reflect a definitive outcome.

Second, the external environment remains very powerful. On the regional scale, the very proximity to Kenya, where leaders seem better rewarded, where shortages of basic supplies seem less frequent, and where consumer goods seem more available, is itself a constraint. If Tanzania's development strategy is to be preferred to that of Kenya, Tanzanians must see the better results. The willingness to delay gratification, to work hard now for a better life some generations in the future, is conditioned by visible and apparently viable alternative models. If people elsewhere are eating better now, why should we have to wait? On the global scale, the incorporation of Tanzania into the world economy is manifested concretely within the educational system by the extent to

---

[42] Academics apparently share that perception—in this arena, what academics choose to document not only reflects but may well influence the policy agenda.

which new projects, and even recurrent expenditures for regular operations, rely on external funding. Although there is a great sensitivity in Tanzania to subtle donor influences and a firm resolve by Tanzanians to set their own priorities, nonetheless the goals and concerns of external partners often become the bounds within which Tanzanian choices are made.

Third, in exploring problems to be addressed through educational reforms, it is essential to ask whether or not the appropriate remedies lie elsewhere. It is useful here to recall the earlier discussion of the unemployment and underemployment. What many educators (and others) see as an educational crisis, is primarily a problem of employment creation. Admitting more students to secondary school might keep them out of the labor market for a few years more, but their extended education would not in and of itself create more jobs. At the same time, both the development process, which, however defined, involves increased agricultural productivity and thus fewer farmers feeding more of the populace, and industrialization, which, however halting, requires a larger settled labor force, foster urban migration. This movement of young people to towns and cities is likely to continue, irrespective of public policy. That movement will be even stronger where secure urban life, however difficult to achieve, appears to be so much better rewarded and more highly regarded than rural farming. Teachers' exhortations to remain at home are unlikely to keep all the young people in the village, especially if they find it difficult to obtain sufficient land and/or capital to set out on their own. There does not seem to be persuasive evidence that vocational skills are better acquired a few hours per week in school than all week at the job site. The point here is that it is important to maintain a sense of what can, and what probably cannot, be accomplished in and by schools.

Fourth, it is important to retain a sense of humility about the state of knowledge and control. Although the evidence does seem to show that increased education is associated with increased production and productivity, there is at best limited clarity on exactly how that association works and on which dimensions of education matter. Put somewhat differently, in the complexity of the relationships between education and development, it is both naive and arrogant to assert confidently that, say, the provision of textbooks or teacher training is the critical factor. The conditions within which particular reforms operate are likely to be more important than the content of the reforms themselves.

Correspondence and Contradiction

To make sense of a situation where apparently successful radical and fundamental educational reforms have thus far seemed more to maintain than to transform the social relations, inequalities, and attitudes of peripheral capitalism, we must recognize that there is both correspondence and contradiction in Tanzanian education.[43]

Schools function to reproduce a particular social order, more through institutional arrangements than through curriculum content, though both are involved. Reproducing peripheral capitalism in Tanzania requires identifying and differentiating a new elite generation, reinforcing and legitimizing its claim to power, and at the same time permitting sufficient social mobility to reinvigorate the ruling group and to defuse potential discontent. The bulk of the citizenry must be equipped with basic skills in a manner that restrains their aspirations and reminds them of their largely rural agricultural future. There must be nurtured an ideology that promises extensive change, that attributes delays in those changes to external factors (both human and ecological) or to the inadequacy of citizens' own efforts, that certifies the leadership potential and responsibility of the new elite, and that, where those in power are largely drawn from and rely heavily on administration, portrays development as a technical process best managed by those with the relevant technical and administrative expertise. All of these elements of the reproduction process are reflected in Tanzanian schools.

But that reproduction is neither perfect nor complete. In part, that has to do with institutional and individual incapacities. The curriculum, for example, even in a centralized system, is molded by teachers as they implement it. The intended message—of both content and process—is never exactly what was intended. Socialization is always imprecise and can never be entirely controlled. Symbols have varying meanings across cultures and in different contexts.

Failures of reproduction also have to do with contradiction. Schools in Tanzania, like their counterparts in core capitalist states, have contradictory roles. They must channel most students toward rural agriculture, making that seem desirable and rewarding. At the same time, they must identify and select a small group of students to receive more extended schooling, to be encouraged to be critical, innovative, and anxious to succeed, and to develop the skills and self-confidence required of leaders. Especially in the context of an ideology that emphasizes egalitarianism

---

[43] I am drawing here on notions elaborated especially in critical work on education in capitalist society. "Correspondence" refers to the processes through which schools reflect and reproduce the political structures, social relations, and dominant attitudes of the larger society. "Contradiction" refers to the necessary tension within educational systems that are expected both to contribute to the reproduction of the social order and at the same time to develop and nurture critique and innovation, which are also essential to the maintenance of the social order. For useful overviews and references, see Apple 1978, 1982c; and Giroux 1984.

and merit and that calls for basic education and productive labor for all students, it is difficult to separate the two tasks. Sustained inquiry and probing critique require a skeptical attitude toward received wisdom, toward the usual way of doing things, toward the established order. Success in developing an inquiring orientation and critical attitudes generates rising expectations among the school population as a whole and increases the quality and the quantity of the discontent at the differential reward system. By contrast, the common pedagogy requires compliant students who acquiesce in their subordinate status and help to maintain it. Success in channeling the school population toward rural agriculture through a hierarchical and authoritarian school structure reduces the likelihood that the new adults will have the critical attitudes and self reliant skills required to transform Tanzania's dependent political economy. Similarly, closer integration of schools into their local communities and a more participatory school environment will promote greater self reliance but will also reduce the ability of the schools to reproduce current power and economic relations. Fostering critique is thus developmentally sound but politically destabilizing, while reproducing the existing order is politically more secure and developmentally self-limiting. Schools are expected to do both.

In addition to its incapacities and contradictions, reproduction confronts resistance. Understanding, values, and spirit are never quite as malleable as leaders (and some educators) expect. Precisely because of their central role in maintaining and reproducing the social order, schools become sites for challenges to that order.

As I have noted, schools reflect larger social patterns, but they do so neither completely nor perfectly. Hence, schools are not autonomous institutions independent of conflict and power within society that can be used mechanically as a fulcrum for transforming society. At the same time, to perform their tasks adequately, and especially to maintain their legitimizing role—to project an image of equality and merit while organizing differentiation and stratification—schools and teachers must have some autonomy. That autonomy, in turn, makes schools both a focus for conflict and a terrain for conflict. Control of the educational system does matter. Since that is clear to all groups contending for power, disputes over school organization and content have societywide roots and ramifications. For the observer, that means that each interplay of proposal, response, and counterproposal must also be understood as a phase of a broader struggle. Ostensibly technical issues, such as the length of the basic education, or the prerequisites for entering a postprimary technical program, or the allocation of time and resources to self-reliance projects, are also political issues, and must be understood—by observers as much as by participants—as such.

At first glance the educational agenda in Tanzania seems to revolve around tensions among the need to develop higher-level skills, public demand for school expansion, and the national commitment to reduce inequalities. As we have seen, however, attention to reproduction, contradiction, and resistance in Tanzanian education reveals an underlying conflict: that in which initiatives toward socialist construction confront efforts to entrench peripheral capitalism. Our study of educational policy returns us to the transition state.

Education and the Transition State in Tanzania

Nominally and legally supreme, the party in Tanzania (CCM) does not directly rule. More an alliance of contending groups and ideological orientations than a tightly organized and highly centralized institution, it is able to facilitate and legitimize rule. As it does, it, too, is both a focus and terrain for conflict. Apparently currently dominated by a technocratic-administrative orientation and often controlled at the local level by a coalition of administrators and larger-scale farmers, the party lurches between developing peripheral capitalism and challenging it.[44] That alternation is reflected in educational policy.

The thrust of recent educational policy changes reflects the technical-administrative orientation that has in the past few years come more visibly to dominate the national leadership and national policy. To employ a rough but convenient shorthand, in the struggles among the contenders for power in Tanzania, the experts have displaced the politicians: The relative dominance in the late 1960s and mid-1970s of a political perspective that regarded development as essentially a political process and that emphasized politicization, mobilization, and, to some extent, socialism was by the early 1980s supplanted by a return to the view that development is principally a technical process, although, of course, one requiring a supportive political environment. Again put crudely, in the popular perception, the politicians had simply failed to produce and, as a consequence, suffered an erosion of legitimacy. The need to import cereal grains in the mid-1970s weakened their base, though it was restored somewhat by the economic recovery and military victory of the late 1970s. The continuing difficulties in meeting the demand for both basic foods and consumer goods in this decade have further weakened that political base, or, rather, have reinforced the political claims of the technocratic orientation.

Although it is impossible here to assemble extensive evidence for or

[44] For a more extended presentation of this perspective and relevant references, see Samoff 1981, 1987b.

discuss in detail the sources and consequences of this transition, its symbolic manifestations are, I think, reasonably clear. Academics and individuals widely regarded as relatively apolitical have been appointed to head key ministries, parastatals, and other organizations. The visible portions of public policy debate, in which at other times political concerns have been paramount (for example, arguments about which proposed policy is more clearly socialist), are now more often dominated by discussions of ostensibly apolitical policy alternatives, defended in terms of their technical merit. The recent relaxation of restrictions on consumer goods and luxury imports (a policy thrust often labeled "liberalization," to the delight of critics of Tanzanian socialism), for example, has been defended largely in terms of economic rationality, not socialist construction (notwithstanding the socialist terminology employed).

Within education, the recommendations of the presidential commission appointed in 1980 were developed and presented in terms of attention to the (academic) quality of education, its costs, and its training roles, rather than in terms of education for socialist construction, or redistribution, or equality. In large part, the policy thrust preferred by the professional educators—including the introduction of fees for government secondary schools, doubling government secondary schools, and encouraging private educational institutions—prevailed over the objections of those concerned that charging fees for admission to the key recruitment mechanism for high-level positions and leaving much of its development in private hands were inconsistent with basic egalitarianism, democratic participation, and socialism. Strong opposition to some of the recommendations, apparently centered in the party's National Executive Committee, did effectively delay for two years the adoption of the new policies. Some proposals, including a revision of the school cycle (essentially, shortening primary education to permit expanded access to junior secondary school) were rejected. Ultimately, however, it was the party that acquiesced. The ministry responsible for education, which a decade ago was renamed the Ministry of National Education to assert the importance of the political role over the technical responsibilities of education, has again become the Ministry of Education. At the same time, Colleges of National Education have resumed their former name: Teachers' Colleges. Regarding education in primarily technical-administrative rather than political terms has also been a central tenet of most of the numerous external educational advisers to Tanzania, especially the World Bank and UNESCO.

This transition—from the proudly political to the aggressively apolitical, from self-consciously socialist to dispassionately neutral, from education as social transformation to education as the transmission of skills and attitudes—is nicely captured in the contrasting language of the 1974

Musoma Resolution (officially titled "Directive on the Implementation of 'Education for Self-Reliance' ") and the 1984 report of the Presidential Commission. Both begin with a reference to Nyerere's 1967 paper, *Education for Self Reliance*. At Musoma in 1974, it was essential to go beyond that paper: "[T]he main purpose of education is to enable man to liberate himself" (TANU 1974, 103). By 1984, it was deemed essential to return to it: ". . . to provide Tanzanians with a proper education, that is, knowledge and understanding, important skills and attitudes . . ." (Tanzania 1984, 1–3).

It would, of course, be quite erroneous to assume that what I have termed here the political orientation is unconcerned with issues of technique and administration or is indifferent to the academic quality of educational institutions. It would be equally erroneous to assume that the current political configuration is either immutable or immortal. My point here is simply that recent educational policies correspond to the current dominance of a more technical-administrative and less political perspective in national politics.

Tanzania's transition is stymied. Its socialist vision is regularly obscured and often overwhelmed by its capitalist practice, both within and outside education. Frequently denounced, the modernization orientation is equally frequently reasserted, with both local and foreign support. Although—as I have argued throughout—the current political trajectory is neither unchallenged nor invulnerable, the Tanzanian experience points to the powerful obstacles, and perhaps the limits, of a nonrevolutionary transition. Where the workers and peasants have yet to seize power, where the political revolution has yet to be completed, schools cannot be primarily a vehicle for constructing a new order. Their central role in reproducing the current order and their necessary relative autonomy do permit schools to be sites for revolutionary initiatives. At the same time, where the educational system relies heavily on external funding and advice, schools are unlikely to be primarily concerned with promoting social transformation or laying the foundation for Tanzanian socialism. Just as the revolution cannot occur without attention to the schools, so the educational system cannot, by itself, be the revolution.

CHRONOLOGY OF EDUCATION AND POLITICS IN TANZANIA

	Economy, Polity, Society	*Education*
1954	TANU formed as national liberation party	TANU Constitution: Promise No. 6 commits leadership to educate selves and to use that education for the benefit of all
1958		TANU Annual Conference: commitment to establishing a leadership training institution (becomes Kivukoni College in 1961)
1961	Independence (United Kingdom Trusteeship) Three-Year Plan for Economic Development (based on World Bank Report)	University College, Dar es Salaam, opened (Law School)
1962	Trade Disputes Act of 1962: effectively bars most strikes	Initial decolonization of curriculum
1963	Independence of Zanzibar	
1964	Army mutiny Union with Zanzibar First Five-Year Plan (FFYP) for Economic and Social Development (1964–1969) Workers' Committees established (Security of Employment Act) Tanganyika Federation of Labour (TFL) replaced by National Union of Tanganyika Workers (NUTA)	FFYP: major emphasis placed on high-level skills training by the educational system, particularly secondary schools and the university Secondary school fees abolished
1965	One-Party Interim Constitution adopted	Swahili becomes language of instruction in primary schools Phaseout of Standard VIII (eighth year of primary school) and Standard IV examination, and merging of upper (V–VII) and lower (I–IV) primary schools begun
1966		University students demonstrate against required National Service

(*Continued on next page*)

EDUCATION AND POLITICS IN TANZANIA—*Continued*

Economy, Polity, Society	*Education*
1967 Arusha Declaration: clarifies and strengthens Tanzania's commitment to ujamaa socialism; nationalizations; leadership code Creation of Permanent Labour Tribunal, limiting worker's ability to strike and negotiate contracts	Education for Self Reliance Policy: emphasis on mass education, particularly primary schools—both increasing enrollment and changing curriculum to provide skills for rural agricultural development strategy Phaseout of Standard VIII completed National Literacy Test: 69% illiterate
1968	Entrance examination to Standard V eliminated (all primary school pupils able to remain in school for seven years) UNESCO/UNDP-supported World Oriented Adult Literacy Project (WOALP)—Mwanza Functional Literacy Project—initiated
1969 Second Five-Year Plan (SFYP) (1969–1974)	SFYP: directs that all primary schools will become adult education centers and directs that the main emphasis of adult education will be on rural development National Education Act: government assumes control of all schools First mass education campaign: To Plan is To Choose (focus: new Five-Year Plan)
1970 Workers' Councils established in every public corporation/enterprise (Presidential Circular No. 1)	Party declares 1970 Adult Education Year Second mass education campaign: The Choice is Yours University of Dar es Salaam created (dissolution of University of East Africa)

(*Continued on next page*)

EDUCATION AND POLITICS IN TANZANIA—*Continued*

Economy, Polity, Society	*Education*
1971 TANU Guidelines (Mwongozo)	Six Districts Literacy Campaign TANU 15th Biennial Conference: Resolution 23 calls for the eradication of illiteracy in the next four years and directs that worker education be carried out within working hours Third mass education campaign: A Time for Rejoicing National Forms 4 and 6 examinations replace Cambridge examinations
1972 Decentralization policy adopted TANU Annual Conference: Iringa Resolution finds agricultural productivity too low and declares politics and agriculture inseparable	National Literacy Campaign, planned for three years, is initiated in response to 1971 TANU Conference Resolution Fourth mass education campaign: Politics is Agriculture
1973	Primary school fees abolished TANU 16th Biennial Conference: Resolution 29 declares that students in classes VI and VII should be taught skills directly useful for work in villages Prime Minister's Directive on Worker Education National Examinations council established (localization of examinations) Fifth mass education campaign: Man is Health

(Continued on next page)

EDUCATION AND POLITICS IN TANZANIA—*Continued*

Economy, Polity, Society	*Education*
1974 TANU National Executive Committee (Musoma) Resolutions Villagization campaigns Workers' Committees become Union (NUTA) Field Committees (that is, union branches)	Musoma Resolutions directed accelerated progress toward universal primary education (by 1977), elimination of illiteracy (by 1980), and self-sufficiency in high-level skills (by 1980); instituted vocational orientation in all secondary schools; required village or factory work experience and recommendation and party endorsement for admission into university Initial (four) zonal Kivukoni Colleges opened
1975 Third Five-Year Development Plan postponed Village Development Act	Folk Development Colleges established Sixth mass education campaign: Food is Life and Death National Literacy Test: 39% illiterate
1976 Third Five-Year Development Plan (1976–1981)	Universal primary education accelerated Adult literacy progress extended and intensified
1977 TANU and Afro-Shirazi parties merged to form the Chama Cha Mapinduzi (CCM) Collapse of the East African Community National Union of Tanganyika Workers (NUTA) becomes Jumuiya ya Wafanyakazi wa Tanzania (JUWATA)	National Literacy Test: 27% illiterate
1978 War with Uganda (1978–1979)	
1980	Presidential Education Commission formed to evaluate past nineteen years of education and plan the next twenty

(*Continued on next page*)

EDUCATION AND POLITICS IN TANZANIA—*Continued*

	Economy, Polity, Society	*Education*
1981		National Literacy Test: 21% illiterate
1982		Presidential Education Commission reports to president and party
1983		National Literacy Test: 15% illiterate
1984		Sokoine University of Agriculture, Morogoro, opened Primary school fees restored as "development levies"
1985	Ali Hassan Mwinyi succeeds Julius K. Nyerere as President of Tanzania	Initial implementation of approved recommendations of the Presidential Education Commission, including introduction of secondary school fees, plan to double the number of government secondary schools, and encouragement to private secondary schools
1986		National Literacy Test: 9.6% illiterate

CHAPTER 8

The Mozambican State and Education

Anton Johnston

THIS CHAPTER ANALYSES the developments, changes, and tensions in the Mozambican education system since Independence in 1975.[1] The principal phases of these developments are closely associated with the phases of conflicts in and around the state: the armed takeover of state power from the Portuguese by the Mozambican Liberation Front, FRELIMO; the transformation of the Front into a Marxist-Leninist vanguard party (the Frelimo party); and its struggle to lead the society through the transition to socialism. Two concerns are central here. First, the social and economic legacy of the past, left the revolutionary forces in control of an exploited and underdeveloped country with large but unused or badly used resources, and a much-misused population. The legacy of Portuguese colonialism was forced labor and a 93 percent illiteracy rate. Only a tiny handful of cadres trained beyond four years of primary schooling existed at independence. Second, there have been constant aggressive counterrevolutionary activities fomented by neighboring South Africa. Effectively, violence has reigned in Mozambique for several centuries, and the country has experienced constant, shifting warfare over the past twenty years. All the trials and errors inherent in the social transformation of an underdeveloped colony have been made in the context of armed conflict, crisis management, and social upheaval.

[1] I am indebted to Martin Carnoy, Agneta Lind, Judith Marshall, Joel Samoff, Carlos Torres, and Jeff Unsicker for long discussions and detailed criticisms of earlier drafts of this chapter; the views represented are my own. I had the honor of being employed in the Mozambican Education Ministry's Adult Education Department from 1976 to 1983, where I had the privilege of participating in the inspiring process of social transformation unleased by Frelimo. This opportunity gave me a unique chance to experience the revolution, and especially the educational revolution, from inside. Unavoidably, this means that I had privileged knowledge of what was happening, which cannot but influence the views and opinions expressed in this discussion. I have tried throughout to use information that has been published or publicized openly, primarily in the Mozambican media or in my SIDA/ministry of education–commissioned works (Johnston 1984, 1985). Nonetheless, the views expressed here do not necessarily coincide with those of the Mozambican government.

THE COLONIAL LEGACY

Mozambique as a Colony

Mozambique fell under Portuguese influence in the sixteenth century. The Portuguese completed their occupation and defeated most armed resistance by about 1920 (TEMPO/UEM 1982).[2] The nature of colonial power itself defined and limited Mozambique's development after the Portuguese asserted direct control. Portugal was a state dependent on British capital and covering for British interests in Africa, with a fascist government and a weak capitalist class. All this limited or even prevented the Portuguese state from making serious development investment in its colonies. Even at the end of the colonial period, the "development plans" were (under)financed by loans debited to Mozambique's perennial deficit with Portugal.

The colonist population, often illiterate and without either skills or capital, remained small until near the end of the colonial period, when it grew to about 165,000, mostly in the towns. Very little of the Portuguese bourgeoisie was actually to be found in Mozambique. The colonists were the lieutenants and sergeants of the metropolitan bourgeoisie, as managers, traders, skilled workers, or civil servants.

A mixed middle stratum of petite-bourgeoisie arose gradually, composed of Asian commercial capitalists, *mestizos* (people of mixed race), and *assimilados* (assimilated Africans). Together, the largely urbanized colonist and middle stratum totaled about 2.5 percent of the population in 1964 (Mondlane 1967).

Colonial economic policy falls into three phases: a first *concessionary* phase, when foreign companies took over large areas; a second, *nationalistic* phase from 1928 to 1960, when Portugal excluded direct foreign investment from the colony to protect its own bourgeoisie; and a third, *open-door* phase, when foreign investment was encouraged to bind the West into direct interest in and support of Portuguese colonialism. In spite of the long closed period, the economy of the country remained connected to foreign capital through the provision of services, such as labor, transport, energy, and tourism, to the countries inland. These services represented Portugal's major income from its colony.

With the commercial exploitation of gold in South Africa, by 1900 migrant labor to the mines reached an annual figure of around 100,000 males, mostly from the south of Mozambique, for which the mining capitalists paid part of the wages in gold directly to the Portuguese state. Mozambicans also migrated to other South African economic sectors. In

---

[2] Useful studies describing and analyzing the colonial period are Isaacman and Isaacman 1983; Saul 1985; and Mondlane 1967.

the center of the country, a similar number of Mozambicans migrated to Rhodesian farms and mines.

All the neighboring countries used rail and port links through Mozambique for imports and exports. The dues for this service constituted a second major source of revenue for Portugal.

Common to all activities of infrastructural development, industry, and plantation farming was the system of forced labor. By law, Mozambicans had to pay taxes and demonstrate their productive activity, without which they were declared "idle" and forced into employment. This translated into internal migrant labor, forced labor conscription to farms and plantations, and forced cultivation of export crops at the place of residence. Only a very small African proletariat grew up internally, largely concentrated in the ports and railways. That proletariat was involved in most of the recorded direct confrontations with the colonial system before 1960, in the form of stoppages and strikes. The colonial state always put these down forcibly, by shooting some workers, imprisoning or firing others, and replacing the work force with forced labor recruits (Isaacman and Isaacman 1983).

The Colonial State and Education

In their colonial propaganda, the Portuguese claimed to be exercising a civilizing mission in their overseas territories, "acculturating the savage" and "teaching the native the path of human dignity and the grandeur of the nation which protects him."[3] The ideal was that the educated "native" who spoke "proper" Portuguese and was sufficiently "civilized" would be considered assimilated, with Portuguese citizenship and exemption from forced labor (for extracts from colonial propaganda, see Mondlane 1967). By 1961, when, in the face of international pressure, everyone became Portuguese overnight by decree, less than 1 percent of the population had been assimilated.

The education system was divided into three parts: official schools and private schools for the colonists and the assimilados, and mission primary schools for the "natives." From the beginning it was clear that the mission-run system was vastly inferior to the other two. Its teachers had far less training, and it required several additional years to complete, because of extra initial classes for teaching Portuguese and the Catechism. In many areas, even these schools did not exist. Where they did, school

[3] It is difficult to find good published sources on colonial education in Mozambique, and education statistics vary widely in the sources available. Mondlane (1967) includes a chapter on the subject, while Lisboa has a chapter in Rose (1973). Lisboa (1967) and Ministerio de Educação (Mozambique) MEC (1979) are unpublished but contain more detailed information.

fees were charged. Exams were administered in every grade, with an average pass rate of less than 30 percent. Most missions did not offer the crucial final primary grade required to proceed to secondary school. Secondary schools were located in the towns, required passing an entry exam, and had an age restriction for entrance (Lisboa 1967).

In most ways, colonial education provision corresponded directly to the nature and organization of colonial exploitation. As the colonial economy changed, so did its schools. During the concessionary phase, there was virtually no education. In the nationalistic phase, the education that was provided served primarily the colonists. Mission schooling for Africans grew only very slowly during most of the period. In the open-door phase, there was a sudden rush to expand education.

The Portuguese Catholic mission education appears to have achieved its aims quite well, as it provided the only accessible avenue for individuals to become assimilated, which provided some protection against forced labor and limited possibilities to move up into better-paid employment. Indeed, the later explosive growth of education after independence can be attributed largely to the demand created by colonialism.

On the other hand, the other types and levels of education had effects very contrary to those the colonial state considered desirable. Early assimilados were often openly critical of the colonial situation. A few other mission denominations were grudgingly permitted to operate schools, usually with rather more humane methods. A disproportionate number of FRELIMO's educated cadres seem to have passed through these schools. Once pupils got through into the secondary school level, they often entered the political arena through student associations. Those sufficiently successful in their examinations to be sent to a university in Portugal met nationalists from the other colonies and came into contact with Portuguese students opposed to fascism and energetically exploring Marxist ideas. Other early FRELIMO cadres came from the half-million refugees from the colony in the neighboring countries, often having received their education outside Mozambique.

Thus, in one sense, the limited application of the colonial state's professed ideology of assimilation produced some of the crucial few who would organize the overthrow of colonialism. At the same time, the education of the few often did assimilate them to colonial ideology in subtle ways, which complicated the armed struggle and still fuels the conflict over how to go about constructing socialism. For many, educational experience outside the system seems to have had more radical effects than did schooling within it. Furthermore, the exclusion of the majority from the system, accompanied by the exploitation and suffering imposed by the colonial power, served to stoke the fires of popular anger and made it possible to organize the peasantry to overthrow colonialism.

The decolonization of Africa and the founding of FRELIMO changed Portuguese colonial tactics drastically. Suddenly the doors were opened to foreign investment in order to try to involve the Western powers in the direct defense of Portuguese colonialism and their investments in it. Various cosmetic measures were taken to counter the growing wave of international and internal opposition to colonialism. One of these was a sudden drive for educational expansion and reform, such as the apparent scrapping of so-called "adaptive" classes for Africans at the beginning of primary schooling. The reality of expansion and reform can be better understood by the figures provided by Lisboa (1967, 17): In 1964–1965, 72 percent of total African primary enrollment was in the preprimary grade, and the pass rate in that grade that year was 21.7 percent. In the same year, only 1.5 percent of total African primary enrollment was in the final (fourth) grade. By 1972, the Portuguese claimed to have reached a coverage of about 36 percent of the primary age group—probably rather less, in fact. Even so, most of the expansion went into the preprimary and first two primary grades, so that even in 1974–1975 over 51 percent of enrollment was in the preprimary grade. Dropout and failure rates were still enormous, and the overall results were hardly impressive. In 1940, 99.9 percent of Mozambique's population were illiterate. The 1970 census put the level at 89.7 percent. In 1973, only 40 of the students in Mozambique's 3,000-place university were black. In 1970 only 1.07 percent of the population covered by the census (including colonists) had completed more than four school grades.

The Armed Struggle for National Liberation

Precipitated by the massacre of 600 peacefully protesting peasants at Mueda, FRELIMO was founded in 1962 through the unification of three exile Mozambican groups.[4] It was at first a broad front, pulling together disparate groups of exiles, students, some of the petite bourgeoisie, workers, and peasants, with the principal common goal of liberating Mozambique from colonialism. It began the armed struggle for national liberation in 1964, reaching Mozambique through Tanzania, with the initial strategy of attacking the colonial repressive apparatus and economic infrastructures. The weak colonial government in the north quickly collapsed, permitting FRELIMO to occupy large liberated zones.

In the late 1960s, internal struggles broke out over the policies to be adopted in the struggle, ending with the expulsion of one faction and the affirmation of a socialist political orientation. From 1970 on, FRELIMO's

---

[4] Good coverage of the armed struggle and the liberated zones is to be found in Saul 1979 and 1985; Isaacman and Isaacman 1983; and Munslow 1983.

strategy focused on establishing, securing, and gradually extending liberated zones. Increasingly, the armed struggle, political work, and administration were integrated. Services to the people in health, education, and marketing were extended and placed under popular control. The guerrillas participated in the production of food; the peasantry participated in military and defense operations and in feeding the combatants; and small hidden communal villages were set up to organize and protect the population. Tribalism and racism were actively combated, and the long process of women's liberation began with the creation in the army of a women's detachment, an initiative that the reactionary faction had solidly opposed. Thus, FRELIMO moved through a whole set of practical experiences toward the adoption of Marxism-Leninism as its guiding ideology. By the early 1970s, FRELIMO began to organize army cadres as members of a revolutionary party. It adopted the administrative method of democratic centralism, and involved the guerrillas and the peasants in the nascent self government by setting up organs of People's Power (see Munslow 1983).

In 1974, Portugal's military collapse and bankruptcy were confirmed by the April revolution, and hostilities ceased in September of that year. The collapse took FRELIMO by surprise. It had expected the struggle to continue through the gradual extension of the liberated zones throughout the countryside, finally leaving the Portuguese army isolated in the towns. Indeed, the FRELIMO leadership noted that it was almost a pity that victory came so soon, since it had been learning so much and since it was in the struggle that both the leadership and the populace confronted the colonial ideas and practices they had internalized. Certainly, it was a big step for FRELIMO, with a cadre strength of about 12,000, to move from the administration of rural liberated zones, which included about 10 percent of the population, under wartime conditions to the administration of a whole country and its economy.

Education in the Parallel State

From early on, FRELIMO dedicated a great deal of attention to mass education in the liberated zones and to the education of cadres.[5] It was important to set up educational activities to inform the population and cadres about the objectives and meaning of the struggle and to secure their more effective and conscious participation in it. The provision of education served as a concrete demonstration to Mozambicans and for-

[5] The references in note 4 cover education in the liberated zones to a varying extent. Ganhão (1978) represents an accessible summary by a participant; MEC (1979) is more detailed. Documents on the "struggle between lines" are to be found in de Bragança and Wallerstein (1982).

eigners alike that life under FRELIMO would be better. At the same time, demands for education from students in FRELIMO and from the peasantry seem to have made its expansion a rapid process under very difficult conditions.

The education system FRELIMO operated in the liberated zones and in Tanzania was at the beginning subject to exactly the same kinds of ideological conflict as the Front was facing in other spheres. The same essential questions arose: Education for what? Education for whom? Should resources be concentrated on basic education for many or higher education for the few? Why?

This policy debate, which was to continue after the end of Portuguese rule, highlighted a tension between FRELIMO and the movement's higher-level students. The representatives in FRELIMO of the secondary students' organization, NESAM, and the university student group, UNEMO (most of whose student members were studying overseas), argued that the first priority was to develop needed high-level skills. From the leadership's perspective, the students' self-interest had overwhelmed their revolutionary zeal, and their involvement in FRELIMO was more a strategy for securing senior positions after independence than a commitment to popular liberation. A particularly outspoken group of students sought to avoid service at the front line of the struggle, arguing that their potential role as future leaders made them too valuable to lose in combat. These students also articulated a racially conscious African nationalism, opposing the participation of whites and mestizos in the struggle, especially as teachers. When FRELIMO tried to assert its authority over the students, they complained that they were refused scholarships and further educational opportunities overseas because the FRELIMO leadership was afraid it would lose its power if better-educated members should emerge. In the course of this conflict, the U.S. branch of UNEMO broke away from FRELIMO, and in 1968 rioting and attacks against non-black teachers broke out at the Mozambican Institute in Dar es Salaam, a FRELIMO secondary school. The institute was surrounded and then closed, and about 80 percent of the students left. This led the FRELIMO to a fundamental reevaluation of its education policy (Ganhão 1978).

FRELIMO reorganized its secondary schools in Tanzania and continued to send cadres overseas to study, but turned its primary attention toward education within the liberated zones. Education was to become a major element of the democratic parallel state being established there. By 1972, there were some 160 primary schools operating, with 20,000–30,000 pupils, mostly in the first and second grades. By 1974, FRELIMO secondary school enrollment reached approximately 500, and FRELIMO was sponsoring 70 students in universities overseas (Collins 1977).

Secondary students in schools in Tanzania had a common program.

During their school holidays they were sent into the liberated zones in brigades to do various kinds of work, notably teaching adult literacy. Literacy classes' content focused around the meaning of the struggle and the new way of life in the liberated zones, and were taught by guerrillas, local literate people, some pupils from the primary level, and the secondary school brigades. One estimate put the number who became literate during this period at 20,000 (Johnston 1984, 22). In general, the schoolteachers had similar origins. Schooling also relied on assistance provided by pupils in each grade to the grade below. To upgrade teachers, seminars were held, and collective study and lesson preparation were organized. Under the pressures of war, the schools generally led a precarious existence, often having to change locality or stop entirely during periods of attack.

A Ministry of Education study (Ministerio da Educação [MEC] 1979) summarized the lessons of the education experience in the zones as follows:

- counting on your own resources;
- the duty of everyone to teach and to learn;
- the application of content and methods to local circumstances and realities;
- the fostering of a sense of Mozambican nationality and of combating tribalism, regionalism and racism—hence, the decision to use Portuguese in school and literacy classes and as the official "language of national unity";
- the linking of education to production and to the community;
- the school as a democratic center, where new types of relations between teacher and pupil should evolve; and
- combating superstition through education with a scientific base, designed to produce the "new person."

In the final stages of the armed struggle, FRELIMO seems to have made its education system correspond rather well with the demands and conditions of carrying on a popular-based war. The education principles listed above are still used as an important point of reference for education today. However, some of them are now played down, as we shall see shortly.

TEN YEARS OF INDEPENDENCE: THE ECONOMY, CLASS, AND THE STATE

Mozambique's first decade of independence was marked by enormous difficulties and intense upheavals, accompanied by a state of war and destabilization actively promoted by foreign powers.[6] The shifting balance

---

[6] The sources cited in note 4 and Hanlon 1984 provide detailed accounts and analyses of

of forces and material conditions has resulted in complex alignments and rapid policy changes and restructurings.

Relations of Production

Defensive and offensive nationalizations in the period 1975–1978 placed the state in the position of owning directly almost the entire modern economy: industry, large-scale agriculture, rented housing, banks, insurance, commerce, hotels, transport, fishing companies. By 1982, the state claimed to produce 70 percent and plan the production of 85 percent of marketed production. Most of the rest of production was in the hands of the family sector, and the capitalist class had been effectively dismantled (FRELIMO 1983b).

In 1980, 85 percent of the population, mostly women, worked in agriculture as peasants not employing labor. About 6,900 farmers employed labor. Cooperativists were few, and overwhelmingly in agriculture. Employment in the export sector and in the public services was overwhelmingly male and highly concentrated in the urban areas (which contained 10 percent of the active population but offered 38 percent of all salaried employment). The state sectors employed 10–12 percent of the active population in addition to part-time migrant workers on state plantations. Apart from farmers, only about 7,000 others were registered as employers of labor, half of these in commerce (Comissão Nacional do Planos [CNP] 1982).

In 1980, 87 percent of the population lived in the rural areas. Of the rural population, by 1982, 19 percent lived in communal villages, but this was not accompanied by the development of cooperative production (Frelimo 1983b).

Major structural changes have therefore included the creation of communal villages, the growth in the economic role of the state as owner, producer, and employer, and consequently the reduction in the ownership of means of production by private and foreign capitalists. Compared to 1970, those employed full time in agriculture had doubled and those employed full time in industry had tripled by 1980. The civil service itself had grown rapidly over the same period, though exact figures are not available.

Some steps were taken to create a collective mode of production, but much remained to be done. Among the peasantry, organized cooperative production had hardly taken root. The state had effective ownership of the dominant, once-capitalist productive sectors of the economy, but

---

various aspects of Mozambique's postcolonial experiences. Ottaway 1981 offers a less sympathetic view.

their integration into a collective mode was limited in two ways. Much of the produce was for export, and therefore the price and the distribution were not under state control, but rather under that of the world (capitalist) market (Frelimo 1982). The economy's export orientation also tended to impose capitalist organizational forms on the relations between the owner-state and the workers.

Also, throughout its history, Mozambique has principally come to serve as a labor reserve for neighboring capitalist countries, and labor is the country's most valuable export. The new state found itself selling its labor in a foreign market characterized by capitalist relations of private ownership and hired wage labor and at the same time attempting to develop new collective relations at home. Essential for the state's revenue, foreign wage (often, essentially indentured) labor has tended to undermine collectivization and cooperativization. Since its independence, Mozambique's exports have earned only a little more than 50 percent of what its imports cost only in 1974, and the ratio declined rapidly from 1979 onwards. This deficit had previously been made up through the sale of migrant labor and other services to South Africa and Rhodesia. Receipts from Rhodesia were totally cut off in 1976, when Mozambique imposed United Nations sanctions on that settler state. Those receipts did not reach their former level after Zimbabwe's independence, because of changed labor relations within Mozambique and attacks on transport by a guerrilla opposition created by Rhodesia and subsequently supported by South Africa. This organization, the Mozambican National Resistance (MNR), has continued to wreak terror and economic destruction in Mozambique since that era. In addition to its direct and indirect military interventions, South Africa heightened Mozambique's dependence by unilaterally reducing its use of Mozambican services, with an immense destabilizing effect on the Mozambican economy. Simultaneously, then, Mozambique was subjected to direct aggression from Rhodesia and South Africa, to the effects of the world economic recession, and to floods and drought. From about 1983 on, Mozambique's dependence on capitalist countries was being further reinforced at the expense of the diversification of its foreign markets and trading partners.

Mozambique calculates the cost of subversion ("destabilization"), direct attack, world recession, and natural disaster in 1975–1983 as MT 195,587,000 (approximately U.S. $5.5 million). Notwithstanding the speculative components of this estimate, it indicates that the costs were high—amounting to the value of about twenty years of exports at the best level ever reached (1981). South African reductions in labor recruitment and transport use accounted for nearly 61 percent of the total. The wave of MNR destruction and terrorism has generated an ever-continuing drain of resources into military activities, including the purchase of military supplies with scarce foreign exchange. Between 1981 and 1984, the Gross Social Product declined by some 33 percent; MNR attacks on electricity supply lines and the lack of foreign exchange to import raw materials and parts reduced industrial production in 1984 to half that in 1981. A 1986 press release (AIM, October 1986) claims that the damages caused by MNR/South African aggression alone now amount to the sum of U.S. $5.5 million (for 1982–1986). The national debt stands at U.S. $2 billion.

In the face of this level of catastrophe, any analysis of the Mozambican experience has to be made against a background of crisis management. Mozambique's attempt to withdraw from dependence on world capitalism has been severely punished. However, the facts that thus far all attempts to overthrow the Frelimo party have failed and that there has not emerged any feasible alternative force to replace it are evidence of the party's deep societal roots. The MNR, in spite of its destructive capacity as a surrogate of the South African army, has revealed no capacity to govern anything and has achieved no international legitimacy (reflected in the report commissioned by the U.S. State Department, Gersony 1988).

This represents a situation that is, at the least, paradoxical. On one hand, the state has been under continual attack from outside, and is associated with a rapidly declining economy. It has made large-scale economic errors of its own, including relative inattention to providing economic support and incentives to the large majority of the society—the peasantry. On the other hand, it has retained power in a situation where external support was not available to the same extent as, for example, in Angola. Thus the state is to a degree both dependent and autonomous in relation to the economy and to the outside world and both strong and weak in relation to internal forces.

Initial Experiments with Direct Democracy

On accession to state power, FRELIMO had achieved widespread national legitimacy and support. However, it was a fairly small organization that had been successful in cleaning out and unifying its own ranks and in overthrowing Portuguese colonialism without having directly occupied the whole country. Its administrative experience was limited to about 10 percent of the population, and that under wartime conditions. From the time of the Transitional Government, FRELIMO set about establishing organs of direct democracy throughout the country. The first form this took was in the creation in all sectors of Dynamizing Groups (GDs), mostly chosen by the people themselves. This provided an experience of democracy and participation not known during the long period of European rule. The GDs both represented FRELIMO and carried out administrative functions at the base that the formal state apparatus was unable to manage. The GDs had mixed success. To them goes the credit for the prevention of much economic sabotage, for the maintenance of popular mobilization at a high level, and for the maintenance of some life in the modern economy (Frelimo 1977a).

But they were hampered by a number of factors. FRELIMO was too small to be able to support them properly. Their members did not have the necessary administrative skills and experience, especially where intersectoral coordination was necessary to maintain operation. Also, in some of the GDs a momentum developed contrary to what FRELIMO (or their own constituencies) desired. In some cases, revenues from collective production and consumer cooperatives disappeared into private pockets. In others, literacy classes purveyed an anti-FRELIMO content, and populist actions were precipitated against individual enemies, against traditional culture, or against local figures of status in the community.

Vast voluntarist programmes were begun without adequate preparation or possibility of follow-up. For instance, cooperative production was initiated with large numbers of people on small areas of land, and literacy classes were started en masse with no curriculum, materials, or teacher preparation. Thousands of schools were built by local communities in the expectation that a teacher would be assigned, and communal villages were built in areas of low fertility or low fuel or water supplies. FRELIMO's antireligious and antitribalist stance alienated important sectors of the populace, especially when local cadres used heavy-handed methods in nationalizing missions or acting against traditional customs and practices.

Consolidating a Vanguard Strategy

At its Third Congress in 1977, FRELIMO constituted itself as the Frelimo party, the Marxist-Leninist Vanguard Party of the Worker-Peasant Alliance, and launched a "Campaign for the Structuring of the Party" to broaden its base by incorporating militants at every level. Strict recruitment criteria were employed, and candidates were subject to the scrutiny of existing FRELIMO organs and of the local populace. In 1982, the party revealed that it had a membership of 110,000, of whom 53.5 percent were peasants, 18.9 percent, workers, and 27.6 percent, functionaries from mass organizations and the administration, or members of the security forces.

The adoption by Frelimo of a vanguard strategy automatically placed the party in a position of central political power, and it took care to create and institutionalize its own apparatuses throughout the state and the economic sectors. It regarded the central administration as being the most important executive instrument in its economic and social development strategy, and thus focused much attention on it. The administration had gradually been building up on the ruins of its colonial predecessor, and included among the personnel some of its functionaries. After 1977, central planning became a major element of the party's development strategy. This additional responsibility added substantially to the power that the administrative institutions already held by virtue of their size, central position, and direct supervisory role over economic and social units. It made them de facto enormously influential in policy formulation and execution at all levels. That the senior administrators were often senior party officials as well further enhanced the power of the administration.

Centralism and Democracy

For administrative purposes, the party implemented a network of elected People's Assemblies at village, locality, district, city, provincial and national levels. For the same reasons, new GDs were created in urban areas at the suburban level. The election of deputies took the form of a national campaign. At the lowest levels, the party proposed suitable candidates, who were then presented to the Village Assemblies for scrutiny and voted on one by one. These Assemblies elected representatives to vote on the constitution of the Assembly at the next level, and so on up the chain to the top. In 1977, just over 1,000 Assemblies were elected, with 27,040 deputies. About 10 percent of the candidates were rejected. At all levels of the Assemblies, workers and peasants made up between 49 percent and 60 percent of elected deputies. Women comprised 27 percent of all deputies (see Isaacman and Isaacman 1983, 131).

The creation of the Assemblies and other people's power organs and mass organizations was intended to enable every community to manage its own affairs directly and to create a large degree of direct democracy in the workplace. Given the number of such structures and their varying degree of competence and distance from the center, there has been wide variation in the manner and effectiveness of their functioning. One problem has been the lack of experience, self-confidence, and even basic literacy in these organs, which has meant that questions that could have been resolved locally got referred upwards, or instructions from above were followed that were not suitable to local conditions. The combination of "double subordination"—subordination in decisionmaking to national authorities and one-rank-higher local authorities—with the mechanisms of planning has reinforced this relationship of subordination and deference. The base organs have become renderers of accounts upwards, especially when planning was an office-based bureaucratic procedure. In places of both work and residence, the formal division of powers between party and government created confusion about responsibility and authority. Who was responsible for what? Which organ was really superior to which? The most senior leadership seemed occasionally to shift its position on these issues. This problem led some party cells, production councils, and Assemblies to function poorly or even to become moribund. The GDs and Administrative Commissions had usually united the party and government functions into one organ, avoiding the problem. Contrary to its stated purpose, at least in workplaces, the restructuring laid the ground for reducing direct democracy and for emphasizing central steering by appointed management.

Economic Policy and Practice

The party sought to build a more modern economy on the foundation of collectivization. The nationalized state sectors were to be crucial in the short run to developing production and meeting the people's needs. Agriculture would be the base, and industry the leading sector. Economic independence would result from the development of heavy industry. The education system was assigned an important role in creating new democratic relations, as well as in providing skills for running a modern, collectivized economy (Frelimo 1977c).

The rather abstract formulation of "agriculture is the base" embraced two principal forms of collectivized agriculture in party thinking: the state farms and the cooperativization of peasant agriculture. The fact that the nationalized farms already existed, were large and more developed, and demanded resources and attention made it certain that more investment and effort would be dedicated to state-owned agriculture. In particular, that seemed to offer the major avenue to increasing and developing the Mozambican proletariat. In addition, it was in the interest of the officials and apparatuses entrusted with their management to attend to the state farms before all else.

Giving Priority to the collectivized peasants had the effect of leaving the rest of the peasantry out of state programs. The effects of the implementation of the policy can be deduced from the practice of education. In adult education, cooperatives and communal villages were included in the priority groups. Primary education was to be developed, and trained teachers were to be placed first and foremost in communal villages. This was expected to stimulate collectivization, which, in turn, would create the conditions for effective concentration and organization of the population for education and create the need for literacy and numeracy skills. But such priorities also tended to leave out the dispersed peasantry from (easy) access to education services.

Over time, however, the relative priority assigned to the collectivized peasantry was itself eroded. The gradual growth in the economy from 1977 onwards gave new confidence in the planning process and in central management. The previous dual policy, within the framework of a vanguard-directed, state-based development strategy, of trying to maintain some harmony between developing new relations and new forces of production simultaneously, gradually gave way to a development policy characterized by central economic direction and technological solutions. The ten-year plan and its implementation in 1981–1982 mark the high point of this line. All too often the large, the modern, the technocratic, and the centralized were preferred. In Hanlon's analogy, when it came to the choice between importing hoes and importing tractors, it was the hoes that got left out (Hanlon 1984, 195).

This gradual distancing of the state from the peasantry stemmed in part from a major economic problem in Frelimo's analysis of the peasantry, reflected in the words "subsistence production" used by the party to characterize the peasant economy in its Third Congress analysis. Indeed, a large proportion of the peasantry produced for its own subsistence. But colonialism had thoroughly incorporated the peasants into the capitalist economy in various ways. Dolny argues that there is not really "a Mozambican peasantry," but rather several peasantries, depending on their different ownership of means of production and their differing relations to migrant labor, plantation work, and cash crop production (in Saul 1985). Many peasants produced principally for the market according to prices and needs. Others combined family production with selling their labor in neighboring countries. Furthermore, especially in slack seasons, hundreds of thousands were interested in selling their labor internally for short periods. Major export crops, such as cashews and cotton were produced almost entirely by the peasantry, while major plantations were dependent on seasonal workers, particularly for harvesting. In these ways, the peasant sector was in fact the backbone of the whole economy.

In this situation, state control of prices, inadequate provision of marketing networks, and lack of consumer and producer goods on the market all stimulated the black market and inflation, discouraged collective production, made money transactions unattractive, and over time promoted a large-scale withdrawal from active participation in the market economy. On the state plantations, money wages became increasingly unattractive. In colonial times, plantation profitability had depended on low-wage seasonal labor, whom the Portuguese forced to work at peak periods. The Mozambican state found its plantations increasingly operating at a loss, as it reduced their profitability by increasing wages, by mechanizing, or by stabilizing the work force. It did not want to force labor participation, and the peasantry was not interested in selling its labor at peak periods when their own harvest was due and money had little value.

All of this resulted in dwindling production for the market and angry peasants, a situation hardly improved by South Africa's destabilizing policy of reducing employment of Mozambicans, a receding world economy, natural disasters, and insurgent attacks aimed at worsening the situation. Collectivization had not been accompanied by "higher forms of production," and the noncollectivized were reducing their production, at least for the official market. The state's de facto focus on its own sectors led to major public investments in looking for technical solutions to production problems. This absorbed surplus, incurred international debt, reduced employment and profitability, and diverted support from the peasantry.

Party Policy and Government Practice

As the vanguard, the party has often been the forum for the emergence of disquiet over such tendencies. Despite the responsibility of the party's vanguard policy for the centralization of authority in the state, in its composition and practice, the party is a more representative and democratic organization than the civil service. Besides, the administration tends to compete for influence with the party, and tends in its structure to prioritize its own controlled sectors, rather than taking overall responsibility for political developments at all levels in the nation. Thus, one major trend deriving from conflicts between the party and the government, or within the party itself, over the balance between one line and another has been to blame the government apparatuses (which, indeed, developed their own dynamics in their own self-interest).

The struggles within the state have been intense. Along one dimension, there has been constant friction over the balance between modernization and democratization, between centrally planned technical development and the development of people's power. In parallel, there has been a constant effort by the party to retain the development dynamic in its own hands, and constant attempts to mould and influence the administration into effective compliance, through coercing and cajoling officials, restructuring apparatuses, and reshaping the party's relationship to them. At some times there has been extreme centralization of power in the hands of top strata, especially through the mechanisms of central planning. At other times, there have been moves to limit the individual power and privileges of leaders, democratize decisionmaking, and decentralize. The creation of the vanguard party in 1977 gave particular impetus to the fractions of the ruling group that saw their interests as best served by the combination of central leadership and the use of technological solutions to development problems. However, in the "condensation of class relations" in the state, the democratic dynamic has always been present.

Decentralization, Liberalization, Mobilization

By the 1983 Fourth Congress, the technocratic and centralizing orientation in the party and in the government had suffered severe setbacks. It was obviously not only not working, but also directly counterproductive and lending strength to the enemy. This led to the adoption of much more modest planning targets. Planning was to cover fewer areas and to be done at the base itself. A variety of decentralizing and privatizing efforts were implemented.

Perhaps the major error in party policy was to assume that the transition from the inherited pattern to a locally appropriate socialism in Mozambique required an orthodox socialist strategy, to be led from the very beginning by the proletarian vanguard in alliance with the peasantry, as represented by vanguard peasants with a developed collective consciousness. The proletariat, however, was not very large, very strong, or very class-conscious. Even though thousands of Mozambicans had experienced wage labor in neighboring countries and in the national economy, they had always been organized on a temporary migrant basis in order to maintain and even reinforce their ties to the land. Peasants with a collective consciousness were only a small fraction among the various peasantries. In time, the Leninist vanguard strategy distanced the party—which had no large proletarian base—from the bulk of the peasants. In an important sense, the state apparatus became the class base for the development strategy, promoting authoritarian steering.

TRENDS IN EDUCATION

Frelimo placed enormous faith in the education system, which is reflected in the prominent place it occupied in party documents, in the 1980 Prospective Indicative Plan (PPI), and in the continuing investment of scarce human and material resources to build it up.[7]

The nationalization of education in 1975 laid the ground for macropolitical reforms in the system (using the terminology proposed by Carnoy and Levin 1985, 218). The reforms included introducing coeducation,

---

[7] Accessible references to postcolonial education are few. Judith Marshall (1985) presents a broad participant's view of the system, while my own work (Johnston 1984, subsequently revised, updated, and translated into Portuguese in MEC 1985) provides a more detailed description of the educational system and its development since 1984. Searle (1981) offers a useful record of a teacher's experience in a Mozambican secondary school between 1977 and 1979.

adult education, new curricula at all levels, and democratic school management structures; expanding access enormously at all levels; improving teacher training and employment conditions; promoting new teacher-pupil relationships in pedagogy and school administration; establishing productive activities in all educational institutions; and enhancing school-community links. Professional teachers became state employees, and teaching for private gain was prohibited. The discriminatory age restrictions on access were relaxed or removed, and all colonial textbooks and programs abolished. FRELIMO and the GDs mobilized enormous attendance at literacy classes taught by volunteers; it is believed that over a million people participated. However, with almost no textbooks or teacher preparation the activity was often not academically rewarding. In 1978, the state launched the First National Literacy Campaign, to enable 100,000 people in political and economic priority sectors (cadres, workers and collectivized peasants) to become literate.

However, the implementation of these reforms over the 1975–1979 period was partial and uneven. Primary enrollment doubled over two years, but universal primary coverage was not achieved. Curriculum transformation was hasty and largely unaccompanied by teacher preparation and textbooks, while the books that were produced had serious defects. Production was implemented in a patchy fashion, and often school-community links were not established in the ways intended. Teachers' previous limited education and training proved resistant to reform. Academic quality as measured by the examination system in every grade did not improve; learning quality was low, and the dropout and failure rates were high. Democratic organization of school management did not always lead to democratic practice. Adult education results were seen as disappointing. All of these problems corresponded very closely to parallel developments in the implementation of other reforms in the society and the economy.

The party response was also similar to its response in other policy areas. By 1979, dissatisfaction arose with the results of the reforms and with the quality of schooling in general; in response, macrotechnical reforms (again, in Carnoy and Levin's terms) began to be implemented (MEC 1982). Planning was tightened and began to serve as the central mechanism for maintaining direct control over the system. Cost-effectiveness was pursued, administration was centralized and director power emphasized, and a massive process of technical restructuring of the system was started, accompanied by grade-by-grade curriculum reform. In line with the development prognoses of the PPI for 1980–1990, priority was assigned to a rapid increase in the number of graduates from the higher levels of the system. Educational expansion thus moved up to the higher levels, quality of schooling was stressed, the entry level to teacher training was raised and its duration lengthened, and the lowest level of technical education was phased out. Adult education was made more formal and selective. Primary and lower secondary enrollment was cut by 8 percent by reducing the coverage of optional preprimary classes and by closing down small schools with few classes or low enrollment.

The macropolitical changes in 1975–1979 were thus neither total nor totally implemented. But they were not totally forgotten in the macrotechnical reform plans, as indicated by the importance assigned to eradicating illiteracy and to achieving universal primary education. The macrotechnical educational reforms initiated in 1983 have also been only partially implemented, largely because of the worsening military situation. Nearly 2,000 rural schools have been destroyed; teachers have been murdered by the MNR; and there have been great difficulties in distributing materials and new programs and preparing teachers for their use. It remains to be seen how and to what extent the reforms will be changed again in response to struggle and crisis in the state and in the economy.

TENSIONS AND PROBLEMS IN THE EDUCATIONAL SYSTEM

Developing a New Ideological Hegemony

In Mozambique, the school's first ideological role was and is to serve as an alternative to the colonial model. One important feature of the colonial school was that it excluded and treated people differentially on the basis of their sex, race, and class. At the same time, the colonial school did offer access to very high material rewards for those who passed through it successfully. This had accorded schooling a very high value and created a large demand for education. The school system exercises its ideological influence most directly by incorporating as many people as possible. These factors, coupled with FRELIMO's general mobilization for participation in education, marched all one way: The school system doubled in two years, and adult education classes mushroomed. Much more problematic, however, is what all those people were to learn once they were in school.

In theory, the school should become a model for the creation of new relations, values, and skills that correspond to those developing, and required, in the new society. Ideally, from it should emerge the new person, imbued with collective values and class consciousness. In practice, few ready recipes exist for the rapid creation of new persons (or the new society). One decision was made, in line with FRELIMO's Leninist vanguard strategy: The state, and within it the party, would exclusively lead and direct that training.

A profoundly different model (loosely described as "popular education") is theoretically possible and was perhaps emerging in embryo during the first years of independence. Communities everywhere were in fact building their own schools, mobilizing and supporting their own teachers, and attending classes. However, the state was determined to exercise a tighter control than this model allows by monopolizing the curriculum and teacher training and employment, by separating child from adult education, and by global educational planning. It was never on the state's agenda that an important ideological instrument should be "non-state." It was regularly reiterated (for example, Machel 1977) that private schooling, or teaching for private gain, was unacceptable, using as examples such colonial practices as racially exclusive private schools and the exploitative system of private tutors, which had developed to enable children to cram for exams. The policy perspective did not entirely preclude community, or even private, schools, but once it was clear that all teachers would be civil servants, or volunteers without pay, and that there would only be one official curriculum, the popular model had no future.

Notwithstanding the state's dominant role in education, conflicts still arose over the management of, and participation in, the educational process and over curricular issues, such as the kind of ideology to be transmitted and the ways of doing so. Initially, the objective of "the school as a democratic center, where new types of relation between pupil and teacher should evolve" (MEC 1979), was seen to require a number of profound changes in schooling. Among them were the democratization of education management, the development of party cells and mass organization units in educational institutions, the linking of study with production and of school with community, the adoption of new teaching methods, a generally politically oriented curriculum, and political education as a school subject.

Democratization of education management was effected in the education administration (as elsewhere in the state administration), by the creation of management collectives at each hierarchical level to direct the formulation of policy and its implementation. These were supplemented by general meetings of all workers in each institution to influence policy and to maintain democratic work relationships. Political study was obligatory once a week. In the schools, management was the responsibility of a school commission, teachers, and student representatives. Each class in the school also had elected student representatives for classroom issues. Adult education had a similar educational pattern.

A special section was set up in each school to manage school-community relations. This meant regular meetings with parents, reliance on parents to help in school maintenance, pupil-teacher work parties to help out in the community, and a literacy section to train, allocate, and support pupils teaching adult literacy in the neighbourhood. Parents were urged to take responsibility for their children's school discipline and study. A totally new school curriculum and the first-ever adult literacy curriculum were introduced, built around Mozambican realities and history and Frelimo policies and ideology, all from the perspective of dialectical materialism. Political education was introduced into the schools as a nonexamination subject, usually taught by local Frelimo cadres. On the basis of the experiences of the liberated zones, Portuguese was retained as the only language of instruction to create greater national unity. This decision raised little controversy in the state, though it certainly made it harder for non-Portuguese speakers (notably the peasantry, and especially women) to get through the system.

The school-community link proved to be difficult to establish and difficult to maintain. Often, the relationship between the school and its community was expected to consist largely of local citizens' participation in school construction and maintenance and in school productive projects. Not surprisingly, some parents were restive about this limited sense of their role.

This provide-labor-but-not-decisions sense of the community's role in education was consistent with a history of detaching schools and their students from the local community. At least a part of the party leadership, however, sought to extend parental participation in education. In 1982, for example, President Machel opened the school year by addressing himself almost exclusively to pupils' parents, indicating that too many now considered the education of their children to be entirely the state's responsibility, in which they felt they had no role (Machel 1982). The literacy teaching by the pupils was one good way to keep the link a living one. Even that declined over time, however. As schools were pressed for good exam results, the ministry of education became increasingly reluctant to permit upper-level students to participate in adult literacy programs, regarding such participation as a hindrance to their studies.

Struggles around the new curricula to serve as the base for the macro-technical reforms that began in 1983 also reveal some of the opposing lines and different interpretations of educational policy. These conflicts led to a more formal, directive, and academic approach to education in both adult and child curricula. In the curriculum for adults, the emphasis was to be on political content and relevance to a rural environment. For the school curriculum, the emphasis was to be on a kind of "back to basics" approach and on an urban environment. However, more recent curriculum revision for the upper primary grades has returned to focusing on developing more relevant contents for rural life and production, especially given the current catastrophic economic situation.

As has been stressed throughout this discussion, the general trend in all these aspects of the education system closely follows overall trends in state policy, from direct democratic approaches to centralized techno-cratic approaches, and back to recent attempts at what might be called decentralized functionalist approaches. Underlying all these shifts and trends is another important set of tensions: those around the need for skills training to raise economic productivity.

Economic Production and Reproduction

Mozambique inherited a 93 percent illiteracy level in 1975, and the assumption of power was accompanied by the flight of almost all the better-educated people in the country, since almost all postprimary education access and skilled work posts had been reserved for the colonists by the colonial state. It is not surprising, therefore, that Frelimo saw education as an immediate and pressing economic need.

On one hand, and within the strategy of the time, schools were expected to provide to the economy people who would fit into new democratic relations of production. Adult education was to mobilize and politicize the working masses, on the basis of both their experience (and hatred) of colonial exploitation and their political consciousness. On the other hand, people with technical skills were desperately scarce. Thus, while at the beginning of the period of independence it was ideologically important to the changing of the relations of production, and important to the legitimacy of the new state in showing its response to the demands of the people, to incorporate as many people as possible into the education system, it was also important to increase the number of graduates from the upper levels of the system as quickly as possible. After an initial preoccupation with the rapid expansion of the base of the system, within a short time the upper levels began to receive greater attention, in parallel with the gradual crystallization of a development strategy which especially emphasized the growth of the forces of production.

At the primary level, enrollment initially exploded, doubling in the space of a year and reaching its highest level in 1979 (see Table 8–1). In that year, the ministry of education moved to rationalize the school system by strict planning in order to improve quality, the efficient use of human resources, and teachers' working conditions. By reducing enrollment in the preprimary grade and closing down small schools with low attendance levels, total enrollment was reduced; it declined again slightly in 1981. Since then, enrollment has continued to fall, mostly as a result of the MNR's brutal attacks.

Table 8–1 indicates a difficult situation. The ratio of graduates to enrollment indicates high rates of failure and dropout. The planned rationalization began to prioritize first-grade entry for 7-year-olds and reduced the pupil-teacher ratio and class size. Thus, it is possible that the lower

TABLE 8–1

Mozambique: Enrollment, Graduates, Teachers, and Number of Schools by Schooling Level, 1974/75–1984

	1974/75	1977	1979	1980	1982	1984
Primary						
Enrollment	671,600	1,363,000	1,494,700	1,387,200	1,333,100	1,303,700
Graduates, Grade 4	19,700	39,600	74,000	82,600	58,800	72,700
Teachers	10,300	16,100	16,800	17,000	20,600	21,000
Schools	5,200	7,100	7,200	5,700	5,700	5,000
Grades 5–6						
Enrollment	20,400	43,500	85,400	79,900	80,700	104,000
Graduates, Grade 6	3,600	10,200	12,300	18,200	14,200	20,200
Grades 7–9						
Enrollment	4,600	4,400	7,400	9,700	12,500	17,500
Graduates, Grade 9	600	900	300	1,000	1,700	1,800
Grades 10–11						
Enrollment[a]	1,300	300	800	800	1,200	2,000
Graduates, Grade 11	200	200	300	300	300	400
Secondary						
(Grades 5–11)						
Teachers	n.a.	1,900	2,500	2,100	2,400	3,100
Schools	31	94	97	100	116	146
Technical Elementary						
(Grades 5–6)						
Enrollment	1,000	3,000	3,500	2,800	2,000	1,500
Graduates, Grade 6	n.a.	n.a.	500	500	300	500
Teachers	n.a.	200	200	200	100	100
Schools	10	18	16	13	11	9
Technical Basic						
(Grades 7–9)						
Enrollment	7,100	6,400	9,000	9,900	10,000	9,700
Graduates, Grade 9	n.a.	n.a.	[800][b]	1,600	2,000	1,500
Teachers	n.a.	400	500	500	700	700
Schools	13	13	18	19	23	23
Technical Intermediate						
(Grades 10–11)						
Enrollment	800	n.a.	[600]	1,000	1,400	1,600
Graduates, Grade 11	n.a.	n.a.	100	[200]	400	300
Teachers	n.a.	n.a.	n.a.	100	100	100
Institutes	3	3	3	3	3	4

Sources: Johnston 1985; Ministerio da Educação 1985; Comissão Nacional do Plano 1985.

[a] Enrollment figures for 1977, 1979, and 1980 include the preuniversity course at the university.

[b] Brackets indicate incomplete data.

enrollment after 1979 represents a better coverage of the 7–11 age group than does the earlier larger (total) enrollment. However, the reductions in 1980–81 reduced the number of schools by 20 percent and particularly affected the dispersed peasantry and the schools they had built themselves.

The planned cuts represent the turn towards schooling quality and efficiency, to some extent at the cost of quantity. The definition of quality was largely based on academic results in the exam system.

The system of exams in every grade provides some legitimacy to a situation where only a minority of entrants complete primary education. That legitimacy, however, is fragile. Students and their parents—indeed, all citizens—recognize that schooling provides the most direct route to social mobility and an improved standard of living. In this setting, low exam scores do not quench the popular demand for expanded educational opportunities. This partially explains the government's intention to extend the primary level to seven years of education (to be made compulsory in the future) as part of the current reform. This proposed extension also stems from a concern with improving the quality of schooling for all students and from a sense that students who leave school at age 14 or older will be better able to begin work and assume adult responsibilities immediately. The maintenance of the exam system benefits urban dwellers and groups already favored under colonialism, notably the public sector, but it also underlines that the schools-are-for-selection ideology has fairly wide acceptance, even in revolutionary Mozambique.

The chaos caused by MNR activities from 1982 onwards has clearly cut back access to primary education. In the period 1982–1985, over a thousand primary schools were destroyed or had to cease functioning.[8] In line with reform plans to introduce universal education, although the problems in the countryside persist, efforts to achieve full primary education in the cities and towns have been increased, surely in part to gain and maintain urban support.

Whereas in 1980, in parallel with cuts at the primary level, spending at the lower secondary level was also reduced, the more recent trend in all secondary levels has been one of expansion. Some schools were created by local initiative and presented as a fait accompli, while others reflect the concrete demands of the 1980 PPI for more graduates from the higher levels of the system, to take posts in the state and the modern economy.

Education expansion at higher levels has produced some tensions. Higher levels cost much more per student, raising the overall costs of the

---

[8] Johnson and Martin (1986) indicate that 1,863 schools were destroyed by April 1985, displacing 313,766 pupils and nearly 5,000 teachers.

system (for education costs, see Table 8–2). At the same time, in Mozambique's situation upper-level education expansion becomes at least self-limiting and perhaps self-destructive in terms of government capacity. Expanded education requires more teachers, which in turn requires more teacher training with more highly qualified graduates; this further increases the costs. Consequently, investment in higher-level schooling yields results that are felt only in the long term. All of these factors help explain why the Fourth Congress directives on education concentrate on cost-effectiveness and efficiency (Frelimo 1983b).

"Literacy Is Production"

Adult education experienced tensions similar to those in other parts of the education system. Literacy classes mushroomed after Independence (see Table 8–3), and adult night schools flourished. Over time, the state worked to take control of the adult education movement in a planned way. Literacy and postliteracy campaigns were implemented annually from 1978, with both political and economic objectives. They were structured selectively to serve political and economic priority groups. The

TABLE 8–2

Mozambique: Education Costs, 1975–1984 ('000,000,000 of escudos/meticais and percent)

	1975	1977	1979	1980	1982	1984
Global Social Product (GSP) (1980 constant prices)	711	750	779	821	788	582
GNP (current prices)	n.a.	n.a.	n.a.	789	916	1,094
Current state budget	61	83	107	141	195	229
For education	11	16	19	25	37	41
State investment budget[a]	18	27	40	99	143	106
For education[b]	1	1	1	4	2	2
Education as % GNP	n.a.	n.a.	n.a.	3.7	4.3	4.0
Education as % GSP	1.5	2.1	2.6	3.5	4.1	3.8
Education as % budget	13.9	14.2	12.8	12.2	11.5	12.9

Source: Comissão Nacional do plano 1985.

Notes: n.a. indicates data not available. U.S. $1 = 29$00 (1975) − 40MT (1984).

[a] Values for 1977 and 1979 are estimates. Available sources give the GSP in 1980 constant prices; others give it in current prices.

[b] Values for 1975 and 1977 are my estimates, as above.

TABLE 8–3
Mozambique: Adult Education, 1978/79–1984 ('000)

	1978/79	1980	1981	1982	1983	1984
Literacy						
(Grade 2 equivalence)						
Enrollment[a]	260	325	310	200	143	150
Number passing	140	120	61	38	16	13
Postliteracy						
(Grade 4 equivalence)						
Enrollment	—	87	143	87	40	41
Number passing	—	26	28	25	15	8

Source: Johnston 1985.

[a] Values for 1983 and 1984 indicate sum of enrollments in the expanded two-year literacy course.

state was manifestly disappointed with the skills levels achieved and the pass rates, and moved from a period of mass enrollment in 1980 to a formalization of the curriculum and tighter prioritization of selected target groups. This occurred in spite of the general aim of eradicating illiteracy, which was stated as a priority of the 1980–1990 plan. Once the machinery had been put in place for mounting mass campaigns, however, the gradual fall in enrollment and targets, the lower priority assigned to literacy in practice, and the increased concentration on priority sectors, meant that the cost per student rose sharply. As the emphasis on the volunteer nature of literacy teaching was toned down and more and more teachers came to be remunerated through full-time or part-time employment, fees, or cash or in-kind incentives, the costs of adult education rose still further.

Adult education had been assigned a high priority in the period immediately after the end of colonial rule. Incorporated in its structure was the tension between education to prepare and train productive workers on one hand and education to mobilize citizens and reinforce the regime's legitimacy on the other. When the academically measured results turned out to be lower than had been expected, literacy and postliteracy programs lost their priority in practice, especially as mass campaigns, in the atmosphere of technological solutions, became increasingly focused on the export and urban sectors of the economy, a tendency reinforced by the Fourth Congress directive to make the curriculum more directly functional. Notwithstanding its expected mobilizing and politicizing role, the state looked to adult education to raise production and productivity directly by providing technical skills, and in that way to repay the investment made in it.

Production in Education

In Mozambique, the attitudes of teachers, pupils, parents, and administrators to production at school has been affected by the colonial experience. The mission schools used production at the primary level to extract surplus from the pupils and to initiate them into forced labor. The colonial education system also included technical schooling from a very low level as an alternative track for the lower social classes to the various levels of general secondary education. Some technical school programs did not offer any equivalence to the academic curriculum; they were a dead-end siding rather than a parallel track. Thus, for most Mozambicans, school production was an activity for the lower strata.

Four main streams of interest emerged in the debate around school production after independence:

1. Theory-practice as a *methodological* issue: Practice for pupils is advocated as a means of understanding the content of the curriculum.
2. Cognition-skill as a *relevance* issue: The curriculum should be built around providing relevant theory and practice for the pupils' future. An agriculture-linked curriculum would be urged for rural areas, and a factory- or office-linked curriculum for urban areas.
3. Study-work as a *subsistence* issue: First and foremost, pupils should produce at school to feed themselves better, to pay for school improvements or operating expenses, and the like, that is, production should be undertaken in order to be profitable.
4. Study-production as a *class consciousness* issue: Pupils' engagement in production (and in related decisionmaking) is essential in itself, irrespective of the kind of production, its relevance to the curriculum, and its profitability (although if all these subsidiary aims can be achieved, so much the better). The aims of the production are to make pupils accustomed to and respectful of manual labor, production, cooperative effort, and the producer and to counteract the division between mental and manual labor.

In the liberated zones, and immediately after Independence, class consciousness (issue 4 above) was at the core of educational policy; the other objectives were subsidiary. In the wave of collective voluntary work following liberation, and in terms of directives of the time, each school and boarding institute set up its own fields. With a few exceptions, this experience was not satisfactory. On one hand, since the schools had no funds to invest, their production practices were identical to those of the local peasantry, with the same tools, methods, and crops—and with rather poorer results. On the other hand, in many places school authorities decided that work in the fields was a good way to punish malefactors, which hardly elevated the activity in the pupils' eyes. The teachers, often overworked and with their own schooled disdain for hard manual labor, were also not particularly enthusiastic or energetic participants.

By 1977, ideas on school production were changing. President Machel (1977) put emphasis on school production to pay for the costs of education (issue 3 above). However, as the ministry of education assumed increasing control over curriculum organization and scheduling, production became more and more an extracurricular activity. In theory, pupils' political conduct, including participation in production, was to be an important criterion for evaluation. However, this expectation was never incorporated into formal evaluation procedures, and an assessment of political conduct probably influenced selection and promotion in only a few cases.

By 1980, attitudes toward school production had changed further. President Machel (1980) declared that in the cities, small plots were neither attractive nor relevant, and that pupils should concern themselves with gardens and school maintenance. At the general secondary level, it was decided that existing production was not serving any of the objectives outlined above, and that it was taking time away from studies. Thus, it was decided that emphasis should be placed on assigning pupils to factories and other places of work during the holidays (issue 2 above). At the primary level, it was decided that since pupils were too small to develop proper plots on the peasant model (and would probably do some of this at home anyway), attention should be turned to gardens and small vegetable plots of some relevance to such subjects as natural science (issue 1 above). Gradually, the issue was swept under the carpet, all priority in practice going to academic results, with a few exceptions. Some pilot centers maintained good production levels; boarding institutes often retained a plot for food (issue 3 above); and in the big reform debates during the period 1979–1982, school production activities were considered in terms of the technical education subsystem (issue 2 above).

As has often been the case, the debate over technical and polytechnical education resulted in two different outcomes. First, up to this time, after finishing middle secondary schooling, almost all pupils had been assigned to jobs, with only a few going on to preuniversity training in Maputo, usually for teacher training. Most people in university courses were worker-students with jobs in the state. It was decided however, that most of those entering the academic track should in the future go directly on to further studies or training at the preuniversity or university level, in order to expand rapidly the output of graduates from higher levels. At the same time, an accelerated, preuniversity Faculty for Workers and Combatants was opened to ensure a better class composition among university students, and curriculum planners were given the task of introducing a different, more industrial form of production in academic secondary schools as a subject in the curriculum (as of 1988, not yet implemented).

Second, it was decided that technical education should take priority over general education. Again rather contradictorily, the lowest level of technical schooling was phased out (it would be bypassed by the creation of a seven-year compulsory primary level) and the schools thus released were upgraded to expand the next level (basic level). In practice therefore, the basic level produced as many graduates as did the equivalent ninth grade of the general track. Thus, technical education, in which productive practice is a necessary component of training, has taken over the functions of school production for the present. It remains to be seen whether its priority in enrollment will be accompanied by a de facto change in its status in the eyes of primary level graduates. The liberalization of the labor market in 1985 and the continuing role of the academic track as the fast route to the university and to jobs in the state make this somewhat unlikely.

Problems in financing education and its expansion, allied to the overall crisis in the country, brought attention back to school production in general after 1983, and many schools began producing again on a larger scale (issue 3 above). The fourth-grade natural science syllabus was revised to be more directly relevant to agriculture. A plan to turn some technical schools into schools for cooperativists was adopted, though as of 1988, it has not yet been implemented.

Reproducing the Petite Bourgeoisie?

In its analysis of the class development and economic performance of the country during its Fourth Congress, Frelimo identified as problematic the growth in the state of what was referred to as "aspirants to the bourgeoisie." At least some of those aspirants felt that the schools had become too democratic and accessible, creating too much competition from other classes for their own privileges, threatening the advancement of their children and themselves. Since their main avenue of mobility is through the higher levels of education into the state, they may well try to influence state policy toward reducing this competition. The party response thus far has been to make a compulsory allocation of graduates to careers or further schooling, to demand use of class criteria in selection for levels where access is limited, and to set up special facilities for promoting cadres, workers, and peasants (a special preuniversity faculty, adult education boarding centers, party schools).

This challenge by an aspiring petite bourgeoisie has expressed itself in the conflict between specifically nationalist and explicitly socialist policies. While language policy (Portuguese as the national language), curriculum policy (the same for all), and planning policy (equitable regional distribution, access for all citizens) are intended to promote national unity and nationalism, so curriculum policy (content and pedagogy), network planning (priority to communal villages), and stated selection policies (priority to the working classes) are intended to promote collectivization. This uneasy synthesis potentially threatens the aspiring petite bourgeoisie, which has managed so far to maintain its position through its advantage in Portuguese, through the operation of the very traditionally academic examination system, and through the ambivalent application of the category "worker" to include civil servants.

Women and Education

In colonial times, discrimination against women in general and in the education system in particular was a matter of public policy. Women were expected to be homestead-bound producers of cash crops and reproducers of the family, a reinforcement of their subordinate place in the earlier era. Fewer schools were available for girls. The enrollment ratio for girls was less than 1:2, while a larger percentage of girls than of boys dropped out or failed. Only in the more privileged strata of colonial society were the gender differences in educational access relatively smaller, narrowing the gap at the top of the system.

In the liberated zones, one of the most heated issues in the struggle between the two lines in FRELIMO was over the status and role of women. The victory of the revolutionary line led to the establishment of the Women's Detachment in the armed forces and the Organization of Mozambican Women (OMM). After Independence, FRELIMO moved swiftly toward redressing the double exploitation of women, mobilizing against the bride-price and premature marriages, making women equal legal persons, and enshrining sexual equality in the constitution. In education, enlightenment campaigns were carried out to persuade the society to enroll girls in school and to persuade husbands not to interfere with their wives' participation in adult education. Primary education, made coeducational, saw a swift rise in girls' participation, to over 40 percent of enrollment in 1980, while in the same year women's participation in adult literacy classes comprised 54 percent of the total. Through the persistent action of the OMM, supported by the party, women began to assert their rights and to enroll in education to achieve better status. Women became everywhere the most determined supporters of Frelimo, formed the majority of cooperative producers (56 percent in 1980), and joined the OMM. Women were also significant participants in the People's Assemblies and the party. This led to some uproar in the traditionally oriented society and, apparently, to increased instability of marriages. Faced with this situation, in 1980 the party toned down the OMM's policy by putting more emphasis on the role of women as mothers and the maintainers of families. This seems to have reduced the OMM's status and influence. The OMM national conference in 1984 was notable for pressure from above for women to follow the more traditional line in relation to family role and pressure from below for new steps forward to women's liberation, with the latter line coming through more strongly in the conference's decisions. In adult education, the concentration of literacy and postliteracy courses in areas of the country producing export crops seems to have reduced women's access and enrollment. In formal schooling, the dropout and failure rates remain higher for girls than for boys, and girls' participation in higher levels, though in absolute terms vastly increased, is at a lower rate than at lower levels (for relevant data, see Table 8–4). This reflects both traditional perceptions of women's roles and male dominance of the labor market—in 1980, though the proportion of female workers was much increased over colonial times, only 10 percent of employed labor was female.

It is odd that the struggle for independence should have reduced women's participation in lower grades and increased it in upper ones, while the present struggle does precisely the opposite. Mozambique's new rul-

TABLE 8–4
Mozambique: Women in School, 1974/75–1984 (enrollment figures in '000)

	1974/75		1979		1984	
Grade	Total Enroll.	% Fem.	Total Enroll.	% Fem.	Total Enroll.	% Fem.
Preprimary	3,418	37.2	1,887	46.8	633	46.9
1	1,605	31.5	5,843	46.7	4,790	46.0
2	879	30.4	3,628	42.3	3,605	43.7
3	502	28.0	2,274	34.3	2,165	40.5
4	312	28.7	1,315	26.6	1,402	35.1
5	124	42.2	557	28.8	618	32.5
6	80	46.1	297	27.9	430	31.3
7	20	46.0	47	30.4	88	28.7
8	17	49.3	22	29.8	50	30.4
9	9	53.0	16	40.7	35	29.7

Source: MEC 1985.

ers have managed to reduce the gender division considerably and look to women at the base as a major constituency. At the same time, it may be that women with higher education represent threatening competition for available employment.

Who Teaches the New Person?

Teachers occupy the crucial position in the education system, as they largely determine the manner of its functioning and its successes and failures. Once in the classroom, they are largely uncontrolled and unobserved. Their own backgrounds, views, and experience, as translated into their social class practice, dominates. Furthermore, although by no means well paid, they are continually employed and have status in their community, to whose demands they may be more responsive than they are to those of a distant bureaucracy. Nevertheless, few pupils in the schools want to become teachers, having set their sights elsewhere. All of this translates into a cluster of problems which the state addresses mainly in selection and training of teachers.

At Independence, the primary schools were staffed by *monitores* with fourth-grade schooling and little, if any, formal training. Their colonial experience was with a Portugal-oriented curriculum, teaching by dictation and repetition, and harsh discipline. All of these were exaggerated by their own previous exposure to the same kind of schooling and by their own elevation in status by assimilation. Consequently, they were under some suspicion as agents of colonial ideology, and in the first few years after Independence, much attention was spent on upgrading and retraining them. At the same time, the state decided to cease employing untrained teachers and to begin new teacher training on a large scale. However, by 1980 still only 7,000 of the 17,000 teachers had more than fourth-grade qualifications, and fewer still any lengthy training. It is clear that the retraining process and political mobilization eliminated some of the most drastic aspects of teacher behavior, such as corporal punishment. Although the new curricula went some way toward revising the content and methods of instruction, primary schooling remains strongly characterized by rote learning and choral repetition. Meanwhile, the more subtle aspects of teachers' attitudes hardly support enabling their pupils to become dedicated cooperative producers or well-formed new persons. Examples are the teachers' own pursuit of further schooling and their desire to get away from the countryside for that purpose, and their reluctance to work in the schools' fields. At higher schooling levels, hundreds of foreign *cooperantes* were hired to fill the gaps left by colonist teachers, and pupils from higher grades were removed to teach lower grades. The preuniversity Grades 10 and 11 were suspended from 1977 to 1980, apart from a course at the university at this level to train teachers. One problem came to light at once: Far fewer pupils in the system wanted to become teachers than the numbers required.

Beginning in 1977, Frelimo began to mobilize tenth- and eleventh-graders to teach younger pupils and to mobilize practicing and future teachers. Still, however, few teachers were forthcoming. The ministry's power to allocate new graduates to teacher training was unpopular and produced reluctant recruits.

With the spread of what has been termed here the technocratic orientation in the state and its concern with high (academic) quality in the schools, the educational growth strategy reaffirmed by President Machel in 1977—pupils in each grade teaching those in the grades below—was abandoned, and in the reform work of 1979–1982, a more formal approach was evident. Teacher training was to be raised in entry level and duration, a costly decision and a policy that promotes disquiet among existing teachers, who see their own qualifications and salaries falling behind, notwithstanding their longer service. They thus press for their own retraining and further schooling, become disgruntled with their workload or their rural posting, and vote with their feet by leaving the education system. This tendency becomes more prominent in the countryside, as money salaries come to be worth less and less and barter is the order of the day, as local demand for schooling drops in the face of subsistence problems, as access to further schooling is difficult, and as the teacher's role as a target for the MNR makes rural placement dangerous. These problems increase the difficulty of providing schools throughout the rural areas. The partial response has been to raise teachers' salaries and to form a National Teachers Organization (ONP), to improve teachers' conditions, and to expand political mobilization. Even this is not likely to stop teacher dropout, although many teachers have held on under terrible conditions.

It is also doubtful that lengthening teacher training will effectively change the teachers' classroom approach in the direction indicated by policy documents. A 1983 research project (Centro de Estudos Africanos [CEA] 1984) on teacher training preparatory to the introduction of new reforms revealed that the same old pedagogical approaches were being transmitted, that the curriculum content was still being taught in a similar theoretical and definitional way, with little clear linking to the daily lives and experiences of the students, that prospective teachers' political training did not equip them with a materialist approach to and understanding of society, and that no useful experience in production was being acquired. Clearly, improving the quality of the teacher corps is difficult to accomplish without the prior training of extremely good teacher educators.

Similar problems have plagued the selection and training of adult educators. It became successively harder to mobilize volunteer teachers, and their dropout rate has been a constant problem. Their qualifications have remained low, and their practices have mirrored their own schooling experience. One solution tried was to send graduates to longer training courses and post them to the communal villages as paid educators with the tasks of teaching postliteracy classes and mobilizing and supporting voluntary literacy teachers, but this has not functioned very well. In sectors that can afford it, more literacy teachers are being employed. Recently, there have been efforts to change significantly the training of adult educator trainers and of voluntary and professional educators, but the problems of finding and keeping educators in the countryside are likely to worsen. Furthermore, all these training and utilization strategies have the immediate effect of raising the costs of education.

CONCLUDING OBSERVATIONS

The state's policies and strategies for social collectivization and economic transformation largely account for the direction of education policy in Mozambique. Those policies and strategies were themselves bounded and influenced by three major forces. First, the historical legacy meant that the intended social transformation would have to be based on conditions of severe under- and undevelopment and on relations of dependence on a hostile capitalist neighbor. The process of collectivization and transformation of the economy would have to involve not only the creation of new relations and attitudes, both internally and with the outside world, and the development of new productive forces but also disentangling the web of historical relations and structures.

Second, Mozambique was not left in peace to get on with these tasks. Rhodesia, South Africa, and Malawi were not well disposed towards the changes taking place next door. The resulting damage has been immense. During the same period, the world capitalist economy went into decline and oil prices rose, which severely reduced Mozambique's terms of trade. And, to cap it all, in every year since its independence, one part or another of the country has been shaken by natural disaster in the form of large-scale flooding or extensive drought. The long-term result of all this has been to slow, or even reverse, the social transformation program and to increase the country's poverty, indebtedness and dependence.

Third, even if better external conditions had prevailed, the construction of a revolutionary state would not have been simple. The primary dynamic of development was lodged in the state and its institutions, led by a vanguard party, but this did not mean that it was clear which policies were best, or that the state would perfectly implement those that were adopted. In the main, the conflicts of emphasis did not directly challenge the party's collectivist objectives. Rather, they revolved around the relative emphasis to be given to political participation and economic development: in a word, whether to emphasize the forces or the relations of production, and what *kind* of emphasis to give them.

The argument here has been that FRELIMO's initial need was to mobilize the population to defend the revolutionary conquests, first from sabotage and the threats of a colonist coup, and then from threats of invasion from neighboring countries. In this phase, FRELIMO implemented a form of direct democracy in all sectors of society. As these major threats were overcome, FRELIMO constituted itself as a Marxist-Leninist vanguard party and created organs of representative democracy in a hierarchical form. Attention shifted to ensuring state control over the economy, a process that reduced workplace democracy and emphasized efficiency of labor. Once the overshadowing military aggression from Rhodesia was ended, the state concentrated on developing the forces of production and further reduced its mobilizational activities and popular participation in decisionmaking. After the Frelimo party's largely conventional military response to this aggression had failed to stop the MNR, and vast damage had been done to the economy, the party returned to more popular mobilization tactics, such as rejuvenating party cells, mass organizations, and local People's Assemblies and redynamizing people's militias. There was also a turn to reengaging peasant support by economic measures, such as restocking the market with goods, price liberalization, and limited privatization. The change in tactics was hampered by the economic crisis that the MNR had caused and by the resulting reduction in party credibility. As a result, policy orientation has swung further and further away from the original collectivist goals in an urgent attempt to mobilize more external financing and to find some way of improving the economy.

The adoption by the liberation movement of a vanguard strategy as the political form for directing social and economic development gave the central organs of state a monopoly on decisionmaking. There is no doubt that a social transformation cannot be realized without a good measure of centralism. However, the subordination and virtual emasculation of people's democracy by central steering permitted an embryonic privileged class in the state to entrench and extend its own power and prestige, and was thus promoted and supported by this class. In spite of frequent official recognition of this problem by the party, the "bureaucratic" class (or "aspirants to the bourgeoisie") remains a powerful and antidemocratic force within the state.

Developments in the field of education are a microcosm of the broader political process. The pent-up demand for education in the society was very great, and satisfying it was fundamental to the legitimacy of the new state. The state is in a veritable educational minefield. The leadership's ideological economic development strategy can hardly afford to see large sectors of the population left out of the ideological influence of schooling. In practice, the experiences of participants in education do not directly convert them to the state's way of seeing things, but rather may raise unattainable expectations, notably of employment. When access to further schooling or paid work is not forthcoming, frustration, not legitimacy, is the result. The aspirants to the bourgeoisie, well represented within the state itself, have pursued their own interests, including making education a highly selective instrument of their own reproduction.

Given all these tensions and problems in the society and in the education system, it is important to explore how education fared in relation to its goals. During the first postcolonial years, education performed a valuable function as a site for the mobilization and expression of popular participation in unleashing the process of social transformation. It served to inform the people about the changes under way and to transmit important parts of FRELIMO's message. It suddenly included on equal terms masses of previously excluded people from the oppressed classes, most notably women. As a Portuguese official recently admitted, more people were included in education and graduated during the first 10 years of independence than during the entire 500 years of Portuguese sovereignty.

Although mass education is still a long way from including everyone, it has created a situation where the workers and peasants in the collectivized economic sectors and in the organs of the state are considerably better educated, better trained, and more politically conscious than ever before. The system also advanced numbers of people to the higher levels of the system, to positions in state organs, and to employment. In this way, it has served to maintain and increase the struggles between groups in the state over alternative policies, maintaining alive in the various institutions a democratic process of discussion and debate.

But the most significant contribution made to Mozambican social transformation by the educational system has been its performance as a mobilizer, as an avenue for collective consumption and political participation, and as a provider of popular legitimacy for the state. It has not created the new person, but it has at least created a different person, who enters the political economy with more tools for collective and conscious participation in society. Despite all efforts, the system has not developed adequate technical skills for increased production, in either quantitative or qualitative terms. In a period of crisis in the economy, the state will be tempted both to save on education and to increase the system's "productivity" by putting more people through the higher levels with better results on academic examinations. Nonetheless, it seems more important for the state, also facing a crisis of legitimacy, to use to the utmost the potential of the system to mobilize and incorporate the mass of Mozambicans and thereby to confer renewed legitimacy on itself, especially through investing in mass basic education.

CHRONOLOGY OF EDUCATION AND MAJOR POLICY CHANGES IN
MOZAMBIQUE

	Politics, Economy, Society	*Education*
1974	Transitional government Flight of colonists, and economic sabotage Directive to set up Dynamizing Groups (popular selection)	Upper education levels fall into disorder Widespread appearance of literacy classes and small schools
1975	Independence Collectivize, mobilize: "Unity, work, vigilance" Nationalization of many social and economic sectors	Nationalization of all education Macroreforms (curriculum, entry regulations, school calendar)
1976	Sanctions on Rhodesia South Africa cuts back on use of ports and labor	School system doubles Mass adult literacy participation
1977	Frelimo third Congress: plan and restore economy, construct bases for socialism, collectivize Constitution of elected people's assemblies and vanguard party	Education planning Mass primary teacher recruitment and upgrading Preuniversity level closed
1978	Extensive Rhodesian attacks Economy recuperates, but low growth in agriculture More nationalizations and investment in giant state farms	First national literacy campaign for collective sectors and cadres
1979–1980	Lancaster House, peace, and Zimbabwean independence Attack the Internal Enemy, emphasize top-down command Create conventional army Prepare plan for "Leap Forward" to construct material base for socialism over 1980–1990 Eliminate inequities in salary structures Founding of nine-country SADCC for regional cooperation and economic independence from South Africa	Preparation of new education reform Highest-ever school enrollment (1979) and adult enrollment (1980) Preparation of ten-year education plan Rationalization of education system; lower-level school enrollment cut by 8% Law 4/80 links schooling level and salary

(Continued on next page)

EDUCATION AND MAJOR POLICY CHANGES IN MOZAMBIQUE—*Continued*

	Politics, Economy, Society	*Education*
1981	South Africa attacks and intensifies economic sanctions Large investment in large development projects Best year for production and export Harsh security laws passed	Preparation of curriculum reform emphasizing quality Law 1/81 regulates adult education, emphasizes modern productive sector, rules that classes must function outside work time
1982	Large-scale South African launch of MNR Purge of security forces; emphasis on citizens' rights Calls for revitalizing party, restructuring government Economic decline; black marketing	Adult education enrollment drops Expansion of secondary education Big rise in education budget
1983	Frelimo Fourth Congress: Defend the Country, Combat Hunger, Build Socialism Some privatization Attention to family producers Reduction in scale of large projects Decentralization Operation to evacuate the "unproductive" from the cities War, drought, and floods	First year of implementation of reforms, in first grade and literacy program Large decline in primary enrollment as rural schools burnt by MNR
1984	Widespread MNR destruction; 33% GNP decline 1981–1984 Growth of black market Nonaggression pact with South Africa Increased dependence on the West IMF/IBRD membership	Reform implementation delayed and compromised Destruction of schools, kidnapping and assassination of pupils and teachers Further adult education decline

(*Continued on next page*)

EDUCATION AND MAJOR POLICY CHANGES IN MOZAMBIQUE—*Continued*

	Politics, Economy, Society	*Education*
1985	South Africa continues support to MNR Debt burden 175% (U.S. $2 billion) "War economy" Market and wage liberalization Revitalization of mass organizations Strengthening of Party organs Limited growth in agriculture	Crash in exam results 1,900 schools closed, 5,000 teachers and 314,000 pupils displaced
1986	War spreads in the North South Africa threatens to attack Mozambique threatens Malawi sanctions Nationwide elections to new term for People's Assemblies President Machel killed in plane crash in South Africa President Chissano promises to continue the same policies	20% cut in budget and thus in local staff Primary expansion in the cities, partly to cope with stream of refugees

CHAPTER 9

Education and Social Transformation in Nicaragua, 1979–1989

Martin Carnoy and Carlos Alberto Torres

THE SANDINISTA-LED REVOLUTION that overthrew the Somoza dictatorship in July 1979 made educational expansion and reform top priorities in its overall attempt to transform Nicaraguan society. The educational effort faced extraordinary difficulties. It had to make up years of educational neglect by the Somozas and shortages of teachers and materials. A counterrevolutionary guerrilla war killed hundreds of teachers, forced youth to serve in the military instead of pursuing their studies, and effectively closed much of the countryside to educational activities. Even so, the revolution succeeded in bringing many more children and adults into school, lowered the illiteracy rate, and has begun to reorient the schools to develop new values and skills consistent with the changing vision of what it means to be a Nicaraguan.

Why were educational changes such an important issue for the Sandinista revolution? What political and social forces influenced these changes? We argue that education as an issue and its subsequent expansion and reform were and continue to be directly shaped by the process of reconstitution of the Nicaraguan economy and state and, more recently, by the preservation of the process against armed intervention. The Sandinista reconstitution is based on incorporating the mass of peasants and low-income urban workers into national political and social life. Education, in turn, plays a key role in this process and is shaped by it.

But reconstitution faces important constraints. The Nicaraguan revolution is a contested concept, even within the Sandinista movement. Counterrevolutionary groups—with the direct support of the United States—have tried to overthrow Sandinismo altogether. Educational policy, as a crucial element of reconstitution, is therefore marked by considerable conflict—conflict that reflects the broader social and political struggle. And educational expansion, which depends on state resources, is also affected by the massive military spending required to fight the war. Nicaraguan education is now inexorably intertwined with the nature of the Sandinista revolution itself. Both the political struggle over educational policy and the diversion of human and physical resources away from education to the war effort, have had enormous influence over educational change since 1979.

THE REVOLUTION AND THE LEGACY

Historical Development

Nicaragua was a prime target for social revolution. It had a revolutionary past linked with the figure of Augusto Cesar Sandino, and an intransigent series of corrupt dictators (Anastasio Somoza and his two sons), who were intimately associated with a foreign power—the United States. The Somozas had a brutal private army (the Guardia Nacional, or National Guard), which had forced large numbers of peasants off their land in the 1930s and again in the 1950s. Finally, through their direct control of much of the Nicaraguan economy, the Somozas had even repressed important fractions of the local bourgeoisie.

Even so, the revolution was long and difficult. When the fighting was over, 40,000 of Nicaragua's 2.7 million people were dead, 100,000 had been wounded, 150,000 were homeless, and hundreds of millions of dollars of material assets had been destroyed ("Prospects for the Sandinista Revolution" 1979, 426).

The Sandinistas came to power on a wave of popularity. They were committed to redistributing land to the peasants and developing a socially oriented economy; at the same time, political alliances and disastrous economic conditions bound the Sandinistas to a mixed economy that would include an active private sector. As a victorious revolutionary army, they gained control of the political and repressive apparatuses of the state, and were thrust into the role of reconstituting it.

But there are enormous difficulties in carrying out this project. The Sandinistas inherited one of the lowest-income economies in Latin America, an economy tied closely to primary exports and foreign loans to the United States and corrupted by forty years of a single family's repressive control. The Sandinistas had no political experience outside of guerilla warfare and very few cadres who could actually carry out government plans. There were few well-trained professionals in Nicaragua in 1979, even outside the Sandinista movement, leaving the new government with only a relatively small group of people to take on the enormous task of rebuilding and reform.

The Sandinistas also inherited one of the least developed educational systems in Latin America. Nicaragua's 1960 and 1970 enrollment rates were the second lowest (after Guatemala's) in Central America, and, in the rest of Latin America, only Haiti's enrollment rate (18.8 percent in 1960) was lower. In the mid-1970s, half the population were illiterate, and more than three-fourths of the rural population unable to read or write. About 65 percent of Nicaraguan children aged 7 to 12 attended primary school; preprimary education was available to a mere 5 percent of children, mostly in private, fee-paying centers. Only 22 percent of those who entered schools finished the sixth grade—only 6 percent in rural areas.

Finally, within two years of the triumph over Somoza, the Sandinistas had to go to war again, this time against remnants of the Guardia Nacional and some former Sandinista allies supported by the U.S. government.[1] The military struggle for survival created even greater obstacles to achieving economic growth and the expansion of social services. A high percentage of human and material resources had to be and continues to be devoted to defending the country against armed intervention.

The Conditioned Inheritance of Contemporary Nicaragua

The revolution inherited a political economy that had seen the rapid acquisition of important sectors of the economy by the ruling Somoza family over the previous forty years (in 1979, approximately 15 percent of the arable land and other productive assets belonged to the Somozas). Although Nicaragua has a small population (less than 3 million) relative to its territory and its arable land, this land had systematically been taken out of peasants' food production and turned into successive export crops. Sugar was the first of these, but in the 1870s, a still self-sufficient agricultural system was replaced by an export-oriented coffee agriculture in the hands of coffee capitalists. The benefits of the coffee booms were highly concentrated, while the small farmers who lost their lands became a rural proletariat. During the 1940s, exports became diversified, particularly through the introduction of cotton plantations in the rich valleys of northwestern Nicaragua. Again, this diversification increased rural proletarianization by displacing peasants from their land. The Somozas were heavily involved in the land expropriations that put increased acreage into cotton (under the family's ownership). Finally, in the 1960s and 1970s, feed lots for beef became a new source of export earnings, in both

[1] The FSLN (Frente Sandinista de Liberación Nacional), which is the formal name of the Sandinista movement, was composed of three wings: The GPP, or Prolonged Popular War wing, which was headed by Tomas Borge, fought a rural guerrilla war on the Vietnamese model; the Proletarian wing, headed by Jaime Wheelock, and most traditionally Marxist, focused on organizing the urban proletariat; the Tercerista wing, organized in 1976 and headed by the Ortega brothers, pushed for a wide, anti-Somoza national front, including elements of the anti-Somoza bourgeoisie. Some of this latter group, including Eden Pastora (Comandante Zero), formed anti-Sandinista groups in 1980–1981. All but Pastora had joined forces with the groups led by former National Guardsmen by 1984. Pastora himself ended his anti-Sandinista activities in 1985.

beef and cattle exports (Vanlanduyt 1985, 42–47). In 1977, Nicaragua exported $162 million of cotton, $95 million of coffee, $53 of sugar, and $38.5 million of meat and live cattle (Dumont 1983, 199).

Industrialization was slow after World War II, despite attempts, in the 1960s, by the Central American Common Market to spread manufacturing from El Salvador and Guatemala into Honduras and Nicaragua (see Grunwald, et al. 1972). In the 1970s, the Nicaraguan manufacturing sector produced 23 percent of the gross national product with less than 10 percent of the labor force (Vanlanduyt 1985, 53). Most industry was related to the agricultural sector—food processing, fertilizers, and pesticides—with some textiles and furniture manufacturing; much of it was owned by the Somozas. The Nicaraguan bourgeoisie operated at the fringe of this family empire and was sharply constrained by it. Indeed, in the Nicaraguan free enterprise system, the state was at one and the same time the public sector and the largest group of private enterprises. The state was personalized as the Somoza family.

Under the Somozas the Nicaraguan state was oriented primarily to maximizing the economic returns of the Somozas and their friends. Rather than seeking any widespread legitimacy through popular public projects, the Somozas used their monopoly over the repressive apparatus—in the form of the National Guard (trained in the United States)—to terrorize and control the population. Elections, when they were held, were totally manipulated to ensure that Somoza candidates won. Even so, some of the political parties cooperated with this sham, going through the motions of elections and passing legislation (Vanlanduyt 1985).

The Catholic Church played an ambiguous role during the Somoza dictatorship. On one hand, it cooperated with the Somozas and thrived. Under the conditions of poverty and landlessness in rural Nicaragua, the traditional Church provided the poor with a spiritual home without questioning the state's violence and economically exploitative practices. In that sense, a "feudal" Church was complementary to the state. On the other hand, the Church represented a political power center outside the state. The newer interpretations of Catholic philosophy increasingly conflicted with dictatorial practices, particularly the Bishops' meeting in Medellin, Colombia, in 1968. The spread of liberation theology throughout Latin America also reached into the Nicaraguan Church, and a number of priests joined the Sandinista revolution against the wishes of the Church hierarchy.[2] Even the latter pressed for Somoza's resignation dur-

[2] An important example of this religious opposition to Somoza was the community of Solentiname organized in the early 1970s on an island in the Lake of Nicaragua, led by the Kentucky-trained Trappist monk, Ernesto Cardenal, today the Minister of Culture.

ing the last eighteen months of his regime, contributing to his eventual downfall.

This form of conditioned capitalism, where the state, as a private family, accumulated a significant portion of national capital, was unique. Individuals, or groups of individuals, in conditioned bureaucracies do regularly amass wealth as part of their public role in the conditioned state. Yet, the Somozas achieved this through direct private ownership of the means of production and used the state to expand their private holdings. They also acquired or developed businesses that could be logically operated as state enterprises—large cotton plantations, the national airline, a cement factory, park facilities, banks, etc. In this case, the surplus accumulated by the state from such activities was not used for financing broader social development or subsidizing the private sector (outside of the Somoza holdings). Somoza profits were used to further the family fortune (which reached $600 million by the mid-1970s). Foreign direct investment played a relatively small role in this model, but foreign loans were important. The Somozas, as the state, borrowed heavily abroad in the 1970s to finance manufactured imports, but also used such financing to add to their private investments in other countries.

Typical of conditioned states, the economy was organized to benefit a relatively small group of people: a bourgeoisie and professional class tied in with the export sector and state activities. In 1980, the top 5 percent of income earners in Nicaragua earned 28 percent of the nation's total income, and the bottom 50 percent earned 15 percent. The average overall income of the top 5 percent was almost 20 times the average $286 earned annually by Nicaraguans in the bottom 50 percent (Vanlanduyt 1985, 57).[3] On the other hand, the income distribution was not as unequal as in El Salvador (Carnoy and Levin 1977), for example, because of the more equal distribution of land and the relatively low population density in Nicaragua. According to Baumeister and Neira Cuadra (1986, 172), "One does not find in Nicaragua, as in other revolutionary societies, a large peasant mass, weakly linked to the market, with archaic technology. Neither does one find a large rural proletariat linked to plantation agriculture, nor haciendas nor peasant communities. Rather than any single productive arrangement, small, medium, and large producers coexisted side by side, producing for export and the internal market."

The performance of the Somoza regime in education during the late 1960s and the 1970s was consistent with its unwillingness to provide so-

---

[3] The income distribution in Nicaragua in 1980 was as follows: Top 5% of population— 28% of country's income (GDP), average income 5,409 cordobas; next 15% of population— 32% of GDP, average income 2,062 cordobas; next 30% of population—25% of GDP, average income 805 cordobas; bottom 50% of population—15% of GDP, average income 286 cordobas (mean national income 966 cordobas) (Vanlanduyt 1985, 57).

cial services that did not directly benefit the particularistic state.[4] Table
9-1 shows that primary school enrollment between 1965–1966 and 1977–
1978 grew at only 3.9 percent annually, or slightly more rapidly than the
3.3 percent annual increase in population during that period. But enrollment in universities grew rapidly under Somoza, from 4,000 students in
1966 to 24,000 in 1978. Although the percentage of GDP spent on education grew, from 2.2 percent in 1970 to 2.7 percent in 1978, the figure was
low by Latin American standards, and an increasing fraction of this
spending went to university education, that is, to the higher income
groups in Nicaraguan society.

ECONOMIC AND SOCIAL CHANGE AFTER THE TRIUMPH

Political Change

When the pressure for social and economic reforms increased in the
1970s, the Somoza family was unwilling to give up control of the repressive apparatus of the state—an apparatus that was crucial for maintaining
the family's economic holdings. Military overthrow of the family state
became the only possible alternative to continued dictatorship and repression.

The Sandinista forces that conquered Managua on July 19, 1979, were
both a guerilla army and a social movement, much like the 26th of July
movement in Cuba. They were not a political party, and consequently
not at all organized to take political power. Yet that was precisely what
was handed the movement in its triumph over the National Guard and
the Somozas. Since existing political apparatuses were so intimately connected with the Somozas, the Sandinistas essentially had to begin from
scratch, reconstructing a state on the basis of the massive participation of
the Nicaraguan population in the war of liberation.

The National Guard had either fled the country or were in prison
(many were later to be released), so the Sandinista forces were the de
facto new army and police. But the FSLN in 1979 was not organized politically to nearly the degree it was as a military force. At best, it was a
diverse group of activists and sympathizers capable of mobilizing the urban population. Once in power, however, and particularly when the
movement's leaders had accepted (in 1981) the principle of election, the
FSLN transformed itself slowly into a political party (Duflo and Ruellan
1985, 177). The ideological base of the party was, and continues to be
Marxist, but its politics (strategy) are much less Marxist than anti-imperialist and nationalist, rooted profoundly in the Nicaraguan experience it-

---

[4] In addition to education, health care was deplorable in Somoza's Nicaragua. Life expec-
tancy was only 52.9 years in 1977, primarily because of high infant mortality.

TABLE 9–1

Nicaragua: Primary School, Secondary School, University, and Adult Education Initial Enrollment at Beginning of Academic Year, 1965/67–1988

Academic Year	Level of Schooling			
	Primary[a]	Secondary	University	Adult
1965/67	233,255	30,276	4,080	—
1970/72	297,518	53,653	10,415	—
1976/78	368,550	80,241[b]	23,791[c]	—
1979/80	431,164 [411.3]	110,726	29,739[d]	—
1980/81	503,497 [472.2]	139,743[b]	34,710[d]	167,852
1982	534,996 [500.9]	139,957[b]	33,838	148,369
1983	564,558 [536.3]	158,215	35,585	166,208
1984	534,317	161,845	33,062[e]	129,290
1985	517,811	130,000[f]	n.a.	104,165
1986	563,925	142,790	n.a.	120,851
1987	590,906	167,600	23,448	n.a.
1988	621,000	188,400	26,176	180,000

Sources: 1965/67–1982: Ministry of Education, *Situación del Sistema Educativo después de 45 Años de Dictadura Militar Somocista y Perspectiva que Plantea la Revolución Sandinista* (paper presented to the Conferencia Regional de Ministros de Educación y de Ministros de Planificación Económica de los Estados Miembros de America Latina y del Caribe, Managua, December 1979). Figures for 1965/67, 1970/72, and 1976/78 are annual averages for those years. 1983–1984: Secondary and higher enrollment—*Anuario Estadístico de Nicaragua 1984*, 1986; primary and adult enrollment—ministry of education figures provided to the authors. 1985–1988: Ministry of education figures provided to the authors by the ministry.

[a] Figures for primary enrollment in Nicaraguan sources are extremely confused on the issue of whether they include preprimary enrollment (for example, the *Anuario* states that they do). In the latest figures we have received from the ministry of education (1986), primary school enrollment is lower than the figures in *Cinco Años de Educación en la Revolución 1979–1984* (Managua: Ministry of Education, 1984) by approximately the amount of preprimary enrollment. We have put these lower figures in brackets. Our sense is that the lower figures are the correct ones (though they may reflect dropouts); we also use these in calculating cost per student in Table 9–4.

[b] The figure from *Cinco Años de Educación en la Revolución* (p. 126) is 98,042.

[c] This figure is for 1978 only, rather than an average.

[d] This figure is from *La Educación en Cuatro Años de Revolución* (Managua: Ministry of Education, 1983). It is somewhat higher than the *Anuario*'s 28,759 figure.

[e] This figure is considerably lower than the programmed number of students for 1984 (about 37,000).

[f] Approximated from secondary enrollment (99,984) for 1985 plus 1986 figures for technical and normal school.

self (Wald 1987, 8). Further, party leadership (particularly the Tercerista wing) has shown itself willing to experiment with alternatives to traditional Marxism to fit the present Nicaraguan conditions.

The collapse of the Somoza regime also required the guerilla movement to organize a political-administrative apparatus capable of transforming the economy and reconstructing the state. We can divide this transition during the first seven years into two stages: the first, when the FSLN ruled the country as a movement, from 1979 to January 1985; and the second, when the FSLN ruled a reconstituted state as the major political party in the legislature and with control of the executive branch.

In both stages, the FSLN has been able to maintain considerable hegemony despite strong opposition from the hierarchy of the Catholic Church; much of the small, but politically active, business community; and the remnants of the National Guard, who had fled to the United States in 1979. Revolution always engenders counterrevolution from those national elites and their international allies who benefited from the old order. In Nicaragua, counterrevolution turned into a full-scale, U.S.-sponsored armed intervention. Whatever the revolution might have been, it was made to become a fight for survival by the FSLN against its Nicaraguan opponents and the U.S. state.

When the revolution triumphed in 1979, the old (Somoza) constitution was annulled, and a new state apparatus created: the government Junta, with executive and legislative powers; the Council of State, with colegislative power; the Supreme Court; the popular armed forces; and the police. One member of the Junta and several ministers in the first period belonged to the opposition parties. Four Catholic priests were also ministers (in addition to those ministers who were FSLN comandantes).

Even though the country was ruled formally in this period by the coalition government, the coalition was dominated from outside the government by the FSLN. The FSLN representatives on the Junta and in the Council of State had behind them the political hegemony of the Sandinista movement through its mass organizations (capable of mobilizing large numbers of workers, peasants, youth, women, and so forth in various activities) and its control of the army and police. The only opposition organization that had the same level of contact with the mass of Nicaraguans was the Catholic Church, but it was limited in the degree and nature of political organizing it could undertake. Effectively, the nine "comandantes de la revolucion"—who still control the FSLN and decide FSLN policy by consensus—explicitly directed government policy in this stage.[5] Decisions made by the comandantes were passed on to the Junta

---

[5] The internal structure of the FSLN is hierarchical, with the comandantes making all major decisions. All disagreements among them are also kept out of the public record.

and the Council of State. In turn, Junta policies were carried out at the local level through the mass organizations, the army, and the police, all controlled by the FSLN.

It rapidly became clear that although the local bourgeoisie was represented in the state, the armed forces would not serve specifically to protect the bourgeoisie's interests, nor would the ministry of labor favor employers in conflict with the unions. In addition, the Junta and the Council of State directed the nationalization of banking, insurance, foreign commerce, mining, and the fishing industry, as well as the former Somoza agricultural lands, despite opposition by some bourgeois representatives in those two government bodies. This separation between the bourgeoisie's important role in production and its reduced political role—particularly its inability to control the state apparatuses so that they would act to favor bourgeois economic interests—created increased difficulties for the new economy/polity. The Sandinista regime attempted to harness the bourgeoisie's skills in accumulating capital and even was willing to favor the bourgeoisie politically and economically by resisting early demands for land redistribution.[6] Nevertheless, the regime did act to redistribute income, and placed greater control of economic development in the hands of the state and the popular sectors, including—eventually—the landholding peasants.

Important elements of the bourgeoisie were not willing to accept such changes. Baumeister and Neira Cuadra (1986) show that the agrarian bourgeoisie, concentrated in cotton production, reduced the volume of their output 7 percent annually in 1980–1983; coffee growers maintained their plantations but did not expand output; sugar and rice producers, alone among the larger growers, cooperated with the revolution. "All in all, the capitalist sector is in a sense 'on hold,' producing with generous credit and little of their own working capital" (p. 186). While on hold, some of the agrarian and urban bourgeoisie have turned to tacit support of an overthrow of the Sandinista-dominated state; apparently, however, a much smaller percentage of this class is directly counterrevolutionary

---

Decisionmaking is secretive and, outside of the comandante group itself, undemocratic. In the first stage, once political decisions were made by the ruling group, the FSLN attempted to mobilize popular support around these general policies and hoped to have the mobilization solve problems of implementation at the local level.

[6] The Sandinistas immediately nationalized land held by the Somoza family and their friends and turned it into coops and state farms. The primary recipients of such redistribution were landless peasants. As late as December 1984, the ministry of agriculture suspended the agrarian reform law in an attempt to reassure large private producers. But in mid-1985, rural pressure for land, political opposition to agricultural price and trade policies, and resistance of certain sectors in the countryside to the cooperative movement forced the government to begin redistributing the land of large private owners and from the inefficient state sector to landholding peasants (Torres and Coraggio 1987, 98).

than in other transition societies because of the willingness of the state to share the economic pie with the large private agricultural producers (Marchetti 1986, 327).

In analyzing the conflict between the private sector and the Sandinista state, it is important to distinguish class differences in the private sector itself. Even after the revolution and the nationalization of the mining industry (the only prerevolutionary stronghold of transnational capital), the sector included "latifundistas," the small and medium-size agricultural producers, a very limited number of local monopoly businesses, the petty merchants, and the craftspeople. The heterogeneity of this private sector differs from that in the larger Latin American countries, which have a much more dominant bourgeoisie and large landowning class in the agricultural sector.

The Sandinistas have shifted their economic policy vis-à-vis these groups substantially even in the short period since taking power. After taxing the peasantry and favoring urban workers (and the urban commercial petite bourgeoisie) through agricultural pricing policy, and holding back on peasant demands for more land to avoid frightening the large agricultural producers, in 1985 the FSLN freed up agricultural prices and began distributing underutilized private land and state farmland; both measures shifted income to the peasantry (Torres and Coraggio 1987).[7]

The role of the traditional Nicaraguan Church hierarchy is also important in this private sector-state conflict. The traditional Church is closely allied with the business and agricultural bourgeoisie. The Church has adopted a strategy of confrontation with the FSLN.[8] One expression of this was the removal of Catholic priests identified with the revolution from important positions in the Church hierarchy; there were at least twenty such cases in 1980–1985 (Serra 1985, 270). Others have been the call by the hierarchy (supported by the Pope) for religious discipline, the order for priests in the government to give up their positions as public officials (for example, Ernesto Cardenal, Fernando Cardenal), and the dissolution of religious organizations that cooperated with the Sandinistas (for example, the Asociación del Clero Nicaraguense). The Church has

---

[7] As discussed below, in part, this policy shift was due to the war with the Contras, who operated in peasant areas and hence could build an effective countermovement where the peasants were dissatisfied, but the shift was also due to poor production results on state farms.

[8] It should be noted that the FSLN has also adopted a policy of confrontation with the Church. This was never more evident than when the Pope celebrated a public mass in the Plaza 19 de Julio, on March 4, 1983. That day, 700,000 people attended the mass, and the Pope was interrupted several times by the huge crowd chanting Sandinista mottos. The Church later argued that the government provoked the crowd's reaction to the Pope. The Sandinistas contended that the reaction was a spontaneous response to the Pope's failure to recognize the validity of the revolution and what it meant to the people of Nicaragua.

also opposed military conscription, (instituted in 1983), arguing that it is illegal and that Christians should have the right to conscientious objection. Furthermore, the Church hierarchy has taken a clear anti-Sandinista position regarding education: It supports the continuation and expansion of a privately run, state-subsidized educational option; the Sandinistas would like to eliminate aid to private (largely Church-run) schools and to secularize publicly funded education (an analogous conflict to the one in France in the mid-1980s under the Mitterand government).

The election of 1984 changed the FSLN from a general political movement to a ruling political party. The Council of State was replaced by an Assembly with deputies elected through a system of proportional representation (parliamentary lists). The FSLN has 64 percent of the deputies in the Assembly; 6 percent belong to other left parties, and 30 percent to the bourgeois parties (the Democratic Conservative party has 15 percent, the Independent Liberal party, 9 percent, and the Popular Social Christian party, 6 percent). The Nicaraguan Democratic Coordinating Coalition (CDN), led by Arturo Cruz (now part of the Contra organization), did not participate in the elections.

The Assembly was charged with drafting a new constitution, and, in theory, is supposed to provide a counterbalance to the executive. But just as in the present French system, when the executive and the legislative branches are led by the same party, it is the executive that has real power. The FSLN's winning candidates for president and vice president, Daniel Ortega and Sergio Ramirez, now head the state, and along with certain members of the cabinet (for example, Tomas Borge, Jaime Wheelock, and Humberto Ortega), are the principal decisionmakers under the new system. Although party decisions are still made by the comandantes, it is the policymaking of the comandantes as members of the executive branch of the state that count in this second stage. The FSLN is now the government of the country and exercises power directly through the state apparatuses.

The comandantes still occupy key positions in the state: Daniel Ortega is president; Victor Tirado is responsible for the unions; Carlos Nuñez is president of the national assembly; Jaime Wheelock is responsible for agrarian reform and economic questions; Henry Ruíz is responsible for foreign cooperation; Bayardo Arce is responsible for party matters; and Humberto Ortega, Tomas Borge, and Luis Carrión, representing the three historical tendencies of the Front, divide responsibility for national security (Duflo and Ruellan 1985, 77).

The army is not only a professional force tied to the state; it also remains the popular armed force of the FSLN. On one hand, this ensures the fidelity of the military to the revolution and to social change (and avoids the possibility of a counterrevolution coming from the military, as in Chile, or as almost happened in the Philippines in November 1986). On the other hand, this mixture of party and official government identities raises the serious issue of what the role of the army would be if the FSLN should lose an election. The larger question is whether the military apparatus can ever remain neutral in a period of transition, that is, outside the transition itself. Can a military organized to protect particular class interests stand back and watch those interests being eroded? In the Nicaraguan case, the destruction of the National Guard was crucial to the construction of a new state. The new state was the outcome of a successful revolution, built on a revolutionary army. The revolutionary army is organized to defend the revolution. Thus, any attempt to undo the revolution and reverse the transition must confront the existence of an armed force organized in the context of that revolution.[9]

The popular forces called upon to implement many of the state's policies also have close ties to the party, although their relation to the state is much more elusive. The mass organizations are independent of the FSLN financially and organizationally, but they receive ideological and political guidance from the party (Ruchwarger 1985, 94). On the other hand, they must depend on the state to carry out their projects. When the state was governed by the Junta and Council of State in which Sandinistas were one (and the most important) element, the FSLN was willing to give the mass organizations a certain leeway to operate as an alternative pole of power. According to Vilas (1986), the presence and strengthening of these mass organizations was a prerequisite for constituting popular power in Nicaragua, within and without the Sandinista state, depending on how that state is defined.

It appears, however, that the mass organizations increasingly became implementors of FSLN policies between 1981 and 1985, as the FSLN halted land occupations by peasants, resisted women's demands to participate in the draft, and so forth.[10] These decisions were usually politically necessary because of pressures to maintain pluralistic support for

[9] This raises a series of important questions: Does the revolution, which the army is organized to defend, include elections that might allow non-FSLN parties—even if such parties are committed to the continued social transformation of Nicaraguan society—to gain executive power over the state? Are popular (as compared with "bourgeois") "democracy" and hegemony necessarily tied to a one-party state, in part because the revolutionary armed forces are inseparable from the revolutionary party? How do citizens (rather than the party apparatus) in such a system sanction political leaders who do not respond to the economic and political needs of the society?

[10] When the draft was instituted in 1983, the national women's association, AMNLAE, opposed the initial draft law because it excluded women. A compromise was reached with the government whereby women could volunteer for regular service. Although some women do now serve in the army, most do militia duty and civil defense activities (Arnove 1988a, 7).

Sandinista policies, but it had the result of distancing the mass organizations from their constituencies, since the organizational leadership could not meet the demands of its membership (Torres and Coraggio 1987, 108). Part of this pluralistic process was the move to "officialize" the FSLN as the official ruling government party by holding the 1984 elections. As a result of all these factors, many of the organizations seem to have lost their dynamic as representatives of groups working to influence state decisionmaking. Furthermore, as members of mass organizations have become voters, they have tended to become redefined as individual political units, and the political power of mass organizations as expressions of collective will has necessarily been reduced.

The war against the Contras, on one hand, required more centralized decisionmaking and greater adherence (allegiance) by mass organizations to state-directed policy, but, on the other, required greater mobilization through the mass organizations. There has therefore been an increasing reenergizing of the mass organizations since 1985. A good example of this is the success of the National Organization of Farmers (UNAG). It specifically demanded more land for its peasant members and realized its demands—more land was distributed in 1985–1986 than in the previous five years (Torres and Coraggio 1987).

This pattern of potential conflict between the mass organizations and the Junta-governed state also applied to some extent in education and educational policy. Such organizations "outside" the state but closely tied to the FSLN, such as the Sandinista Youth Organization, were highly critical of the ministry of education and of the low quality and traditional type of education being provided. And as in other matters, the influence of the "outside-the-state" movements on educational policy also declined between 1980 (the year of the literacy campaign) and 1985, but now may be in the process of some revitalization through policies within the ministry of education (MED) itself, particularly as the MED decentralizes educational administration to the regions and has to rely on the Sandinista Youth Organization to fill teacher shortages in rural areas (Arnove 1988a, 14).

Economic Change

When the FSLN took over the Somoza state, the revolutionary forces inherited Somoza's lands and enterprises. The forces also inherited an impoverished economy, ravaged by two years of heavy fighting (1978–1979), and a capital city that had never recovered from the devastating earthquake of 1972 and the subsequent corruption during reconstruction. Real gross domestic product fell 7 percent in 1978 and 25 percent in 1979 (see Table 9–2). In real terms, by the end of 1979, the country's per capita

GDP had fallen to 1962 levels. More than $500 million in foreign exchange was exported between January 1978 and June 1979, which, added to the 33 percent drop in exports in 1978 and the service on the debt incurred by Somoza, caused a massive foreign exchange shortage in 1979–1980.

The critical situation in the economy narrowed greatly the choices available to the Sandinistas. They were committed to restructuring the economy away from its extreme export dependence and unequal distribution of land and economic output. They were also committed to raising social wages (money wages paid plus social services) to the mass of agri-

TABLE 9–2

Nicaragua: Real Gross Domestic Product (GDP), GDP per Capita, and Exports, 1960–1984 ('000,000,000 of 1980 cordobas and 1980 cordobas)

Year	Real GDP ('000,000,000 of cordobas)	GDP/Capita (cordobas)	Exports ('000,000,000 of cordobas)	Exports/GDP (%)
1960	10.3	7,280	2.6	25.2
1965	16.4	10,171	5.3	32.4
1970	20.1	10,805	6.2	30.8
1975	26.3	11,950	9.1	34.6
1977	27.9	11,731	9.0	32.2
1978	26.0	10,500	9.7	37.2
1979	19.3	7,500	6.4	33.0
1980	21.9[a]	8,193	5.0	23.0
1981	23.0	8,365	5.5	23.9
1982	22.8	8,030	4.5	19.7
1983	23.9	8,111	6.2	25.9
1984	23.6	7,730	7.2	30.5
1985	23.0	7,274	n.a.	n.a.

Sources: 1960–1979: World Bank, World Statistics, 1983. 1980–1983: International Monetary Fund, International Financial Statistics 1986. 1984–1985: Central American Bulletin, December 1986, 32—GDP growth rates for 1984 and 1985 applied to 1983 figure from IMF. See also for 1984: INEC, Anuario Estadístico de Nicaragua 1984, 51. Anuario Estadístico (51, tab. 2) figures for 1980–1984.

[a] The IMF has a slightly different series for the GDP in 1960–1979, because of the GDP price deflator used. Therefore, the figure shown here for 1980 should not be compared with the figure for 1979. The actual growth rate of real GDP in 1979–1980 was 4.6% (see Central American Bulletin, December 1986, 32).

cultural and urban workers. But the weakness of the new state apparatuses, particularly the lack of skilled cadres, the very structure of agrarian
production with the relatively large proportion of small and medium-size
producers, and a commitment (and need) to maintain the alliances developed in the fight against Somoza argued against socializing the entire
economy. Neither could the FSLN count on the large "public" enterprises, formerly Somoza-owned and the most dynamic elements in the
Somoza economy, to change the nature of the economic structure. The
new dynamic for economic growth—if the basis for that growth were to
change—had to come from elsewhere.

Furthermore, the traditional agriculture export sector, concentrated
heavily in sugar, coffee, and cotton, brought in 75 percent of export income, accumulated more than 80 percent of the country's surplus, occupied almost one-half of its cultivated land, and was responsible for more
than one-third of the economy's capital investment. Maintaining the alliance with that group of private agricultural entrepreneurs who were
willing to cooperate was therefore an economic necessity. A rapid conversion to a largely publicly owned and state-controlled economy, even
one based on large and dynamic public enterprises, presented risks of
serious further impoverishment of an already impoverished economy,
something the FSLN could ill afford. Neither could the new regime afford
to alienate foreign lenders—continued foreign borrowing was essential to
import necessary manufactured goods for restoring growth. As a result,
the Sandinistas applied several economic paradigms (nationalization of
Somoza's land holdings and the family's assets in other sectors, some
cooperativization, and a policy of giving state credit to private agricultural
producers) at once as part of the economic transformation in the transition.

At one level, the strategy worked: real GDP increased 4.6 percent (1.5
percent per capita) in 1980 and 5.4 percent (2.1 percent per capita) in
1981 (see Table 9–2). But the private sector became increasingly critical
of FSLN economic policy, in part because it was working, but primarily
because the relationship between private sector economic power and its
control of the state had been broken. In the new political economy, the
business community was asked to invest capital and produce without the
quid pro quo of political control, which put it in an even worse position
than under the Somoza regime, where at least it had had the state repressive apparatuses (the courts and the police) on its side in protecting
property and in labor disputes. Private agricultural producers were willing to take government credit and make profits, but not to invest in the
future. The "capitalized" sector was not willing, under Nicaraguan political conditions, to act as the dynamic pole of capital accumulation, and

the other parts of the private sector (latifundia and the informal economy) were characterized by low productivity.

By 1981, this resistance, a number of management errors in state-run agriculture and the inefficiency of small peasant agriculture (Dumont 1983)[11] combined with the world recession to slow down growth (-4.0 percent per capita in 1982). This pushed the government to begin nationalizing private lands that were not being used, and to employ other measures of control in the economy. The resistance of the private sector, however, was not the only pressure being put on the government. Peasants wanted land and workers wanted higher salaries. As part of the emergency measures, the government implemented a no-strike law and stopped peasants from occupying lands.

Under these conditions, the economic growth paradigms focusing on the mechanization (increasing productivity) of the state sector and on providing credit to the private sector were somewhat deemphasized (although not abandoned) and greater emphasis was placed on distributing land to landless peasants and developing cooperative production. The FSLN, therefore, through a land reform based on newly (1981–1982) confiscated, abandoned, and underutilized holdings, put its emphasis on the development of a cooperative sector in agriculture, whose growth was expected to form the basis of a new economic structure and would eventually be a major source of capital accumulation: "Beginning in 1983, state farms that could not be managed efficiently as part of a given productive unit were turned into cooperatives and state farmlands were increasingly given to individual producers. These developments responded to the growing organizational capacity of the mass organizations, the demands of the workers and peasants, and also to the military and economic pressures of the counterrevolution" (Deere 1986, 115). Although still a small part of the total agrarian economy (in 1983, agricultural coops had only 22 percent of cultivated land, and in industry, their number was minor), in the long term, coops were planned to be the dominant form of peasant agriculture and an important form of industrial production.

Contra operations made the government even more sensitive to the demands of peasants for the escalation of the agrarian reform, particularly the titling of lands into the hands of individual peasants. The military itself urged the more rapid implementation of the reform to increase the defense capabilities of the war zone (Deere 1986, 128). In 1983, as much land was redistributed and titled as in the previous eighteen months: "By . . . July 1984, the rapid pace of titling had raised the total amount of

---

[11] José Luís Coraggio writes: "So-called institutional feudalism, bureaucracy, and the corrupt tendencies of the state's agents did not disappear with the triumph. Instead, a permanent tendency arose to reproduce and even extend this behavior, against which the revolutionary political leadership fought, and continues to fight" (Coraggio 1986, 155).

redistributed land to . . . nearly 20 percent of the cultivable land. At that point 42 percent of the land had gone to production cooperatives, 4 percent to indigenous communities on the Atlantic coast, and 54 percent to individual producers" (Deere 1986, 129). In 1985–1986, this process was even more accentuated in favor of individual peasants: "To provide food for the whole country and win rural support, the government has turned to a small farmer-based development strategy" (Cutting 1986, 34).

The mixed economy is an attempt by the FSLN to maintain production in an economy devastated by the earlier civil war and characterized by very low levels of labor and management skills. The existence of a capitalist production sector helps the FSLN postpone the enormous costs involved in training a whole new generation of farmer-managers, costs that would set the economy back even further and would require repressive measures to control consumer dissatisfaction. Expanding the state sector is clearly constrained under these conditions. Experience in that sector suggests just how difficult it would be to maintain production without individual private farmers. Dumont (1983) has documented the inefficiency of ill-prepared cadres on the state farms. Eventually these problems could be solved, but if the political structure is to be at all open and democratic, the economy must function reasonably well so that the level of dissent does not threaten "revolutionary hegemony" as interpreted by the FSLN.

At the same time, the private capitalist sector cannot be relied upon to increase production when the bourgeoisie are fundamentally opposed to the revolution and the political limitations placed on capitalist influence over the state. This has led the Sandinistas to rely increasingly on the private peasantry organized in cooperatives and as small and medium-size individual producers for economic growth. The land reform has been the primary instrument of this shift of reliance. But, according to Deere, it is also a shift of political necessity: The counterrevolution necessitates the mobilization of the peasantry and titling peasant land is fundamental to tying the peasants to the Sandinista cause (1986, 129). Titled by the Sandinista state, peasants are incorporated into the revolutionary nation. And the land distribution also reflects the commitment of the FSLN to "popular participation and the role of the mass organizations in shaping the agrarian reform" (Deere 1986, 129).

In addition to the agricultural reform, the major success for Nicaragua in this period has been the shift of foreign commerce from almost total dependence on the United States to a much more diverse trade pattern. Since the U.S. trade embargo of 1984, this shift has been mandatory. The major failures of the revolutionary economic policy have been in industrial growth recovery, with consequent continued high urban unemployment rates and inflation (see Table 9–3), and lack of control over black markets. The latter has made planning difficult and has diverted scarce resources into speculation in currency and illegally imported goods. In February 1985, the government freed the exchange rate and eliminated subsidies to private producers of basic agricultural products. Prices of goods and services rose rapidly, improving market prices for peasant agricultural production and eliminating the enormous cost to the state of subsidizing private production. The reforms were aimed at reducing inflation by reducing demand, a demand that had been rapidly increased by increased salaries for agricultural labor. Real purchasing power fell by one-half and inflation continued because of the U.S. embargo, which caused serious shortages in many imported goods. These new policies again showed the FSLN's commitment to a mixed economy, but the problems of such an economy during a war and even with the end of the fighting remained unresolved.

In 1985, military expenditures rose to 50 percent of the state budget and the coffee harvest of 1984–1985 was one of the worst since 1979, as the Contras systematically sabotaged coffee-growing areas. Much of industrial production was oriented toward military production, and a high percentage of human resources were also directed toward the war.[12]

TABLE 9–3
Nicaragua: Economic Indicators, 1978–1985 (percent)

Year	GDP Growth	Per Capita GDP Growth	Infla-tion	Unemploy-ment	Defense Spending	Fiscal Deficit
1978	− 7.2	− 10.5	4.3			
1979	− 25.9	− 28.6	70.3			
1980	4.6	1.5	35.3	18.3	7	8.8
1981	5.4	2.1	23.9	14.8	7	11.8
1982	− 0.8	− 4.0	24.8	14.5	13	—
1983	4.4	1.0	31.1	18.9	19	27.7
1984	− 1.4	− 4.7	35.4	21.4	33	24.8
1985	− 2.6	− 5.9	219.5	22.2	50	22.2

Source: *Central American Bulletin*, December 1986, 32. Figures for 1978 and 1979 per capita growth rates taken from Table 9.2, above.

Note: Defense spending is expressed as a percentage of the national budget; fiscal deficit is expressed as a percentage of GDP.

[12] More recent estimates place the proportion of the state budget going to the war effort as "more than 50 percent" (*Jornal do Brasil*, July 20, 1986, 26) or "55 percent" (*Central American Bulletin*, December 1986, 32).

After a recovery in 1983, growth rates were down sharply in 1984 and 1985. Inflation was over 200 percent in 1985 and 1986, and as high as 1200 percent in 1987 (Arnove 1988b, 23). Nicaragua is suffering through major shortages of both production and consumption goods.

The question is whether Nicaraguan politics (the FSLN nationalist, anti-imperialist ideology) will sustain the government in its simultaneous struggle against the counterrevolution and against any dissension at home among its principally peasant and worker base. The growth of education and health care play an important role in providing social benefits to these groups where none existed before. To some extent, the longer the Sandinistas can stay in power, the more young people will have grown up in a revolutionary society, which may change attitudes toward the type of society that Nicaraguans want and expect. The war itself (and military service) has also created an ideological commitment to the revolution among youth, which may be much more permanent than more traditional educational socialization. Mothers of those who serve in the military are also among the most fervent supporters to the revolution (Angel and Macintosh 1987). Yet material and social conditions are also important to the FSLN's legitimacy, especially now that the Contras have ceased to be a direct threat. Without an improvement of the economic situation, that legitimacy would certainly have eroded.

The ending of U.S. congressional support for Contra military aid and the agreement among the Central American presidents in Sapoa in 1988 had both positive and negative effects for the Sandinistas. On one hand, the fighting stopped, making it easier to get on with the economic tasks needed to resume economic growth. On the other hand, the austerity measures imposed in 1988 did not stop the inflation. This failure delegitimates the Sandinista regime. With elections promised for February 1990, there are growing possibilities for the opposition to make a good showing. Much depends on economic improvements before those elections and the ability of the opposition to organize itself. The election will be, in effect, a test of whether the Sandinistas have succeeded in creating a new concept of people-nation with which Nicaraguans identify.

THE NEW EDUCATION: POSSIBILITIES AND CONTRADICTIONS

In revolutionary Nicaragua, educational expansion and reform is conditioned by the basic need to defend the new state, accumulate capital, and deliver social services as part of the larger goals of implementing the revolution and transforming Nicaraguan society.[13] Both the structure of the

---

[13] "Development and transformation, [FSLN members] believed, depended in the short run on national reconstruction and in the long run on a transition to socialism . . . according

economy and the educational system are transformed simultaneously, but both are conditioned by the short-term need to expand production and to defend the country against externally financed counterrevolutionaries.

Consistent with this model of development, the new leadership of the ministry of education envisaged "the expansion, improvement, and the transformation of education as, respectively, contributing to the democratization of basic social services, the independence of the Nicaraguan economy from foreign domination and the development of a new model of capital accumulation based on different social relations of production and forms of public and cooperative ownership. The overriding goal has been to contribute to the formation of the 'new man (and woman) and the new society' " (Arnove 1988b, 4).

But, as Arnove and others have noted, there are conflicts generated by such attempts at rapid change, and the solution of one set of problems usually leads to the emergence of other problems. As education develops in the context of revolutionary change, contradictions emerge in the society as a whole that affect education, and contradictions also emerge in the educational reform process. The most important of such contradictions is the opposition of those who lose power because of the changes unleashed by the revolution. In the Nicaraguan case, in contrast to China, Cuba, and Mozambique, some opposition groups have stayed in the country as a legitimate opposition. These have continued to fight against educational reform through the Church and have made the formal educational system particularly difficult to change. In addition, an illegitimate opposition, with U.S. arms, has tried to destroy schools and, through a protracted war, to destroy the revolution's financial capacity to provide education. The counterrevolution hits hard at precisely those institutions that are most closely linked to the revolutionary project and most involved in social democratization—for example, the "popular education" schools for adults in the countryside.

Contradictions in educational change also emerge from within the revolutionary process itself. We highlight two examples: First, the demands of the revolution for rapid educational democratization (rapid educational expansion for youth and adults) tends to reduce the "quality" of education; second, the pressure to develop skills for economic growth tends to push the educational system into more "traditional" modes, sacrificing revolutionary socialization and more socially ideal curricula and educational methods. To the extent that the expansion of social services conflicts with capital accumulation, that expansion will be slowed, with a

to this view, attainment of such a society required economic growth, extensive redistribution of power and wealth, and broad-based citizen participation" (Miller 1985, 30).

resulting ideological (transformational) cost. To the extent that democratizing formal education and the work process appears to restrain capital accumulation, a tension also develops in the transformation of social relations.

Yet, although the pressures of counterrevolution and the high resource cost of providing "traditional" education have hurt the expansion of formal schooling (and academic skills), they may also have accelerated its democratization and the revolutionary socialization project. In Nicaragua, much of the extension of education to adults and children has been carried out through student mobilization and through turning recently literate Nicaraguans into rural teachers. Such lower-cost forms of education are more open and informal and often use teaching techniques and curricula that are innovative and perhaps more responsive to community demands. Popular education is difficult to sustain, as is all adult education, particularly in the harsh economic reality of war-torn Nicaragua. Such education is voluntary and does not lead to better jobs. But the war has shifted revolutionary socialization from popular adult education in schools to popular education in the military and to the ideological impact of the military effort itself.

Educational Reform, 1979–1988

From the outset, the new education in Nicaragua was defined as *popular*.[14] Sandinista educational policy, according to government statements, was, and continues to be, based on three general objectives: (1) to expand the educational system; (2) to promote a qualitative change in education; and (3) to transform the system. Expansion means an increase in enrollment and a corresponding increase in teachers, school buildings, and school supplies. It represents the clearest expression of democratization of access, primarily because most of the increase in spending and personnel is intended to go to those who had least access before the revolution.

[14] "Popular education" is not a conventional term for American and English readers. However, in Latin American education, the use of the term is widespread. In revolutionary Nicaragua, it means that education is a right for all (particularly the peasant and working classes), and that this education cannot be constructed without the active and conscious political participation and mobilization of the mass organizations. Second, popular education is considered a powerful ideological weapon in the process of ideological class struggle (Vallecillos 1983). Third, it means that the revolution is an immense and continual political workshop, where revolutionary politics becomes a pedagogy for the mass and the Sandinista leadership. Finally, popular education means following Sandino's pedagogical principles that a learning process can be carried out only through practice and struggle (Tunnerman 1983, 15). For a thoughtful discussion of popular education in Latin America, see Gajardo 1983; Varios 1982; La Belle 1986.

The Sandinistas termed the expansion "the right to education for everyone."

For the people of Nicaragua, the expansion of education represents not just the possibility of social mobility in material terms, but also access to power—the political and social power associated before the revolution with the dominant groups in Nicaraguan society (Arnove 1986). For the Sandinista regime, delivering education to rural areas and to those in urban areas who had not had access to primary schooling under Somoza was a political necessity. Education was and is the principal direct means for the Sandinistas of reaching the population with revolutionary ideology and simultaneously of legitimizing the new regime with that large fraction of the population desiring access to schools.

The FSLN began expanding education soon after their victory under the constraints of limited resources. This meant using nonformal education to reach children and adults in rural and marginal urban areas; training secondary and university students as volunteer teachers for a literacy campaign and subsequent primary education expansion; and turning over a significant portion of primary education, especially in rural areas, to mass-base organizations. Indeed, as La Belle points out, "in post-revolutionary guise, nonformal education can be used to solidify a new government's existence and to politically socialize the population to support the viability of the accompanying institutions and ideology" (La Belle 1986, 10–30). Although this educational goal of contributing "to the formation of the new man [person] and the new society" (Ministry of Education, quoted in Arnove 1986, 138) was not achieved in the relatively short seven years since the Sandinistas took power,[15] it appears that the expansion and reform after 1979 have been an important factor in legitimating the Sandinistas' revolutionary program of economic and social change and in consolidating their control over the state. The most important single policy was the national literacy crusade, but educational expansion in general, even in more limited terms at the university level, has delivered desired services to various groups in the population and has been impressive, given available resources. In the mid-1980s, with the tremendous increase in resources needed for military defense, the Sandinista government has faced declining gross domestic product and

[15] Arnove argues (correctly, in our view) that change in school systems "typically lags behind economic and political changes; the recruitment and training of teachers and the revision of curriculum takes years, and does not always lead to the desired outcomes. . . . The political content of education may change, but old attitudes, beliefs, and behaviors may not. The education system may provide more opportunities to behave in new ways, but the greatest socializing impact on system-relevant values and conduct is more likely to be effected by the revolutionary changes in society itself, by the demands placed on youths by structurally altered circumstances" (Arnove 1986, 138–39).

has had to struggle to keep up educational spending. Enrollment growth slowed down at all levels, but considering the circumstances of the war economy, school expansion has been a surprisingly positive feature of the 1984–1988 period, reflecting again the high priority given to education by the Sandinista government. The government still devotes approximately 5 percent of GDP to education and apparently has somewhat increased spending per student in school. The program that has suffered most because of the war has been adult education, since it is the popular education centers (CEPs) that are the target of Contra attacks.

As we discuss the details of these policies, we must keep in mind that whatever problems the Sandinista government may be having in other aspects of its economic and educational policies, including the quality of the education delivered, and whatever other positive effects the expansion of education may have in the future (such as in increasing productivity or creating the "new person"), Sandinista educational reform has been visibly successful as a political action in and of itself.

THE NATIONAL LITERACY CAMPAIGN

One of the first acts of the new government was to plan (in October 1979) and carry out (in March-August 1980) a national literacy campaign, known as the Cruzada (Lacayo, in Torres 1983, 555–80; see also Torres 1985; Miller 1985; Arnove 1986). The campaign involved more than 50,000 youth brigade members and 30,000 literacy teachers. It made literate more than 400,000 people, reducing the illiteracy rate from 50.3 percent to 12.9 percent.[16] It was conducted not just in Spanish, but in Miskito, Sumo, and Creole English. All in all, like its Cuban predecessor, the literacy campaign was a remarkable achievement. It reached out to the many adults and young people who had previously been denied a fundamental prerequisite of participation in modern life—the ability to read and write.[17] At the same time, it brought tangible evidence to the most marginalized groups of Nicaraguans that the revolution was going to include them and change their lives for the better: "Widely acclaimed as the most important educational event in the history of the country, the

[16] A more accurate figure is that illiteracy was reduced to 23 percent, since the lower figure of 12.9 percent cited here is based on "the government's decision to subtract from the target population of illiterate adults approximately 130,000 individuals who were considered unteachable or learning impaired" (Arnove 1986, 27).

[17] In 1978, only 68 percent of Nicaraguan children 7–12 years old were enrolled in schools. This was in sharp contrast to other countries of the region (for instance, Costa Rica, Mexico, Venezuela, Chile, Peru, Panama, Colombia, and Cuba), which all had a 100 percent gross rate of schooling for that age group by the end of the 1970s (UNESCO/CEPAL.PNUD-DEALC 1981, Vol. 4, Table IV, 13, p. IV-21). In Nicaragua 50.3 percent of the total population 10 years of age and older were illiterate in 1979. In some rural areas, 80–90 percent of the adult population were illiterate.

crusade was viewed as a second mass uprising—a 'cultural insurrection' that was a sequel to the armed struggle against the Somoza family dictatorship" (Arnove 1986, 17). In August 1980, a second campaign also reached out to the populations of the Atlantic zones of the country, permitting 12,500 Indians to become literate in their native language (Duflo and Ruellan 1985, 240–418).

The evaluations of the campaign vary widely. There are those who considered it a successful educational project for an underdeveloped society despite a number of problems (Arnove 1981; Saenz n.d., 3–4) or a remarkable political achievement promoting Sandinista political ideology and national culture (Miller 1985). Others doubt the pedagogical effectiveness of the campaign, given the questionable educational value of national, mass-oriented literacy campaigns elsewhere in the world (La Belle 1986, 10–28).

Nevertheless, even though the campaign's lasting impact on literacy gains and ideological change in the individuals involved is, indeed, questionable, the Cruzada produced some clear and significant results, which have endured. It was critical in reducing the high degree of inequality between countryside and city, males and females, and the Atlantic and Pacific coasts. It mobilized previously marginal populations into new roles related to national reconstruction. It strengthened mass organizations, notably the Sandinista Youth Organization, the teachers' association (ANDEN), and the Nicaraguan Women's Association (AMNLAE). It was the first national task in which women had equal participation, and it provided the opportunity for women to take the lead in other activities. It helped reduce the hostility that existed between teachers and those youth who had participated in the guerrilla struggle of the previous few years. It created a national publishing industry, in that the Cruzada produced and distributed over 1 million texts and pamphlets. It initiated the process of administrative decentralization of the country, dividing it into nine regions and delegating substantial authority to local government entities and the mass organizations (Arnove 1986, 35–36).

POPULAR BASIC EDUCATION

After the Cruzada, the regime launched a postliteracy program intended to carry newly literate adults on to the equivalent of primary education. The ministry of education increased the funds going to popular education from less than 4 percent of its budget in 1980 to perhaps as high as 12 percent by 1984 (see Ministerio de Educacion (Nicaragua) 1984), and then appears to have dropped the allocation to 8 percent in 1986.

This system of nonformal education, called Popular Basic Education for Adults (PBEA), had, by 1984, six educational levels (grades), plus an ad ditional introductory level designed to make permanent the literacy acquired during the initial crusade. Approximately 400,000 adults finished literacy training during the campaign, and by the mid-1980s, about 100,000 to 120,000 adults and young people were still enrolled in some 13,000 PBEA popular educational collectives (CEPs), taught by secondary and university students and, in rural areas, almost entirely by new teachers from peasant backgrounds, some of whom had only become literate themselves during the crusade. According to Torres (1985), 4 percent of the teachers had become literate during the literacy campaign, 16 percent were studying the first level of adult education, and 32 percent had completed only a few years of primary schooling. All these teachers were trained under a new program specifically for the PBEA. The training program enrolled 23,000 teachers in 1983.[18]

The basic unit in the PBEA is the popular education collective, consisting of about fifteen adults in the city units and five in the rural ones, who meet in a private house, a school (after school hours), or a church. Each CEP is animated by a "coordinator" assisted by a "promoter." Both are considered adult education teachers. Teaching and learning of academic skills is organized around problems of interest for the student-participants, such as agricultural production, health care, and so forth. Periods of study may also be geared to the needs of the students, taking into account their work schedules. Although directed at adults, during the first four years of PBEA's existence, approximately 20 percent of its students were under 15 years old and another 20 to 25 percent were 15 to 19 years old; this was largely the result of the need for youth to contribute to the earnings of very poor families.

The popular education collective is an innovative approach to schooling in a country with relatively limited resources available for education. The concept of highly motivated young people (during the first four years of PBEA, only 30 percent of the popular educators were over 25 years old, and over 40 percent were 19 years old or less) and adults volunteering to teach their neighbors is, indeed, revolutionary and has, according to some, been an antibureaucratic force in education and shown that creative, committed, nonauthoritarian teaching can be developed by use of nonprofessionals (Torres 1983). With the high proportion of youth attending the PBEAs, it is apparent that many young people would not have received any education had it not been for this kind of after-work opportunity.

Despite its achievements, however, there are many problems with the

[18] One claim, probably exaggerated, is that "Seventy percent of the 23,000 adult education teachers are peasants . . . [and they] participate every day in a workshop with the purpose of raising their schooling level" (Myrian Mercado, "Reportaje, en vivo y en directo: educacion en la zona de guerra," *Nuevo Diario*, July 8, 1983, 16 [our translation]).

PBEA. These include disruption by Contra attacks, high dropout rates due to students' work and militia commitments, inadequately trained teachers, and lack of dovetailing with the formal school system.

Since 1984, the PBEAs have been threatened extensively by the war in rural areas. The coordinators and promoters have been special targets of the Contras, and many peasants have been unwilling to risk their lives to attend classes in the centers. Many potential PBEA teachers have also had to enter the army. Thus, popular education has been singled out (along with health care programs) as an object of destruction by the Contra guerrillas (Duflo and Ruellan 1985, 242–43).

Because of students' work and militia commitments, the collectives are often characterized by high dropout rates and frequent absences. With the constant disruptions caused by the war and with the high dropout rate, many adults are lapsing back into illiteracy or are achieving levels of literacy inadequate to the new demands placed on them—the illiteracy rate rose 10 percent in 1982–1987 (Arnove 1988b, 16).

Although the teachers are highly motivated, their abilities to teach are stretched beyond the breaking point (Arnove 1986, 55). It is unlikely that most popular educators have adequate knowledge to teach beyond the course's introductory levels. The pedagogy to be used—based on notions of dialogue and active, inquiring learners—also requires teaching skills that are beyond the preparation of the popular educators, and are rarely implemented (Arnove 1986, 55). Furthermore, there is no equivalence between the levels of PBEA and those of the formal school system, so PBEA students do not obtain an equivalent primary school diploma, and have a difficult time shifting over to conventional schools. This puts pressure on the PBEA to expand to higher levels, even further beyond its teachers' capacities (PBEA has now been expanded to nine levels, with the last three cycles concentrated on teaching vocational skills). Since so many of the PBEA students are young, however, unless this expanded vocational training is tightly coordinated with expanded work possibilities, the end result of the PBEA will be to create an even greater demand for formal secondary education. "The lack of clear definition and design has resulted in what was supposed to be a parallel education system closely tied to community and work place needs gradually beginning to resemble in some respects traditional schooling—namely, a bureaucratic, centralized, credentialling system not closely tied to local circumstances and learner needs" (Arnove 1988b, 12).

Notwithstanding these problems, adult education and new opportunities opened up by the revolution have enabled tens of thousands of previously illiterate adults to play new and important roles at all levels of Nicaraguan society. Furthermore, reforms in adult education are taking place in the context of new realities: The program will be reduced from six to three levels of instruction. In 1987, the ministry of education and the Sandinista Workers' Central agreed to organize CEPs in Managua's major factories. Intensive literacy instruction is also being organized in coops specifically aimed at increasing agricultural production (Arnove 1988b, 13).

THE EXPANSION OF FORMAL EDUCATION

Enrollment in formal schooling has fallen short of the goals set in the early 1980s, but has continued to increase, even in the war economy. The number of students grew rapidly in the period 1979–1984, slowed down significantly in 1984–1986, and began growing again in 1986–1988 except at the university level. Compared with 1978, there were twice as many students in Nicaraguan schools and universities by 1984—more than one-third of the Nicaraguan population was enrolled in some form of publicly supported instruction. The initial enrollment in 1988 was over 800,000 students in formal schools and almost 200,000 adults in various forms of adult education (see Table 9–1). Only 65.5 percent of primary school–age children were enrolled in schools in 1978; by 1984, the percentage had risen to over 80 percent. Enrollment in preschools increased from 9,000 pupils in 1978 to almost 77,000 in 1987 and was estimated to be 81,000 in 1988. In 1978, there were less than 500 children enrolled in special education. By 1984, the number had risen to 1,500 handicapped children and youth and was 2,300 in 1987 and in 1988.

Between 1978 and 1984, 1,400 new primary schools were built, mostly in rural areas, with 3,300 classrooms. Almost 700 new secondary classrooms were constructed. Before the revolution, the total teacher force was less than 13,000. In the next five years, the number of primary school teachers increased by more than 6,000, and the number of secondary teachers increased, by 2,500. Including the 2,000 Cuban teachers of the Augusto Sandino Brigade,[19] by 1984, there were 16,000 teachers working in almost 5,000 centers of basic education. The number of centers dropped significantly between 1984 and 1986 (whether through the reduction of double shifts or for some other reason is unclear), but the number of teachers rose to more than 17,000. Secondary education was also expanded, with increased emphasis placed on teacher training, agriculture, and industrial technical training, although the number of students

[19] In March 1984, *Barricada Internacional* reported that the first of thirty-six education brigades from Cuba had arrived in Managua. Since 1979, 2,000 Cuban teachers have been incorporated into the Nicaraguan teaching force. In 1983, these volunteer teachers, working with 80,000 students, built 2,000 classrooms and participated in almost 25,000 different educational programs in the country. Cuba has also helped Nicaragua in teacher training. In 1983, 1,600 Nicaraguan teachers attended an education workshop in Cuba.

in technical schools (industrial and agricultural) has not grown significantly since 1984.

There is little question that the war has hurt formal schooling. In 1984, there were only 75,000 children without access to schooling; by 1988, the number had increased to 200,000, as a result of "destruction and damaging of schools, dangers of traveling to schools in the war zone, displacement of rural populations, and the economic necessity for children to work" (Arnove 1988b, 18). The MED has not been able to provide schooling throughout the national territory; teachers have faced such erosion of their salaries through inflation, that it has been difficult to recruit people into teaching; and the real spending per student has dropped. Even so, there have been major improvements in the quality of education: In the 1987 school year, despite a chronic shortage of paper goods, 3.7 million school texts were produced; curricula have been revised; and new methods of instruction have been devised, particularly in the language arts and sciences. Transformations in teaching and learning have centered on "fostering more collective, participatory, inquiry-oriented, and work-related approaches . . . a number of classroom assignments involve group efforts . . . steps have also been taken to involve the schools more directly in their surrounding communities . . ." (Arnove 1988b, 19–20). Average retention rates for each grade in primary school, according to MED figures, were 84 percent in 1987; and in secondary school, 76 percent. These are among the highest in Central America.

HIGHER EDUCATION

Two particular characteristics were inherited by the higher education system from the Somoza period: a growing process of privatization (in 1979, there were twelve institutions of higher education, and only the UNAN was publicly funded), and an orientation of academic training that tended to serve the service sector and not the manufacturing and agriculture sectors (Dettmer 1983, 108). If we analyze the distribution of students in higher education during 1980, we find that 23 percent were enrolled in economic sciences, 18 percent in education, 18 percent in humanities and law, 16 percent in technology, and 25 percent in medical sciences, agricultural sciences, physical sciences, and mathematics (Dettmer 1983, 113).

After initially allowing a rapid expansion in 1979–1980 as part of its need for legitimacy among the urban middle classes, the Sandinista government began to curtail university enrollment growth. In that first year of the revolution, the two principal Nicaraguan universities, Universidad Nacional Autonoma de Nicaragua (UNAN) and Universidad Centroamericana (UCA), together had less than 1,000 professors, and only 400 were employed full time (Dettmer 1983, 114–15). With an enrollment of

27,000 students in both universities (94 percent of the total national enrollment in higher education), this translated into a student-professor ratio of 28:1. Because of the lack of professionals, the shift of intellectual effort from the university to the government bureaucracy, and the rapid growth in demand for university education after the revolution, this ratio increased in 1981. One attempt to solve this shortage involved making the best students in the upper levels student-teachers (*alumnos-ayudantes*) to teach to their younger colleagues. In 1981, there were approximately 600 of these student-teachers teaching in higher education. This was a stopgap measure at best, although it did provide firsthand teaching experience for those involved in the Sandinista movement. By 1984, there were 1,630 faculty and almost 800 students working as teaching assistants for an estimated 33,000 to 37,000 students[20] in four universities (a new national engineering university was opened in 1983) and twelve technical training centers, an overall reduction in the student-professor ratio to about 23:1. Furthermore, almost 70 percent of teaching contracts were full time by 1984. And in 1983, the government began sending students abroad to countries that offered scholarships for Nicaraguans. Most went to Eastern Europe, the Soviet Union, Scandinavia, Cuba, or Mexico. Also, some regional institutions, such as the Facultad Latinoamericana de Ciencias Sociales (FLACSO), became involved in curriculum planning (especially in social sciences) and training of university teachers, as well as in the development of publications and libraries. Finally, UNESCO offered help in technical and teaching issues through a number of programs in the National University, and some of UNESCO's top experts worked as advisors for program development.

The university is changing significantly under the Sandinistas. They have introduced state planning to address the increasing demand for higher education and to modify the concentration of enrollment in liberal professions. For the first time in Nicaragua, university enrollment and spending in the academic year 1980–1981 was part of a national development plan. Among that plan's principal points was the restriction of enrollment in the first year of the UNAN and UCA to the 1980 level (that is, a quota restricted to 2,000 new students in UNAN and 800 in UCA). Nevertheless, with the expansion of specific career-oriented training centers (see Arnove 1986, 108) and the opening of the new Polytechnic University, university enrollment continued to expand (in contrast to Cuba in the first ten years of the revolution), but the expansion was much slower than in the first two years after the triumph, and the enrollment

[20] The *Anuario Estadístico de Nicaragua 1984* (p. 186) reports the lower figure (shown in Table 9–1), whereas the Consejo Nacional de la Educación Superior, Dirección de Planificacion, in its *Programa de 1984*, projects 37,304 students. Since the former figure (33,000) is more recent, it is probably closer to the actual enrollment in 1984.

was much more oriented toward those professions needed in the new technically and mass social services–oriented economy. This change in professional orientation was not as precipitous as in Cuba in the 1960s, but by 1984, enrollment in economic sciences had dropped from 23 to 20 percent of the total, and in humanities and law, it had dropped from 18 to 5 percent. Enrollment in education stayed at 18 percent, and enrollment in technology, medicine, agricultural, natural, and physical sciences, and math rose from 41 to 53 percent of the total. Among new entrants in 1984, the figures are even more striking: 38 percent in medicine, natural sciences, and math, 20 percent in technology (total = 58 percent); only 4 percent in humanities, 11 percent in economic science, and 23 percent in education. The other 4 percent in both years were in the preparatory course.

The Sandinistas also reduced university fees. This necessitated a larger public subsidy for higher education, which came to include both public and private institutions (by 1984, state financing of higher education accounted for 94 percent of all expenditures). In 1979, the last year of the Somoza government, 58.3 million cordobas had been authorized for the following year's higher education expenses (the total actually spent in 1979 was about 80 million cordobas); by 1984, the amount of current expenditures on university was 382 million cordobas, almost five times that spent by the state on higher education in 1980, or, correcting for the rapid inflation in the five years, more than double in real terms. In addition to current expenditures, another 25 percent of the budget for universities is spent annually on capital investment (CNES 1984).

With less than 4 percent of total school enrollment in 1984, higher education received 25 percent of total public spending on education (including capital spending): "The state spends more than eight times as much on a higher education student than on a high school student, and ten times more than on a primary school student" (Arnove 1986, 109). Public spending (not including capital costs) per student on higher education in the five years after the triumph also increased twice as rapidly as that on primary and secondary education, although the ratio was lower for normal and technical education (where per student cost increased about 20 percent more rapidly than for general secondary education). All this suggests that, unlike Cuba, which deemphasized university education while building up its primary and secondary system, Nicaragua is placing much more of its effort into developing highly schooled cadres— cadres with specific skills relevant to the revolutionary project.

The pattern of this expansion (at least until 1984) has been to increase per student spending in the university relative to other levels while reducing the growth of enrollment relative to other levels (see Tables 9–1 and 9–4). The relative expansion of primary and secondary enrollment has been more rapid than university enrollment expansion in the postrevolutionary period, despite the much smaller absolute number of students at university. Much of the increase in spending per student is related to (1) the shift from relatively low per-student costs in economic sciences, humanities, and law to the relatively expensive fields of physical sciences, technology, and medicine; and (2) the state's assumption of more than 90 percent of the costs of university education. The state appears to have increased its spending per student partly in order to increase access to university education and democratize it by charging no tuition. In addition, the university has instituted a quota system to guarantee enrollments from all regions of the country, and has provided an accelerated high school program ("preparatory faculty") to students who otherwise would not be able to attend university (Arnove 1986, 109). But the polit-

TABLE 9-4

Nicaragua: Government Spending per Student on Education by Level, 1979–1988 (cordobas)

Year	Primary	Total Secondary	Secondary Technical	University[a]	Adult[b]
1979/80	543 [569]	1,205	2,661	2,872	—
1980/81	616 [656]	1,265	2,633	4,663	360
1982	[765]	1,470	2,204	7,515	576
1983	907 [954]	1,588	2,033	10,435	785
1984	1,012 [1,164]	2,232	3,412	10,244	1,305
1985	n.a.	n.a.	n.a.	n.a.	n.a.
1986	20,823	34,745	89,367	n.a.	14,114
1988	188,000	307,774	487,052	n.a.	91,453

Source: MED, *La Gestión Educativa en Cinco Años de Revolución* (Managua: MED, May 1984), tabs. A-1 and A-3. Figures in brackets show estimates based on budget figures from tab. A-3 for primary school and number of students from MED data provided to the authors in 1987 (excluding preprimary students)—see Table 9–1, above.

[a] University per student costs are estimated by taking total education spending from MED, *La Educación en Cuatro Años de Revolución* (Managua: MED, 1983) 147, subtracting the total MED budget, and then multiplying by 0.75 (this figure is based on actual capital/total costs in 1984) to get current costs. These are then divided by the number of students from Table 9.1, above.

[b] The per student costs for adult education are extremely approximate because the actual number of students enrolled in adult education are so approximate. Thus, we have used the figures in *La Gestión Educativa*, tab. A-1, except for 1984, because the *Anuario Estadístico 1984* reports an enrollment of 129,000 in 1984 versus the 195,000 in tab. A-1, and it is likely that the *Anuario* figure is closer to reality, since projections by the Dirección General de Educación de Adultos show projected enrollments of 122,000 in 1985, 136,000 in 1986, and 157,000 in 1987 ("Cifras Directivas del Programa de Educación de Adultos para 1987" [Managua: 1986]). This is corroborated by MED figures provided us in 1987.

ical role of higher public spending on universities to subsidize the predominantly middle-class students who attend university also has to be taken into account, especially under present pluralist conditions.

The war has hit universities especially hard, because students are of draft age. Enrollments are down sharply, from a high of 35,000 in 1983 to about 25,000 in 1988. Another outcome of the draft is that in 1984, for the first time, women comprised a majority of higher education students. But, according to Arnove (1988a, 8), the "constant mobilizations of youth for military service and participation in the production brigades . . . to a certain extent have transformed the university milieu. . . . [T]here is a greater sense of purpose, a more profound seriousness, and even joy, at being a university student than prior to the establishment of the new regime."

CHANGES IN THE CONTENT AND METHOD OF FORMAL SCHOOLING

As in Cuba, the new education in Nicaragua is supposed to "overcome the gaps that exist between theory and practice, intellectual and manual work, schooling and community. . . . The new person that emerges from this system is to be altruistic, cooperative, participatory, and self-abnegating for the collective good" (Arnove 1986, 91). According to Arnove, Nicaraguan schools from kindergarten on do attempt to emphasize a more cooperative and collective approach to work and life (Arnove 1986, 95). But these efforts are considerably more limited than in Cuba, and, as in Cuba, there is still principal emphasis on individual performance in school and the classroom is still very much teacher dominated. Nevertheless, the school is a place where revolutionary ideology is taught and the very ambience of education is collective, nationalistic, and anti-imperialistic.

Although there is no evidence that Sandinista schooling alone is producing a different kind of person, the school in the context of a society in the process of transformation and a state fighting for its survival does, in all likelihood, have a considerable impact on young people's attitudes and norms, even though perhaps not great enough to serve as the sole basis of transformation of social relations. The intense social involvement of youth and their key role in production and defense activities must be a much greater influence on their values and self-definition than anything they learn in school. Young women's roles in society also are being transformed by the war. Thousands of them participate in the militia and civil defense, and they necessarily play a greater role in production. There are now more women than men at university, which means that, in the future, they will also fill more professional positions.

Conflicts in Nicaraguan Educational Reform

The confrontation between "traditional" and "revolutionary" educational expansion is an expression of the conflicts in Nicaragua's transitional state. This conflict is played out on two levels. First, it is expressed in the struggle between groups opposed to the Sandinista revolution—the hierarchy of the Catholic Church and elements of the business and other middle classes—who support the class-based, narrowly defined education of the Somoza period (and oppose any revolutionary ideology in the curriculum) versus those groups who support the ideological message and the significant educational changes proposed by the Sandinista state. Second, there are conflicts within the Sandinista project itself, especially between those who feel that education should be built on a revolutionary, participative pedagogy—the popular education model developed in the literacy crusade and the popular education centers—and those who see traditional curricula as the most efficient model for building skills.

EDUCATIONAL REFORM AND INTERNAL OPPOSITION

Even though it belatedly supported the overthrow of Somoza, the Church hierarchy (with the support of business groups) almost immediately opposed Sandinista educational reform. It presented this opposition in terms of two issues: early on, in terms of the role of politics and ideology in education (opposition to the expansion of public education); later, in terms of the right to educational choice (opposition to any reduction in public aid to Church schools).

The Church and its business allies opposed expanding public education from the very beginning of the Sandinista regime. They viewed school expansion as spreading an ideology among the poor that would challenge the Church's ideological hegemony in many rural and marginal urban communities.

The Sandinistas moved quickly (early 1980) to overcome this opposition by taking a nationwide survey on educational demand. The National Survey of the New Education's Means and Objectives established that there was an overwhelming desire for educational expansion and reform among the mass of Nicaraguans (Vilas 1982). The survey addressed three main themes: popular democracy, nationalism, and anti-imperialism (La Belle 1986; Arnove 1986). Its results showed that Church opposition to expanding education was at odds with deep-seated demands in its own constituency. Thus, the survey demonstrated to the Church hierarchy that opposing educational reform could well reduce its own legitimacy, not that of the Sandinista regime.[21]

[21] The survey was carried out in a two-stage process: the training stage in September—

That failure forced opposition groups into the seemingly contradictory position of fighting for continued support for private education within the state's educational expansion program. Part of the revolutionary state's legitimacy in Nicaragua lies in its commitment to the mixed economy and to a constrained political pluralism. As part of this commitment, the state has maintained the rights of parents (guaranteed under the previous constitution) to send their children to private (in this case, Church) schools and even subsidizes most of those schools. The ministry of education has signed more than twenty contracts of association with religious communities that provide education. In 1984, 15 percent of primary and secondary school students were attending private schools. Of 298 private primary schools, 217 were subsidized. The Church hierarchy that exerts pedagogical control over many of these schools is openly opposed to the Sandinista government. In terms of the government's goal of developing, through the schools and mass organizations, a new, revolutionary concept of nation in which collective needs take primacy over individual needs and in which the defense of the revolution and transformation of Nicaraguan society is fundamental to the collective project, Church control of a significant portion of the educational system—when the Church has a high degree of political legitimacy and is directly opposed to this goal— poses a serious problem. Nevertheless, for the moment, the state is unwilling (and probably unable) to take the political risk of eliminating subsidies to Church schools.

In early 1984, the Bishops' Conference strongly criticized the ministry of education for its religious intolerance and for its interference in Catholic education. The Union Nicaraguense de Padres de Familia de Colegios Cristianos (UNAPAFACC) and the Federación Nacional de Escuelas

November 1980, and the data collection stage during January and February 1981. The preliminary results were published by the ministry of education in August 1981. Some political organizations did not agree to participate in the survey (for example, the Partido Conservador Democrata [PCD], the Partido Social Cristiano, the Partido Popular Social Cristiano [PPSC], and the Confederación de Unificación Sindical). Others withdrew before the data collection process started (for example, the Central de Trabajadores de Nicaragua [CTN], which, despite, its name is not the principal representative of workers in Nicaragua, the Confederación de Camaras de Comercio, the Unión de Productores Agrícolos de Nicaragua, the Instituto Nicaraguense de Desarrollo, and the Movimiento Democrático Nicaraguense). Finally, two organizations delivered the information either later than the deadline or in an improper form (these were the Cámara de Industrias de Nicaragua, a private-sector organization, and the Confederación Nacional de Asociaciones Profesionales [CONAPRO], a Sandinista organization). A total of thirty organizations participated in the survey, representing approximately 53,000 individuals. Surprisingly enough, all the associations linked to the Catholic Church participated (for example, the Federación Nicaraguense de Educación Católica, the Union de Padres de Familia de Colegios Cristianos, the Union de Padres de Familia por la Educación Cristiana, the Conferencia Episcopal de Nicaragua, the Asociación del Ciero Nicaraguense, and the Conferencia de Religiosos de Nicaragua), as well as many other Christian organizations.

Católicas (FENEC) threatened a strike in Catholic schools. These and many other conflicts led one analyst to contend that by mid-1983 the Catholic Church was engaged in a counterrevolutionary discourse,[22] confronting Sandinista policies in every sector of society, including education (Ezcurra 1984, 120).

THE CONFLICT BETWEEN EDUCATIONAL EXPANSION AND OTHER GOALS

The rapid growth of formal and nonformal education in the first years of the Sandinista revolution reflects both the important symbol that education has come to be in developing societies and its key ideological role in a regime attempting to counter traditional political forces and to build a new basis for capital accumulation. In delivering educational services, the Sandinistas have tended to favor the poor and the rural over better-off Nicaraguans, through emphasis on adult and primary education and by shifting secondary education to a more technical agricultural/industrial orientation.

Despite their accomplishments in expanding education, the Sandinistas have been constrained in delivering more and better education by the more pressing needs of capital accumulation and the defense of the country. The growing emphasis on these other goals is reflected in both the slowdown in the growth of the overall education budget after 1981 and the more rapid growth of the budget (until 1983) for university education relative to primary and secondary education. Even though university education is being democratized, the students who attend are still from a higher social class than the average Nicaraguan.

Simultaneously, adult education, although expanded, still being taught largely by paraeducators, and rural primary schooling—except that taught by Cuban volunteers—is still of questionable quality. As Arnove points out, school completion rates "remain low and not noticeably different from the Somoza epoch" (Arnove 1986, 76). Secondary technical schools are now not being expanded more rapidly because of lack of resources (enrollment since 1983 has even apparently declined significantly). The government has increased educational spending to more than 4 percent of GNP, but that is far short of the much higher percentage of GNP spent by Cuba in the mid-1960s.[23] Nicaraguan policymakers, even

[22] Nicaragua's private university, the Universidad Centro-Americana (UCA), owned and operated by the Jesuit order, has been collaborating closely with the revolutionary government. There is an informal division of labor between the UCA and the National University. For example, both are financed by the government, and each one develops different university careers. At the higher-education level, then, private and public education function side by side, largely because the Jesuits have chosen to work with rather than against the social changes promoted by the Sandinistas.

[23] We hesitate to provide an exact percentage for Cuba because Cuba's output figures are

before the war economy, had to make a choice between delivering more and better social services to the mass of Nicaraguans and developing highly trained cadres as well as increasing agricultural exports and food production. Part of the difficulty of this choice was softened by turning to cheaper forms of education and by shifting responsibility for education away from the ministry of education to mass-base organizations. This democratized control over educational decisions enabled many Nicaraguans to receive schooling who otherwise would not have received it, but it has also raised questions about the level of quality of that type of education and its impact on the economic productivity of those taking it. Once the war began soaking up public resources and human capital, as well as inflicting severe damage to education in rural areas, a different set of conflicts emerged. In part, those conflicts were resolved through the socialization of youth in the military; but declines in the quality of academic training and adult literacy were exacerbated.

The development of three parallel subsystems of education—the public formal one, the public nonformal one, and the publicly subsidized private one—has been necessary in part because of political factors and in part because the state lacks the resources to defend the country against the Contras, satisfy the high consumer demand for material goods, and still supply formal public education for all who desire it.

But the existence of a formal educational system alongside a nonformal system creates problems of competitiveness between the two, in terms of their pedagogical and administrative styles, between the formal education teachers and the popular educators, and, to a lesser extent, in the sense of "second-classness" among the high percentage of nonadult students in the PBEA vis-à-vis formal schools. Participative ideology and the development of FSLN-tied mass organizations as a logical outgrowth of the Sandinista mobilizations of 1978–1979, have catalyzed and taken responsibility for mass demands for education, but also injected those demands with a "popular" nonstructured form. This popular form reaches into grass-roots culture and, simultaneously, is inherently much more democratic than bureaucratized formal schooling. Despite agreement on overall goals for the revolution, there is little agreement on strategy and form between the two state subsystems.

The conflict within the educational system itself (which, as in the case of many such discussions, is taking place simultaneously in the hierarchy of the FSLN and in the mass organizations) concerns the optimum "revolutionary" strategy of expanding public formal schooling. There was and continues to be, profound disagreement between those who view such a

---

not comparable to traditional gross domestic product data. The percentage is therefore not equivalent.

strategy as consisting of delivering high-quality traditional formal schooling, with an emphasis on academic skills taught in a traditional fashion,
and those who believe that delivering that high-quality education requires changing the nature of pedagogy, making it more participative and
coherent in the Nicaraguan context.

These different views existed from the beginning of the revolutionary
state and were accentuated by the mobilization and attempts at alternative pedagogies during the literacy campaign. The campaign created a
group of new teachers and mobilized students who believed in popular,
participative education. When data showing extraordinarily poor performance by students on math and language examinations became available at the end of the 1982–1983 school year, the concerns about the
quality of education were in part translated into a critique of traditional,
formalistic schooling by the proponents of pedagogical alternatives.[24]

The conflict between traditional and popular education is primarily
ideological, but it also has economic roots. The Sandinista leadership
might prefer, for organizational and perhaps technical reasons, to provide
a high-quality, scientifically oriented education that would, in the longer
run, develop the basis for training the skilled cadres, technicians, and

[24] The debate on educational performance that surfaced in the summer of 1983 represented a sharp divergence between two alternative projects in the transition state. On one
hand, the "technocratic" group in the ministry of education and the National Council of
Higher Education (CENES), as well as in the FSLN—concerned with the economy's personnel needs and committed to the development of traditional schooling—wanted to modernize, make more efficient, and expand existing public schools, with practices that did not
differ greatly from education in the 1970s. Supporting them were the more traditional
teachers, many of whom had taught in the Somoza era. On the other hand, the newer group
of teachers, developed in part through the literacy campaign, and others in the ministry
and the FSLN who wanted to introduce new kinds of pedagogy and take a more "revolutionary," consciousness-raising, participative approach to education in general were joined
by the Sandinista Youth movement (MJS) in criticizing the ministry's policy. Their underlying view was that the schools should be an apparatus that would build a new hegemony
based on popular culture and political action (interview in Managua, February 1984, with a
former high official in the ministry of education; see also Barricada, Nos. 1431–1437, August 3–9, 1983, and No. 1440, August 12, 1983).

One result of the debate was a greater emphasis on quality of schooling. A second was a
political shake-up in the ministry of education. A Jesuit priest, Fernando Cardenal, the
former national coordinator of the literacy campaign and the vice-chairman of the Sandinista
Youth movement, was ultimately appointed minister of education. The Cardenal appoint-
ment was logical in terms of assuaging the proponents of a "new education." As a leader in
the "liberation" wing of the Church, Cardenal had been instrumental in introducing participative, popular education among the poor during the Somoza period. He could, therefore,
be expected to cast a sympathetic eye on the criticism of the ministry's more traditional,
technocratic approach to education. Indeed, beginning in 1985, and consistent with a new
emphasis on revitalizing mass organizations as a source of dynamic in Nicaraguan politics,
Cardenal attempted to gradually introduce innovative, more participative pedagogies into
formal public schools (Torres and Coraggio 1987).

administrators needed for planned economic development. But this type of expansion is expensive and constrained by lack of resources. The need of the new state to gain legitimacy by incorporating adult peasants and workers into the revolutionary project (and concept of nation), plus the commitment of the Sandinista government to education per se, as a means of imparting basic academic skills, raising consciousness, and providing a common, uplifting, revolutionary, and democratic experience (much as Cuba had done twenty years before), resulted in the literacy crusade and the PBEA groups. This was relatively inexpensive education, based on participation rather than traditional hierarchies, and oriented much more than formal schools to raising revolutionary consciousness. But, at the same time, popular education puts considerable responsibility for educational decisionmaking into the hands of local branches of mass-base organizations. While this decentralization of political power helped transform Nicaragua's conditioned capitalist society, it also strengthened mass organizations opposed to the traditional, bureaucratic form of public education—a form that was still dominant in the overall revolutionary educational system.

Accomplishments and Conflicts in Nicaraguan Education

The Sandinista revolution has had a profound effect on Nicaragua's educational system. From one of the lowest rates of enrollment and literacy in Latin America, Nicaragua has now reached levels that are much more consistent with the more developed countries in the region. In addition to rapid growth in primary, secondary, and university formal education, the Sandinistas have created popular education schools, which reach out to rural and marginal urban populations, both adult and youth. Considering that the country has had to defend itself against externally financed guerrilla forces since 1982, the government's ability to sustain a relatively high level of educational spending is remarkable. It reflects a deep commitment by the new government to the development of Nicaragua's human resources capability and a recognition of the importance of education among those who never had access to it and of its role in promoting Sandinista ideology.

In the early stages of the revolution, the emphasis was on mobilization through popular education, first in the form of the literacy campaign and later as popular basic education. At the same time, however, because of the commitment by the Sandinistas to keep the middle class in the revolution and the desperate need for highly trained cadres, the government expanded university education and began more formal technical training at the secondary level. The growth of university enrollment and spending in this period appears especially anomalous, but can be explained politically by this underlying social demand for doctors, teachers, engineers, and technicians and the continued strength of the middle class.

By the revolution's fourth year, despite a significant conflict in the FSLN and some of its organizational elements over the nature of formal education, there was a relative slowdown in the weight given to nonformal adult education (even though some new initiatives began to appear from the ministry in "popularizing" the lower levels of formal schooling) and an increased emphasis on increasing technical training at the secondary and higher levels. Part of the change in emphasis was directly the result of the war. There was a much more urgent need to increase material output, and this, in turn, seemed to require more specific skills. Only spending per student on normal and technical secondary education in 1984 kept up with the more than 30 percent inflation of the previous year (see Table 9–4). Even with this commitment, enrollment has slowed down since 1983–1984 in technical education (although the budget allocation to technical education as a percentage of the budget has stayed constant at 7.3 percent). Normal school enrollment has kept up, however, and the normal schooling allocation now (1988) represents 4.3 percent of MED's budget (versus 2.5 percent in 1984).

But this pattern can also be looked at another way: If secondary technical and normal education is considered another form of popular education, in the sense that it trains primarily youth from the popular classes, it can be argued that spending on popular education as a whole (preprimary plus primary plus adult plus normal and technical secondary) has risen as a percentage of total spending on education even during the period of most intensive fighting against the Contra threat. Approximate estimates indicate that the proportion spent on those categories of education was 57 percent in 1979, 41 percent in 1980, 46 percent in 1981, 44 percent in 1982, 45 percent in 1983, 51 percent in 1984, and apparently more than 60 percent in 1986 and 1988. The percentage going to higher education also rose between 1980 and 1983, but dropped from its high of 23 percent in 1983 to 19 percent in 1984.

The Sandinistas have therefore continued to invest in the expanded education of the popular classes throughout the revolutionary period, but have had to face an increasing struggle in the face of war and a declining economy to maintain educational expansion. Much of the socialization of youth is taking place outside schools in the military and through the very nature of the struggle for physical survival.

In the immediate future, the principal problem for the government is to accumulate capital more rapidly and to get its austerity program to stop the inflation. The economy's ability to continue expanding schooling is declining as per capita income declines, even though, as a percentage of GDP, education continues to remain important. At the same time, the war and now lack of funds have made it difficult to maintain popular education centers in rural areas. These were primary targets for the Contras. The short-term future of educational expansion depends very much on the Sandinista government's ability to get the economy on its feet, but in the longer run, the underlying conflicts about the nature of education—its "quality"—will continue, and will continue to be very much part and parcel of the nature of the revolutionary process itself.

CHRONOLOGY OF ECONOMIC CHANGE AND EDUCATIONAL POLICY IN NICARAGUA

	Economic Strategy	Mobilization Strategy	Economic Performance	Education Policy
1979	Nationalization of Somoza lands and businesses Some cooperativization	Coalition government Mass organizations	27% drop in GDP	Expansion of primary schooling
1980	Mixed economy Continued foreign borrowing State credit for private agricultural producers	Income redistribution	*1980–1981* Increase in GDP	National literacy campaign Expansion of university
1981	Some nationalization of private lands Mechanization of state lands deemphasized	Conflict with Catholic Church		Popular education for adults
1982	Credit to private farms reduced Increased cooperativization of unused private agricultural land		Decline in GDP as part of world recession	Continued expansion of primary and secondary schools Expansion of teacher and technical education
1983	Inefficient state farms turned over to peasants (coops and individuals)	Increased reliance on mass organizations Military conscription	Increase in GDP growth	Slower growth in university education Shift to medical, science, and teacher education

(Continued on next page)

ECONOMIC CHANGE AND EDUCATIONAL POLICY IN NICARAGUA— *Continued*

	Economic Strategy	*Mobilization Strategy*	*Economic Performance*	*Education Policy*
1983 *(cont)*	Rapid land re- form Gradual shift of trade away from reliance on U.S.			
1984	Increased titling of land to coops and in- dividual peas- ants U.S. trade em- bargo forces further trade diversification	General elec- tions for As- sembly and President	*1984–1985* Increasing infla- tion Rapid decline in GDP/capita	PBEA Centers attacked by Contras Reduction of adult educa- tion
1985	Emphasis on ti- tling land to individuals Small farmer– based devel- opment strat- egy War economy Freed exchange rate and elim- ination of sub- sidies to pri- vate producers Freed agricul- tural prices	New constitu- tion drafted More power given to mass organizations in rural areas Anti-Contra mo- bilization		Slower growth in primary and secondary education
1986	Intensification of war economy		Rising inflation Commodity shortages	Renewed expan- sion of formal primary and secondary ed- ucation

(*Continued on next page*)

ECONOMIC CHANGE AND EDUCATIONAL POLICY IN NICARAGUA— *Continued*

	Economic Strategy	*Mobilization Strategy*	*Economic Performance*	*Education Policy*
1987	Continued reliance on individual peasant agriculture	Continued mobilization for the war	Negative economic growth	
1988	Attempts to control currency black markets Austerity measures to combat inflation		Runaway inflation Negative economic growth	Sharp drop in university enrollments
1989	Cuts in government spending	Agreement to hold elections in 1990	Major shortages of production and consumption goods	Reduction in spending for education

PART III

Conclusions

CHAPTER 10

Education and Social Transformation: Theory and Practice

Martin Carnoy and Joel Samoff

WE BEGAN by asking whether education in societies undergoing rapid social transformation plays a role different from that in conditioned capitalist societies, and if so, why. We suggest that it does, for two specific reasons. First, in the transition, there is a fundamental shift in the primary social dynamic, from the previously capitalist economy to the transition polity—from the economic to the political. Second, the transition state, which is the product of that social dynamic, is necessarily oriented toward the development of labor, in contrast to capitalist states' emphasis on capital.

These are the general characteristics that provide the setting for the differences between transition and conditioned capitalist education discussed in the case studies. But we have also found that each transition is set in a particular historical and cultural context, with its own process of change and conflict, conditioned by its prerevolutionary (or preindependence) history, its geopolitical situation, its physical size, and its available resources. Global similarities are rooted and shaped in national and historical uniqueness.

At the same time, we have stressed that the social transformation that characterizes the transition is not simply a change from one type of economy to another. Nor is it solely a shift of the center of gravity from the economy to the polity. The conditioned capitalism that a revolution or independence attempts to replace is not just a mode of production but a mode of life:

> We cannot separate either the forces of production (narrowly conceived) or the purely legal forms of property control, from the richly variegated texture of political, cultural and other social relations which made that capitalist production possible. And this texture is the more complex still in these societies where the transformation into capitalist forms was only partial.
>
> (Marshall 1986, 5)

Social transformation must be accomplished through multiple struggles on multiple fronts, all linked, but each distinct. As the locus of action shifts from the economy to the polity, the old order must be confronted, and the new order fashioned, in the worldview, in the attitudes and expectations, and in the daily practices of the citizenry. The process of social transformation is thus both heroic and mundane. In the cases we have studied, relative inattention to the struggle on the small scale has regularly jeopardized the transition on the large scale. The new leadership generally assumed that the conquest of the economy, with appropriate revolutionary guidance, would carry with it the transformation of other sectors and the resocialization of the populace. Nowhere did that occur. The conquest of the economy itself was often halting and partial and, with the exception of China and perhaps Cuba, remains incomplete. Having seized the reins of power (or perhaps more accurately, having occupied the offices of authority), the new leadership was initially inclined to focus on production at the expense of mobilization. Although increased output and productivity were, and are, essential for the transition, the preoccupation with production obscured the durability of the old understandings and social relations and undermined the politicization necessary to challenge them.

This contextual analysis draws another conclusion: It is difficult to measure or even discuss how *much* "socialism" each of these transition societies has or has not achieved, even though the leadership in each of the countries we studied has declared its intention to build socialism. We suggest that the important issue is less whether or not a particular society is socialist and more the extent of its concrete social transformation, its political participation, its development of human capacities, its improvement of the material conditions of life, and its citizens' internalization and elaboration of a sense of worth and self-identity. Whatever the content of the socialism under construction, what matters is what each of these societies is or is not achieving in these concrete terms. We therefore focus in the case studies on what is actually happening in each country's efforts to transform its social, political and economic relations.

Studying educational policy is essential to understanding the reality of this transformation. The case studies confirm that education in transition states is viewed, much more than in capitalist countries, as the key to economic and social development. After the takeover of the conditioned state, whether by revolution or independence, there has been a rapid expansion of both formal schooling and nonformal adult education. The expansion has included and especially focused on those segments of the population least empowered in the conditioned political economy.

In addition to the rapid expansion, both to increase skills and to reduce inequalities in access, education in such societies is expected to play a key role in the transformation of social relations. This role is shaped by the ideal of making educated labor the keystone of a more productive, modernized, participative economy, based on a collectivist or socialist ideology. Educational expansion and content are also shaped by the ideal of developing a new, indigenous, and revolutionary sense of national history. Part of that ideal is to give a prominent place in creating history to groups marginalized by conditioned capitalism.

But our case studies show that the reality of revolutionary transition in a world dominated by capitalist financial institutions, transnational manufacturing and service enterprises, core countries' dominance of technological creativity and their conflict with the Soviet Union (which translates into potential conflict with all "socialist" states) has required important compromises with these ideals by the revolutionary leadership, including compromises on educational expansion and content. These compromises have consequences for the transition process.

They may help explain, for example, why educational expansion and reform do not appear to develop, at least in the short term, a new consciousness among those who attend school. Nor do they appear to lead directly to social transformation. In part, slower than expected progress toward these goals is attributable to the demand for traditional skills in order to meet short-term production and organizational needs—needs accentuated by economic sanctions, political subversion ("destabilization"), and military intervention. In part, it also seems to be the result of conscious government decisions regarding education and political participation. Education in transition states, for example, continues to be characterized by formality and hierarchy. In part, this reflects the emphasis on the development of basic skills and the importance of maintaining centralized control in a situation of persisting external threat. In part, it stems from the uncritical adoption of external models. And in part, it is due to the tendency by revolutionary leaders to increase bureaucratization and control. Our analysis suggests that whatever its proximate origins, there seems to be a clear relationship between increased bureaucratization in the transition state and increased reliance on traditional hierarchical formal schooling as the principal means of defining and transferring knowledge.

ACCOMPLISHMENTS AND SHORTFALLS

Education in these societies differs from education in capitalist states largely because the state in all of the countries we have studied is committed to building a mass society, in which individual gain is subsumed to national needs and objectives and social transformation is the basis for economic growth and for increased political participation. Apparently, the rapid equalization of income and wealth and the disconnection of wealth from political power are crucial to realizing such a society. So is the enhancement of human capacity to contribute economically and socially. Hence, increasing human capital in the masses becomes an important element in the transition project.

The educational changes that have been implemented are part of this effort to equalize social position and access to knowledge, and to develop a new basis for political power. This basis is rooted in labor instead of the ownership of capital. We have argued throughout this book, however, that the process of change does not end once this initial reduction of inequalities and the development of a new basis for state power is achieved. For one thing, even though there have been drastic changes in the relation of labor to capital and hence of different social groups in society to one another and to the state, economic growth and political participation have not necessarily followed. Further changes in social relations are needed for increases in production and participation.

Second, slow improvement in the material conditions of life in these poor countries and limits on political participation have important implications for the legitimacy of their state leaders, who promise rapid increases in both growth and (implicitly if not explicitly) participation. Third, although education has moved toward equalized access to knowledge, it has failed to create the kind of social and political consensus imagined by the leaders of these transition states. This has made vanguard and mass parties face the unpleasant reality that either education has to be made devoid of all critical analysis (and that critical analysis has to be suppressed in general)—severely limiting further social transformation—or political organizations have to be made participative and accountable, and thus potentially threatening to those in power. In other words, increased participation is neither necessarily socialist nor sufficient for social transformation. As these and other cases have shown, the major capitalist states are quick to nurture dissidence and to recruit, finance, and arm dissidents. Internal opponents to the transformation may be able to draw on racial, ethnic, religious, and regional ties, on their patronage relationships, and on frustration at the apparently slow pace of change to mobilize support for their challenges to the new order. More generally, populist demands may be fundamentally conservative. As Mao, Cabral, and others have observed, the peasantry's strongest resistance to the capitalist state is often fueled by an image of restoration, not revolution: the desire to re-capture what is perceived as the solidarity and stability of an older order. In addition, the coalition that becomes the new leadership is itself fragile. Allies who submerged their differences in their attack on the old order become enemies, with dramatically different visions of the desired future.

Consequently, the gains initially achieved remain insecure. Put somewhat differently, social transformation is not simply a struggle, but a continuing struggle. Each progressive advance alters the terrain of conflict—especially by extending the boundaries of legitimate political participation—but must be defended to endure. That defense must be mounted in multiple arenas simultaneously, and it must be supported by an increasingly productive economy. It must, as well, be sustained by a transformed understanding of what is desirable, what is possible, and how to get there. For that, education is central.

The variation in economic and political outcomes found in the case studies and the different nature of the economic and political transitions in the five societies suggest that different inherited conditions, the availability of resources, the degree of armed external opposition, and the size of the country (and consequently its relationship to the rest of the world economy), as well as the nature of the leadership that emerges from the revolutionary movements, all influence the effects of social transformation on economic and political change.

The studies also suggest that there is a constant tension in transition states between political forces that want to tighten controls and promote technocratic reforms to increase economic growth and groups that want to promote increased equality and socialist ideals. The leadership fluctuates between considering economic growth as the single most important objective, both in terms of national objectives and in terms of the leadership's own security of tenure, and (for the same reasons), pushing for greater equality in social relations.

Moving dialectically between these partly competing objectives, each of the countries studied has been able to transform its society's fundamental economic and political relationships. With that transformation has come rapid educational expansion, an expansion that is successfully reaching into rural areas and into the poorest regions of the country. All of these countries have made significant strides toward eliminating illiteracy and raising the average level of schooling in their populations. They have increased investment in education much more rapidly than have other countries at the same level of economic capacity. They have emphasized the growth of primary and adult education, thus developing an inclusive educational expansion model, which is aimed at the rural and urban poor—thus, their educational investment has made explicit and central the goal of transforming the lives of the mass of peasants and workers.

These changes do not take place overnight. The data presented in the China study suggest that thirty-seven years after the revolution, China still has not achieved universal literacy, nor do all Chinese children attend primary school. Three decades of commitment to literacy training and universal primary education have not made all Tanzanians literate or primary educated. Of the five countries we studied, Cuba has achieved the highest levels of mass schooling (grade ten) and lowest levels of illiteracy, but Cuba enjoyed relatively high educational levels before the triumph of the revolution in 1959 and, in addition, Cuba's investment in education in the 1960s and 1970s was massive, supported by its economic relationship with the Soviet Union.

Nevertheless, the educational accomplishments of these transition states (even the two youngest, Nicaragua and Mozambique) are impressive, especially considering the military and economic pressure that all but Tanzania faced (and that Cuba, Nicaragua, and Mozambique are still facing) in the early years of their postrevolutionary development.

The single most important of their achievements is the ability to reach out to adult populations and incorporate them into the newly defined nation through literacy campaigns. Even though the goals of the literacy campaigns were not solely educational, they showed the powerful relationship between political mobilization and educational outcomes. In every case, the campaigns were intended to bring masses of rural and urban illiterates (usually the most marginalized elements in the prerevolutionary society) into the revolutionary project and to raise the consciousness of already schooled teachers and students participating in the campaign. Mobilizing the schooled and unschooled in the teaching and learning of reading and writing has been effective in (1) developing a new concept of nation in both groups; (2) creating an identification with the revolutionary or independence movement, even among those who did not participate directly in the country's liberation; and (3) empowering politically, through literacy—an important symbol of political power in conditioned capitalist society—the previously illiterate.

Tanzania's vacillating policy in this regard is instructive. With support from UNESCO Tanzania launched what came to be regarded as a model functional literacy project. Successful implementation of that project in one region became the basis for its extension throughout the country. Extraordinary resources, both internal and external, were mobilized. The major literacy campaigns had all the elements of a national crusade: The literate were sent out to the countryside, rural teachers and volunteers were recruited and trained and became themselves the trainers, and the party effectively made participation in a literacy program a condition of citizenship. Continuation programs and village libraries were created to serve the newly literate. An entirely new educational institution was created—the Folk Development Colleges (more than fifty were opened within a few years)—to provide additional educational and vocational programs to what was expected to be a new sort of rural elite, the newly literate. Yet when the village libraries decayed, or when the Folk Development Colleges were challenged, it was not the newly literate peasants who rallied to their defense. In the effort to eliminate illiteracy rapidly, the dominant voices were those—both Tanzanians and others—who were inclined to regard literacy more as a functional requisite for economic growth than as a political foundation for social transformation. Freire's liberation pedagogy was more often cited than employed. Literacy class participants were more often required to memorize the names for agricultural implements than asked to label their social environment. The precepts of modernization had overwhelmed the generative process of political and social transformation. Illiteracy had been sharply reduced, and new participants had entered the political arena. But they did so with little sense of their own role in that entry, either actual or potential. Unlike the other cases we discuss here, the pressures on Tanzania to compromise its socialist agenda did not appear primarily in the form of armed attack or economic boycott (though there was some of each). Rather, the struggle occurred at the level of conceiving what was to be accomplished, what were to be the priorities. That the siege of modernization focused on ideas rather than arms returns us again to the importance of education in the transition.

The second achievement is the relatively rapid development of a mass educational system for children and adults. The degree of this achievement varies from country to country, but it is universal in the sense that each of the societies we studied has been committed in practice to mass education and to improving the quality of that education. The pressures of serious military interventions have influenced that commitment in Mozambique and Nicaragua, but even there, the percentages of students in primary school have continued to rise in recent years and overall spending on education has been maintained. There are also differences in the priority given mass education relative to university education, not only among the countries studied but also within a country during different historical periods. The clearest case of shifting priorities is China, where higher education was relatively important in the early years after the revolution, then was effectively shut down during the Cultural Revolution, and has now been restored to high priority, whereas primary schooling in this most recent period has received much less emphasis. At the other extreme is Tanzania, which achieved essentially universal primary education by 1978, but has severely limited access to secondary schools even until today, despite pressures from the population for more postprimary education (reflected in the recent rapid growth of private secondary schools). Cuba maintained a tight rein on the growth of university education until the early 1970s, when a large fraction of students were completing the lower level of secondary schools. Nicaragua, with its mixed economy (including a politically active small middle class) and desperate shortage of skilled cadres, has continued to expand the university system, particularly in the technical and medical fields.

The third achievement is the equalization of access to knowledge both among social classes and between genders, and, to some extent, the demystification of expertise (or, put another way, a decrease in the separation between manual and mental work). The rapid increase in primary schooling and adult education, together with the slowed higher education enrollment growth increases the relative social wage of peasants and workers. Except for China in the last six years and for Nicaragua to the extent that capital spending on higher education has raised the portion of the public budget allocated to that level, the countries we studied did increase their investment in lower levels of education relative to higher levels until these lower levels became almost universal. Similarly, these countries invested heavily in equalizing access to schooling for males and females. Gender equalization has clearly gone farther than in comparable conditioned societies.

The fourth achievement—developed in large part through the expansion of the educational system—is the increased capacity for self-government. Particularly through the literacy campaigns and the development of popular (adult) education and rural primary education, the transition state in each of these countries developed (and, with the exception of Tanzania, continues to develop) the mass organizations that are the key to these operations. At the same time, the literacy campaigns and the expansion of adult education produced embryonic local leadership in the form of newly literate teachers and rural cadres. The war against counterrevolutionary forces in Cuba, Mozambique, and Nicaragua also has spawned new leadership, which plays a role at the local level. All in all, the process is precisely the opposite of that which prevailed in the previously conditioned state, where old alliances, family ties, and material wealth were determining factors in local power (and hence access to the central administration). In the transition, participation and performance in mass organizations, dedication to the politics of social transformation, and a certain amount of competence allow new leaders to develop from even the poorest, least empowered groups in society. Structures are in flux; organizations are in motion; the threats are concrete and need immediate responses.

What education has not been able to achieve in the cases we analyzed is to create a totally different consciousness—a "new person," collectively oriented, putting social goals ahead of personal ambition, rejecting materialism, and developing new concepts of gender relations. In large part, this follows directly from the failure of the vanguard party's cadres to provide role models for this new person and of the vanguard party's decisionmaking structure and gender composition to lead in providing the context in which such consciousness can develop. Ascending the ladder of political power in these societies (as in capitalist societies) requires individual ambition and fierce competition. Party hierarchies are male dominated and party policies have (except in Cuba and in earlier phases of the Chinese revolution) had little to say about the need to alter family relations and have in general failed to translate their progressive rhetoric into concrete efforts to transform the status of women. Even in the goals and structure of the educational system itself, the criterion of individual academic excellence as a necessary (if not always sufficient) condition for access to higher levels of schooling is contradictory to the development of a collective and egalitarian consciousness. And, other than in the context of family planning, gender relations outside the workplace have received scant attention in efforts to theorize the transition and in the school-based socialization process.

Here, again, we find that the concern with economic growth often overwhelms other goals. The focus on modernization in periods of technocratic reform breeds inattention to the significant role(s) of culture and ideology (other than in the narrow sense of expecting schools to inculcate official values) in organizing and governing the transition state. Even the Mozambican leadership's clarity on the importance of integrating the different dimensions of the transition and on considering culture a source of strength rather than an obstacle to change seems to have succumbed to the imperatives of modernization: Access to education was reduced in order to address schooling's perceived decline in quality.

China during the Cultural Revolution and Cuba in the 1960s put greater emphasis on political behavior than on academic and practical skills in developing its cadres, contending that socialist consciousness had to precede economic development. Yet later both countries' party hierarchies rejected this policy (the Chinese through a power struggle within the hierarchy won by the more technocratic, modernizing faction; the Cubans through a gradual shift in policy, apparently influenced by the Soviets) and opted for economic growth through more traditional skill formation and academic selection. Cuba still stresses collective competition in school and at work, but now provides individual incentives, uses pricing mechanisms for exchange between productive units, and has somewhat deemphasized the physical work aspect of schooling. The Cubans and the Chinese have acknowledged the importance to their citizens of material consumption—the Cubans by offering imported Japanese color television sets and other appliances at high prices (Cubans had accumulated large savings because of relatively high salaries combined with a lack of available consumer goods) and, in the early 1980s, by relaxing a prohibition on private markets and private artisan services. The Chinese now permit private family production and commerce. Tanzania's insistence that villages be organized around cooperative production and that leaders live austere lives has also been relaxed. In most villages, farmers

maintain family plots. Though still enjoined from the extremes of con-
spicuous consumption common elsewhere in Africa, leaders can now legitimately expand and employ labor on their farms, operate private businesses, and acquire expensive consumer goods. The trajectory, however,
is not unilinear. In 1986 Castro overturned his earlier decision on private
markets in the wake of "corruption" and a recent recession and harked
back to the "socialist morality" and collective ideals of the 1960s.

But even in failing to develop the completely new person, these countries have been able to achieve some change of consciousness—a *different* person—and they have been highly creative in using popular (nonformal, participative) socially based education to reach this goal. The
literacy campaign has been one form of this kind of education. Rural,
somewhat participative adult primary education has been another form.
In both, volunteer or low-wage, highly politically motivated student-
teachers have formed the basis of the effort. And the effort has been
couched in the context of building new concepts of the individual, of the
nation and the meaning of membership in the nation-state, of law (the
reconstitution of the state on other than its relationship to property owners), and of knowledge. The very basis of education in all these countries
is that all individuals have the right to a basic education and have the
capacity to learn the fundamental elements of reading, writing, and
mathematics.

In addition, formal and nonformal (popular) education in these societies stresses social commitment (to the nation, to the revolution, to the
community) through social service (military, community, neighborhood)
and work. Several educational systems have been designed around the
combination of academic and physical, productive work. All have
stressed vocational training over solely academic pursuits—the higher
the educational level, the more that academic work is joined to the practice of a profession in an actual workplace. The exceptions to this are
Tanzania and, to some extent, Nicaragua. Although all educational institutions in Tanzania operate productive projects, usually farms, on which
students provide the labor and, to some extent, the management, the
selectivity of postprimary education and the significantly higher remuneration its graduates receive combine with its European heritage and its
external orientation to preserve its elitist character. In Nicaragua, the
existence of a significant number of private schools makes the implementation of work-linked academic secondary training more difficult. At the
university level, however, Nicaraguan university students do begin working by the third year as part of their studies (Arnove 1986, 123–24).

The Cubans have been the most systematic in attempting to combine
study and work, mental and manual activities, the moral and the cognitive. Both the primary school gardens and the secondary schools in the

countryside make organized, collective work an integral component of the educational experience. For entering the best schools and for advancing from secondary school to the university, attitudes and leadership displayed by students in work are important over and above their academic work. There has been a gradual shift in Cuba away from the earlier goal of an agricultural and rural experience for all urban secondary school students. Nevertheless, a significant fraction of urban students do continue to take their secondary education in the countryside, working twenty hours a week in the fields as part of a student brigade.

TENSIONS AND TENDENCIES

The expansion of education and its reform, particularly in the context of creating a new society, are set in the context of a development process characterized by considerable conflicts and contradictions. These translate into significant tensions over educational policy. We have discussed these in some detail earlier, but it is worth reviewing them again here as we explore these societies' future direction.

In transforming itself through the revolutionary transition, the transition state has three principal purposes: (1) to change the social relations that underlie economic and political interaction, stressing collective rather than individual gain and a definition of the nation-state as one that takes collective responsibility for the welfare of all individuals rather than one that represents the collective self-interest of groups of powerful individuals; (2) to increase the material productive capacity of the collective nation-state and the material consumption of its individual members; and (3) to distribute material consumption in a manner that is related as much to need as to individual capability.

Our studies suggest that the path to achieving these goals has not been easy or obvious. In each country various alternatives have been tried. Conflicts occur in the state over the proper or best alternative to pursue. The conflicts derive from different interpretations of the relation between collective social relations (in the broadest sense) and increases in material production and consumption, and of the relation between the leadership of the transition (including the state bureaucracy) and the civil society.

The long-standing (and Soviet) understanding of these relationships regards the development of material production and consumption as a precondition of developing collective social and political consciousness. The development of material production requires, in turn, the development of a skilled labor force, considerable political control and worker discipline, and centralized decisionmaking in the hands of politically proven experts. In return for being subjected to social discipline and control from above, the citizen-worker-peasant receives from the state guaranteed material support (the right to work for a living wage, housing, education, health care, social security) to the extent that the economy can provide it.

Yet this understanding has been contested in every transition society, including the Soviet Union and the five Third World cases we have examined here. Early on, both the Chinese and Cubans attempted strategies that were intended to build collective consciousness in the masses as the basis for increasing material productive capacity and consumption. The strategy was not particularly successful in raising productivity and economic growth, but it appears to have gone far in creating collective identification with the new, revolutionary nation-state even among the previously most marginalized groups. For the Cuban leadership, especially Fidel Castro himself, the concept of developing new social relations continues to be an important goal, despite its shift to the more traditional Soviet model in the early 1970s.

The strategy of centralizing power, decisionmaking, and expertise and *limiting* the development of civil society has also been contested by dissident groups. Part of the conflict is centered on opposition to social transformation. But even in the context of a transformation which separates economic from political power, there are alternative interpretations of what the relation between the state and civil society should be. One of these interpretations focuses on the role of markets and the introduction of foreign investment and technology. It is increasingly understood in transition societies that where politics and the state are the source of the social dynamic, markets (economic arrangements in civil society that function autonomously from state decisionmaking) might increase productivity without necessarily changing social relations. A second interpretation challenges the decisionmaking monopoly of the state administration and attempts to democratize politics, including the decisionmaking in economic units controlled by the state. The Czech spring of 1968, *Solidarity* in Poland and its success in the 1989 elections there, the current Gorbachev political reforms in the Soviet Union, and the elections and attempts to revitalize the mass organizations in Nicaragua, are all versions of this challenge to a state which limits the political development of civil society.

Such conflicts make clear the underlying contradictions of development at the periphery of a world capitalist system and of organizing the transition. First, these economies' limited material capacity requires that the transition state place primary emphasis on material development. This necessity is usually accentuated by external military actions (or, in Eastern Europe, the threat of military actions) opposed to the social transformation that is at the heart of the transition. The commitment to material development, especially in the short term, strengthens the hand of those in the revolutionary leadership who want to centralize political control and direct economic growth through expertise, whether in the central administration or in a combination of central administration with more decentralized factory and party economic management. In either case, the decisionmaking process becomes extremely hierarchical. Such hierarchy, particularly when combined with guaranteed employment and the low availability of consumer goods (because of an emphasis on the production of exports and capital goods), undermines workers' motivation to increase productivity, consequently limiting increases in output per worker and economic growth.

Second, tendencies toward bureaucracy, hierarchy, and *dirigisme* gradually reduce the capability of the state to mobilize citizens to innovate and reenergize society. The reduction of commitment and activism tends to produce a new individualism, where workers draw guaranteed material and social benefits from the collective but channel their creative energy into defending themselves against the collective or into defining an individual space for overcoming collective inefficiency. This separation of the creative, active individual from the collective deadens collective action and makes social renovation difficult.[1]

---

[1] Such contradictions differ from those that emerge in capitalist development. In capitalism, the locus of the social dynamic is in the private economy, and capital accumulation and economic growth are inherent objectives of capitalist development. Because of capitalism's ability to discipline and reward individualized labor, increasing productivity and entrepreneurial effort has not been a fundamental problem of capitalist development. Although collective identity and nationalism have occasionally played a role in motivating workers to work harder in capitalist societies (during wars, for example), it is the fear of unemployment and the competition for readily available material consumption that drives workers to produce more. For businesspeople, there is also a direct link between material success and political power. The contradiction emerges from the unequal distribution of the fruits of increased productivity and the decisionmaking process concentrated in private capital, which determines the conditions under which increased productivity occurs, who gets to participate in it, and how.

This is not wholly different from the contradiction that emerges in transition development, to the extent that productivity increases are affected in both cases. But in capitalism, the contradiction arises because the process of capitalist production is necessarily highly unequal, both economically and politically; in the transition, the contradiction arises when the political process is hierarchical and undemocratic. It is this political process that reaches down to reduce the effectiveness of socialized production.

Where capitalism has been associated with a democratic state, it is the state that democratizes capitalism by acting as an arbiter (a procapital arbiter, but an arbiter nonetheless) between the demands of social movements (including, but not limited to, labor) and the requirements of capital to accumulate. Again, there is a similarity between the contradictions that arise in the transition and in capitalism: The successful capitalist or transition state can create for individuals a sense of membership in the collective people-nation by allowing them the power of political participation and political sanctions. The state must then control the range of those sanctions within allowable limits. The unsuccessful state creates difficulties that may jeopardize economic and social stability and its own reproduction. But even

Conflicts over educational policy reflect these larger conflicts and contradictions. We have argued that the commitment to increase material
productive capacity and worker productivity requires both the development of human capital and investment in physical infrastructure. All the
countries we studied insisted on spending heavily on education and training despite the competition from other projects (including military defense) for physical and human resources. This suggests an overall faith in
the long-run role of increased worker skills in economic development and
an ideological bias toward relying on enhanced labor skills relative to improved capital as the basis for that development.

But there are conflicts within this pattern of educational expansion. A
strategy which emphasizes material growth will tend to reduce the rate
of educational expansion, particularly at lower levels (including adult education) and focus more on directly productive investment. Except for
Cuba, which has been able to count on regular, substantial assistance
from the Soviet Union (in the form of guaranteed sugar prices and low-
cost crude oil refined and sold by Cuba), each of the countries has slowed
educational expansion once the initial literacy campaigns and political
mobilizations were successfully completed.[2] Direct, productive investments appear to take precedence in the second period. In Nicaragua and
Mozambique, it is more difficult to identify lower educational spending
increases with increased emphasis on raising material consumption since
sabotage and the destruction of guerrilla war have lowered economic
growth and played a crucial role in reducing the resources available for
education, since an increased fraction of the public budget goes to defense.

Strategies that emphasize economic growth over the development of
new social relations (including more equal distribution of goods and services) will also tend to spend relatively more on university education and
less on raising everyone—both children and adults—to high levels of basic education. The underlying argument is that without highly trained
cadres, economic efficiency is impossible to achieve. In each of the countries studied, the leadership appears to have made conscious decisions
(in the case of China, a series of decisions) about university expansion

in politically democratic and relatively successful capitalist societies, the underlying contradiction between the inherently private, individual control of the dynamic of capital accumulation and the needs and aspirations of those who work and vote remains. In the transition, even if the state is successful in raising material consumption, an underlying
contradiction exists between power concentrated in the state and the needs and aspirations
of those who produce.

    [2] Tanzania's enrollment expanded most rapidly in the 1970s, a decade after indepen-
dence. However, the articulation of the content and direction of Tanzanian socialism was
formalized only in 1967, precisely the era of the commitment to the literacy campaign and
educational expansion for political mobilization.

precisely in these terms, and the decision reflects considerable tension between different social strategies.

Notwithstanding the enormous need for highly trained cadres, university expansion was generally limited almost immediately after the triumph of each revolution. This supports the view that the extension of the revolution and the creation of new social relations through mobilization of the population is the overriding strategic objective in this initial period. In Cuba, the initial period was rather long—ten years. In China, university expansion was controlled until the 1960s, and then eliminated during the Cultural Revolution; it was not until the end of the 1970s that university education was expanded rapidly as part of a drastic shift to increasing material productive capacity. In Mozambique, university training had already been expanded in the mid-1970s to replace the Portuguese cadres whose departure left the country with little managerial expertise. Similarly in Tanzania, the university was allocated considerable resources (with the help of foreign assistance) to develop high-level cadres, even while secondary education was severely restricted. In Nicaragua, restrictions on university expansion were compromised even in the initial period because of the pluralist political model followed by the Sandinista revolution and the resulting importance of middle-class support—from a middle class that demanded expanded university access. Subsequently, however, spending on university-level education was sharply curtailed.

The second tension we observe in education is also the result of the larger conflict over the primary objectives of transition development, or at least the order in which those objectives are to be realized. In the countries we studied, we observe a historic conflict between education for greater political participation and social consciousness on one hand and a formal academic and technical education on the other. Their goals differ sharply. Participatory, liberating education seeks to increase equality in the access to knowledge (indeed, redefining the meaning of knowledge itself) and to continue to transform society, including developing higher levels of productive capacity and material consumption through greater participation. Academic education seeks to increase skills in order to raise the standard of material consumption and to do so by relying on hierarchically organized expertise, on the assumption that social consciousness and participation in decisionmaking and in the definition of knowledge are possible only after high levels of traditional education and material consumption have been achieved.

In none of the societies we studied has the content of formal education been changed significantly to reflect a participative ideal or a participative redefinition of knowledge that allows this ideal to be reflected in the learning process (although apparently there has been an effort in Nicaragua to undertake such a reform in the past two years). Formal schooling in all of these countries still selects children for higher levels on the basis of traditional criteria, and years of schooling are still an important determinant of status, probably of consumption (but less so), and perhaps of political power (but other important factors are involved here). There have been exceptions to this pattern. For example, in China during the Cultural Revolution, being highly educated increased the likelihood of being sent to a reeducation camp. There have been periods in all five countries when education counted for less than did revolutionary commitment and organizational competence. These periods have reflected a dominant strategy of emphasizing equality and social consciousness (creating the new person) as a precondition for economic development. Similarly, educational policy in these periods has been concerned with inclusiveness (reaching out to the illiterates, the rural poor, and adults with little schooling) and, simultaneously, has focused on education through mobilization (bringing the schooled together with the unschooled, the urban with the rural, youth with adults, students with teachers), requiring the full commitment of the society to revolutionary ideals.

In those periods when the focus changes from mass mobilization to technical competence, the vanguard or mass party's dominant strategy has shifted to achieving economic growth in a more traditional fashion, placing much more responsibility on hierarchy and hierarchical definitions of knowledge. It is striking that in both Cuba and China the reduced emphasis on popular participation in the production of knowledge was accompanied by decentralization of economic (technical) decisionmaking. The two moves are both associated with economic efficiency. But, as we suggested in our introduction to the case studies, they are also associated with a concentration of expertise and a distancing of the experts from the ideal of changing social relations.

Our studies raise serious questions, however, about whether competent, technocratically oriented bureaucrats can produce economic growth in these societies without a highly mobilized population that has already learned basic skills and that is committed to increasing output. And mobilization probably requires high levels of political participation, that is, a state that places much of the burden of decisionmaking on locally based organizations. Yet it is also evident that political commitment without competent planning, organization, and management has not worked. The argument that education must develop technical skills and focus on quality (high academic performance in traditional terms) is also valid. Nevertheless, the move to a high-quality technical orientation is not always possible for the educational authorities even when they feel that this is what is needed for economic growth. Often, they lack resources to develop this technical education. And the expansion of alternative, participative education is not always possible either, because of other constraints, including guerrilla activities that make rural popular education centers and teachers the targets of their destruction (as in Mozambique and Nicaragua) and young people and their families who view traditional education as the means to better jobs. This preference for academic schooling is part of a circle that is difficult to break. Reacting to continued differences in social status and material consumption that are associated with different amounts of traditional formal schooling, students and their parents seek just that sort of education.

What Tendencies for Education in the Transition?

Education is used in the transition to redefine and equalize access to knowledge as the basis for a new type of participative development. It is also used to improve academic and technical skills for a more rational, systematic economic growth. The tension between these two types of education is at the heart of the development problem itself. Knowledge for what purpose? is not just an idealistic or rhetorical question, even in these low-income societies. Yet, although this question has certainly been raised in practice through literacy campaigns, mass mobilizations, adult education, student work brigades, and participation in mass organizations, the tendency has been to focus increasingly on traditional performance-based learning, vocational, skill-based training, and the bureaucratization of the educational system and educational decisionmaking.

This tendency is, we argue, in part the result of practical, short-run necessity. These are low-income societies in which the population needs, first and foremost, to be fed, clothed, and housed. The newly defined revolutionary nation-state must protect itself against externally financed counterrevolutionary guerrillas. Technical and managerial skills are crucial to meeting these needs. But so are political participation, responsive political organizations, and the motivation that comes from a highly mobilized, politically dedicated society.

Why, then, the tendency to technical, performance-based learning and hierarchical education? First, the societies we studied are all heavily influenced by a dominant ideology that regards academic and technical knowledge (expertise) as the principal basis of economic growth and economic growth as the key to social development. This is not just the influence of the Soviet concept of polytechnic education, but also an ideology imported from advanced capitalist countries, particularly the United States, where the highest-status knowledge is scientific, managerial, and functional. Second, in these societies, the concentration of political power in the hierarchy of the vanguard or mass party creates an inherent bias in what knowledge is valued and how knowledge is defined. This bias has tended to push education toward formalization, hierarchization, and technicalization, that is, toward narrowly specified expertise, especially once the initial mobilizational period is over.

However, there are important exceptions to this tendency, indicating that groups exist in the party hierarchy who are more willing to respond to pressure from the population for greater political participation and decentralization of economic and political decisionmaking. The Chinese study shows, for example, that three different models of decisionmaking have been in competition since the early days of the revolution: Maoist, Stalinist, and Titoist, each with a different degree of decentralization. And each has been the dominant model in some period of China's postrevolutionary history. In this most recent phase, it is the Titoist version of increasingly decentralized economic decisionmaking that serves as the basis for transition development. Cuba has also fostered increased political participation at the local level (*poder popular*) and decentralized economic decisions to the factory level, but it has simultaneously centralized overall economic planning. Mozambique, under pressure from a disintegrating economic and military situation, vacillates between the technocratic tendency and a more mobilizational model. Nicaragua's pluralistic system is tending toward technocracy, but in the context of a mixed economy. Were the guerrilla threat to end, it is unclear in what direction the political system would move.

In terms of what the members of revolutionary societies need and want, the emphasis placed by the transition state on economic growth and on the development of technical skills is not necessarily incorrect. Developing the forces of production and accumulating capital is particularly important in such societies because it is the mass of peasants and workers who are the political base of the transition state. The state is committed to increasing their standard of living rather than that of relatively small upper and middle classes. Economic stagnation necessarily cuts into the political base, undermining the leadership's legitimacy. Positive growth has to be relatively large and sustained to alleviate the lack of proper nutrition, poor housing, and low level of health care and education in the rural and marginal urban areas.

Furthermore, technical and managerial skills associated with advanced capitalist society are especially necessary in those small countries we have studied, which must trade to survive. Cuba, Nicaragua, Mozambique, and Tanzania cannot pursue autarkic development. Rather, they must diversify trade, produce new products that can compete in world markets, and continue to import technology and capital goods for their agricultural and limited industrial sectors. For China, the options are much more varied. Although China is now in the throes of developing industries that will ultimately export, it could continue to develop in significant isolation from the world economic system.

There is a logic to technically specialized knowledge and even hierarchical education. But it is not evident from our studies (or any others) that economic growth follows from an emphasis on such knowledge and education. And there are serious questions as to whether economic growth and increased material consumption, were they to result from such education and the bureaucratic political structures that promote them, would satisfy all the basic needs of people in these societies.

Economic growth in transition societies results not just from increasing skills, but also from the commitment of their members to work hard and be socially responsible. Since individual material incentives are reduced because of smaller differences in material consumption and status associated with different positions in the labor force, social commitment is an even more significant factor in an individual's productivity in these societies. Identification with the state's social and political project is the basis of this commitment. Some people, of course, make that commitment to gain individual power and status in the political hierarchy. But this route is open to only a relatively few even in a highly democratic society. Mass political identification with the nation-state therefore must come from the political process that achieves increased material consumption. Whereas hierarchical, expertise-based economic growth in transition societies may be possible in the short and medium term, the monopolization of political power and absence of mass-based political participation inherent in such an arrangement distances the state from the mass of the peasants and workers whose labor must produce the growth. The members of the expert hierarchy become a new class, defining knowledge in their own terms, reproducing themselves by securing for their children advantaged access to elite schools, and—unable to produce consensus for their policies—tending to repress dissent and reduce the autonomy of mass organizations. Not only does economic growth suffer in this scenario, reducing the population's material consumption, but other important social needs related to control over individual and collective destiny are neglected.

The development of a participative, popular educational system in transition societies ultimately depends on the development of a participative state. We have argued that in the transition, politics is in command. For the state to mobilize, it must diffuse political power. In all the societies we studied, mass organizations served this function in the early revolutionary years. To continue to mobilize the population, democratic institutions with real decisionmaking power will have to continue to serve as important elements of the organized state. To the degree that this occurs, the educational system will focus as much on participative, inclusive definitions of knowledge (discourse and process) as on its technical, hierarchical dimensions. The state, not education per se, is the key issue here. We cannot separate how education develops in the transition—or even what education is—from the nature of the transition state.

At the same time, education serves as a primary terrain of conflict over the form of the state. Precisely because the nature of the state determines the character of education, the schools become sites for conflicts about the character of and control over the state. It is no accident that in all these countries "red" versus "expert," the "new person," popular education, the "quality" of education, literacy campaigns, and the role of universities are fundamental political issues. They reflect the much larger conflict over the way politics will be defined.

Selected Bibliography

Adams, J. 1982. "The Contribution of Education for Self-Reliance to Manpower Development in Tanzania—A Critical Appraisal," *Journal of International Educational Research*.

Adamson, Walter. 1980. *Hegemony and Revolution: A Study of Antonio Gramsci's Political and Cultural Theory*. Berkeley: University of California Press.

Adelman, Irma, and S. Robinson. 1978. *Income Distribution in Developing Countries*. Stanford, Cal.: Stanford University Press.

AIM: Mozambique News. Monthly Mozambican Information Bulletin. Maputo: Agencia Informativa de Mocambique.

Ake, Claude. 1976. "The Congruence of Political Economies and Ideologies in Africa," in Peter C. W. Gutkind and Immanuel Wallerstein, eds., *The Political Economy of Contemporary Africa*. Beverly Hills: Sage.

————. 1984. "Ideology and Objective Conditions," in Barkan 1984, 127–39.

Allen, Garland. 1974. "Education in Revolutionary Cuba," *The Education Digest* 40 (October): 51–54.

Almond, Gabriel, and Sidney Verba. 1963. *The Civic Culture*. Princeton: Princeton University Press.

Althusser, Louis. 1971. *Lenin and Philosophy and Other Essays*. New York: Monthly Review Press.

Amin, Samir. 1970. *L'Accumulation à l'Échelle Mondiale: Critique de la Théorie du Sous-Développement*. Paris: Editions Anthropos.

————. 1980. *Class and Nation*. New York: Monthly Review Press.

————. 1981. *The Future of Maoism*. New York: Monthly Review Press.

————. 1983. "A. G. Frank and the Crisis," *Monthly Review* 35, (6)(November): 52–58.

Amnesty International. 1984. *China: Violations of Human Rights Report*. London: Amnesty International Publications.

Anderson, Perry. 1979. *Lineages of the Absolutist State*. London: New Left Books, Verso edition.

Angel, Andriana, and Fiona Macintosh. 1987. *The Tiger's Milk: Women of Nicaragua*. New York: Seaver Books.

Annual Joint Review of the Swedish Support to Education and Vocational Training 1983. 1983. Stockholm and Dar es Salaam: Swedish International Development Authority and Tanzania Ministry of Education.

Anyon, Jean. 1983. *Social Class and Gender in U.S. Education*. London: Routledge & Kegan Paul.

Apple, Michael W. 1978. "The New Sociology of Education: Analyzing Cultural and Economic Reproduction," *Harvard Education Review* 58(4) (November): 459–503.

————. 1982a. *Cultural and Economic Reproduction in Education: Essays on Class, Ideology and the State*. London: Routledge & Kegan Paul.

Apple, Michael W. 1982b. *Power and Ideology*. London: Routledge & Kegan Paul.

——. 1982c. "Reproduction and Contradiction in Education: An Introduction," in Apple 1982a, 1–31.

Arnove, Robert. 1971. *Student Alienation: A Venezuelan Study*. New York: Praeger.

——. 1981. "The Nicaraguan National Literacy Crusade of 1980," *Comparative Education Review* 25(2) (June): 244–60.

——. 1986. *Education and Revolution in Nicaragua*. New York: Praeger.

——. 1988a. "The Impact of War on Educational Policy and Practice in Nicaragua." Bloomington: Indiana University, School of Education. Unpublished (May).

——. 1988b. "Education and Revolutionary Transformation in Nicaragua." Bloomington: Indiana University, School of Education. Unpublished (October).

Arrien, I., et al. 1977. *Educación y Dependencia*. Managua: Instituto de Promocion Humana.

Assembleia Popular. 1980a. *Decreto-Lei 4/80*. Maputo: Boletim da Republica.

——. 1980b. *Resolucao sobre a Ofensiva Politica e Organizacional*. Maputo: Instituto do Livroe Disco (INLD).

Avirgan, Tony, and Martha Honey. 1983. *War in Uganda: The Legacy of Idi Amin*. London: Zed Press.

Bachrach, Peter, and Morton S. Baratz. 1962. "Two Faces of Power," *American Political Science Review* 56(4) (December): 947–52.

——. 1963. "Decisions and Nondecisions: An Analytical Framework," *American Political Science Review* 57(3) (September): 632–42.

——. 1970. *Power and Poverty: Theory and Practice*. New York: Oxford University Press.

Balazs, Etienne. 1964. *Chinese Civilization and Bureaucracy: Variations on A Theme*. New Haven: Yale University Press.

Baran, Paul A. 1957. *The Political Economy of Growth*. New York: Monthly Review Press.

Barkan, Joel D. 1971. "African University Students: Presumptive Elite or Upper-Middle Class?" in Kenneth Prewitt, ed., *Education and Political Values: An East African Case Study*. Nairobi: East African Publishing House.

——, ed. 1984. *Politics and Public Policy in Kenya and Tanzania*. Rev. ed. New York: Praeger.

Barkin, David. 1973. "Cuban Agriculture: A Strategy of Economic Development," in Barkin and Manitzas 1973.

Barkin, David, and Nita Manitzas, editors. 1973. *Cuba: The Logic of Revolution*. Andover, Mass.: Warner Modular Publications.

Bastid, Marianne. 1984. "Chinese Educational Policies in the 1980's and Economic Development," *The China Quarterly* 98: 189–219.

Baume, Carol. 1983. "Self-Reliance Activities in Tanzanian Schools." Unpublished. Stanford: Stanford University, School of Education.

Baumeister, Eduardo. 1985. "The Structure of Nicaraguan Agriculture and the Sandinista Agrarian Reform," in Harris and Vilas 1985.

Baumeister, Eduardo, and Oscar Neira Cuadra. 1986. "The Making of the Mixed Economy: Class Struggle and State Policy in the Nicaragua Transition," in Fagen et al. 1986.

Becker, Gary S. 1962. "Investment in Human Capital: A Theoretical Analysis," *Journal of Political Economy* (Supplement) 52 (October): 9–50.

———. 1964. *Human Capital*. New York: Columbia University Press.

Bender, Lynn Darrell. 1975. *In the Politics of Hostility: Castro's Revolution and United States Policy*. Hato Rey, Puerto Rico: Inter-American University Press.

Bernardo, Robert. 1971. *The Theory of Moral Incentives in Cuba*. University, Ala.: The University of Alabama Press.

"Beyond Unions." 1985. *Business Week*, July 8, 72–77.

Bienefeld, Manfred. 1982. "Tanzania: Model or Anti-Model?" in Manfred Bienefeld and Martin Godfrey, eds., *The Struggle for Development: National Strategies in an International Context*, 293–322. New York: Wiley.

Black, George. 1988. "Cuba: The Revolution Toward Victory Always, But When?" *The Nation*, October 24, 373–86.

Blakemore, Kenneth, and Brian Cooksey. 1981. *A Sociology of Education for Africa*. London: Allen & Unwin.

Blaug, Mark. 1970. *Introduction to the Economics of Education*. London: Penguin Press.

Bobbio, Norberto. 1977. "Existe una Doctrina Marxista del Estado?" in *El Marxismo y el Estado*. Barcelona: Editorial Avance.

Bodde, Derk, and Clarence Morris. 1967. *Law in Imperial China*. Cambridge, Mass.: Harvard University Press.

Boorstein, Edward. 1968. *The Economic Transformation of Cuba*. New York: Monthly Review Press.

Borge, T. 1984. "Revolucion y Religion: Frente a la Teologia de la Muerte, la Teologia de la Resurreccion," in De Lella, C., ed., *Cristianismo y Liberacion en America Latina*, 137–49. Mexico: Nuevomar.

Borghi, Lamberto. 1958. *Educazione e scuola nell'Italia d'oggi*. Florence: La Nuova Italia.

———. 1974. *Perspectives in Primary Education*. The Hague: Nijhoff.

Borthwick, Sally. 1983. *Education and Social Change in China*. Stanford, Cal.: Stanford University Press.

Bourdieu, Pierre, and Jean-Claude Passeron. 1977. *Reproduction in Education, Society and Culture*. Beverly Hills: Sage Publications.

Bowles, Samuel. 1972. "Education and Socialist Man in Cuba," in Martin Carnoy, ed., *Schooling in a Corporate Society*. New York: David McKay.

Bowles, Samuel, and Herbert Gintis. 1976. *Schooling in Capitalist America*. New York: Basic Books.

———. 1982. "The Crisis of Liberal Democratic Capitalism: The Case of the United States," *Politics and Society* 11(1): 51–93.

———. 1986. *Capitalism and Democracy*. New York: Basic Books.

Branch, Taylor, and George Crile III. 1975. "The Kennedy Vendetta," *Harper's Magazine*, August, 49–63.

Braudel, Fernand. 1982. *The Wheels of Commerce*. New York: Harper and Row.

Broccoli, Angelo. 1977. *Antonio Gramsci y la Educación Como Hegemonia*. Mexico: Editorial Nueva Imagen.

Brundenius, Claes. 1984. *Revolutionary Cuba: The Challenge of Economic Growth with Equity*. Boulder, Colo.: Westview Press.

Buci-Glucksmann, Christine. 1980. *Gramsci and the State*. London: Lawrence and Wishart.

Buci-Glucksmann, Christine, and Goran Therborn. 1981. *Le defi social democrate*. Paris: Maspero.

Capela, Jose. 1974. *Mocambique pelo seu Povo*. Porto, Portugal: Martins Editora.

Cardoso, Fernando Henrique, and Enzo Faletto. 1979. *Dependency and Development in Latin America*. Berkeley: University of California Press.

Carnoy, Martin. 1974. *Education as Cultural Imperialism*. New York: David McKay.

———. 1977. *Education and Employment*. Paris: International Institute of Educational Planning.

———. 1984. *The State and Political Theory*. Princeton: Princeton University Press.

———. 1986. "Educational Reform and Planning in the Current Economic Crisis," *Prospects* 16(2): 205–14.

Carnoy, Martin, in collaboration with Jose Lobo, Alejandro Toledo, and Jacques Velloso. 1979. *Can Educational Policy Equalize Income Distribution in Latin America?* Westmead, England: Saxon House, for the International Labour Office.

Carnoy, Martin, and Henry M. Levin. 1976. *The Limits of Educational Reform* (New York: David McKay).

———. 1977. *Estudio de la Educación Secundaria y Superior en el Salvador, las Tendencias en los Requerimientos de Mano de Obra con Educación Secundaria y Superior, y las Implicaciones para la Politica de Educredito*. Palo Alto, Cal.: Center for Economic Studies.

———. 1985. *Schooling and Work in the Democratic State*. Stanford, Cal.: Stanford University Press.

Carnoy, Martin, Henry M. Levin, Reginald Nugent, Suleman Sumra, Carlos Torres, and Jeff Unsicker. 1982. *The Political Economy of Financing Education in Developing Countries*. Ottawa: International Development Research Center.

Carnoy, Martin, Richard Sack, and Hans Thias. 1978. *The Payoff to "Better" Schooling: A Case Study in Tunisian Secondary Schools*. Washington, D.C.: World Bank. Mimeographed.

Carnoy, Martin, and Derek Shearer. 1980. *Economic Democracy*. Armonk, N.Y.: M.E. Sharpe.

Carnoy, Martin, and Jorge Werthein. 1977. "Socialist Ideology and the Transformation of Cuban Education," in A. H. Halsey and J. Karabel, eds., *Power and Ideology in Education*. London: Oxford University Press.

———. 1980. *Cuba: Cambio Economico y Reforma Educativa (1955–1978)*. Mexico City: Nueva Imagen.

Carr-Hill, Roy A. 1984. *Primary Education in Tanzania: A Review of the Re-*

search. Stockholm: Swedish International Development Authority, Education Division Documents No. 16.

Carter, Michael. 1976. "Correspondence and Contradiction," in Carnoy and Levin 1976.

Castro, Fidel. 1974. *La Educación en Revolución.* Havana: Instituto Cubano del Libro. Speeches of Fidel Castro related to education.

———. 1976. *La Experiencia Cubana.* Barcelona: Editorial Blume. Fidel Castro's speech to the First Congress of the Partido Comunista Cubano.

Centro de Estudos Africanos (CEA). 1984. *A Formação do Professor Primarioe sua Actuação no Meio Social.* Maputo: University Eduardo Mondlane.

Chama Cha Mapinduzi (CCM). 1981. *Mwongozo wa Chama cha Mapinduzi.* Dar es Salaam: Printpak Tanzania.

Chauncey, Helen R. 1982. "Education and Social Mobilization: Tradition and Radical Transformation in Central China." Ph.D. diss., Stanford University.

Chesneaux, Jean. 1979. *China: The People's Republic, 1949–1976.* New York: Pantheon Books.

Chidzero, B.T.G. 1961. *Tanganyika and International Trusteeship.* London: Oxford University Press.

Cliffe, Lionel. 1978. "A Non-Revolutionary Transition to Socialism?" in Palmberg 1978, 38–43.

CNES (Consejo Nacional de la Educación Superior). 1984. *Programa 1984.* Managua: CNES.

Collins, C. 1977. "Mozambique: Education for the People," *Southern Africa* (June/July): 21–23.

Comissao Nacional do Plano (CNP). 1982. *1- Recenseamento Geral da População: Informação Pública.* Maputo: Comissao Nacional do Plano.

———. 1984. *Economic Report.* Maputo: Comissao Nacional do Plano.

———. 1985. *Informação Estatística, 1975–1984.* Maputo: Comissao Nacional do Plano.

———. 1986. *Informação Estatística, 1985.* Maputo: Comissao Nacional do Plano.

"Conscripts Come Home, Well-Drilled Sandinistas." 1986. *New York Times,* September 12, 8.

Cooksey, Brian, and Abel Ishumi. 1986. "A Critical Review of Policy and Practice in Tanzanian Secondary Education Since 1967." Dar es Salaam. Unpublished.

Coombs, Philip. 1985. *The World Crisis in Education: the View from the Eighties.* New York: Oxford University Press.

Coraggio, Jose Luis. 1986. "Economics and Politics in the Transition to Socialism: Reflections on the Nicaraguan Experience," in Fagen et al. 1986.

Coulson, Andrew, ed. 1979. *African Socialism in Practice.* London: Spokesman.

———. 1982. *Tanzania: A Political Economy.* Oxford: Clarendon Press.

Court, David, and Kabiru Kinyanjui. 1980. "Development Policy and Educational Opportunity: The Experience of Kenya and Tanzania," in Gabriel Carron and Ta Ngoc Chau, eds., *Regional Disparities in Educational Development.* Paris: UNESCO/IIEP.

Croll, Elisabeth. 1979. *Women in Rural Development: The People's Republic of China*. Geneva: International Labor Office.

Cuba, Ministerio de Educacion. 1979. *La Educación en Cuba*. Havana: Ministerio de Educación.

Cunha, Luis Antonio. 1975. *Educação e Desenvolvimento Social no Brasil*. Rio de Janeiro: Francisco Alves Editora.

Cutting, Hunter. 1986. "The Countryside: Burnt Fields and Sowing Hope," *Central American Bulletin* 6 (December): 30–35.

Dahlman, Carl J. 1973. The Nationwide Learning System of Cuba. Princeton: Princeton University, Woodrow Wilson School. Unpublished (July).

Davies, Robert. 1984. South African Strategy towards Mozambique in the Post-Nkomati Period. Maputo: CEA, University Eduardo Mondlane. Unpublished.

Davin, Delia. 1976. *Woman-Work: Women and the Party in Revolutionary China*. Oxford: Clarendon Press.

de Bragança, Aquino, and Immanuel Wallerstein, eds. 1982. *The African Liberation Reader*, Vols. 1, 2, 3. London: Zed Press.

De Castilla, M. 1977. *La Educación en Nicaragua*. Managua: El Pez y la Serpiente.

———. 1980. *Educación y Lucha de Clases en Nicaragua*. Managua: Publicaciones del Departamento de Filosofia, Universidad Centroamericana.

Deere, Carmen Diana. 1986. "Agrarian Reform, Peasant and Rural Production, and the Organization of Production in the Transition to Socialism," in Fagen, et al. 1986.

De Lella, C., ed. 1984. *Cristianismo y Liberación en América Latina*. Mexico: Nuevomar.

Deng Xiaoping. 1984. "Respect Knowledge, Respect Trained Personnel" (May 24, 1977), in *Selected Works of Deng Xiaoping: 1975–1982*. Beijing: Foreign Languages Press.

Dettmer, J. 1983. "Nicaragua: La Revolución en la Educación Superior" *Revista Latinoamericana de Estudios Educativos* 13 (1st quarter): 102–30.

Dewey, John. 1966. *Democracy and Education*. New York: Free Press.

Dilger, Bernard. 1984. "The Education of Minorities," *Comparative Education* 20(1): 155–64.

Dore, Ronald. 1976. *The Diploma Disease: Education, Qualification and Development*. Berkeley: University of California Press.

Duflo, Marie, and Francoise Ruellan, eds. 1985. *Le Volcan Nicaraguayen*. Paris: Editions La Decouverte.

Dumont, Rene. 1983. *Fini les lendemains qui chantent, I*. Paris: Seuil.

Duyvendak, J.J.L. 1963. *The Book of Lord Shang: A Classic of the Chinese School of Law*. Chicago: University of Chicago Press.

Edelman, Murray. 1964. *The Symbolic Uses of Politics*. Champaign-Urbana: University of Illinois Press.

———. 1971. *Politics as Symbolic Action: Mass Arousal and Quiescence*. Chicago: Markham Publishing Company.

Edquist, Charles. 1985. *Capitalism, Socialism, and Technology: A Comparative Study of Cuba and Jamaica*. London: Zed Books.

La Educación Popular en América Latina: ¿Avance o Retroceso? 1982. Mexico: Centro de Estudios Educativos.

Education in China: The Past Five Years. 1983. Materials prepared by the Information and Documentation Unit of the Ministry of Education, PRC, for the Regional Office for Education in Asian and the Pacific of UNESCO.

Entwistle, Harold. 1978. *Class, Culture, and Education.* London: Methuen.

———. 1979. *Antonio Gramsci: Conservative Schooling for Radical Politics.* London: Routledge & Keegan Paul.

Enzenberger, H. M. 1976. "Portrait of a Party: Prehistory, Structure, and Ideology of the PCC," in R. Radosh, ed., *The New Cuba.* New York: Morrow. © 1975.

Evans, Peter. 1979. *Dependent Development: The Alliance of Multinational, State, and Local Capital in Brazil.* Princeton: Princeton University Press.

Ezcurra, A. 1984. *Agresión Ideologica contra la Revolución Sandinista.* Mexico: Nuevomar.

Fagen, Richard. 1969. *The Transformation of Political Culture in Cuba.* Stanford, Cal.: Stanford University Press.

———. 1980. *The Nicaraguan Revolution.* Washington, D.C.: Working Papers of the Latin American Program No. 78, The Wilson Center.

———. 1986. "The Politics of Transition," in Fagen, et al. 1986, 249–63.

Fagen, Richard, R. A. Brody, and T. O'Leary. 1968. *Cubans in Exile: A Demographic Analysis of Social Problems.* Stanford, Cal.: Stanford University Press.

Fagen, Richard R., Carmen Diana Deere, and Jose Luis Corragio, eds. 1986. *Transition and Development: Problems of Third World Socialism.* New York: Monthly Review Press.

Fagen, Richard, and James Nelson Goodsell, eds. 1975. *Fidel Castro's Personal Revolution in Cuba: 1959–1973.* New York: Alfred Knopf.

Fanon, Frantz. 1968. *The Wretched of the Earth.* New York: Grove Press.

Flora, J., et al. 1983. "The Growth of Class Struggle: The Impact of the Nicaraguan Literacy Crusade on the Political Consciousness of Young Literacy Workers," *Latin American Perspectives* I 10(36) (Winter): 45–61.

Foster, Philip J. 1965. "The Vocational School Fallacy in Development Planning," in C. Arnold Anderson and Mary Jane Bowman, eds. *Education and Economic Development,* 142–66. Chicago: Aldine.

Frank, Andre Gunder. 1967. *Capitalism and Underdevelopment in Latin America.* New York: Monthly Review Press.

———. 1978. *Dependent Accumulation and Underdevelopment.* New York: Monthly Review Press.

———. 1979. Economic Crisis and the State in the Third World. Development Discussion Paper No. 30, University of East Anglia (England) (February).

Freire, Paulo. 1970. *Pedagogy of the Oppressed.* New York: Herder and Herder.

Frelimo. 1977a. *Estatutos e Programas do Partido.* Maputo: Departamento do Trabalho Ideologico da Frelimo.

———. 1977b. *Relatorio do Comité Central ao 3- Congresso.* Maputo: Departamento do Trabalho Ideologico da Frelimo.

Frelimo. 1977c. *Directivas Económicas e Sociais do 3- Congresso*. Maputo: CEDIMO. Official translation.

———. 1977d. *Guía para o Estudo das Teses do 3- Congresso*. Maputo: FRELIMO Press.

———. 1982. *A Situação Actual no Nosso Pais*. Maputo: INLD.

———. 1983a. *Relatorio do Comité Central ao 4- Congresso*. Maputo: Frelimo.

———. 1983b. *Directivas Económicas e Sociais do 4- Congresso*. Maputo Frelimo.

———. 1983c. *Estatutos e Programas do Partido*. Maputo: INLD.

Friedman, Edward. 1984. "Three Socialist Paths within A Socialist Conundrum," in Solinger 1984.

Fuenzalida, Edmundo F. 1983. "The Reception of 'Scientific Sociology' in Chile," *Latin American Research Review* 18(2): 95–112.

Gadotti, Moacir. 1987. *Pensamento Pedagógico Brasileiro*. Sao Paulo: Editora Atica.

Gajardo, M., ed. 1983. *Teoria y Practica de la Educación Popular en America Latina*. Ottawa: IDRC-MR81s (August).

Gallo, M., et al. 1975. *La Educación en Cuba*. Buenos Aires: Editorial Convergencia.

Galt, Howard Spilman. 1929. *The Development of Chinese Educational Theory*. Shanghai: The Commercial Press. Ltd.

———. 1951. *History of Chinese Educational Institutions*. London: Arthur Probsthain.

Ganhão, Fernando. 1978. "The Struggle Continues: Mozambique's Revolutionary Experience in Education," *Development Dialogue* 2: 25–36.

Gao Weizhen. 1986. "Dui Waikaifang ru Gaoxiao de Gaige" (On the Opening Relations with Foreign Countries and the Reform of Higher Education), *Jiaoyu Yanjiu* 2: 14–17.

Gersony, Robert. 1988. *Summary of Mozambican Refugee Accounts of Principally Conflict-Related Experience in Mozambique: Report Submitted to Ambassador Jonathan Moore, Director, Bureau for Refugee Programs and Dr. Chester A. Crocker, Assistant Secretary of African Affairs*. Washington, D.C.: Bureau for Refugee Programs, U.S. Department of State.

Gillette, A. L. 1976. *Beyond the Non-Formal Fashion: Towards Educational Revolution in Tanzania*. Amherst, Mass.: University of Massachusetts Center for International Education.

Gillette, Arthur. 1972. "Cuba's Educational Revolution," Fabian Research Series, No. 302, London, June.

Gilly, A. 1980. *La Nueva Nicaragua (Antiimperialismo y Lucha de Clases)*. Mexico: Nueva Imagen.

Gintis, Herbert. 1975. "The New Working Class and Revolutionary Youth," in Martin Carnoy, ed., *Schooling in a Corporate Society*, 2d ed. New York: David McKay.

Giroux, Henry. 1981. *Ideology, Culture, and the Process of Schooling*. Philadelphia: Temple University Press.

———. 1984. "Theories of Reproduction and Resistance in the New Sociology of

Education: A Critical Analysis," *Harvard Education Review* 53(3) (August): 257–93.

Gramsci, Antonio. 1971. *Selections from Prison Notebooks.* New York: International Publishers.

Green, Reginald Herbold. 1977. *Toward Socialism and Self Reliance: Tanzania's Striving for Sustained Transition Projected.* Uppsala: Scandinavian Institute for African Studies, Research Reports, No. 38.

————. 1979. "Tanzanian Political Economy Goals, Strategies, and Results, 1967–74: Notes Toward an Interim Assessment," in Bismarck U. Mwansasu and Cranford Pratt, eds., *Towards Socialism in Tanzania,* 19–45. Toronto: University of Toronto Press.

————. 1981a. " 'Once More Into the Breach . . .': Tanzania's 1979–81 Political Economic Crisis," *Contemporary Review* 238 (1380) (January): 25–30.

————. 1981b. " 'A Time of Struggle': Exogenous Shocks, Structural Transformation, and Crisis in Tanzania," *Millennium: Journal of International Studies* 10(1) (Spring): 29–41.

————. 1983. " 'No Worst There is None'? Tanzanian Political Economic Crises 1978–????," in Jerker Carlsson, ed., *Recession in Africa,* 108–40. Uppsala: Scandinavian Institute of African Studies.

Green, Reginald Herbold, et al. 1980. *Economic Shocks and National Policy Making: Tanzania in the 1970s.* The Hague: Institute of Social Studies.

Griffiths, John, and Peter Griffiths, eds. 1979. *Cuba: The Second Decade.* London: Writers and Readers Books.

Grunwald, Joseph, Miguel Wionczek, and Martin Carnoy. 1972. *Latin American Integration and U.S. Policy.* Washington, D.C.: The Brookings Institution.

Hall, Budd L. 1975. *Adult Education and the Development of Socialism in Tanzania.* Kampala: East African Literature Bureau.

Hanlon, Joseph. 1984. *Mozambique: the Revolution under Fire.* London: Zed Press.

Harnecker, Marta. 1975. *Cuba: Dictadura o Democracia?* Mexico: Siglo XXI.

Harris, Richard, and Carlos M. Vilas, eds. 1985. *Nicaragua: A Revolution under Siege.* London: Zed Books. Also published as *La Revolución en Nicaragua.* Mexico: Era.

Hawkins, John D. 1983. *Education and Social Change in the People's Republic of China.* New York: Praeger.

Hayhoe, Ruth. 1984. "The Evolution of Modern Chinese Educational Institutions," in Ruth Hayhoe, ed., *Contemporary Chinese Education.* New York: M. E. Sharpe, Inc.

Hayhoe, Ruth, and Marianne Bastid, eds. 1987. *China's Education and the Industrialized World.* New York: M. E. Sharpe, Inc.

Henze, Jürgen. 1987. "Educational Modernization as a Search for Higher Efficiency," in Hayhoe and Bastid 1987.

Hinzen, H., and V. H. Hunsdorfer, eds. 1979. *Education for Liberation and Development: The Tanzanian Experience.* Hamburg: UNESCO Institute of Education and Evans Brothers, Ltd.

Hirji, Karim F. 1973. "School Education and Underdevelopment in Tanzania," *Maji Maji* 12: 1–22.

Hirschmann, Albert O. 1977. *The Passions and the Interests*. Princeton: Princeton University Press.

Holt, Pat. 1974. "Cuba." Washington: U.S. Government Printing Office. Report prepared for the Committee of Foreign Relations of the U.S. Senate.

Hooper, Beverly. 1985. *Youth In China*. Victoria, Australia: Penguin Books.

Hu, C. T. 1984. "The Historical Background: Examinations and Control in Premodern China," *Comparative Education* 20(1): 7–27.

Hu Shiming and Eli Seifman. 1976. *Toward A New World Outlook: A Documentary History of Education in the People's Republic of China, 1949–76*. New York: AMS Press.

Huang Shiqi. 1987. "Contemporary Educational Relations with the Industrialized World: A Contemporary View," in Hayhoe and Bastid 1987.

Huntington, Samuel. 1975. "The United States," in Michael Crozier, Samuel Huntington, and Joji Watanuki, eds., *The Crisis of Democracy*. New York: The Trilateral Commission and New York University Press.

Huteau, Michel, and J. Lautrey. 1973. *L'Education à Cuba*. Paris: Maspero.

Hydén, Göran. 1979. " 'We Must Run While Others Walk': Policy-Making for Socialist Development in the Tanzania-Type of Polities," in Kwan S. Kim et al., eds., *Papers on the Political Economy of Tanzania*, 5–13. Nairobi: Heinemann.

———. 1980. *Beyond Ujamaa in Tanzania: Underdevelopment and an Uncaptured Peasantry*. Berkeley: University of California Press.

———. 1984. "Administration and Public Policy," in Barkan 1984, 103–24.

Iliffe, John. 1979. *A Modern History of Tanganyika*. Cambridge, England: Cambridge University Press.

Ingrao, Pietro. 1977. *Massa e potere*. Rome: Editore Reuniti.

Inkeles, Alex, and David Smith. 1974. *Becoming Modern*. Cambridge, Mass.: Harvard University Press.

International Labour Office, Jobs and Skills Programme for Africa. 1978. *Towards Self-Reliance: Development, Employment and Equity Issues in Tanzania*. Addis Ababa: International Labour Office.

International Labour Organization. 1982. *Basic Needs in Danger: A Basic Needs Oriented Development Strategy for Tanzania*. Addis Ababa: International Labour Office, Jobs and Skills Programme for Africa.

Isaacman, Allen, and Barbara Isaacman. 1983. *Mozambique: from Colonialism to Revolution*. Boulder, Colo.: Westview Press.

Ishumi, Abel G. M. 1981. *Community Education and Development*. Nairobi: Kenya Literature Bureau.

Jackal, Robert, and Henry M. Levin. 1984. *Worker Cooperatives in America*. Berkeley: University of California Press.

Jallade, Jean-Pierre. 1988. *Financiamento de la Educación y Distribución del Ingreso en America Latina*. Mexico: Fondo de Cultura Económica.

Jencks, Christopher, et al. 1979. *Who Gets Ahead*. New York: Basic Books.

Johnson, Phyllis, and David Martin, eds., 1986. *Destructive Engagement: Southern Africa at War*. Harare: Zimbabwe Publishing House.

Johnston, Anton. 1984. *Education in Mozambique, 1975–84*. Stockholm: Swedish International Development Authority.

———. 1985. *Educação em Moçambique, 1975–84*. Stockholm: Swedish International Development Authority.

Jolly, Richard. 1964. "Education," in Dudley Seers, ed., *Cuba: The Economic and Social Revolution*. Chapel Hill, N.C.: University of North Carolina Press.

———. 1971. "Contrasts in Cuban and African Educational Strategies," in J. Lowe, ed., *Education and Nation Building in the Third World*. New York: Barnes and Noble.

Kahama, C. George, T. L. Maliyamkono, and Stuart Wells. 1986. *The Challenge for Tanzania's Economy*. London: James Currey.

Kaniki, M. H. Y., ed. 1980. *Tanzania under Colonial Rule*. Singapore: Longman. © 1979.

Kassam, Yusuf O. 1978. *The Adult Education Revolution in East Africa*. Nairobi: Shungwaya Publishers.

Kimambo, I. N., and A. J. Temu, eds. 1969. *A History of Tanzania*. Nairobi: East African Publishing House.

King, Edmund J. 1984. "Chinese Educational Development in Comparative Perspective," *Comparative Education* 20(1): 165–81.

King, Kenneth. 1983. *The End of Education for Self-Reliance?* Edinburgh: Centre of African Studies, Edinburgh University, Occasional Paper No. 1.

———. 1986. "Evaluating the Context of Diversified Secondary Education in Tanzania: Preliminary Comments." London: University of London, Institute of Education, Vocationalising Education Conference.

Kraus, Richard. 1981. *Class Conflict in Chinese Socialism*. New York: Columbia University Press.

———. 1983. "The Chinese State and Its Bureaucrats." in Nee and Mozingo 1983.

Kraus, Richard, and Reeve Vanneman. 1984. "Bureaucrats, Peasants and the Paradox of State Building in the Third World." Unpublished manuscript.

———. 1985. "Bureaucrats versus the State in Capitalist and Socialist Regimes," *Comparative Studies in Society and History* 27(1): 111–22.

Krupskaya, Nadezhda K. 1955. *Ausgewahlte Padadgogische Schriften*. Berlin: Volk und Wissen Verlag.

Kuznets, Simon. 1955. "Economic Growth and Income Inequality," *American Economic Review* 45(1) (May): 1–28.

Kwong, Julia. 1979. *Chinese Education in Transition: Prelude to the Cultural Revolution*. Montreal: McGill-Queen's University Press.

La Belle, T. 1986. *Nonformal Education and the Poor in Latin America and the Caribbean: Stability, Reform or Revolution?* New York: Praeger.

Lacayo, F. 1982. "La Cruzada Nacional de Alfabetizacion en Nicaragua," in Carlos A. Torres, ed., *Ensavos sobre la Educación de los Adultos en América Latina*, 555–80. Mexico: Centro de Estudios Educativos.

Legge, James. 1865–1895. *The Chinese Classics*. Oxford: Clarendon Press. Vol. 1, 1893; vol. 5, 1872; reprinted 1939.

Leiner, Marvin. 1973. "Major Developments in Cuban Education," in Barkin and Manitzas 1973.

———. 1974. *Children Are the Revolution: Day Care in Cuba*. New York: Viking.

———. 1975. "Cuba: Combining Formal Schooling with Practical Experience," in Manzour Ahmed and Phillip Coombs, eds., *Education for Rural Development: Case Studies for Planners*. New York: Praeger Publishers.

Lenin, V. I. [1917–1920] 1978. *On Socialist Ideology and Culture*. Moscow: Progress Publishers.

Levenson, Joseph. 1966. *Confucian China and Its Modern Fate*. Berkeley: University of California Press.

Levin, Henry M. 1976. "The Meaning of Educational Reform," in Carnoy and Levin, 1976.

Li Kejing. 1980. "Is Education a Superstructure or a Productive Force?" *Social Sciences in China* 1(3) (September): 16–25.

Lian Ruiqing. 1986. "Xiandaihua yu Jiaoyu Tizhi Wenti" (Some Problems of Modernization and the Educational System), *Jiaoyu Yanjiu* 2: 8–13.

Lipset, Seymour Martin. 1963. *Political Man*. New York: Doubleday Anchor Books.

Lisboa, Eugenio. 1967. "Ensino em Moçambique." Lourenco Marques: TEMAS ESTUDANTIS, Associacao Academica de Mocambique.

Lockheed, Marlaine, Dean Jamison, and Lawrence Lau. 1980. "Farmer Education and Farm Efficiency: A Survey," *Economic Development and Cultural Change* 29(1) (October): 37–76.

Lofchie, Michael F. 1978. "Agrarian Crisis and Economic Liberalisation in Tanzania," *Journal of Modern African Studies* 16(3) (September): 451–75.

Löfstedt, Jan-Ingvar. 1980. *Chinese Educational Policy: Changes and Contradictions 1949–79*. Stockholm: Almqvist & Wiksell International.

Lombardi, F. V. 1969. *Idee pedagogiche di A. Gramsci*. Brescia: La Scuola.

Louie, Kim. 1984. "Salvaging Confucian Education," *Comparative Education* 20(1): 27–38.

Louzada, Nilson. 1986. "A Lingua Portuguesa em Mocambique." Unpublished.

Lunacharsky, V. E. 1970. *The Commisariat of Enlightenment: Soviet Organization of Education and the Arts under Lunacharsky, October 1917–21*. Cambridge, England: Cambridge University Press.

Luxemburg, Rosa. [1905] 1961. *The Russian Revolution and Leninism or Marxism?* Ann Arbor: University of Michigan Press.

MacEwan, Arthur. 1975. "Incentive, Equality, and Power in Revolutionary Cuba," in R. Radosh, ed., *The New Cuba*. New York: Morrow.

———. 1981. *Revolution and Economic Development in Cuba*. New York: St. Martin's Press.

Macfarquhar, Roderick. 1960. *The Hundred Flowers Campaign and the Chinese Intellectuals*. Hong Kong: F. A. Praeger.

Machel, Samora. 1971. *Produzir e Aprender: Aprender para Produzir e Lutar Melhor*. Maputo: Frelimo.

———. 1974. *Fazer da Escola uma Base Para o Povo Tomaro Poder*. Maputo: Imprensa Nacional.

———. 1977. "Empenhar Toda a Capacidade de Trabalho para a Vitoria na Frente Educacional," *Noticias* [Maputo] (March 9).

———. 1979. *Façamos da Decada 1980–1990 a Decada da Vitoria sobre o Subdesenvolvimento*. Maputo: Frelimo.

———. 1980. *Desalojemos o Inimigo Interno do Nosso Aparelho do Estado*. Maputo: Frelimo.

———. 1982. "Organizar a Sociedade para Vencer o Subdesenvolvimento," *Noticias* [Maputo] (February).

———. 1983. *A Nossa Força está na Unidade*. Maputo: INLD.

———. 1985. "Mistakes and Deviations Persist," *AIM: Mozambican News* 114 (January).

Makarenko, Anton S. 1951. *The Road to Life*. Moscow: Foreign Language Publishing House.

———. 1961. *Lectures to Parents*. New York: National Council of American-Soviet Friendship.

Malekela, G. A. 1983. "Access to Secondary Education in Sub-Saharan Africa: The Tanzanian Experiment." Ph.D. diss., University of Chicago.

Maliyamkono, T. L., A.G.M. Ishumi, and S. J. Wells. 1982. *Higher Education and Development in Eastern Africa*. London: Heinemann.

Malya, S. 1979. "Literacy—A Work-Oriented Adult Literacy Pilot Project and a National Campaign," in Hinzen and Hunsdorfer 1979, 141–52.

Manacorda, M. A. 1966. *Marx e la pedagogia moderna*. Roma: Editora Riumiti.

———. 1970. *Il principio educativo in Gramsci*. Roma: Armando.

Manitzas, Nita. 1973. "The Setting of the Cuban Revolution," in Barkin and Manitzas 1973.

Mao Zedong. 1940. "On New Democracy," in *Selected Works of Mao Zedong*, Vol. I. Beijing: Foreign Languages Press, 1961.

Marchetti, Peter. 1986. "War, Popular Particpation, and Transition to Socialism," in Fagen, et al. 1986.

Marini, Ruy Mauro. 1977. "Estado y Crisis en Brasil," *Cuadernos Politicos* 13 (July-September): 76–84.

Marshall, Judith. 1985. "Making Education Revolutionary," in Saul 1985, 155–210.

———. 1986. "Mozambique and Nicaragua: The Politics of Survival." Paper presented to the 1986 Conference of the *Review of African Political Economy*, Liverpool, September, 1986.

Mauger, Peter, ed. 1974. *Education in China*. New York: Anglo-Chinese Educational Institute.

Mbilinyi, Marjorie J. 1972. "The Decision to Educate in Rural Tanzania." Ph.D. diss., University of Dar es Salaam.

———. 1973a. "Education for Rural Life or Education for Socialist Transformation?" in Council for the Social Sciences in East Africa, *Proceedings, Annual Social Science Conference* 2: 437–64.

———. 1973b. "Education, Stratification and Sexism in Tanzania: Policy Implications," *African Review* 3(2): 327–40.

———. 1979. "Contradictions in Tanzania Educational Reform," in Coulson 1979, 217–27.

McCarthy, D.M.P. 1981. *Colonial Bureaucracy and Creating Underdevelopment: Tanganyika, 1919–1940.* Ames, Iowa: Iowa State University Press.

Meisner, Maurice. 1977. *Mao's China: A History of the People's Republic.* New York: Free Press.

Memmi, Albert. 1968. *The Colonizer and the Colonized.* Boston: Beacon Press.

Mercado, M. 1983. "Reportaje en Vivo y en Directo: Educación en la Zona de Guerra," *Nuevo Diario*, July 8, 16.

Mesa-Lago, Carmelo. 1969. "The Economic Significance of Unpaid Labor in Socialist Cuba," *Industrial and Labor Relations Review* 22 (April): 339–57.

———. 1972. "The Labor Force, Employment, Unemployment, and Underemployment in Cuba: 1899–1970." New York: Sage Professional Papers.

———. 1974. *Cuba in the 1970s.* Albuquerque, N.M.: University of Mexico Press.

———. 1981. *The Economy of Socialist Cuba: A Two-Decade Appraisal.* Albuquerque, N.M.: University of New Mexico Press.

Miller, Valerie. 1985. *Between Struggle and Hope: The Nicaraguan Literacy Crusade.* Boulder, Colo.: Westview.

Ministerio da Educação (Mozambique) (MEC). 1979. "Sistemas de Educação em Moçambique." Maputo: INDE/MEC. Mimeographed.

———. 1982. "Linhas Gerais do Sistema Nacional de Educação." Maputo: INDE/MEC. Mimeographed.

———. 1985. "Alunos Existentes No Inicio do Ano Lectivo por Classes e Sexo." Maputo: Direcção de Planificação, MEC. Mimeographed.

———. 1986. "Avaliação da Implementação do SNE." Maputo: INDE/MEC. Mimeographed.

Ministerio de Educación (Nicaragua). 1979. *Situación del Sistema Educativo después de 45 años de Dictadura Militar Somocista y Perspectivas que Plantea la Revolución Sandinista.* Paper presented to the Conferencia Regional de Ministros de Educación y de Ministros de Planificación Económica de America Latina y del Caribe, Managua, December 1979.

———. 1981. *Consulta Nacional para Obtener Criterios que Ayuden a Definir los Fines y Objetivos de la Educación Nicaraguense.* Managua: Informe Preliminar, Ministerio de Educación (August).

———. 1982. *La Educación en Tres Años de Revolución.* Managua: Ministerio de Educación (July 19).

———. 1983. *La Educación en Cuatro Años de Revolución.* Managua: Ministerio de Educación (July 19).

———. 1984a. *5 Años de Educación en la Revolución.* Managua: Ministerio de Educación (July 19).

Ministerio de Educación (Nicaragua). 1984b. *La Gestión Educativa en Cinco Años de Revolución.* Managua: Ministerio de Educación (May).

———. n.d. "La Educación antes y después del 19 de Julio de 1979." Managua: Ministerio de Educación. Mimeographed.

Ministry of Education (People's Republic of China). 1984. *Achievement of Education in China: Statistics 1949–1985.* Beijing: Ministry of Education, Department of Planning.

Ministry of National Education (Tanzania). 1981. *The Primary School Sub-Sector Review.* Dar es Salaam: Ministry of National Education.

Mohiddin, Ahmed. 1981. *African Socialism in Two Countries.* London: Croom Helm.

Molyneux, Maxine. 1982. "Socialist Societies, Old and New: Progress toward Women's Emancipation?" *Monthly Review* 34(3) (July-August): 56–100.

———. 1986. "Mobilization without Emancipation? Women's Interests, State, and Revolution," in Fagen, et al. 1986, 280–302.

Mondlane, Eduardo. 1967. *Struggle for Mozambique.* London: Penguin.

Moore, M. P., et al. 1981. *Smallholder Food Production in Tanzania.* Brighton: Institute of Development Studies, University of Sussex.

Morrison, David R. 1976. *Education and Politics in Africa: The Tanzanian Case.* Montreal: McGill-Queen's University Press.

Mosha, H. J., ed. and trans. 1982. *Report of the Research on the Process and Impact of Folk Development Colleges in Tanzania.* Dar es Salaam: Ministry of National Education.

———. 1983. "United Republic of Tanzania: Folk Development Colleges," *Prospects* 13(1): 95–103.

Mozingo, David. 1983. "The Chinese Army and the Communist State," in Nee and Mozingo 1983.

Msekwa, Pius, and T. L. Maliyamkono. 1978. *The Experiments in Educational Policy Formation in Tanzania before and after Arusha.* Dar es Salaam: University of Dar es Salaam.

Mueller, Susanne D. 1980. "Retarded Capitalism in Tanzania," in Ralph Miliband and John Saville, eds., *Socialist Register 1980*, 203–26. London: Merlin Press.

Munslow, Barry. 1983. *Mozambique: The Revolution and Its Origins.* Essex: Longmans.

———. 1984. "State Intervention in Agriculture: the Mozambican Experience," *Journal of Modern African Studies* 22(2): 199–221.

Mushi, S. S., and K. Mathews, editors. 1981. *Foreign Policy of Tanzania 1961–1981: A Reader.* Dar es Salaam: Tanzania Publishing House.

Mwiria, Kilemi. 1985. "The Kenya Harambee School Movement: An Historical Perspective." Ph.D. diss., Stanford University.

Naciones Unidas (United Nations), Comission Económica para América Latina (CEPAL). 1979. "Nicaragua: Repercusiones Económicas de los Acontecimientos Recientes," *Comercio Exterior* 29(9) (September): 1020–26.

Nazzari, Muriel. 1983. "The Woman Question in Cuba," *Signs* 9: 246–63.

Nee, Victor, and David Mozingo, eds. 1983. *State and Society in Contemporary China.* Ithaca, N.Y.: Cornell University Press.

Nellis, John R. 1972. *A Theory of Ideology: The Tanzanian Example*. Nairobi: Oxford University Press.

Nelson, Lowry. 1971. "The School Dropout Problem in Cuba," *School and Society* 99 (April): 234–35.

Newman, Philip. 1965. *Cuba Before Castro, an Economic Appraisal*. New York: Foreign Studies Institute.

Nicaragua en Cifras [1983] 1984. Managua: Instituto Nacional de Estadísticas y Censos.

Nivison, David S. 1975. "Protest against Conventions and Conventions of Protest," in Arthur Wright, ed., *Confucianism and Chinese Civilization*. Stanford, Cal.: Stanford University Press.

Nnoli, Okwudiba. 1978. *Self Reliance and Foreign Policy in Tanzania*. New York: Nok.

Norton, Theodore Mills, and Bertell Ollman. 1978. *Studies in Socialist Pedagogy*. New York: Monthly Review Press.

Noticias (Maputo daily newspaper).

Nyerere, Julius K. 1967. *Education for Self Reliance*. Dar es Salaam: Government Printer.

———. 1968a. *Essays on Socialism*. Dar es Salaam: Oxford University Press.

———. 1968b. *Freedom and Socialism / Uhuru na Ujamaa*. Dar es Salaam: Oxford University Press.

———. 1969. "To Plan is To Choose." Speech to the TANU Conference, May 28, 1969, reprinted as the Introduction to the *Second Five-Year Plan for Economic and Social Development, 1st July, 1969 – 30th June, 1974*, Vol. I, vii–xxiii. Dar es Salaam: Government Printer.

———. 1985. "Education in Tanzania," *Harvard Educational Review* 55 (February): 45–52.

Offe, Claus. 1973 "The Capitalist State and the Problem of Policy Formation," in Leon Lindberg, ed., *Stress and Contradiction in Modern Capitalism*. Lexington Mass.: D.C. Heath.

Ollman, Bertell. 1979. *Social and Sexual Revolution*. Boston: South End Press.

Omari, I. M. 1968. "Role of TAPA (Tanganyika African Parents Association) as an Educational Institution," *Mbioni* 4(12): 3–25.

Omari, I. M., et al. 1983. *Universal Primary Education in Tanzania: A Continuation of the Educational Revolution*. Dar es Salaam: University of Dar es Salaam.

Othman, Haroub, ed. 1980. *The State in Tanzania: Who Controls It and Whose Interest Does it Serve?* Dar es Salaam: Dar es Salaam University Press.

Ottaway, David, and Marina Ottaway. 1981. *Afrocommunism*. New York: Holmes & Meier.

Paine, Lynn Webster. 1985. "Reform and Balance in Chinese Teacher Education." Ph.D. diss., Stanford University.

Palmberg, Mai, ed. 1978. *Problems of Socialist Orientation in Africa*. Uppsala: Scandinavian Institute of African Studies.

Paulston, Rolland. 1971. "Education," in Carmelo Mesa-Lago, ed., *Revolution-*

ary Change in Cuba: Economy, Policy, and Society. Pittsburgh: University of Pittsburgh Press.

Pepper, Suzanne. 1984. *China's Universities: Post Mao Enrollment Policies and Their Impact on the Structure of Secondary Education.* Ann Arbor: Center for Chinese Studies, University of Michigan.

Ping Wen Kuo. 1918. *The Chinese System of Public Education* New York: Columbia Teachers College.

Poulantzas, Nicos. 1975. *Classes in Contemporary Capitalism.* London: New Left Books.

———. 1980. *State, Power, Socialism.* London: New Left Books, Verso edition. © 1978.

Pratt, Cranford. 1976. *The Critical Phase in Tanzania, 1945–1968: Nyerere and the Emergence of a Socialist Strategy.* Cambridge, England: Cambridge University Press.

"Prospects for the Sandinista Revolution." 1979. *Comercio Exteriór* 25 (November): 422–28.

Przeworski, Adam. 1979. "Economic Conditions of Class Compromise." Chicago: University of Chicago. Unpublished.

Przeworski, Adam, and Michael Wallerstein. 1982. "The Structure of Class Conflict in Democratic Capitalist Societies," *American Political Science Review* 76(2): 215–38.

Psacharopoulos, George. 1985. "Returns to Education: A Further International Update and Implications," *Journal of Human Resources* 20(4): 583–604.

Psacharopoulos, George, and William Loxley. 1985. *Diversified Secondary Education and Development: Evidence from Colombia and Tanzania.* Baltimore: Johns Hopkins University Press, for the World Bank.

Psacharopoulos, George, and Maureen Woodhall. 1985. *Education for Development.* Baltimore: Johns Hopkins Press.

Rama, German. 1984. *Educación, Participacion, y Estilos de Desarrollo en América Latina.* Buenos Aires: CEPAL Kapelusz.

Rawski, Evelyn Sakakida. 1979. *Education and Popular Literacy in Qing China* Ann Arbor: University of Michigan Press.

Read, Gerald. 1975. "The Revolutionary Offensive in Education," in James Goodall, ed., *Fidel Castro's Personal Revolution in Cuba: 1957–1973.* New York: Alfred Knopf.

Resnick, Idrian N., ed. 1968. *Tanzania: Revolution by Education.* Arusha: Longman.

———. 1981. *The Long Transition: Building Socialism in Tanzania.* New York: Monthly Review Press.

Ritter, Archibald. 1974. *The Economic Development of Revolutionary Cuba.* New York: Praeger.

Rose, Brian, ed. 1973. *Education in Southern Africa.* London: Collier-Macmillan.

Rosen, Stanley. 1985. "Recentralization, Decentralization and Rationalization: Deng Xiaoping's Bifurcated Educational Policy," *Modern China* 11(3): 301–46.

Rousseau, Jean Jacques. [1762] 1967. *The Social Contract and Discourse on the Origin of Inequality.* New York: Pocket Books.

Rubin, Vitaly. 1976. *Individual and State in Ancient China* New York: Columbia University Press.

Ruchwarger, Gary. 1985. "The Sandinista Mass Organizations and the Revolutionary Process," in Harris and Vilas 1985.

Sack, Richard, Martin Carnoy, and Claudia Lecaros. 1980. "Educación y Desarrollo Rural en América Latina," in *El Problema del Financiamiento de la Educación en América Latina*, 310–55. Mexico City: Interamerican Bank and Government of Mexico.

Saenz, R. n.d. "Solidarity as an Alternate Form of International Cooperation: The Experience of the National Literacy Crusade in Nicaragua." German Foundation for International Development & International Council for Adult Education.

Samoff, Joel. 1974. *Tanzania: Local Politics and the Structure of Power.* Madison, Wis.: University of Wisconsin Press.

———. 1980. "Underdevelopment and Its Grass Roots in Africa," *Canadian Journal of African Studies* 14(1): 5–36.

———. 1981. "Crises and Socialism in Tanzania," *Journal of Modern African Studies* 19(2) (June): 279–306.

———. 1982a. "Class, Class Conflict, and the State in Africa," *Political Science Quarterly* 97(1) (Spring): 105–27.

———. 1982b. "On Class, Paradigm, and African Politics," *Africa Today* 29(2): 41–50.

———. 1982–1983. "Pluralism and Conflict in Africa: Ethnicity, Institutions and Class in Tanzania," *Civilisations* 32(2)/33(1): 97–134.

———. 1983. "Bureaucrats, Politicians, and Power in Tanzania: The Institutional Context of Class Struggle," *Journal of African Studies* 10(3) (Fall): 84–96.

———. 1987a. "School Expansion in Tanzania: Private Initiatives and Public Policy," *Comparative Education Review* 31(3) (August 1987): 333–60.

———. 1987b. "Single-Party Competitive Elections in Tanzania," in Fred Hayward, ed., *Elections in Independent Africa*, 149–66. Boulder, Colo.: Westview.

Sanshiwu Nian Lai Wo Guo Jiaoyu Shiye de Juda Chengjiu (Assessment of Thirty-Five Years of Our Nation's Great Achievements in Education). 1984. Beijing: Educational Science Press.

Saul, John S. 1979. *The State and Revolution in Eastern Africa.* New York: Monthly Review Press.

———, ed. 1985. *A Difficult Road: The Transition to Socialism in Mozambique.* New York: Monthly Review Press.

Saviani, Dermeval. 1983. *Escola e Democracia.* Sao Paulo: Cortez Editora.

Schmitter, Philippe. 1983. "Democratic Theory and Neocorporatist Practice," *Social Research*, 50(4) (Winter): 886–928.

Schultz, Theodore. 1961. "Investment in Human Capital," *American Economic Review* 51 (March): 1–17.

Schurmann, Franz, and Orville Schell. 1967. *Imperial China.* New York: Random House.

Searle, Chris. 1981. *We're Building the New School! Diary of a Teacher in Mozambique.* London: Zed Press.

Seers, Dudley. 1964. *Cuba: The Economic and Social Revolution.* Chapel Hill, N.C.: University of North Carolina Press.

Selden, Mark. 1982. "Socialism or 'Post-Revolutionary' Society?" in Christoper Chase-Dunn, ed., *Socialist States in the World System.* London: Sage Publications.

Selser, G. 1984. "Expediente 1 y 2: Cinco Anos de Agresiones Estadunidienses a Centroamerica y el Caribe (1979–1984)," *El Dia* (Mexico), June 1984, special twenty-second anniversary supplement.

Serra, Luis. 1985. Ideology, Religion and Class Struggle in the Nicaraguan Revolution," in Harris and Vilas 1985.

Seybolt, Peter. 1969. "Yenan Education and the Chinese Revolution, 1937–1945." Ph.D. diss., Harvard University.

———. 1973. *Revolutionary Education in China/ Documents and Commentary.* New York: International Arts and Science Press.

Shao, John. 1985. "Politics and the Food Production Crisis in Tanzania," *Issue* 14: 10–24.

Sheringham, Michael. 1984. "Popularisation Policies in Chinese Education from the 1950s to the 1970s," *Comparative Education* 20(1): 73–80.

Shivji, Issa G. 1976. *Class Struggles in Tanzania.* New York: Monthly Review Press.

———, ed. 1985. *The State and the Working People in Tanzania.* Dakar: Codesria.

Siddiqui, Rukhsana. 1984. "Ideology and Socialist Transition in Tanzania." Ph.D. diss., University of Pennsylvania.

Simmons, John, and William Mares. 1983. *Working Together.* New York: Alfred Knopf.

Skocpol, Theda. 1979. *States and Social Revolution: A Comparative Analysis of France, Russia, and China.* New York: Cambridge University Press.

———. 1985. *Bringing the State Back In.* Cambridge, England: Cambridge University Press.

Smith, Adam. [1776] 1937. *The Wealth of Nations.* New York: Modern Library.

Smith, Arthur A. 1907. *Village Life in China.* New York: Young People's Missionary Movement.

Smith, William Edgett. 1971. *We Must Run while They Walk: A Portrait of Africa's Julius Nyerere.* New York: Random House.

———. 1986. "A Reporter at Large," *New Yorker*, March 3, 72–82.

Solinger, Dorothy, ed. 1984. *Three Visions of Chinese Socialism.* Boulder, Colo.: Westview Press.

Spalding, R. 1984. "La Expansion Economica del Estado en Nicaragua despues de la Revolucion," *Foro Internacional* 25(1) (July-September): 14–32.

Spence, Jonathan D. 1981. *The Gate of Heavenly Peace.* Middlesex, England: Penguin Books.

Stabler, Ernest. 1979. "Kenya and Tanzania: Strategies and Realities in Education and Development," *African Affairs* 78(310) (January): 33–56.

Stacey, Judith. 1983. *Patriarchy and Social Revolution in China.* Berkeley: University of California Press.

State Education Commission (People's Republic of China). 1986. *The Development of Education in China (1984–1986).* Beijing: State Education Commission, prepared for the International Conference on Education, Geneva, 1986.

Stepan, Alfred. 1979. *The State and Society: Peru in Comparative Perspective.* Princeton: Princeton University Press.

Stromquist, Nelly. 1984. "Cuba: Trip Report." Ottawa: International Development Research Center (October).

Suchodolski, Bogdan. 1966. *Teoriá Marxista de la Educación.* Mexico: Grijalbo.

———. 1967. *Fundamentos de Pedagogía Marxista.* Barcelona: Editorial Laia.

Sweezy, Paul, and Charles Bettelheim. 1971. *On the Transition to Socialism.* New York: Monthly Review Press.

Sweezy, Paul, and Leo Huberman. 1969. *Socialism in Cuba.* New York: Monthly Review Press.

Tan, Jee-Peng. 1985. "The Private Direct Cost of Secondary Schooling in Tanzania," *International Journal of Educational Development* 5(1): 1–10.

Tandon, Yash, ed., 1982. *Debate on Class, State and Imperialism.* Dar es Salaam: Tanzanian Publishing House.

Tanganyika African National Union (TANU). 1971. *TANU Guidelines on Guarding, Consolidating and Advancing the Revolution of Tanzania, and of Africa (Mwongozo).* Dar es Salaam: TANU, 1971. Reprinted in Coulson 1979, 36–42.

Tanganyika African National Union (TANU), National Executive Committee. 1974. "Directive on the Implementation of 'Education for Self-Reliance' " (the Musoma Resolution, Dar es Salaam), reprinted in *African Review* 6 (1976): 103–12 (from which the pagination here is taken).

Tanzania. 1981. *Statistical Abstract 1973–1979.* Dar es Salaam: Ministry of Planning and Economic Affairs, Bureau of Statistics.

———. 1984. *Educational System in Tanzania towards the Year 2000: Recommendations of the 1982 Presidential Commission on Education as Approved by the Party and Government.* Dar es Salaam: Ministry of Education.

Tanzania, Ministry of Agriculture. 1982. *The Tanzania National Agricultural Policy [Final Report].* Dar es Salaam: Printpak.

Tanzania, Ministry of Education. 1982a. *Mfumo wa Elimu ya Tanzania 1981–2000, Juzuu la Kwanza.* Dar es Salaam: Ministry of Education. Report and recommendations.

———. 1982b. *Mfumo wa Elimu ya Tanzania 1981–2000, Juzuu la Pili.* Dar es Salaam: Ministry of Education. Tables and supplementary discussion.

Taylor, J. Clagett. 1963. *The Political Development of Tanganyika.* Stanford, Cal.: Stanford University Press.

Tempo (Mozambican weekly news magazine). Maputo: Tempografica.

TEMPO/UEM. 1982–1983. *Historia de Moçambique, Vols. 1 and 2.* Maputo: Tempografica.

Therborn, Goran. 1980. *The Ideology of Power and the Power of Ideology.* London: Verso.

Thias, Hans, and Martin Carnoy. 1972. *Cost-Benefit Analysis in Education: A Case Study of Kenya.* Washington: World Bank.

The 13th Party Congress and China's Reforms. 1987. Beijing: Beijing Review.

Thomas, Clive Y. 1978. "Class Struggle, Social Development and the Theory of the Non-Capitalist Path," in Palmberg 1978, 17–37.

Thomas, Henk, and Chris Logan. 1982. *Mondragon: An Economic Analysis.* London: George Allen and Unwin.

Tomala, Jerzy, Ryszard Borowicz, and Zbigniew Kwiecinski. 1983. "Poland: More Equal Access to Higher Education," in John Simmons, ed., *Better Schools.* New York: Praeger.

Torres, Carlos. 1983. "Educational Policy Formation and the Mexican Corporatist State: A Study of Adult Education Policy and Planning in Mexico (1970–1982)." Ph.D. diss., Stanford University .

Torres, Rosa Maria. 1985. *Nicaragua: Revolución Popular, Educación Popular.* Mexico City: Editorial Linea.

———. 1986 Los CEP: Educación Popular y Democracia Participativa en Nicaragua. Managua: CRIES (April). Unpublished.

Torres, Rosa Maria, and Jose Luis Corragio. 1987. *Transición y Crisis en Nicaragua.* San Jose, Costa Rica: Editorial DEI.

Tunnerman, Carlos. 1983. *El Pensamiento Pedagógico de Sandino.* Managua: Ministerio de Educación (May).

UNESCO. 1977. *Trends and Projections of Enrollment by Level of Education and by Age.* Paris: UNESCO, Division of Statistics.

UNESCO-DEALC. 1981. *Desarrollo y Educación en America Latina, Síntesis General,* Vol. 4. Buenos Aires: UNESCO. Mimeographed.

Unsicker, Jeffrey G. 1987. "Adult Education, Socialism and International Aid in Tanzania: The Political Economy of the Folk Development Colleges." Ph.D. diss., Stanford University.

Vallecillos, E. 1983. "La educación popular. Arma en la lucha ideológica de Nicaragua." Paper presented at the Encuentro Internacional de Educación Popular por la Paz (Managua: August 28–September 3).

Vanlanduyt, Eric. 1985. *Nicaragua: Choix libres ou contraints.* Brussels: Universite Libre de Bruxelles and Paul Didier. Published thesis.

Vecino Alegret, Fernando. 1986. *Algunas Tendencias en el Desarrollo de la Educación Superior en Cuba.* Havana: Editorial Pueblo y Educación.

Vilas, Carlos. 1982. "La educación en Nicaragua: Entre la Reproduccion de lo Viejo y la Producción de lo Nuevo." Unpublished.

———. 1986. *The Sandinista Revolution.* New York: Monthly Review Press.

Wald, Alan. 1987. "Perspectives on the FSLN," *Against the Current* 2 (January–February): 5–10.

Wallerstein, Immanuel. 1974. "Dependence in an Interdependent World: The Limited Possibilities of Transformation within the Capitalist World-Economy," *African Studies Review* 17 (April): 1–26. Reprinted in Immanuel Wallerstein, *The Capitalist World Economy,* 66-94. Cambridge: Cambridge University Press, 1979.

Wang Hsueh-wen. 1975. *Chinese Communist Education: The Yenan Period*. Taipei: Institute of International Relations.

Warren, Bill. 1980. *Imperialism: Pioneer of Capitalism*. London: New Left Books.

Watson, Andrew J. 1973. "A Revolution to Touch Men's Souls: The Family, Interpersonal Relations and Daily Life." in Stuart R. Schram, ed., *Authority Participation and Cultural Change in China*. Cambridge, England: Cambridge University Press.

Werth, Alexander. 1964. *Russia at War, 1941–45*. New York: E.P. Dutton.

Werthein, Jorge. 1976. "El Uso do los Medios de Comunicacion para la Educación en Cuba," *Revista del Centro de Estudios Educativos* 6(4).

———. 1977. "Educational Television in Cuba," in George Gerbner, ed., *Mass Media Policies in Changing Cultures*. New York: Wiley.

White, Gordon. 1984. "The Postrevolutionary Chinese State," in Solinger 1984.

Whyte, Martin King. 1985. "Society," in Steven M. Goldstein, *China Briefing*. Boulder, Colo.: Westview Press.

Williams, Bruce, and Michael Yates. 1974. "Moral Incentives in Cuba," *Review of Political Economics* 6(3) (Autumn): 86–90.

Willis, Paul. 1977. *Learning to Labor*. Lexington, Mass.: Heath.

World Bank. 1981. *China: Socialist Economic Development: Annex G Education Sector*. Washington: World Bank.

Wu Wei. 1986. "Zai Jiaoyu Gaige Shang Gaige He Jiaoqiang Jiaoyu Kexue Yanjiu Gongzuo" (To Improve and Advance Research on the Educational Reforms), *Jiaoyu Yanjiu* 2: 2–7.

Yeager, Rodger. 1982. *Tanzania: A Political Experiment*. Boulder, Colo.: Westview.

Yglesias, Jose. 1968. *In the Fist of the Revolution: Life in a Cuban Country Town*. New York: Vintage.

Zhao Li. 1986. "Jiaoyu Xingxheng Guanli Yuanze Chutan" (Preliminary Study of the Conceptions of the Administration and Management of Education), *Jiaoyu Yanjiu* 5: 69–73.

Zhongguo Baike Nianjian. 1982. Peking: Jiaoyu Kexue Chubanshe.

Zhongguo Gaodeng Xuexiao Jianjie (Chinese Higher Education Yearbook). 1982. Peking: Jiaoyu Kexue Chubanshe.

Zimbalist, Andrew. 1975. "The Development of Workers' Participation in Socialist Cuba." Paper presented at the Second Annual Conference on Worker Control, Cornell University, Ithaca, N.Y., June 6–8.

Index

adult education: in Cuba, 177–78; in Mozambique, 288, 292, 293, 296, 299–300, 308; in Nicaragua, 334, 335, 336, 337, 338–41, 349; in Tanzania, 240, 257
Afro-Shirazi Party (ASP), 215n
agriculture, as economic basis, 31–32, 100
Albania, educational reform in, 99
Althusser, Louis, 16
Amin, Samir, 25, 56
Angola: counterrevolutionaries in, 43; external support for, 285; foreign technological skills in, 32n; nationalism in, 55; private capital in, 43; teachers in, 153; Union for the Total Independence of Angola (UNITA) in, 43
anticolonialism, 20. *See also* Colonialism
Arce, Bayardo, 325
Argentina: conditioned capitalism in, 22; education in, 65
Arnove, Robert, 334, 336n, 349
attendance, 75; and Cuban truancy, 75n. *See also* enrollment
Austria, social democracy in, 16, 19n.2, 27

Bachrach, Peter, 249n
Baratz, Morton S., 249n
Baumeister, Eduardo, 319, 323
Bettelheim, Charles, 42
Black, George, 190n
black marketeering, 44n.18; in Mozambique, 289; in Nicaragua, 331–32
Bobbio, Norberto, 23
Borge, Tomas, 317n, 325
bourgeoisie, 5, 15, 17–18n, 81, 84; in Cuba, 158; in Mozambique, 303–4; in Nicaragua, 316, 318, 319, 323–24; in Tanzania, 212
Brazil, conditioned capitalism in, 22
Brundenius, Claes, 164, 167, 168, 183
bureaucrats: Chinese, 108, 109–11, 112–13, 116–17; Cuban, 186; Nicaraguan, 316. *See also* leadership

capitalism: alternatives to, 15–16, 18, 19n.2; "conditioned," 10, 20–22, 65, 361;

"dependent," 10n; domination of markets by, 95, 363; educational system within, 9–10; law as constituted under, 49–50; Third World opposition to, 5; within transitional states, 34, 44, 369–70
Cardenal, Ernesto, 318n, 324
Cardenal, Fernando, 324, 351n
Carrión, Luis, 325
Castro, Fidel: opinions on education, 144, 176, 177, 191; revolutionary ideology of, 33n, 58, 158, 161, 163, 164–65, 169, 172, 183, 187, 188
Catholic Church, and opposition to transition, 35; in Nicaragua, 71, 72, 318–19, 322, 324–25, 334, 347–49
Chama Cha Mapinduzi (CCM) party (Tanzania), 40, 103, 215, 266
Chang Chihtung, 113
change, outcome of, 11–12
Chiang Kaishek, 114
Chile: education in, 337n; military counterrevolutionaries in, 325–26
China, People's Republic of: American military intervention in, 52; bureaucrats in, 34, 108, 109–11, 112–13, 116–17; Communist party in, 40, 102, 114, 115, 123; competing development strategies in, 57, 139–45; Confucianism in, 107, 108–12, 131; Cultural Revolution in, 39, 47, 61, 71, 85–86, 130–31; curriculum in, 110, 111, 121, 132–33; diversity within, 107–8; economic reform in, 33, 39, 115–16, 120, 124–25; educational reform in, 7, 70, 85–86, 105, 112–13, 116–19, 121–22, 126–27, 128–29, 130–31, 134–36, 137–39, 140–44; enrollment in, 119–20, 121, 122, 123, 126, 133, 136, 365; external technological knowledge necessary in, 34; family relations in, 109, 110, 111, 144; health education in, 114n.10, 128; industrial development in, 122, 125; investments in education by, 79, 82, 121, 138; Japanese imperialism in, 114; key-point schools in, 129, 134; literacy in, 80, 120, 121, 127–28, 133, 135, 365;